SUBSIDIA BIBLICA

22

subsidia biblica – 22

PETER S. WILLIAMSON

Catholic Principles for Interpreting Scripture

A Study of the Pontifical Biblical Commission's *The Interpretation of the Bible in the Church*

Preface by
Albert Vanhoye, SJ

EDITRICE PONTIFICIO ISTITUTO BIBLICO — ROMA 2008

"Principles of Catholic Interpretation in the Pontifical Biblical
Commission's 'The Interpretation of the Bible in the Church' (1993)"
Vidimus et approbamus ad normam Statutorum Universitatis

Romae, ex Pontificia Universitate Gregoriana
die 23 mensis novembris anni 2000

R.P. Prof. JAMES SWETNAM, S.J.
R.P. Prof. JARED WICKS, S.J.

IMPRIMI POTEST

Romae, die 7 novembris 2001

R.P. ROBERT F. O'TOOLE, S.J.
Rector Pontificii Instituti Biblici

ISBN   978-88-7653-617-5
© E.P.I.B. – Roma – 2008

First Edition   *2001*
First Reprint   *2008*

EDITRICE PONTIFICIO ISTITUTO BIBLICO
Piazza della Pilotta, 35 - 00187 Roma, Italia

To my mother, Beulah Pederson Williamson,

and in memory of my father, Reverend Robert S. Williamson,

who together saw to it that "from childhood [I] have known

the sacred writings that are able to instruct…for salvation

through faith in Christ Jesus" (2 Tim 3:15)

PREFACE

It was a pleasant surprise for me to learn that a doctoral student in biblical theology was preparing a dissertation on the teaching contained in the recent Biblical Commission document, *The Interpretation of the Bible in the Church*. Specifically, his research dealt with the principles of Catholic interpretation expressed in that document. The choice of this topic seemed to me particularly felicitous, since it treats the most fundamental aspect of the document, and, furthermore, an aspect that has not received much attention. What has drawn greater attention has been the document's description and evaluation of the various exegetical methods and contemporary approaches to the biblical text. Readers appreciated this description and evaluation because it provides an interesting overview of the current state of exegesis, presented with objectivity and openness of spirit. However, what is more important are the principles that should guide the work of Catholic exegetes and that give Catholic exegesis its specific identity. I am therefore particularly happy at the publication of this study and I gladly accepted the invitation to introduce it with a preface of my own.

First of all I would like to stress the seriousness and the completeness of the study which has been carried out. The document has been analyzed extremely carefully and has been interpreted very well. The author has used every possible means of acquiring a precise and rich understanding of the document. He has not only consulted diverse reviews of the document published in various languages, but he has also interviewed some members of the Biblical Commission to obtain helpful clarifications. The result of the study is the presentation of twenty "principles" of interpretation, grouped in six parts. "Principles" must not be taken in a narrow sense, but must be taken more broadly. Each principle is not defined in a single sentence, but rather each draws together a set of determinations—some general, some particular—pertaining to a particular aspect of the problem of interpretation. In this way the study offers a rich and complete vision of the many aspects of the problem and specifies the orientations for the interpretation of the Bible in the Church set forth in the document of the Biblical Commission.

Obviously, the first "principle" is the most important of all. It is described as "foundational" and it functions as the basis of all the others. It expresses the conviction of the Church's faith regarding the nature of the Bible: it is "the word of God expressed in human language" and must, therefore, be interpreted as such. The immensity and the complexity of the task of the believing exegete immediately become apparent. The exegete finds himself or herself before a paradoxical reality: human words that are at the same time Words of God. These two aspects of Scripture can be distinguished, but they must not be separated. Just as a surgeon who operates on the body of a human person must always have as his ultimate aim the well-being of the person, so must the believing exegete who analyzes biblical texts always have as his or her ultimate aim the service of the transmission of the Word of God. "The ultimate purpose of Catholic exegesis is to nourish and build up the body of Christ with the word of God" (p. 149).

The distinction between the two fundamental aspects of the biblical writings grounds the distinction between two series of "principles": one series pertains to the analysis of the human language of the Bible; the other series pertains to the recognition of the Bible as Word of God. In order to analyze the human language of the Bible the Catholic exegete freely uses all the scientific means and methods that are useful for analyzing ancient texts. In order to perceive the religious message of the Bible accurately and deeply, the Catholic exegete reads the Bible in the light of his faith, which stands in continuity with the faith of the biblical authors and which, therefore, constitutes the pre-understanding that is most conducive to a correct interpretation. Concretely, this means that the exegete situates himself in a great community of faith and does not interpret the Bible individualistically, but in solidarity with his brothers and sisters in the faith. The consequence is that interpretation is carried out, above all, in the light of the entire biblical tradition and, more specifically, in the light of the paschal mystery of Christ according to the living Tradition of the Church.

Parts IV through VI complete the perspective. They contain other series of "principles" which consider the differences among the various senses of Scripture (literal, spiritual, fuller), and then the use of the methods and approaches of interpretation, principally, the use of the historical-critical method—which is indispensable but not exclusive—and finally, the relation of exegesis with the other theological disciplines, the problems of actualization and inculturation of the Bible, and the various uses of the Bible in the Church.

To bring together in a systematic manner all the elements contained in the document of the Biblical Commission that pertain to the principles of interpretation is by itself a very useful work, since these elements are sometimes dispersed in various parts of the document. However, this study does not limit itself to the task of cataloging principles, but contributes—by means of personal reflections, complementary additions, criticisms, suggestions—to a deeper understanding of the issues. For example, on the significance of "history" and "historical," a triple distinction is proposed which clarifies the question (p. 58ff.). On the question regarding philosophical hermeneutics, the observation is made that "the Biblical Commission's necessarily brief and simplified presentation [...] obscures the different uses authors make of different terms" and notes in particular that "the proper object of *understanding* and the relation between understanding and interpretation are among the matters viewed differently". Then clarifications are offered on this point (p. 78n). Some illuminating reflections are also offered on the usefulness of "the insights of philosophical hermeneutics" (p. 88). Some criticisms of the Commission's document regarding its presentation of the relationships between the Old and New Testaments are summarized, and in part, accepted. The various modes in which the concept of the "literal sense" has been understood through the history of exegesis are explained in a very helpful way. In particular it is noted that when Thomas Aquinas says that the literal sense is that intended by the author, he immediately adds that the author of Scripture is God, who understands all things at once (p. 173), in such a way that the literal sense of a text from Scripture can encompass a plurality of meanings. This is a markedly different concept of the literal sense than is commonly accepted in our day and it is also proposed by the document (II.B.1).

Another passage of the dissertation points to a "lack of clarity in the incarnation analogy" applied to Scripture by *Divino afflante Spiritu*: "Just as the substantial Word of God became like men in every respect 'except sin' (Heb 4:15), so too the words of God expressed in human languages, became like human language in every respect except error" (p. 38). In truth, the parallelism is not exact. The idea that corresponds to "except sin" in reference to the Incarnation, should be—in reference to Scripture—"except deceit" rather than "except error". This is because a human error is not sin, while deceit is. It is significant, therefore, that when the Council's Constitution *Dei Verbum* took up the analogy of the Incarnation (*DV* 13) it left out "except error" and expressed its doctrine of biblical inerrancy in another way (*DV* 11).

Other discussions are not without interest. Indeed, more than once perspectives are enlarged. For example, nine "unresolved questions" are listed (p. 248) regarding the relationship between history and exegesis. The conclusion, after indicating the principal merits of the document of the Biblical Commission, proposes a stimulating "agenda for further discussion". It provides a dynamic finale which—like the dissertation as a whole—reveals a strong love for the Bible as the Word of God which leads to communion with Him, as well as a strong love for the Church as the intended recipient of this Word and the privileged context of its interpretation and realization.

It is therefore fitting to hope that very many people will read this work and derive intellectual and spiritual profit from it.

Albert Vanhoye, SJ
Secretary of the Biblical Commission

CONTENTS

ACKNOWLEDGMENTS

This work is the final edition of a doctoral dissertation presented to the Gregorian University in November 2000. I would like to express my gratitude to those who in one way or another helped me to bring this work to completion.

First, I want to express my deep appreciation to the director of my thesis, James Swetnam, SJ, who took a keen interest in this work, read and corrected my drafts with extraordinary rapidity, and gave me much encouragement and sound advice. Likewise, I want to thank Jared Wicks, SJ, the "second reader" of my thesis for his helpful criticisms and comments.

I also want to express my thanks to others who helped me in the course of my research and writing. First among these is Albert Vanhoye, SJ, Secretary of the Pontifical Biblical Commission, who met with me, answered questions by mail, and who reviewed and commented on my first draft of the principles of interpretation. Subsequently, Father Vanhoye agreed to contribute the preface to this work and helped me eliminate a number of minor errors through his very careful reading. I wish to extend special thanks also to Joseph Fitzmyer, SJ, and Brendan Byrne, SJ, members of the Biblical Commission, who spoke with me and offered their comments on the principles of interpretation. In addition, I am grateful to the following persons who either answered questions by mail, or who read and commented on sections of this study: Charles Conroy, MSC, Ignace de la Potterie, SJ, Prosper Grech, OSA, Dr. Mary Healy, Fr. Paul Kreimes, and Dr. George Martin. Finally, I wish to thank the library staff at the Szoka Library at Sacred Heart Seminary in Detroit, and the staff at the libraries of the University of Michigan and the Gregorian University for all their assistance.

I am grateful to those who have taught me to read and interpret Scripture, my parents and my teachers—Elena Bosetti, SGBP, Pietro Bovati, SJ, Scott Brodeur, SJ, Nuria Calduch-Benages, MSFN, Stephen Clark, Charles Conroy, MSC, Prosper Grech, OSA, Fr. Paul Kreimes, Fr. Richard Macey, Stephen Pisano, SJ, Robert O'Toole, SJ, Albert Vanhoye, SJ, and Ugo Vanni, SJ.

I especially want to thank my wife Marsha for her constant support and encouragement in this thesis, for her sound advice and skillful copyediting, and for her prayers and those of her friends whom she enlisted in the cause. I want to thank Laura Baglioni for her gracious hospitality during my visits to Rome and the community members of the Lay Centre of Foyer Unitas for their support over the course of all my studies in Rome. Special thanks is due to my fellow students, Ester Abbattista and Max Bonilla, for their practical help and advice in presenting my work to the University. I am grateful to all my family and friends who prayed for me through this process, especially my morning prayer companions, Stuart Collins, Jack Flanagan, Deacon Gerry Holowicki, and Scott Wright.

I give thanks above all to our Lord whose mercy, grace, and strength I have experienced consistently during these years of writing and research.

Notwithstanding so much excellent help, all responsibility for the shortcomings in this work belongs solely to me.

ABBREVIATIONS

ABD	David Noel Freedman, ed., *Anchor Bible Dictionary* (New York: Doubleday, 1992)
Address	"Address of his Holiness, Pope John Paul II, On the Interpretation of the Bible in the Church", 28 April 1993
CBA	Catholic Biblical Association
CCC	*Catechism of the Catholic Church*
CDF	Congregation for the Doctrine of the Faith
Commento	Ghiberti, Giuseppe, and Francesco Mosetto, eds. *L'interpretazione della Bibbia nella Chiesa: Commento.* Torino: Elle di Ci, 1998.
Conclusion	"Conclusion" of *The Interpretation of the Bible in the Church*
DAS	Pope Pius XII, Encyclical, *Divino afflante Spiritu* (1943)
DBI	R.J. Coggins and J.L. Houlden, eds., *A Dictionary of Biblical Interpretation* (London: SCM Press, 1990)
DFT	René Latourelle and Rino Fisichella, eds., *Dictionary of Fundamental Theology* (New York: Crossroad, 1995)
DS	H. Denzinger and A. Schönmetzer, *Enchiridion symbolorum*, 35th ed. (New York, 1974).
DV	Vatican II, Dogmatic Constitution on Divine Revelation *Dei Verbum* (1965)
EB	Alfio Filippi and Erminio Lora, eds., *Enchiridion Biblicum*, 2nd ed. (Bologna: Dehoniane, 1993)
FI	International Theological Commission, *Faith and Inculturation* (1988)
FOC	Fathers of the Church Series, Catholic University of America
Fr	French
Gk	Greek
GS	Vatican II, Pastoral Constitution on the Church in the Modern World *Gaudium et Spes* (1965)

Heb	Hebrew
IBC	Pontifical Biblical Commission, *The Interpretation of the Bible in the Church* (1993)
IBCom	William R. Farmer, Sean McEvenue, Armando J. Levoratti, et al, eds., *The International Bible Commentary* (Collegeville, MN: Liturgical, 1998)
Intro	Introduction of *The Interpretation of the Bible in the Church*
ITC	International Theological Commission
JBC	Raymond E. Brown, Joseph A. Fitzmyer, and Roland E. Murphy, eds., *The Jerome Biblical Commentary* (Englewood Cliffs, NJ: Prentice Hall, 1968)
Lat	Latin
NJBC	Raymond E. Brown, Joseph A. Fitzmyer, and Roland E. Murphy, eds., *The New Jerome Biblical Commentary* (Englewood Cliffs, NJ: Prentice Hall, 1990)
PBC	Pontifical Biblical Commission
PD	Pope Leo XIII, Encyclical, *Providentissimus Deus* (1893)
Preface	Joseph Cardinal Ratzinger, Preface to *The Interpretation of the Bible in the Church*
RSS	*Rome and the Study of Scripture* (St. Meinrad, IN: Grail, 1962)
SC	Vatican II, Constitution on the Sacred Liturgy *Sacrosanctum Concilium* (1963)
ST	St. Thomas Aquinas, *Summa Theologica*

Unless otherwise indicated, citations in parentheses, e.g., (I.A.1.c), refer to sections and paragraphs in *The Interpretation of the Bible in the Church*. The sections are numbered in accord with divisions in the document, and paragraphs within a section are enumerated by lower case letters.

INTRODUCTION

The interpretation of Sacred Scripture is for Catholics, as indeed for all Christians, of paramount importance for Christian life. Every age of the Church has found it necessary to develop a hermeneutic, a way of interpreting the Bible that corresponds to the needs and mentality of the time, yet remains faithful to the word of God. The earliest Christians needed to interpret the Jewish Scriptures in the light of the death and resurrection of Jesus of Nazareth, whom God had revealed to them as Lord and Messiah. In the second century Irenaeus found it necessary to defend the unity of the Bible, and to distinguish Catholic biblical interpretation from that of the Gnostics, who often used the same Scriptures. In response to the christological controversies, the Fathers of the Church explained the New Testament's teaching about Christ and God in the language of Greek philosophy. Both the Protestant Reformation and the Enlightenment introduced new principles of biblical interpretation. These movements challenged the conclusions of previous generations and forced Christians to consider more deeply the path by which the individual and the Church arrive at the true meaning of the biblical word.

The last century has been a significant one for the interpretation of Scripture as both Catholics and Protestants have encountered, resisted, and then sought to refine and integrate critical methods of exegesis and new hermeneutical understanding. The 1993 publication of *The Interpretation of the Bible in the Church* (*IBC*) commemorates the 100th and 50th anniversaries of two landmark papal encyclicals which treated the interpretation of Scripture, namely, *Providentissimus Deus* (Leo XIII, 1893) and *Divino afflante Spiritu* (Pius XII, 1943). In *Providentissimus Deus* Pope Leo XIII promoted biblical studies at the same time as he sought to defend Scripture against the attacks of rationalism. In *Divino afflante Spiritu* Pope Pius XII opened the doors of the Church to the use of scientific methods in Catholic exegesis[1]. In 1965 the Second Vatican Council confirmed this openness in its Dogmatic Constitution on Divine Revelation, *Dei Verbum*. During the years following Vatican II the historical-critical method has dominated Catholic biblical scholarship.   At the same time this method has provoked dissatisfaction on the part of many and the flowering of various alternative methods and approaches.

New and old questions about interpreting Scripture continue to be posed. What distinguishes Catholic biblical exegesis from Protestant, Jewish or "secular" exegesis?   What is the role of the exegete?   What place should the historical-critical method hold in Catholic exegesis?   What about the new synchronic methods that have been developed in the study of literature? What about patristic exegesis and the "spiritual" meaning of the Bible?   How can the study of the Bible be the "soul" of theology?   How does God speak to men and women today through the Bible?

The ferment regarding these questions and others prompted the Pontifical Biblical Commission to initiate a study of interpretation of the Bible in the Church in 1989.   They published the results of their research and discussions in 1993, *The Interpretation of the Bible in the Church*, with the explicit endorsement of Pope John Paul II.   Exegetes, theologians, and lay people in the Church have received the document warmly.   The *IBC* evaluates the most commonly used scholarly methods at the time of the Biblical Commission's deliberations and articulates what it considers to be the essential characteristics of Catholic interpretation at the conclusion of a hundred-year process of reconciling Christian interpretation with scientific critical methods. This is not to imply that the 1993 document is definitive—the task of articulating an adequate hermeneutic remains as long as the Church continues to confront new intellectual and social circumstances.   Yet for reasons which will become evident in the course of this study, it is possible to recognize a certain maturation in the 1993 Biblical Commission document, perhaps the beginning of a concluding phase in a difficult chapter in the history of the interpretation of the Bible in the Church.

Today, seven years after the publication of the *IBC*, the time is ripe to glean more from the harvest of the Biblical Commission's labors.   The initial round of reviews and critical reflection regarding the Commission's document has appeared in print and can be taken into account.   In addition, with the passage of time it is easier to distinguish elements of passing relevance from those of enduring value.   For example, the Commission's description of what

---

[1] Following the usage of the *IBC*, this study will use the adjective "scientific" to refer to the kind of Scripture study more commonly described in English as "critical" or "scholarly".

it considered the most common methods and approaches in use—a "snapshot" reflecting the time of its writing—is already somewhat dated due to the rapidly changing landscape in biblical studies. On the other hand, the criteria by which the Commission evaluated the various methods and approaches and the *IBC*'s chapter on the characteristics of Catholic interpretation clearly retain their value despite changes in the field.

Finally, a careful analysis of the *IBC* can help to answer a question which has come into clearer focus since the document's publication in 1993. Both the 1997 and 1998 sessions of the Catholic Biblical Association of America featured major addresses on the subject of "What is Catholic about Catholic Biblical Scholarship?"[2]. In light of the scholarly reflection that lies behind the Biblical Commission document and the ecclesial status it enjoys, there appears no better way of defining what constitutes Catholic interpretation than to read the *IBC* attentively with this question in view[3]. The present volume represents the first such attempt.

1. Aim and Method

The aim of this study is to identify the key principles of Catholic biblical interpretation proposed explicitly or implicitly in *The Interpretation of the Bible in the Church* (*IBC*) and to discuss the meaning and significance of each of these principles. "Principles of Catholic interpretation" will be defined as *the presuppositions and procedures appropriate to interpreting Scripture in the life of the Catholic Church*. This thesis will not attempt to present every principle of Catholic interpretation, but only those expressed in the *IBC*[4].

The method of this study has been to formulate, on the basis of a positive analysis of the *IBC*, twenty principles, which succinctly express the presuppositions or procedures found in the Biblical Commission's document.

---

[2] Johnson, "What's Catholic About It?", and Murphy, "What Is Catholic? Revisited". References to books and articles appearing in the footnotes will supply abbreviated titles and, where appropriate, page numbers. Complete information on each work cited is available in the bibliography located at the end of this study.

[3] Roland Murphy suggests that an examination of the *IBC* would provide an "adequate" answer to the question. In his own presentation, however, he opts to offer a more personal response to the topic ("What Is Catholic? Revisited", 112).

[4] Many Catholic beliefs about Scripture which indeed function as principles of interpretation, such as the Bible's inspiration and inerrancy, were assumed by the Biblical Commission (without prejudice to future developments) and not treated. In addition, it would be possible to articulate other principles of interpretation depending on the biblical genre and the interpretive aim. For instance, it would be possible to formulate principles for exegeting parables, or for interpreting the psalms in Christian prayer or the gospels for preaching. Although the Biblical Commission does offer some practical advice that applies to specific instances of interpretation, the *IBC* mainly considers interpretation at a more general level.

Then each of these principles is explained at greater length and the significance of each is discussed.

In order to make the principles reflect the mind of the Biblical Commission as closely as possible, the language of the document has been used whenever possible. When this was not feasible careful paraphrases or summary statements have been formulated. For stylistic and methodological reasons wording taken verbatim from the *IBC* and included in the principles is *not* indicated by quotation marks[5]. Throughout this study the twenty principles (or statements from them) normally appear in indented italics. Since this work depends on deriving a correct set of principles from the *IBC*, three members of the Biblical Commission were consulted regarding the adequacy of these principles[6]. Their suggestions were noted, and for the most part, followed. Nevertheless, the author remains responsible for the principles of Catholic interpretation formulated here, and their validity depends on their consistency with the *IBC* itself.

Besides the *IBC* itself, a variety of other sources provide the basis for further explanation and discussion of each principle. First, writings of the members of the Biblical Commission have contributed to a more reliable interpretation of the document. Second, published commentary on the *IBC* has been consulted. Third, prior magisterial documents on Scripture have been considered, especially the Second Vatican Council's Sacred Constitution on Divine Revelation (*Dei Verbum*) and the two documents commemorated on the occasion of the *IBC*'s publication, *Providentissimus Deus* and *Divino afflante Spiritu*. Finally, contemporary scholarly books and articles on

---

[5] Stylistically it would be awkward for the principles to appear as a mishmash of quotations, ellipses, bracketed insertions and other statements. Methodologically, a quotation of the *IBC* within a principle could appear to claim that the quotation grounds a "principle" of the *IBC* without due consideration of context. Instead parenthetical references indicate the paragraph or paragraphs of the *IBC* which a given principle quotes, paraphrases or summarizes, except when a summary statement expresses a general position which cannot be easily localized.

[6] The Secretary of the Commission, Albert Vanhoye, was kind enough to speak with the author on four occasions (two of which provided the basis for a published interview Vanhoye, "Catholicism and the Bible") and to offer written comments on the twenty principles in December 1998. Commission member Brendan Byrne also met with the author to answer questions about the *IBC* at the Catholic Biblical Association of America's meeting at Notre Dame University in August 1999. Commission member Joseph Fitzmyer shared some of his views in informal conversation at the same meeting. Both Byrne and Fitzmyer were kind enough to give the author their written feedback on the twenty principles in December 1999. None of the Biblical Commission members, however, has read the text of this study except for Father Vanhoye, who read the penultimate version before writing his preface.

interpretation have been consulted in order to contextualize and to evaluate the Biblical Commission's position.

Obviously an exhaustive analysis of twenty principles of Catholic interpretation is beyond the scope of a single study, and therefore this thesis has the nature of an overview. A certain selectivity in deciding which issues to treat is unavoidable. This study will attempt to address the issues most often raised by reviewers of the *IBC*, the issues most raised by critics of contemporary Catholic exegesis, and the issues which seem to the author most important for the future of Catholic interpretation.

Someone may question the legitimacy or usefulness of epitomizing what is already a concise and articulate work in order to formulate principles of Catholic interpretation. After all, the Biblical Commission did not intend or structure the *IBC* to define principles of Catholic interpretation. In its Introduction the Commission indicates that its purpose was to survey the current situation in exegesis, to respond to criticisms which have been made of scientific exegesis, and to clarify the mission of exegesis in the Catholic Church (Intro B.a)[7]. Even chapter III, whose title, "Characteristics of Catholic Interpretation", might lead the reader to expect a list of principles, does not explicitly propose principles. Instead it provides *descriptions—* descriptions of interpretation in the biblical tradition and in the tradition of the Church, of the role of the exegete, and of the relationship of exegesis to other disciplines. Indeed, the persuasive power of the *IBC* may well be due to its descriptive approach[8].

Nevertheless, a careful reading of *IBC* reveals that the Biblical Commission makes its judgements on the basis of consistent principles of interpretation. Sometimes these principles are explicit, for instance, when the document provides precise definitions for the senses of Scripture. At other times they are implicit, for instance, when it evaluates various exegetical approaches in chapter I and offers reasons for these evaluations. Still in other cases, the Biblical Commission's principles emerge as conclusions which follow from descriptive sections, such as the conclusions the Commission draws from the history of interpretation (chapter III).

---

[7] The *IBC* often uses the terms "interpretation" and "exegesis" interchangeably without denying the more inclusive meaning of the former term, and this study will follow the *IBC*'s usage. The document as a whole addresses Catholic interpretation, but gives special attention to exegesis.

[8] As in its most important document prior to this one, which discussed contemporary approaches to christology (see Fitzmyer, *Scripture and Christology*; also Commission Biblique Pontificale, *Bible et Christologie*), the Biblical Commission offers scholarly description and analysis, rather than seeking to define principles on the basis of dogmatic or ecclesial authority.

Someone may point out that by formulating the Biblical Commission document's teaching systematically in principles this study goes beyond the intention of its authors. This is true. Not only does this study re-shape the *IBC*'s material, it takes what was written in a particular historical moment for a particular purpose (see next chapter) and applies it some years later for a purpose, which, though related, is nonetheless distinct. The Biblical Commission intended their document to be a description of Catholic interpretation for the sake of evaluating exegetical methods and approaches, clarifying the role of the exegete, and providing orientations to the use of the Bible in the Church in light of that description. This study analyzes the Biblical Commission's description of Catholic interpretation for the sake of articulating its defining principles. In other words, the *IBC* is an evaluation of exegetical methods in light of an overall account of Catholic interpretation. This study, while not ignoring exegetical methods, concerns itself with the overall shape of Catholic interpretation of Scripture.

What precisely does this writer claim regarding the relationship of this study to the document of the Biblical Commission? This writer maintains that each of the principles identified in this study is grounded in the *IBC* and that this set of principles is complete, i.e., that there are no other principles of the same weight or level of importance to be found in the document. Readers will have to judge for themselves the adequacy of these principles to the *IBC* and to the tradition of Catholic interpretation.

2. *Point of View*

Because this study is a work of interpretation, a word about the point of view of its author is in order. The author acquired his respect for Scripture growing up the son of a Presbyterian minister in an evangelical family. Respect grew into love when, as an undergraduate at the University of Michigan in Ann Arbor, he began to experience the Holy Spirit in the context of a nascent charismatic community. When he graduated from the university in 1972 he entered the Catholic Church, having become convinced of the Catholic understanding of revelation over the Protestant doctrine of *sola scriptura*. From then until the time of this writing, his primary vocation has been the lay apostolate in ecumenical and Catholic settings, in the United States and abroad. These experiences convinced the author of the power of Scripture to nourish and form Christian life. A combination of spiritual desire and pastoral interest led him to graduate studies in theology and Scripture at Sacred Heart Major Seminary in Detroit and the Gregorian University in Rome in the 1990's.

The author's experience of Scripture scholarship over the years was mixed. On the one hand, history, literature, and the biblical languages opened up new vistas of understanding. On the other, it seemed at times that professional biblical scholarship had lost sight of its religious character, or, for some reason, had forgotten how to relate the Bible to life[9]. When he was writing his Masters' thesis on a text from the Gospel of John in 1994, the *IBC* appeared in English and he found it extremely useful, particularly the section on actualization. As he continued to study the Biblical Commission's document, he became convinced that it contained insights that could renew the use of the Bible in the Church. He came to the conclusion that the problem of contemporary biblical scholarship does not reside in its use of the historical-critical method, nor does its hope for the future reside in new methods and approaches. Instead the hope for the renewal of Catholic exegesis lies in clarifying and reappropriating its fundamental principles.

3. *Structure*

A brief chapter is devoted to considering each principle. At the end of the statement of the principle, a footnote refers the reader to the sections of the *IBC* in which the principle finds expression. Each principle receives two kinds of consideration. First, an *Explanation* section provides an exposition of the principle, explaining its meaning, its place in the document, and in some cases illustrates its use in the interpretation of particular texts. Second, a *Discussion* section presents further analysis of some aspects of the principle in the light of published commentary on the *IBC*, prior magisterial teaching on Scripture, or contemporary scholarly discussion of the issues at stake. The *explanations* of the principles are intended to be consistent with what the document says, even if they go beyond what the *IBC* explicitly affirms. The *discussion* sections, however, are not limited to the point of view of the document in what they affirm.

The treatment of the twenty principles of Catholic interpretation forms six parts. Part I introduces the document of the Biblical Commission and considers the foundational principle, that Sacred Scripture is "the word of God expressed in human language". Part II addresses the "human language" dimension and the necessity of "scientific" or scholarly means to interpret it. Part III presents principles which address Scripture as "the word of God", i.e.,

---

[9] Sandra Schneiders reports a similar experience (*Revelatory Text*, 1-2) and elsewhere offers an insightful discussion of the differing interests of the believing community and the methods of Scripture scholarship ("Church and Biblical Scholarship"). The *IBC*, however, recommends an approach to exegesis in the Church that more satisfactorily resolves this tension.

that relate interpretation to Christian faith. Part IV on "the Meaning of Inspired Scripture" treats the senses of Scripture. Part V discusses the human "Methods and Approaches" used by exegesis and the ways in which their use is conditioned by the unique object of their study. Part VI, "Interpretation in Practice" treats the theoretical and practical principles that guide biblical interpretation in the life of the Church. The conclusion sums up the study, highlighting the Biblical Commission's achievement in *The Interpretation of the Bible in the Church* and outlining the challenges that remain for Catholic biblical interpretation at the dawn of the third millennium.

4. Contribution and Limits

The contribution of this work consists in the fact that it is the first book-length work by an individual author devoted to an analysis of the *IBC*[10] and the first study in recent times to propose a set of principles for Catholic interpretation. By distilling and discussing the Pontifical Biblical Commission's principles of Catholic interpretation, this study hopes to serve Catholic exegesis, which, at least since the publication of *Dei Verbum*, has been seeking a fruitful integration of scientific and theological perspectives in its work. These principles can serve not only exegetes, but also can guide the interpretation of theologians, clergy, seminarians and laity. Insofar as these principles faithfully reflect the Biblical Commission's document they can function as criteria for evaluating interpretations, making it easier, for example, to distinguish incomplete treatments of biblical texts from holistic interpretation. Because of their synthetic character, these principles and explanations can perform a pedagogical function for students and professors of Scripture and theology[11]. Furthermore, the formulation and discussion of the Biblical Commission's principles advances the process by which the principles themselves may be evaluated and refined. Finally, the exercise of articulating and reflecting upon principles which sum up the presuppositions

---

[10] That is, not counting Commission member Fitzmyer's one-volume explanatory commentary that accompanies the text of the document (*The Biblical Commission's Document*). A doctoral dissertation by Joseph Prior traces the development of the historical-critical method in Catholic exegesis and devotes about half its pages to the *IBC* (*Historical Critical Method in Catholic Exegesis*). In addition, there are several multi-authored collections of articles considering various aspects of the document, published either as books or in volumes of journals dedicated to discussion of the *IBC* (for a list, see note on p. 13).

[11] There is ample precedent for such hermeneutical guides in the Jewish and Christian tradition. One thinks of the seven exegetical rules (*middôt*) of Hillel or the thirteen *middôt* of Rabbi Ishmael, or of Tyconius' "Book of Rules", which Augustine uses in *On Christian Doctrine*, III.xxx-xxxvi.43-56. See Froehlich, *Biblical Interpretation*, for the texts and an introduction to these ancient principles of interpretation.

and procedures expressed in the *IBC* can bring the reader to an excellent vantage point from which to evaluate what the Pontifical Biblical Commission has achieved, and to reflect on the present status and future needs of Catholic biblical interpretation.

Nevertheless, to avoid arousing false expectations it is important to list at the outset some needs that this study will not fulfill. This work will not provide a commentary on every point in the *IBC*, but confines itself to reflecting on the principles of Catholic interpretation it finds there. Nor will this study treat all the issues raised by any of the twenty principles it sets forth, since each could easily require a monograph in its own right. By design this work provides a bird's-eye view of the forest called Catholic interpretation, rather than a detailed examination of each individual tree. Exegetes will not find applications of these principles to every kind of text; instead, they will find examples that hopefully will stimulate their own thinking. Students will not find a practical guide to the various methods, approaches, and developments in philosophical hermeneutics which the Biblical Commission describes. Other works (some of which will be mentioned in the notes) can meet those needs. Pastors will not find the answers to many practical questions about interpreting Scripture in preaching and catechesis, although hopefully the discussion of these principles will provide a helpful starting point. Finally, those interested in comparing Catholic, Protestant, and Orthodox biblical interpretation will not find a discussion of those differences here, since the Commission did not consider them.

This study intends to be useful to as wide a readership as possible. Therefore, the author has sought to state things as simply as possible, to avoid unnecessary jargon, and at times, for the sake of clarity, to state explicitly matters generally assumed by Catholic scholars. Whenever possible, principles of Catholic interpretation have been illustrated in terms of their implications for specific texts. In addition, the presentation of each principle is intended to accommodate diverse interests and levels of background among readers, generally moving from what is simplest and most fundamental to what is more complex and of specialized interest, giving additional attention to the latter in the notes.

Although this study refers to the principles of interpretation derived from the *IBC* as principles of "Catholic" interpretation, the author by no means intends to use the term exclusively or to imply that they are not shared by other Christians. In fact, most of them are shared by other Christians, and many of them would be shared by believing Jews. Rather, the intent of this study is to address itself positively, like the Biblical Commission document, to the principles of biblical interpretation suited to the faith and life of the Catholic Church.

This dissertation has a practical aim. It is hoped that the principles of Catholic interpretation of the Biblical Commission expounded in these pages may be of service to exegetes, theologians, clergy, seminarians, lay ministers of the word, and to all Christians who seek to understand the message which God himself addresses to them in Sacred Scripture.

PART I

THE INTERPRETATION OF THE BIBLE IN THE CHURCH AND THE FOUNDATIONAL PRINCIPLE OF CATHOLIC INTERPRETATION

INTRODUCTION TO

THE INTERPRETATION OF THE BIBLE IN THE CHURCH

The Pontifical Biblical Commission's 1993 Document

Before identifying and commenting on the principles of interpretation expressed in *The Interpretation of the Bible in the Church*, it is necessary to lay the groundwork for interpreting the document itself[1]. This chapter will discuss the nature and membership of the Pontifical Biblical Commission, the circumstances which occasioned the document, and the process of its composition. Next the chapter will examine the structure and purpose of the *IBC* and its reception, particularly by Pope John Paul II. Finally, this chapter will consider the implications of this background for interpreting the *IBC*.

1. The Pontifical Biblical Commission

The name, the Pontifical Biblical Commission, refers to two quite different entities employed by the popes of this century to take a concern for Catholic biblical scholarship[2]. The original Biblical Commission was

---

[1] Commentaries on the *IBC* include Fitzmyer, *The Biblical Commission's Document*; Ghiberti and Mosetto, *L'interpretazione: Commento*; Loza Vera, "La interpretación"; and Ruppert, "Kommentierende Einführung". Other collections of articles dedicated to considering the *IBC* include Chrostowski, "33 Sympozjum Biblistów Polskich, 1995"; Chrostowski, "34 Sympozjum Biblistów Polskich, 1996"; Houlden, *Interpretation*; Segalla, "Cento anni di studi biblici"; and Segalla, "Scienze umane e interpretazione". *Bibel und Liturgie* carried a series of brief articles on the *IBC* from 1995-1998 found in vols. 68-71. See also Prior, *Historical Critical Method in Catholic Exegesis* and the bibliography at the end of this study.

[2] For background on the PBC see Fitzmyer, *Christological Catechism*, 119-125; Gillman, "Faith and Science Together"; Vanhoye, "Passé et présent de la Commission Biblique"; and *EB* §268-273.

established in 1902 by Pope Leo XIII with the task of promoting biblical interpretation in harmony with his encyclical *Providentissimus Deus* and of guarding against false interpretations.[3] Because of new developments in the biblical sciences, Pope Leo wished to relieve the Holy Office (now the Congregation for the Doctrine of the Faith) of responsibility for decisions regarding Scripture, and to entrust those decisions instead to a group specializing in that field. The members of the Pontifical Biblical Commission were all Cardinals and the commission functioned like other Congregations of the Curia. In addition, the Commission employed the assistance of Scripture scholars and theologians as consultors. In the years that followed, the Biblical Commission functioned as an organ of the Church's Magisterium, and its decisions, once approved by the Pope, were binding like those of other Congregations which concerned doctrine[4]. The Commission began its activity during the Catholic Church's vigorous reaction to Modernism, and its decisions until 1940 had a decidedly defensive character, treating such topics as source criticism (called "literary criticism"), authorship, the integrity of the biblical books, dates of composition, and the historicity of biblical narratives. After Pope Pius XII's encyclical *Divino afflante Spiritu* (1943), however, the perspective changed significantly and the Biblical Commission began to support the scientific study of Scripture.   Clarifications were issued, indicating that earlier decisions of the Commission were to be taken as responding to a particular historical situation, and that Catholic scholars could pursue their research and investigations with full freedom.

After the Second Vatican Council and the first Synod of Bishops, Pope Paul VI decided to change the nature and task of the Biblical Commission "to better coordinate the collaboration of exegetes and theologians with the Holy See and among themselves"[5]. The new Pontifical Biblical Commission is no longer an organ of the Magisterium, but is rather a consultative body, parallel to the International Theological Commission and similarly linked to the Congregation for the Doctrine of the Faith[6]. Instead of Cardinals assisted by scholars, the new Commission consists of twenty "scholars in the biblical sciences from various schools and nations who excel in their learning, their prudence and their Catholic attitude regarding the Magisterium of the

---

[3] Pope Leo XIII, Apostolic Letter, *Vigilantiae*, 30 October 1902, *EB* §137-148.

[4] Pope Piux X, Motu proprio, *Praestantia Scripturae Sacrae*, 18 November 1907, *EB* §268-273.

[5] Pope Paul VI, Motu proprio, *Sedula cura*, 27 June 1971, *EB* §722-739, quotation from §724, author's translation.

[6] One reviewer of the *IBC*, Raymond Collins, described the Commission as "the Church's official 'think tank' for matters dealing with the Bible". See Collins, "Methods of Biblical Interpretation", 8.

Church"[7]. Its President is the Cardinal Prefect of the Congregation for the Doctrine of the Faith, and the Pope chooses its Secretary after consulting the Commission's members.   The President of the Commission presents candidates for membership to the Pope after consulting with the bishops' conferences of the whole world. The Pope chooses and appoints the members of the Biblical Commission for five-year renewable terms.   It is significant that the new Commission is an international group in contrast to the earlier Commission which was entirely resident in Rome.

The role of the Pontifical Biblical Commission is to study various Scriptural topics for the benefit of the Pope and the Congregation of the Doctrine of the Faith. The topics which the Biblical Commission studies may be selected by the Pope, the President of the Commission, the Congregation for the Doctrine of the Faith, the Synod of Bishops, the Bishops' Conferences, or the Commission members themselves. The Biblical Commission submits its conclusions to the Pope and makes them available to the Congregation for the Doctrine of the Faith. The Commission is responsible for maintaining relationships with the various institutes of biblical studies, both Catholic and non-Catholic.   Finally, the Biblical Commission enjoys the right of consultation before the promulgation of any new norms on biblical matters. The current Biblical Commission usually convenes annually for a week-long plenary session and carries out other tasks through committees or by mail[8].

The Biblical Commission's study of biblical interpretation began in 1989, during the last year in which Henri Cazelles was Secretary of the Commission, and was completed in 1993 when Albert Vanhoye was

---

[7] Pope Paul VI, Motu proprio, *Sedula cura*, EB §727.

[8] Since its re-foundation, up to the publication of the *IBC*, the Biblical Commission has studied six themes. The first was the role of women in society and in the Church according to Scripture. This study was presented to Pope Paul VI and was not officially published. (It was, however, leaked and published, revealing that the members of the Commission held that Scripture does not exclude the possibility of ordaining women to the priesthood [*Origins* 6 (1976-1977) 92-96]). The second in 1978 addressed the use of Scripture in the writings on liberation theology, and it also was not published. The third, completed in 1979 and published, was a collection of presentations by Commission members on inculturation within Scripture itself (Pontificia Commissione Biblica, *Fede e cultura alla luce della Bibbia*).   The fourth, completed and published in1984, contained a text of 48 pages on the Bible and christology which was the fruit of the discussion of the Biblical Commission, followed by nine expositions related to the theme by individual members (Commission Biblique Pontificale, *Bible et Christologie*; and Fitzmyer, *Scripture and Christology*. The Fitzmyer volume does not contain the individual presentations, but does include a commentary by Fitzmyer.). The fifth was a study from 1985 to 1988 on the theme of unity and diversity in the Church. The Commission's 20-page synthesis and particular studies by individual members was published in 1989 (Commission Biblique Pontificale, *Unité et diversité dans l'Eglise*).

Secretary. (The Secretary, rather than the President, provides the effective leadership for the work of the Biblical Commission.) The *IBC* was the Biblical Commission's most substantial common effort to date, totaling about 96 pages of text in the original French edition and 102 pages in the official English edition[9]. The members of the Biblical Commission who approved the final draft of the *IBC* included the following: Cardinal Joseph Ratzinger (President); Johannes Beutler, SJ [Germany]; Jacques Briend [France]; N. Balembo Paul Buetubela [Congo Kinshasa]; Brendan Byrne, SJ [Australia]; Marcel Dumais, OMI [Quebec, Canada]; Joseph Fitzmyer, SJ [United States]; Albert Fuchs [Austria]; Jan Lambrecht, SJ [Belgium]; Armando Jorge Levoratti [Argentina]; José Loza Vera, OP [Mexico]; Archim. Antoine Mouhanna [Lebanon]; Domingo Munoz Léon [Spain]; R. Jesu Raja, SJ [India]; Gianfranco Ravasi [Italy]; Hubert Ritt [Austria]; Lothar Ruppert [Germany]; Adrian Schenker, OP [Switzerland]; Giuseppe Segalla [Italy]; Lech Remigiusz Stachowiak [Poland]; Albert Vanhoye, SJ (Secretary) [France]; and Jean-Luc Vesco, OP [France].[10]

Some reviewers have raised questions regarding the independence of the deliberations of the Biblical Commission in view of its close ties to the Congregation for the Doctrine of the Faith (CDF). Some have speculated that Cardinal Ratzinger, the President of the Commission, substantially influenced the contents of the *IBC*, and like good source critics, have even ventured to suggest which nuances come from the Cardinal[11]! However, no evidence supports these speculations. At least two members of the Commission have responded in print to questions about Cardinal Ratzinger's role. In response to an interview question, Commission Secretary Vanhoye described the Cardinal's participation as "admirably" restrained, "not insisting on his criticism. We were completely free to discuss our perspectives on the historical-critical method."[12] Likewise Commission member Lothar Ruppert

---

[9] Pontifical Biblical Commission, *The Interpretation of the Bible in the Church.* See also original French, Italian, Spanish and German versions published simultaneously by the official Vatican publisher.

[10] Besides Henri Cazelles, PSS [France], the members who took part in the initial exploration of the topic in 1989 but did not continue when the membership was renewed in 1990 include the following individuals: Archbishop Pasinya Laurent Monsengwo [Congo Kinshasa]; Bishop João Evangelista Martins Terra, SJ [Brazil]; Jean-Dominique Barthélemy, OP [Switzerland]; Jacques Dupont, OSB [Belgium]; Joachim Gnilka [Germany]; Jacques Guillet, SJ [France]; Augustyn Jankowski, OSB [Poland]; John Francis McHugh [England]; and Joseph Pathrapankal, CMI [India]. The lists are taken from the *Annuario Pontificio*, 1993 and 1989.

[11] See Carroll, "Cracks in the Soul of Theology"; Gillman, "Faith and Science Together"; and Klauck, "Das neue Dokument: Darstellung und Würdigung".

[12] Vanhoye, "Catholicism and the Bible", 35.

insists in his commentary on the *IBC* that the Biblical Commission functions freely and is in no way a mere instrument of the CDF. According to Ruppert, the influence of the President of the Biblical Commission was confined to nuances to the final draft, on which the rest of the Commission had to vote[13].

2. *Occasion*

In their introduction the Biblical Commission recounts the circumstances that led them to address the topic of interpretation in the Church. While interpretation has been important since the times in which the biblical books were written, new problems for interpretation have arisen in modern times. First, the distance in time and culture between modern readers and the original authors and recipients of biblical writings is greater. Second, during the last 100 years scholars have applied new scientific methods of studying ancient texts to the study of the Bible.

The Church's initial caution regarding these methods, due to their often being "wedded to positions hostile to the Christian faith" (Intro A.b)[14], yielded in time to gradual acceptance as the methods were freed from problematic presuppositions. This growing openness to scientific biblical research develops in Leo XIII's *Providentissimus Deus* (1893), Pius XII's *Divino afflante Spiritu* (1943), the Pontifical Biblical Commission's *Sancta Mater Ecclesia* (1964), and finally the Dogmatic Constitution, *Dei Verbum* (1965) of the Second Vatican Council[15]. In the judgment of the Pontifical Biblical Commission the results of applying modern methods of studying texts to the Bible have been positive for the progress of biblical studies in the Catholic Church, for the academic value of Catholic exegesis, for ecumenism and for theology. For those who have been trained in the new methods, a return to pre-critical interpretation is unthinkable (Intro A.c).

Nevertheless, after Vatican II when the leading scientific method, the historical-critical method, seemed to have gained the ascendance, it began to

---

[13] Ruppert, "Kommentierende Einführung", 15.

[14] References to the *IBC* will be appear in parentheses, identifying the heading divisions given by the Biblical Commission (outline numbering), followed by a letter in lower case which specifies the specific paragraph under the heading to which reference is made.

[15] Works that narrate aspects of this development include Asurmendi, "Cien años"; Brown and Collins, "Church Pronouncements"; Curtin, "Historical Criticism and Theological Interpretation"; de la Potterie, "L'Istituto Biblico"; Fusco, "Un secolo di metodo storico"; Gilbert, "Cinquant' anni"; Prior, *Historical Critical Method in Catholic Exegesis*; and Vanhoye, "Dopo la *Divino afflante Spiritu*".

be called into question[16].   Objections came both from scholars, who introduced alternative methods, and from many members of the faithful who found the historical-critical method wanting as regards Christian faith. Many scholars turned their gaze toward a synchronic study of texts, attending to "their language, composition, narrative structure and capacity for persuasion," and lost interest in the diachronic study of texts (Intro.A.d).   Other scholars preferred to interpret texts from within contemporary philosophical, psychological, sociological or political perspectives (Intro A.d).

All of this strengthened the hand of those who opposed scientific exegesis altogether. They judged that the diversity of interpretations showed the uselessness of scientific methods. They saw the negative fruit of doubt and perplexity among the faithful. Finally, it appeared to them that these methods have led "some exegetes to adopt positions contrary to the faith of the Church on matters…such as the virginal conception of Jesus and his miracles, and even his resurrection and divinity" (Intro.A.e). They judged historical-critical exegesis to be sterile for Christian life. It tends to restrict access to the Bible, they said, to a small circle of experts. According to the Biblical Commission, this view led some people to substitute simpler approaches, exclusively synchronic readings, and so-called "spiritual" readings, which are highly subjective. In consequence some people have resorted to simplistic readings of the Bible for "immediate answers to all kinds of questions," or to the interpretation of the sects (Intro.A.e-g).

Since the publication of the *IBC*, some of the Commission members have added details which fill in the picture regarding the motives for the document. In early 1994 the Secretary of the Commission, Albert Vanhoye, published an article explaining the *IBC* in *Civiltà Cattolica*, an Italian Jesuit publication with ties to the Holy See[17]. Vanhoye's account makes clear that leading exegetes and theologians were expressing reservations about the direction of Catholic exegesis. Specifically, Vanhoye refers to articles that appeared in the prestigious *Revue Biblique* in the 1970's[18], and a public address given by Cardinal Ratzinger at a conference in New York in 1988 criticizing what he considered common presuppositions in the use of the historical-critical

---

[16] All of the resources mentioned in the previous note except for Gilbert attend to developments after the Second Vatican Council, especially Curtin (up to 1983), Fusco and Prior.

[17] Vanhoye, "Riflessione circa un documento".

[18] Vanhoye's article in Italian cites only the book which republishes the articles by F. Refoulé and F. Dreyfus in Italian translation (*Quale esegesi oggi?*). The original titles of the articles are Dreyfus, "Exégèse en Sorbonne"; Dreyfus, "L'actualisation à l'intérieur de la Bible"; Dreyfus, "I. Du texte à la vie"; Dreyfus, "II. L'action de l'Esprit"; and Dreyfus, "III. La place de la Tradition"; and Refoulé, "L'exégèse en question".

method [19]. Commission member Ruppert agreed in identifying the upheaval in which exegesis found itself and Cardinal Ratzinger's questions as reasons for the document[20]. Ruppert himself believed that the unreflective use of the historical-critical method, the encroachment of literary perspectives which undermined Scripture's historical and theological dimension, and the multiplicity of methods and approaches required a response from the Biblical Commission[21].

3. *Purpose*

After describing this background in their introduction, the Biblical Commission summarizes the purpose of their document as follows:

> It is, then, appropriate to give serious consideration to the various aspects of the present situation as regards the interpretation of the Bible—to attend to the criticisms and the complaints, as also to the hopes and aspirations which are being expressed in this matter, to assess the possibilities opened up by the new methods and approaches and, finally, to try *to determine more precisely the direction which best corresponds to the mission of exegesis in the Catholic Church*. (Intro B.a, emphasis added)

The Commission goes on to add that its purpose is not to take a position on all the questions which concern the Bible. For instance, theological questions regarding inspiration are excluded (Intro B.b). Although the document includes a section on pastoral and catechetical interpretation in the Church, the primary focus of the document is on the work of exegetes. This interpretation of the Biblical Commission's purpose is confirmed by what the Commission itself says in the *IBC*'s final sentence: "In examining the present state of the matter, the present essay hopes to have made some contribution towards gaining, on the part of all, of a clearer awareness of the role of the exegete" (Conclusion f)[22].

4. *Process*

From Vanhoye's description (confirmed by Ruppert) it is plain that the Commission followed an intensively collegial approach to their study of interpretation in the Church. It began when the former Secretary, Henri

---

[19] Ratzinger, *Schriftauslegung im Widerstreit*; Neuhaus, *Biblical Interpretation in Crisis*.

[20] Ruppert, "Kommentierende Einführung", 15-18.

[21] See also Commission member Segalla, "Storia del documento".

[22] Vanhoye summarizes the purpose of the *IBC* this way: "It has sought to offer an overall vision of current practice in biblical exegesis, and, in addition, a fairly complete and balanced presentation of the Catholic way of practicing exegesis"("Riflessione circa un documento", 15).

Cazelles, asked all the members of the Biblical Commission to prepare presentations on various issues regarding biblical interpretation for the 1989 plenary session. When these papers were presented and discussed it was agreed that a common document should be prepared to present to the Pope to use or dispose of as he wished[23]. Then three subcommittees each drafted a proposed outline for the document. After a pause in their deliberations in 1990 while the membership of the Commission was changed, a Committee of the new Commission met in Milan in January 1991 to examine the three proposals and to establish a provisional outline. The Committee then assigned to each member of the Commission a particular section of the document to draft. At this point I will continue with Vanhoye's account:

> In the plenary session of 1991, all these partial drafts were examined and submitted to an open discussion. After the session each member had the task of revising his own text, taking into account the observations and suggestions received during the discussion, and handing it in to the Secretary. The Secretary, with the help of the Committee, reexamined everything, translating all the contributions into French, and making all the additions and modifications necessary to produce the first draft of the whole.... This draft was mailed in January 1992 to all the members of the Commission with the request that they examine it and send to the Secretary all the criticisms and suggestions they considered useful. The harvest was abundant: fifty pages worth. All this was the object of further discussions in the plenary session of April 1992. The discussions concluded with partial votes on the most important or controversial points.
>
> After the session the Secretary began all over, with the help of the Committee, to re-write the document to conform to all the observations and decisions expressed in the session. This new draft was submitted to detailed voting. Each member was invited to express himself and propose possible amendments to each subdivision of the text. No less than 187 amendments were proposed, which were evaluated by the Committee, and, in the majority of cases, accepted and inserted into the text. The final draft thus attained was submitted to a final vote in December 1992. It was understood that a positive vote did not signify necessarily complete agreement with every detail, but rather, the absence of dissent on any major point. The text of the document, the fruit of a collegial labor conducted with generous commitment and openness of spirit, received a unanimous vote of acceptance...[24].

---

[23] Ruppert, "Kommentierende Einführung", 18.

[24] Vanhoye, "Riflessione circa un documento", 10-11. Unless otherwise stated, quotations in English from books or articles published in other languages have been translated by the author of this study.

Vanhoye goes on to explain that *on only one point* was there a significant disagreement among the members of the Commission which remained unresolved, and that had to do with the last paragraph of the section on the Feminist Approach which contained an exhortation to feminist exegetes. A footnote to that paragraph (I.E.2.m) reveals the vote, since the minority had requested a record of their dissenting votes be published with the text. Although the details behind this vote are interesting[25], what is more significant is the degree of consensus it indicates regarding the rest of the document.

5. *Structure*

The structure of *IBC* yields important clues to its interpretation. Besides an Introduction and a Conclusion, the *IBC* consists of four main sections.

Chapter I is entitled "Methods and Approaches for Interpretation" and is divided into six sub-sections. The first two are devoted to "methods," the next three to "approaches," and the last to what is referred to in French as a "Lecture fondamentaliste" [26]. A descending valuation is intended[27]. A footnote to the Introduction explains the distinction between methods and approaches:

> By an exegetical "method" we understand a group of scientific procedures employed in order to explain texts. We speak of an "approach" when it is a question of an enquiry proceeding from a particular point of view. (Note to Intro B.e)

The first method treated, the historical-critical method, holds pride of place in the Commission's estimation. Yet it is significant that between the initial draft and the final outline of the document, the "literary approaches" were

---

[25] Of nineteen votes, eleven voted in favor of that paragraph, four voted against and four abstained. Vanhoye explains: "The note does not explain the reasons of those opposing the paragraph, whether they considered the text too gentle or too strong. We think we can say, without compromising due discretion, that those who voted against it rejected the paragraph as inopportune, since it was too severe and likely to wound the sensibilities of many women sincerely dedicated to the service of the word of God in the Church. In itself, the thought expressed in the text is true: feminist exegesis must not 'lose sight of the evangelical teaching on power as service'. Those opposing its inclusion were not denying this, but maintained that it was not the responsibility of the Biblical Commission to give feminists this lesson on the spirit of the Gospel" ("Riflessione circa un documento", 11).

[26] The English translation of the section heading "Fundamentalist Interpretation" obscures the Biblical Commission's intention to deny the title of "method" or approach" to fundamentalism, "since it refuses every methodical attempt at interpretation" (Vanhoye, "Riflessione circa un documento", 9).

[27] Vanhoye, "Riflessione circa un documento", 9.

elevated to the status of method, indicating, according to Vanhoye, that the historical-critical method does not exercise a monopoly as a scientific approach to the text[28]. Within the treatment of each of the methods and approaches, the first paragraphs are devoted to a neutral description, and usually, the concluding paragraphs to evaluation[29].

Chapter II, entitled "Hermeneutical Questions", has two parts. The first describes some of the main conclusions of modern philosophical hermeneutics and then evaluates their implications for exegesis. The second offers definitions and explanations of the literal, spiritual and fuller senses of Scripture. According to Vanhoye this chapter

> shows how philosophical reflection on "pre-understanding," "fusion of horizons," and the potential of "symbolic language" liberate exegesis from the excessively narrow confines of the historical-critical method and help to understand better the various levels of meaning traditionally attributed to texts from Scripture[30].

Ruppert refers to the treatment of hermeneutics as a "hinge", joining the exegetical methods of chapter I with their application in the Church in chapter III[31].

Chapter III, entitled "Characteristics of Catholic Interpretation", according to Vanhoye, "defines the orientations of scientific Catholic exegesis"[32]. It discusses interpretation in the biblical tradition, interpretation in the tradition of the Church, the task of the exegete, and the relationship of exegesis with other theological disciplines. For the purposes of deriving principles of Catholic interpretation that apply to exegetes, this chapter is obviously of capital importance[33].

Chapter IV, entitled "Interpretation of the Bible in the Life of the Church", includes sections on actualization, inculturation and the use of the Bible in the liturgy, *lectio divina*, pastoral ministry, and ecumenism. This

---

[28] Vanhoye, "Riflessione circa un documento", 8-9.

[29] The Biblical Commission employed a similar approach in its document regarding various approaches to christology (Commission Biblique Pontificale, *Bible et Christologie*). In that document the Commission employed the awkward structure of devoting the first section to description, and the second—which reviews all of the same approaches—to evaluation, requiring the reader to page back and forth. In this respect the structure of the *IBC* is a considerable improvement.

[30] Vanhoye, "Riflessione circa un documento", 9.

[31] Ruppert, "Kommentierende Einführung", 19.

[32] Vanhoye, "Riflessione circa un documento", 9-10.

[33] Commission member, Giuseppe Segalla, refers to its content as the "frame of reference, the Catholic theological hermeneutic", which is the proper criterion for discerning methods ("Introduzione", 6).

section contains principles of Catholic interpretation that occur beyond the sphere of the exegete in the ordinary life of the Church.

6. Reception and Address by Pope John Paul II

Since the Pontifical Biblical Commission is only a consultative body, its conclusions have weight only insofar as they are received by the Pope or the Congregation for the Doctrine of the Faith (CDF). When the Commission's study of biblical interpretation was completed, it was referred to the Holy See as is customary. At that point there were at least four possible outcomes for the Biblical Commission's document. First, it could have been used by the CDF as the basis for a document of its own. Second, it could have been used as the basis for an encyclical by the Pope. Third, it could have been published under the name of the Biblical Commission, as was the Commission's document on Christology and the Bible. Fourth, the Holy See could have elected not to publish it at all.

The decision was made to publish the *IBC* in the name of the Biblical Commission with an explicit endorsement by the Pope, the first time this had occurred. According to Vanhoye, Pope John Paul II took a keen personal interest in the document, even requesting to read the draft before the Commission had finished its work[34]. Apparently the Holy Father liked the document, since he took the unusual step of not merely receiving the *IBC* at a small audience with the members of the Biblical Commission, but in a solemn gathering of the Cardinals, Diplomatic Corps, and professors of the Pontifical Biblical Institute. This event, which celebrated the 100th and 50th anniversaries of *Providentissimus Deus* and *Divino afflante Spiritu*, took place in the Sala Clementina of the Vatican Palace on 23 April 1993. For the occasion, the Pontiff gave an address recalling those important magisterial documents on the Bible and welcomed the new document of the Biblical Commission. This papal address was published with the *IBC* in its official Vatican publication[35].

In his opening, the Pope speaks of the capital importance of biblical interpretation and recalls the encyclicals *Providentissimus Deus* and *Divino afflante* along with other initiatives of the papal Magisterium touching Scripture during the last 100 years. Then in part I, the Pope points out that these two encyclicals responded to contrasting historical circumstances. *Providentissimus Deus* sought to protect Catholic interpretation from the attacks of rationalistic science; *Divino afflante Spiritu*, on the other hand, defended Catholic scientific exegesis from those who wished to impose a non-

---

[34] Vanhoye, "Catholicism and the Bible", 35.
[35] Pontifical Biblical Commission, *The Interpretation of the Bible in the Church*, 7-21.

scientific "spiritual" interpretation of the Bible. Yet both encyclicals avoided a one-sided mentality. *Providentissimus Deus* urged the study of the ancient languages and scientific criticism of Scripture as a first line of defense against the misuse of these means against Christian faith. *Divino afflante Spiritu* instructed exegetes about the theological significance of the inspired literal sense, yet also placed the study of the spiritual sense within the domain of exegetical science, saying that "one must be able to show that it is a sense willed 'by God himself'" (Address 5). Underlying both encyclicals was a common conviction about the unity of the human and the divine in Scripture, a "harmony with the mystery of the Incarnation" (Address 5).

The heart of the Holy Father's address treats this harmony between the human and divine in Scripture and applies it to the work of Catholic exegesis. He cites a text in *Divino afflante Spiritu*, later restated in *Dei Verbum*, about "the substantial Word [becoming] like men in every respect but sin, [and the] words of God, expressed in human languages, having become like human language in every respect except error" (*EB* §559). The Pope describes Scripture as an abiding "means of communication and communion" between the believing people and God...(Address 6). Because of the "realism" in light of which the Church recognizes the incarnation of the Word in "a determinate historical life," she "attaches great importance to the 'historico-critical' study of the Bible" (Address 7)[36]. Exegetes must study literary genres; they must seek to understand texts in their historical and literary contexts; they must endeavor to penetrate the nuances, possibilities, and the limitations of human language in the Scripture, making use of all relevant science that touches on human communication. This contrasts with the perspective of Christians who mistakenly hold that "since God is the absolute Being, each of his words has an absolute value, independent of all conditions of human language" (Address 8).

Nevertheless, "Catholic exegesis must be careful not to limit itself to the human aspects of the biblical texts. First and foremost, it must help the Christian people perceive more clearly the word of God in these texts..." (Address 9). To this end, the Pope stresses the importance of prayer and the help of the Holy Spirit in the life and work of the exegete. Catholic exegetes are to fulfill their role not individualistically, but as members of the Church, reading Scripture in the light of the great Tradition. Contemporary philosophical hermeneutics confirm the validity of this approach. Catholic exegetes both accept the ultimate judgment of the Church regarding

---

[36] The Pope's translator uses "historico-critical" study for the French expression, "historico-critique"; the translator of the *IBC* uses "historical-critical" for the same term.

interpretation, and by their research they help that judgment to mature. Finally, exegetes should devote part of their time to preaching and other pastoral tasks to avoid becoming lost in abstract scientific research which might cause them to lose sight of the true meaning and goal of the Scriptures, "to put believers into a personal relationship with God" (Address 11).

In the third section of his Address, Pope John Paul II comments on the document of the Biblical Commission itself. New discoveries and developments in scientific methods call for a study of this sort. He praises the document's "spirit of openness" (Address 13) with which it examines and finds the valid elements in so many current methods and approaches.

> Catholic exegesis does not have its own exclusive method of interpretation, but starting with the historico-critical basis freed from its philosophical presuppositions...contrary to the truth of our faith, it makes the most of all the current methods....(Address 13)

He praises it "balance and moderation" since it recognizes the values in both diachronic and synchronic approaches to Scripture, and treats both its human and the divine aspects (Address 14). Finally, he praises the document's concern for the actualization and inculturation of Scripture, its recognition that "the biblical word is at work speaking universally, in time and space to all humanity" (Address 15).

Some months later Cardinal Ratzinger confirmed the Pope's reception and the authority of the *IBC* in an interview with the Italian publication *Il Regno*. In answer to the interviewer who asked why there was not an encyclical to commemorate the centenary of *Providentissimus Deus*, he said,

> The Holy Father was in agreement about the importance of the subject which needed a clear word to update the magisterial teaching. But all in all, it turned out that the voice of the experts—the theologians—confirmed by the Pope, was better suited to meet the current challenges and new questions. I believe this to be a very interesting model. Theologians [referring to the exegetes who comprise the Commission] speak in all their responsibility as believers and pastors of the church, composing a scientific and pastoral work. *Then the Holy Father with a carefully prepared address confirms the essential points, thus assuming the essence of this text (as opposed to its details) into magisterial teaching* [emphasis added][37].

The entire quotation is interesting, but the last sentence, coming from the mouth of the Cardinal Prefect of the Congregation for the Doctrine of the Faith, is significant. On the one hand, it underscores the weight of the *IBC*. On the other, it stands in tension with reports that the Cardinal was

---

[37] Ratzinger, "Modernità atea", 67-68.

dissatisfied with the *IBC* and with phrases in his own preface, which hinted at some reserve about the document[38].

7. *Response*

Since its publication more than a hundred reviews and reflections on the *IBC* have appeared[39]. Not surprisingly, Catholic exegetes wrote most of them, although not a few theologians, journalists, Protestant exegetes and at least one Jewish scholar also offered their perspectives. Almost every review was positive.   Reviewers particularly praised the review of contemporary approaches for its scholarly quality and openness. When the Commission was criticized, usually some specific section was singled out (which varied among reviewers), while the overall effort was commended.

8. *Implications for Interpreting the* IBC

All that has been written above about the authors, occasion, process, structure and purpose, and reception of the *IBC* has implications for its interpretation.

First, as the document's title indicates, *The Interpretation of the Bible in the Church* is oriented to the life of the Church.   The members of the Pontifical Biblical Commission seek to express not merely their own personal views, but to draw upon the Church's tradition and their expertise to respond to Scriptural questions for the good of the Church. This ecclesial orientation suggests, on the one hand, that prior magisterial teaching on Scripture will be useful for understanding the *IBC*, and, on the other, that the document's most immediate relevance will be to biblical interpretation within ecclesial settings—Catholic universities and seminaries, Catholic theology, and the pastoral activity of the Church.

Second, the controversy over the historical-critical method and the other new methods which occasioned this study by the Biblical Commission will be relevant for understanding the *IBC*.

Third, the rigorous collegial process employed by the Biblical Commission and the degree of consensus they achieved, require interpreting

---

[38] In his preface to the *IBC* Cardinal Ratzinger makes a point of saying that the Pontifical Biblical Commission "is not an organ of the teaching office", and that the "struggle over [the historical-critical method's] scope and over its proper configuration…is by no means finished yet". Also, on September 16-19, 1999 the CDF convened leading exegetes and theologians (including several members of the Biblical Commission) to Rome for a symposium entitled, "Interpretation of the Bible in the Church". The participants presented and discussed a dozen papers on major themes of interpretation.

[39] See the bibliography of this study for a list of about 120 articles and books which discuss the *IBC*.

the *IBC* as a unified whole. Of course, compromise formulations will be evident in any document authored by a group of people and this study will note such tensions in the text where they appear.

Fourth, the structure of the *IBC* suggests that some sections will offer more insight than others into the principles of Catholic interpretation. In the light of its unique focus and what Commission members have said about it, this study will attend to principles of interpretation expressed in chapter III, "Characteristics of Catholic Interpretation". In addition, this study will take note of principles reflected in the sections which evaluate various methods and philosophical hermeneutics, and in the document's conclusion.

Fifth, Pope John Paul II's warm reception of the *IBC* and Cardinal Ratzinger's interpretation of that reception, recommends interpreting the *IBC* in harmony with the Pope's Address. This approach will be taken for two reasons: first, because there is no reason to think there is a conflict between the *IBC* and the Pope's Address, and second, because this "reception" by the Pope lends the document its authority in the Church and gives extra reason for regarding its principles as "principles of Catholic interpretation". Nevertheless, when assertions are made on the basis of the Pope's Address rather than on the basis of the Biblical Commission's document, that fact will be indicated.

Finally, broad acceptance of the *IBC* by Catholic exegetes suggests that the work is competent and expresses widely held views. On account of its reception both by church authorities and by the community of Catholic exegetes, the document of the Biblical Commission provides a promising source from which to derive principles of Catholic interpretation.

CHAPTER 1

The Word of God in Human Language

The foundational principle for interpreting Scripture must inevitably be a theological principle which explains what Scripture is. However, the Pontifical Biblical Commission chose not to begin their work with a theological presentation on the nature of Scripture, regarding the theology of Sacred Scripture as belonging to systematic theology, rather than to exegesis (III.D.a-III.D.1.b). Probably they wished to avoid contemporary debate regarding inspiration or inerrancy (Intro B.b)[1]. Rather, the Commission presumed existing Church teaching on the nature of the Scripture that finds its most developed expression in the Dogmatic Constitution on Divine Revelation, *Dei Verbum*.

Nevertheless, an analysis of both the *IBC* and the Pope's Address indicates a kind of functional definition of what the Bible is that is foundational to the other principles contained in the document of the Biblical Commission. There is nothing new in this statement of what Scripture is—it is in complete harmony with *Dei Verbum*—yet it is important to understand the aspects of Catholic theology of the Bible which underlie the Commission's teaching about biblical interpretation.

---

[1] An quotation in the *IBC* from *Dei Verbum* 11 which omitted the part about inerrancy led Avery Dulles to wonder whether the Biblical Commission was intending to back away from the teaching of the Second Vatican Council on that subject ("A Theological Appraisal", 36-37). Vanhoye replied that the abbreviation was only a matter of convenience, and that the Commission had no wish to enter into such questions which are not its field of expertise ("Catholicism and the Bible", 38-39).

Principle #1

Sacred Scripture is the word of God expressed in human language (I.A.a). The thought and the words belong at one and the same time both to God and to human beings in such a way that the whole Bible comes at once from God and from the inspired human authors (III.D.2.c)[2].

It is the canonical text in its final stage which is the expression of the word of God. (I.A.4.f)

Because it is the word of God, Scripture fulfills a foundational, sustaining, and critical role for the Church, for theology, for preaching and for catechesis. Scripture is a source of the life of faith, hope and love of the People of God and a light for all humanity (Intro B.b)[3].

Explanation

1. Two-fold Nature

The two-fold nature of Scripture as the word of God and the words of human beings is a central theme of the *IBC* and receives explicit mention and implicit reference throughout the document. It is based on the analogy between Scripture and the Incarnation of the Divine Word expressed in *Dei Verbum* 13 and in *Divino afflante Spiritu* 37 (*EB* §559)[4]. This principle

---

[2] When a citation from the *IBC* stands outside the final punctuation of a paragraph, the reference is linked to the entire paragraph. When, however, it stands inside the final punctuation of a sentence, the reference pertains only to that sentence.

[3] The *IBC* devotes no section to the nature of Scripture and the implications that follow; rather various elements of this fundamental principle are woven throughout the document's discussion of many issues. Rather than list the references here, they will be given in the explanation of the principle in association with the specific aspect of the principle they substantiate.

[4] Curtin provides helpful background on this analogy in *Dei Verbum* (*DV*) 13. The context of the analogy is *DV*'s allusion to Chrysostom's praise of the divine condescension in Scripture, in which God accommodates his language to our nature. When the citation from *Divino afflante Spiritu* was proposed in the first schema of *DV* in 1962, it appeared in the form which Pope John Paul II cites in his Address, including the sentence, "For as the substantial Word of God became like to men in all things, 'except sin', so the words of God expressed in human language are made like to human speech in every respect, except error." Its presence in the first schema was an implicit argument for a broad interpretation of inerrancy. In the final form of *DV*, the comparison of Scripture to the Incarnation of the Word appears without the phrase comparing Christ's sinlessless with Scripture's inerrancy and without an explicit citation

provided the central theme of Pope John Paul II's Address on the occasion of his officially receiving the *IBC*.

Just as Jesus is fully God and fully human, so Scripture is, at the same time, entirely God's Word and entirely the words of the human authors. Just as the eternal Word took on the limitations of our human nature to reveal God to us, so God has chosen to communicate with the human race through the limitations of human writing and human language. Just as we come to know the Eternal Word through his human existence in a "determinate historical life" (Address 7), so we come to know the divine communication in Scripture through the written words of human authors (Address 6; Conclusion b).

This principle has implications for interpretation. In order to understand the word of God in Scripture, we must first understand the biblical writings as human communication. No "spiritual" bypassing of the human reality is possible. This is the basis for Catholic exegesis' use of the historical-critical method (Address 7; I.A.a). On the other hand, biblical meaning does not end with what the human authors have consciously intended. The guidelines for interpretation given in *Dei Verbum* 12 illustrate this. First a paragraph discusses the need to seek out the sacred author's intention by means of attention to the literary forms and customs of communication of his time and place. The next paragraph, however, begins, "But, since holy Scripture must be read and interpreted according to the same Spirit by whom it was written...[5]. *Dei Verbum* proceeds to insist that "no less serious attention must be given to the content and unity of the whole of Scripture...the living tradition of the whole Church" and the analogy of faith. Catholic interpretation must employ both "scientific" principles, which enable Scripture to be studied like any other human communication, and, "theological" or "spiritual" principles of interpretation, which enable it to perceive what can only be grasped by faith.

---

of *Divino afflante Spiritu*. "Condescendence [sic] now meant the inclusion of human limitation in the writing of Scripture" (Curtin, "Historical Criticism and Theological Interpretation", 84).

According to Curtin, Alonso Schökel's interpretation of *DV* 13 added an extra dimension: "He compared Scripture to an incarnation in language...For Alonso Schökel words are more than vehicles for the transmission of ideas. They involve the person of their originator as well. The movement of condescendence [sic] is therefore an expression of God's will to go down and 'stand alongside' mankind. Alonso Schökel also held that in the same action the reader was raised to the level of the Spirit.... [In this way condescendence] makes God accessible in the Scriptures and underlines their dynamic role in human salvation" (Curtin, 84-85, citing Alonso Schökel, *Commentarios a la constitución "Dei Verbum"*, 488-489).

[5] Citations from *Dei Verbum* and other documents of the Second Vatican Council are taken from Abbott, *Documents of Vatican II*.

This first principle provides the foundation for all of the other principles of Catholic interpretation. In this study the principles enunciated in part II, "Catholic Exegesis and Human Knowledge", and part V, "Methods and Approaches", reflect the fact that the biblical writings are "in human language" and require human means to be understood. On the other hand, the principles enunciated in part III, "Catholic Exegesis and Christian Faith", and in part IV, "The Meaning of Inspired Scripture", reflect the fact that the Scriptures are the word of God, and must be approached in the light of faith to yield their full meaning. The remaining principles in part VI, "Interpretation in Practice", depend on the fact that Scripture both is "the word of God" and comes to us "in human language."

2. The Canonical Text

Furthermore, there is a *specificity* regarding the words which come both from human authors and from God:

> It is the canonical text in its final stage which is the expression of the word of God. (I.A.4.f)

Although neither the Pope nor the Biblical Commission extend the analogy of the Incarnation in this way, it applies nicely: Just as the Word became flesh in one particular historical human being, so God's revelation of himself in written words occurs in one particular book, Sacred Scripture, which has been entrusted to the Church. It is the "text in its final stage, *rather than in its earlier editions*, which is the expression of the Word of God [emphasis added]"[6] (I.A.4.f). In other words, the final text is the inspired text. This is the reason why a historical-critical study that examines the development of a biblical text must be completed by a synchronic study of the text now in our possession (I.A.3.f). Merely to explain the sources behind biblical books, even their respective theologies, falls short of communicating true biblical meaning, which belongs to the inspired final text. The Biblical Commission makes this point on numerous occasions (cf. I.A.1.b; I.C.1.f; Conclusion d).

3. Scripture's Role

Catholic interpretation holds a high view of the authority and power of Scripture.

> Because it is the word of God, Scripture fulfills a foundational, sustaining, and critical role for the Church, for theology, for preaching and for

---

[6] The *IBC* capitalizes "Word of God" in reference to Scripture, while this work reserves capitalization for references to Jesus as the incarnate Word. However, all direct citations in this work will reflect the capitalization used in the works cited.

> *catechesis. Scripture is a source of the life of faith, hope and love of the People of God and a light for all humanity. (Intro B.b)*

Since Scripture witnesses to the origins of our faith and faithfully transmits the original message, it is *foundational* for theology[7] (III.D.2a; IV.C.3.b; IV.D.4.a), preaching and teaching (IV.D.3.b, g-l). Scripture is *sustaining* in that one of its primary roles is the spiritual nourishment of individual Christians and the Church as a whole (Intro B.b; I.E.1.i; II.A.2.a; III.B.3.h; III.C.1.f; III.D.1.a). Finally, Scripture is *critical* in that Scripture is a *norma normans*, a standard that judges all theological expression and church life:

> The Bible has authority over the Christian Church at all times…(IV.A.1.f).

and

> One of the principal functions of the Bible is to mount serious challenges to theological systems and to draw attention constantly to the existence of important aspects of divine revelation and human reality which have at times been forgotten or neglected in efforts at systematic reflection. (III.D.4.e)

Scripture's authority extends also to the Magisterium of the Church which "is not above the Word of God, but serves it" (IV.A.1.f, citing *DV* 10[8]). The very language of Scripture itself bears an authority for faith that no magisterial formulation can equal.   An earlier document of the Pontifical Biblical Commission drew the distinction between the "referential language" of the Scriptures and the "auxiliary language" of all second order faith statements[9].

God has given the Bible to guide the Church's life: "United to the living Tradition… the Bible is the privileged means which God uses yet again in our own day to shape the building up and the growth of the Church as the People

---

[7] "In discerning the canon of Scripture, the Church was also discerning and defining her own identity. Henceforth Scripture was to function as a mirror in which the Church could continually rediscover her identity and assess, century after century, the way in which she constantly responds to the gospel and equips herself to be an apt vehicle of its transmission (cf. *Dei Verbum*, 7). This confers on the canonical writings a salvific and theological value completely different from that attaching to other ancient texts. The latter may throw much light on the origins of the faith. But they can never substitute for the authority of the writings held to be canonical and thus fundamental for the understanding of the Christian faith" (III.B.1.e).

[8] In this context when *DV* 10 speaks of "the word of God" it refers to that word as it is found in both Scripture and Tradition.

[9] "The 'auxiliary' languages employed in the Church in the course of centuries do not enjoy the same authority, as far as faith is concerned, as the 'referential language' of the inspired authors, especially (that) of the New Testament with its mode of expression rooted in the Prior (Testament) [sic]" (in Fitzmyer, *Scripture and Christology*, 20, 57; and, Commission Biblique Pontificale, *Bible et Christologie*, §1.2.2.1).

of God" (III.C.1.f). In addition, Catholic interpretation holds that the Bible as Word of God is addressed not only to the Church but "to the entire world at the present time" (IV.a). "The Word of God transcends the cultures in which it has found expression and has the capability of...reach[ing] all human beings in the cultural context in which they live" (IV.B.b).

Discussion

4. The Pope on the Nature of Scripture

The Pope's Address, which recalls the likeness between the Incarnation of the Word and two-fold nature of Scripture, provides a foundation and a kind of theological commentary for the Biblical Commission document. The Holy Father applied the reality of the two dimensions of Scripture to the exegetical task, insisting on both a historical-critical study and an approach to Scripture in the Spirit, in prayer and in communion with the Church (Address 6-8)[10]. The Biblical Commission itself discusses the nature of Scripture in relation to the doctrine of Incarnation only twice (I.F.d; Conclusion b), both times in the course of contrasting Catholic interpretation to a fundamentalist reading.

In what appears to be a reflection on *Dei Verbum* 21, the Pope explains the specific character of Scripture as the word of God in an interesting way. He speaks of Scripture as "a permanent means of communication and communion between the believing people and God, Father, Son and Holy

---

[10] Lewis Ayres and Stephen E. Fowl criticize the *IBC* for arguing from the two natures of Scripture to the indispensability of the historical-critical method (Ayres and Fowl, "(Mis)Reading the Face of God"). They state, "In the case of Roman Catholic exegetical theory this argument has not yet been deployed in any document that forms part of the ordinary magisterium, but it has appeared in the [*IBC*].... This document has no intrinsic authority, and so cannot be treated as representing an official shift in teaching" (p. 514). They likewise deny any precedent in *Divino afflante Spiritu* and *Dei Verbum* for a christological argument similar to that used by the *IBC*. Ayres and Fowl seem unaware of Pope John Paul's explicit statement of the PBC's position and his attribution of it to *DAS* and *DV* (Address 6-8; see also above, p.29n, regarding *DV* 13).

Nevertheless, Ayres and Fowl make a valuable contribution and raise important issues. Their contribution includes deeper insight into the "educative and redemptive aspects" of the two natures of Scripture, and the ways these aspects are brought out in *Dei Verbum* and discussions of Gregory of Nyssa and John Scotus Eriugena (pp. 522-527). Because their criticism touches on a variety of aspects of the document, this study will take up their arguments in the text or notes in relation to other principles.

Spirit" [11] (Address 6). In the New Testament, written words attest to Jesus' stay among us in a permanent way. What distinguishes this communication is both that it is "permanent" and "verifiable". Other forms of communication and communion between God and his people exist, such as Tradition and the sacraments. But Scripture has "its own consistency precisely as written text which verifies it" (Address 6)[12]. If the meaning of God's other means of communication and communion with his people may at times seem uncertain, the Church has a permanent witness whose message is permanent and verifiable because its content is expressed in the written words which constitute it.

5. Scripture as the Word of God

Although the *IBC* prescinds from presenting a theological treatise on Scripture, in the course of its exposition it repeatedly affirms traditional beliefs about Scripture, including its inspiration (I.B.2.g; I.C.1.f; I.F.d; II.B.1.c), inerrancy (I.F.c), and the fact that Catholics recognize God as its "principal author" (II.B.3.c).

The *IBC* refers repeatedly to the Bible as "the Word of God", or sometimes as "the written Word of God"[13]. The biblical books themselves rarely call Scripture itself the word of God, but use that expression primarily for prophecies and laws which come from the LORD, or in the New Testament, for the proclamation of the gospel[14]. Nevertheless, in referring to the Bible as "the Word of God", the Biblical Commission follows ancient

---

[11] The translation "permanent" in this paragraph is the author's. The French original reads "*stable*", and the official translation, "abiding", suggests the possible connotation of "living", which is not present in the original.

[12] Beyond the fundamental testimony to Jesus as risen Lord, the concept of a revealed content in Scripture that is verifiable is weak in Schneiders, *Revelatory Text*. She writes in the preface to the second edition, "Two major points of the book are that the biblical text does not 'reveal' in the sense of transmitting information from God to humans and that the biblical text is not 'revealed' in the sense of being communicated directly by God to the author" (xviii). Instead Schneiders emphasizes Scripture's role as mediating the believer's encounter with God, an important dimension that the *IBC* treats only indirectly in its discussion of Scripture's use in the liturgy and *lectio divina*. Although Schneiders claims merely to emphasize the interpersonal content and mode of revelation and not to deny its essential cognitive dimension (44-46), she shrinks from affirmations about revealed content beyond the New Testament's testimony to Jesus. Because Schneiders' *Revelatory Text* is the most substantial recent attempt to articulate a Catholic hermeneutic for interpreting Scripture as the word of God, this study will occasionally make reference to Schneiders' positions.

[13] For a brief description of the issues, see Collins, "Inspiration", 1033.

[14] Carlo Maria Martini distinguishes six different senses of "word of God". See *La Parola di Dio*, 56-58.

Christian tradition and *Dei Verbum* 9, which echoes that traditi
Scripture is the word of God inasmuch as it is consigned to wr
inspiration of the divine Spirit"[15]. On the other hand, the word
no means confined to Sacred Scripture, since it is also found equ
Tradition (*DV* 10), and is manifest in the proclamation, teaching and
sacramental celebration of the realities to which both Scripture and Tradition
testify.

By beginning with the recognition that Scripture is a communication
from God to the human race, Catholic interpretation differs radically from
rationalist, positivist, atheist, or materialist interpretation of the Bible which
denies Scripture's transcendent dimension. Similarly, Catholic interpretation
differs radically from interpretation which *ignores* the dimension of divine
communication, and reflects on Scripture for another purpose altogether, such
as literary or historical interests. The reason the Church reads sacred
Scripture is different, her purpose is religious: "The Bride of the incarnate
Word, and the Pupil of the Holy Spirit, the Church is concerned to move
ahead daily toward a deeper understanding of the sacred Scriptures so that she
may unceasingly feed her sons with the divine words" (*DV* 23).

6. Scripture as Human Language

The fact that Scripture expresses the word of God in *human language* has
a number of implications. Many of these are made explicit in the *IBC*'s
critique of fundamentalist interpretation (I.F; Conclusion b; Address 7-8),
since according to the Pope and the Biblical Commission, fundamentalism's
crucial flaw is its failure to accept Scripture's human dimension.

> They [fundamentalists] tend to believe that, since God is the absolute Being,
> each of his words has an absolute value, independent of all the conditions of
> human language. Thus, according to them, there is no room for studying
> these conditions in order to make distinctions that would relativize the
> significance of the words. (Address 8)

At least three characteristics of the human activity in the writing of the Bible
deserve mention, each of which has implications for interpretation. They are
(1) the literary role of the authors and editors in the composition of the
Scriptural books, (2) the historical nature of the process, and (3) the human
limitations of the authors and editors.

First, the biblical books came into existence through the real literary
efforts of human authors and editors; they were not dictated by God. So it is

---

[15] See also *DV* 24: "The sacred scriptures contain the word of God, and, because they are inspired, they truly are the word of God...."

important to understand the modes of literary expression familiar to authors and readers in those times, including the genres they employed. In the case of many biblical books, especially those of the Old Testament, a succession of authors and editors contributed to the final form of the books now in our possession. Although all Scripture and all of its parts are inspired, not every verse or paragraph is of equal theological value. The charism of inspiration does not overwhelm the differences within biblical writings (Address 8). As in every written communication, the point of the message resides more in some parts than in others. Thus a sentence from the Gospel of John describing Jesus' movement from one place to another (e.g., Jn 3:22a) is not nearly as significant as the sentence explaining his mission which precedes it by a few verses (Jn 3:16).

Second, all of the authors and editors who had a hand in the biblical books wrote from within and in response to particular historical circumstances, in forms of thought and expression common to their time. This has two consequences for interpretation. First, later readers must seek to understand as much as possible the patterns of thought and circumstances of the author's or redactor's time in order to grasp their message. For example, in order to understand what is referred to as God's covenant relationship with his people in Deuteronomy and the prophets, one should seek to know as much as possible about the meaning of that kind of relationship in the ancient Near East. Second, what was written in particular historical circumstances is in some measure *conditioned* by those circumstances (III.D.1.b), and "God has [not] given the historical conditioning of the message a value which is absolute" (III.D.2.c). Thus the teaching to Christian slaves and masters (Eph 5, Col 3) is no longer pertinent in its literal sense in societies in which the institution of slavery has long been abolished. Catholic interpretation recognizes that some "elements of the biblical message...are permanent...having their foundation in human nature, and [some] are more contingent, being due to the particular features of certain cultures" (I.D.2.c). On the other hand, historical conditioning does not mean a text is altogether irrelevant:

> It is open both to interpretation and to being brought up to date—which means being detached, to some extent, from its historical conditioning in the past and being transplanted into the historical conditioning of the present. (III.D.2.c)

Thus a modern interpreter might wish to apply the New Testament texts on slavery (with some modifications) to the relations between employees and employers.

Third, the human authors and editors of the biblical books possessed limited capacities and resources (I.F.d), which were not eradicated by the activity of the divine Author in producing the Bible. These limited capacities and resources might be manifest in an erroneous human memory (Mark 2:26 erroneously affirms that David entered the house of God and ate the loaves of the presence when Abiathar was high priest[16]), mistaken views of scientific matters reflecting the age in which they lived, or historical inaccuracies in their sources. It is therefore a mistake to claim inerrancy regarding historical details or scientific facts (I.F.e), or to force harmonizations of differing narrative accounts or to feel the need to defend biblical cosmology (I.F.h). The minor differences in the accounts of the post-resurrection appearances of Jesus, for instance, do not vitiate the overall testimony of the New Testament to the resurrection[17]. It is reasonable to think that neither the human authors nor the divine Author intended absolute precision in historical details or in scientific matters. The human authors had a variety of reasons for writing what they wrote, usually religious reasons.[18] The Divine Author's purpose can be safely said to be religious, to reveal Himself and his salvation and to invite human beings to respond.

7. The Inspired "Final Form" and Source Criticism

The fact that the final form of the text is "the expression of the Word of God" has implications for source criticism, whether of the Old or New Testament. The Biblical Commission's treatment of this issue illustrates the balance of their work. On the one hand, in contrast to fundamentalist interpretation, Catholic interpretation accepts that the Bible comes to us through a long process of development. The *IBC* mentions wide acceptance of (and acknowledges contemporary challenges to) the "Documentary Hypothesis" of the Pentateuch and the "Two Source" Theory of the Synoptics (I.A.1.a). It describes the analysis of sources and the investigation of the personalities of biblical authors as a necessary and useful part of the historical-critical method (III.a). It calls diachronic study "indispensable for making known the historical dynamism...[and] rich complexity" of Scripture, and warns against "neglecting history in favor of an exegesis which would be

---

[16] According to 1 Sam 21:2-7, the priest was Ahimelech, not Abiathar. See Brown, *New Testament Christology* 37-38.

[17] Vanhoye, "Catholicism and the Bible", 39.

[18] Even in the instances in which a religious motive on the part of the human author may be questioned (e.g., the Song of Songs), it is obvious that the biblical authors did *not* intend to write scientific works or scientific histories in the modern sense.

exclusively synchronic" (I.A.4.f)[19]. On the other hand, the Biblical Commission criticizes the kind of literary criticism which focused on sources when "it did not pay sufficient attention to the final form of the biblical text and to the message which it conveyed in the state in which it actually exists" (I.A.1.b). It also criticizes the practice of exegeting a hypothetical historical reconstruction in place of the inspired text (I.E.2.1) and cautions exegetes against substituting the results of their work, i.e., "the reconstruction of ancient sources used by the ancient authors," for the biblical texts themselves (III.C.4.d). The Biblical Commission emphasizes concern for the final text in their conclusion:

> When historical-critical exegesis does not go as far as to take into account the final result of the editorial process but remains absorbed solely in the issues of sources and stratifications of texts, it fails to bring the exegetical task to completion. (Conclusion d)

Commission member A. Levoratti makes the reason clearer: "Whatever earlier developments may be observed within and behind the present text, only the latest theological perspective is authoritative for the Church"[20]. The task before source critics is to bring the fruit of their labors to enrich the understanding of God's word expressed in the inspired final form of the biblical text[21].

8.   Lack of Clarity in the Incarnation Analogy

The christological analogy between the two natures of the Incarnate Word and the divine and human dimensions of Scripture is useful, but ambiguous. The analogy helps the Pope and the Biblical Commission show the necessity of human, scientific methods for interpreting Scripture as human language, and at the same time, the necessity of explaining Scripture's meaning as the word of God. At least two problems have arisen. First, Lewis Ayres and Stephen E. Fowl have shown that for at least some of the Fathers this christological likeness of Scripture had a different implication, namely Scripture's perpetuation of the educative and redemptive mission of the Incarnate Word[22]. This use of the analogy does not necessarily exclude the more recent use (here Ayres and Fowl would disagree), but it deserves more attention and might be the profounder of the two meanings.

---

[19] See the note on the *IBC*'s use of "diachronic" and "synchronic" in the discussion of the necessity of the historical-critical method, p. 221.

[20] Levoratti, "How to Interpret", 31.

[21] It seems fairly clear that the Biblical Commission was concerned about this point. See Vanhoye, "Catholicism and the Bible", 37; Levoratti, "How to Interpret", 30-31.

[22] Ayres and Fowl, "(Mis)Reading the Face of God", 522-527.

The second problem of the analogy is the difficulty of defining its implications regarding Scripture. In *Divino afflante Spiritu* Pope Pius XII teaches that the divine dimension of Scripture is manifest in its inerrancy: "Just as the substantial Word of God became like men in every respect except sin, so too the words of God, expressed in human languages, became like human language in every respect except error" (*DAS* 37, *EB* §559). Pope John Paul II quotes this statement verbatim in his Address (6) [23]. Sandra Schneiders, however, arguing on the basis of the same christological analogy for Scripture, rejects biblical inerrancy: "Attributing inerrancy to the Bible constitutes a kind of biblical Docetism. It is analogous to such christological assertions as that Jesus had all possible knowledge, even that not yet discovered in his day, or that he only appeared to die..."[24]. The problem of the analogy of Scripture to the Incarnate Word is to define in what respects Scripture reflects the perfections of its divine Author and in what respects it reflects the limitations of its human authors.

9. *Reflection*

This first principle of Catholic interpretation which affirms that Sacred Scripture is the word of God in human language provides the foundation for all the other principles. Interpretation must reckon both with the human and the divine nature of its object. "Scientific" procedures must explore the Bible's meaning as written human communication (parts II and IV); procedures grounded in Christian faith must explore Scripture's meaning as a

---

[23] *Dei Verbum*, which taught a carefully nuanced approach to inerrancy, uses the same words but without explicitly citing *Divino afflante Spiritu*, and without the words "in every respect except error" (*DV* 13). The emphasis of *Dei Verbum* is on the "marvelous 'condescension' of eternal wisdom", the educative character which Scripture shares with the Incarnation (thus Ayres and Fowl). Regarding inerrancy, *Dei Verbum* affirms the following: "Therefore, since everything asserted by the inspired authors or sacred writers must be held to be asserted by the Holy Spirit, it follows that the books of Scripture must be acknowledged as teaching firmly, faithfully and without error that truth which God wanted put into the sacred writings for the sake of our salvation" (*DV* 11).

[24] Schneiders, *Revelatory Text*, 54. Schneiders calls for "the discreet but definitive burial of the notion of biblical inerrancy" (55). She believes critical scholarship has discovered the Bible to be "an historical document in the strictly human sense of the term with all the limitations that that implied" (98). At the root of her objection to inerrancy lies Schneiders belief that the Bible contains "theological and moral errors" (54) and is "rife with morally unacceptable material" (175) in regard to slavery, anti-Semitism, and patriarchy. Given this evaluation of Scripture's content, the problem Schneiders attempts to resolve is how a believer may still receive and interpret Scripture as the word of God ("Scripture as Word of God"). The author of this study holds that the difficulties found in Scriptural texts on slavery, Jews, and women can be resolved without abandoning the affirmation of *DV* 11 and without judging Scripture to be "rife with morally unacceptable material".

message from God (parts III and V). The re-affirmation that what matters to Christian interpretation is the final canonical text is important in view of the sometimes excessive interest biblical scholarship has shown in earlier traditions and texts. Finally, the re-affirmation that the orientation of Scripture as the word of God is to nourish and guide the life of the Church and to enlighten humanity grounds the principles regarding the practice of interpretation (part VI).

The Biblical Commission chose to limit their task by not discussing the nature of Scripture and thus avoiding the currently disputed questions regarding inspiration and inerrancy. However, more serious reflection on the nature of Scripture and its implications for interpretation is needed[25]. It is logical that an adequate hermeneutic should begin with serious consideration of the object to be interpreted. This was always the traditional approach to explaining Scripture's interpretation, and Schneiders follows this course in her proposal for interpreting Scripture as the word of God, *The Revelatory Text*. The importance of considering the object of interpretation is especially true in the case of Scripture since the unique characteristics of Catholic biblical interpretation (expressed in *IBC* chapter III, and principles #6-11) depend on Scripture's divine inspiration and relation to revelation. Finally, it is important that Catholic theology and exegesis clarify what it means to affirm a likeness between the Incarnate Word and the divine and human dimensions of Sacred Scripture.

---

[25] A number of reviewers criticized the *IBC* for an underdeveloped theology of Scripture. See Dulles, "A Theological Appraisal", and Vignolo, "Questioni di ermeneutica [*Commento*]".

PART II

"IN HUMAN LANGUAGE": CATHOLIC EXEGESIS AND HUMAN KNOWLEDGE

> In sacred Scripture…the marvelous "condescension" of eternal wisdom is clearly shown, "that we may learn the gentle kindness of God, which words cannot express, and how far He has gone in adapting His language with thoughtful concern for our weak human nature." For the words of God, expressed in human language, have been made like human discourse…. (*Dei Verbum* 13)

Because God speaks to human beings through Scripture in a human way, understanding God's word in Scripture requires human reason, experience and knowledge. To say that human means are necessary to understand inspired Scripture is not the same as saying they are sufficient. Indeed, they are not, as we shall see clearly in part III. Nevertheless, the fact that the Bible comes to us in human words is the foundation for the use of history, the literary sciences, hermeneutics and other fields of learning in the effort to interpret God's word.

CHAPTER 2

Catholic Exegesis and "Science"

Principle #2:

Biblical texts are the work of human authors who employed their own capacities for expression and the means which their age and social context put at their disposal. Consequently, Catholic exegesis freely makes use of scientific methods and approaches which allow a better grasp of the meaning of texts in their literary, socio-cultural, religious and historical contexts. (III.a)

Catholic exegesis should be carried out in a manner which is as critical and objective as possible.

Catholic exegesis actively contributes to the development of new methods and to the progress of research (III.a). In this enterprise Catholic scholars collaborate with scholars who are not Catholic (III.C.a).

Explanation

If God had chosen to communicate to the human race by means of words inscribed on golden tablets, exegesis *might* simply be a matter of semantic analysis, explaining the meaning of the words and their relationship to one another. But the nature of the Christian Scriptures is different from that, and the Biblical Commission explicitly affirms Catholic exegesis' need for scientific[1] procedures at the beginning of its discussion of the "Characteristics of Catholic Interpretation" (III.a):

> [Catholic exegesis] recognizes that one of the aspects of biblical texts is that they are the work of human authors, who employed both their own capacities for expression and the means which their age and social context put at their disposal. *Consequently, Catholic exegesis freely makes use of the scientific methods and approaches* which allow a better grasp of the meaning of texts in their linguistic, literary, socio-cultural, religious and historical contexts, while explaining them as well through studying their sources and attending to the personality of each author (cf. *Divino Afflante Spiritu*: EB 557). (III.a, emphasis added)

The *IBC* illustrates exegesis' use of science and scientific methods and approaches in its first chapter on "Methods and Approaches for Interpretation". There it describes the contribution of historical and literary methods, as well as the value of approaches derived from the social sciences (which the document refers to as "human sciences", i.e., sociology, cultural anthropology, psychology and psychoanalysis), to understanding Scripture. The fact that the Biblical Commission says that Catholic exegesis "makes use of" scientific methods and approaches indicates that exegesis does not belong to any of those disciplines but employs them as instrument to fulfill its particular task of explaining the meaning of the biblical text.

The idea that *Catholic exegesis should be carried out in a manner which is as critical and objective as possible*[2] is indicated by the stress placed on high standards of scholarship throughout the *IBC*. The Commission emphasis on critical and objective procedure appears in the *IBC*'s description of the historical-critical method, which it calls "indispensable" (I.A.a): "It is a critical method, because in each of its steps (from textual criticism to redaction criticism) it operates with the help of scientific criteria that seek to be as objective as possible" (I.A.2.c). In another place the Commission warns against the danger of "attributing to biblical texts a meaning which they do

---

[1] In normal English usage the words "science" and "scientific" tend to be reserved for the natural sciences (e.g., chemistry, biology, physics) or the social sciences (e.g., psychology, sociology, anthropology). Following the usage of the *IBC* itself, this study will employ "science" and "scientific" in their broader sense to refer to any systematic and critical discipline of human knowledge. In most cases the words "scholarship" or "scholarly" would adequately capture the intended meaning.

[2] Although "critical" bears a negative connotation in common usage, obviously, in this context its meaning is positive. Here the adjective, "critical", is close in meaning to the terms "scientific" and "scholarly". "Critical" implies the use of analytical procedures aimed at objectivity and precision. "Critical" sometimes specifically refers to the use of the procedures of historical or literary criticism.

not contain but which is the product of a later development within the tradition" (III.c).   Other statements in the document, particularly in the evaluation of various methods and approaches, illustrate Catholic exegesis' concern for objectivity and scientific rigor (e.g., I.B.1.b, I.C.2.b-d, I.D.a, I.D.3.f, I.E.2.l).

Finally, in its scientific dimension Catholic exegesis belongs to a larger scholarly enterprise interested in the Bible or in the sciences useful for understanding the biblical text. This includes scholars who are not Catholics or not even believers. Insofar as they learn anything true touching the human dimensions of what is found in the Bible—whether historical, literary or anthropological—their insights can serve Catholic exegesis[3]. In the same way, the research of Catholic scholars can and does benefit those who are not Catholic (Intro A.c; III.a). Catholic exegesis does not segregate itself or conduct its research in a religious or cultural ghetto. It is open to truth wherever it may be found and to sharing the results of its own research.

Discussion

Why is Catholic exegesis scientific, and why is this important? Why not adopt instead a method of interpretation which might possibly be more subjectively satisfying, more devotional and religious? The answer has to do with some fundamental Catholic philosophical convictions about truth, the Church's location in a modern scientific culture, and the positive results produced by the scientific study of Scripture.

1.   The Nature of Truth and Scripture

Although the *IBC* nowhere treats it explicitly, Catholic exegesis' scientific orientation is based on Catholic belief in the objectivity, discoverability, and unity of truth.

First, truth, whether in the sphere of the physical sciences or that of morality or the social sciences, is objective[4]. There is a givenness to it, a

---

[3] One may recall that Pope Paul VI's document establishing the new Biblical Commission specifically stipulates that the Biblical Commission may involve non-Catholic scholars in their work (Paul VI, Motu proprio, *Sedula cura*, 27 June 1971, *EB* §731).

[4] John Paul II, *Fides et Ratio*, §25, 56, 82. References will be made to John Paul II, *Fides et Ratio*, a recent restatement of traditional Catholic positions on these issues. Obviously, the argument is not that the Pope's document influenced the Biblical Commission, since it had not yet been written when the Commission did their work! Rather, the point is that a certain view of reality and of the Christian message (believed to be Scripture's essential content) ground Catholic exegesis' commitment to objective "scientific" means of investigating Scripture, even though these scientific means are not considered in themselves sufficient (see principle #6, A Hermeneutic of Faith).

reality which exists "independent of human language, thought and action"[5]. It is simply not true that everything is subjective or that everything is relative. Some statements are true in that they correspond to reality, and some statements are not (assuming due regard for the nature and context of statements). Catholic philosophy has always held to this perspective regarding philosophical truth and factual statements about the physical world. The Church has likewise held that it has been entrusted with the fundamental truth about God and human existence, and on this basis, has sought to evangelize, to communicate her conviction about the truth. When it comes to understanding the meaning of written texts, the notion of objectivity must be qualified by insights from philosophical hermeneutics. Yet the fundamental objectivity of truth is not undermined[6]. Belief in the objectivity of truth, shared by Catholicism and modern science, runs contrary to some popular religious and intellectual fashions.

Second, truth is discoverable[7]. That does not mean that all truth can be discovered by natural human means. Catholics hold that some truths, such as the Trinitarian nature of God, can only be known by revelation[8]. It is also the case that some scientific, historical or even literary facts (e.g., regarding an author's intention) may never be discovered by human beings, due to the limitations of the data available or perhaps of human reason itself. Again, modern philosophy has introduced some qualifications about how humans can know things. Nevertheless, the Catholic tradition is optimistic about reason's ability to discover truth, and in this it tends to side with modern science, and to differ both from fundamentalism and from skeptical movements such as deconstruction and post-modernism. In particular it is optimistic about progress by means of the scientific study of Scripture, expecting critical exegesis to help the Church's understanding of Scripture to become more complete[9].

---

[5] Vanhoozer, "Realism, Reading and Reformation", 24. Vanhoozer, while well aware of the limitations inherent in language and the possibilities of distortion in the reader's perception due to his or her interests, advocates critical realism regarding the meaning of Scripture.

[6] This section does not intend to deny the epistemological challenge of finding an adequate means of coming to know truth or reality. Nor does it intend to convey the impression that language can ever be fully adequate to truth, especially ultimate truth. Yet it maintains that Catholic exegesis' stubbornness about methods which seek to be "as objective as possible" reflect Catholic conviction that a mind-independent reality exists both in the world and in the message of Scripture.

[7] See John Paul II, *Fides et Ratio*, §44, 56,84-85.

[8] Vatican Council I, *Dei Filius* 4, DS 3015.

[9] In his Address (10) Pope John Paul II recalls the expectation voiced by the Second Vatican Council that the work of exegetes will lead "'toward a better understanding and explanation of the meaning of Sacred Scripture [and] that their research may help the Church to

Finally, truth is one[10]. Therefore, there can be no contradiction between truths acquired through human scientific research, i.e., through reason, and the truths received through divine revelation. Christian faith has nothing to fear from science. This idea is very old in Christian tradition and can be found in the Church Fathers who sought to explain the relation of Scripture to the science of their day (Clement of Alexandria, Origen, Augustine, etc.). As regards Scripture, rules were established to cope with apparent contradictions, which were seen as ultimately reconcilable when a proper interpretation of a text and an accurate scientific understanding of a matter were attained. Therefore all dual-truth theory, which distinguishes separate spheres for truths of science and for truths of faith, is to be rejected, as are fideism[11] and rationalism.

The Catholic Church has not always demonstrated its current openness to modern scientific means of studying Scripture. As the *IBC* states in its introduction, in their early stages scientific methods were "wedded to positions hostile to the Christian faith" (Intro A.b). In addition, Catholic scholars did not yet have sufficient competence in the new methods and ancient Near Eastern languages to cope with the challenges brought to traditional belief by historical criticism, while Modernism was offering a false solution to the apparent contradictions between faith and reason[12]. Therefore, for pastoral motivations the Catholic Church took a closed and defensive position towards scientific methods and their conclusions for about forty years, despite the initial open response of Pope Leo XIII in *Providentissimus Deus* in 1893. But due to the progress in Catholic biblical studies and the subsiding of the Modernist threat, the tide began to change with Pius XII's *Divino afflante Spiritu* in 1943. The latter half of the twentieth century has witnessed repeated stands by the Catholic Church to reemphasize its openness

---

form a firmer judgment' (*DV* 12; cf. *Providentissimus Deus*, *EB* §109: 'ut, quasi praeparato studio, iudicium Ecclesiae maturetur')". The original French text of the Pope's remarks follows the Latin citation more closely: "afin que, par leurs études en quelque sorte préparatoires, mûrisse le jugement de l'Église".

[10] See John Paul II, *Fides et Ratio*, §16-17, 34, 43, 51.

[11] Thus, John Paul II, *Fides et Ratio*, §53. The Pope also warns against "biblicism", a contemporary form of fideism (§55). "Fideism" can be defined as "the view that knowledge about God is inaccessible to reason and may be obtained solely through faith". "Rationalism" can be defined as "the philosophical point of view which limits human knowledge to what can be demonstrated by reason alone" (Bonsor, *Athens and Jerusalem*, 182).

[12] For a brief summary of this period, see Gilbert, "Cinquant' anni", 17-33.

to science, symbolically expressed in the Pope's address to the Papal Academy of Sciences on 10 November 1979 regarding the Galileo affair[13].

Not only does Catholic exegesis hold to the objectivity of truth, it also believes in the objectivity of the content of Sacred Scripture[14]. Although insights can be gained by reading Scripture in various contexts, there is an objective content to the biblical message. The *IBC* more often states this fundamental assumption negatively. In what becomes almost a mantra of the Biblical Commission, the point is repeated: interpretation cannot simply be a subjective reading of the text (I.A.g., I.B.2.i., II.A.2.e., II.B.1.g., II.B.2.f.). This applies to so-called "spiritual" or "mystical" readings of Scripture, "guided solely by personal inspiration" (Intro A.g). There is a givenness to the contents of Scripture, and so the discovery of "a Christ of [one's] own personal vision...[to satisfy one's] own spontaneous religious feelings" (Intro A.g) is rejected. Even venerable exegesis of the Church Fathers, which "labored to find a spiritual sense in the minutest details of the biblical text...making use of rabbinic methods" or Hellenistic allegory is judged lacking in "true interpretative value", notwithstanding its pastoral usefulness in its day (II.B.2.h). The truth is out there, inscribed in the written word, and scientific Catholic exegesis strives to understand and expound it. Although the Biblical Commission document in no place explicitly takes up post-modernism, this fundamental assumption of an objective content (c.f.,

---

[13] Cf. Klauck, "Das neue Dokument: Darstellung und Würdigung", 65-66. Other instances of John Paul II's teaching on the relation of faith to science may be found in Neuner and Dupuis, *The Christian Faith*, pp. 67-76, §164-176c. However, Max Seckler cautions against resolving in too facile a manner the tension between science and religion, as though all the difficulties were due to misunderstandings or inappropriate attitudes on both sides. He calls attention to the deeper problem of modern science's apparent need to exclude God as an explanatory factor in order to develop its understanding of natural causality. The consequence is that God is excluded from subsequent thought and language in a way that is problematic in the long run for religion. Seckler provides a brief bibliography on the theme of theology and science ("Theology and Science", 1069-1075). The Biblical Commission did not address itself to this problem which accounts for some of the criticisms the historical-critical method has encountered. The problem arises in biblical studies when scholars define "scientific" or "critical" *a priori* to exclude "God as an explanatory factor".

[14] For example, see John Paul II, *Fides et Ratio*, §82: "The Bible, and the New Testament in particular, contains texts and statements which have a genuinely ontological content. The inspired authors intended to formulate true statements, capable, that is, of expressing objective reality. It cannot be said that the Catholic tradition erred when it took certain texts of Saint John and Saint Paul to be statements about the very being of Christ". This, of course, does not imply that biblical revelation can be *reduced* to propositions or that any proposition about the being of Christ is completely adequate to its subject.

II.A.2.d.) in the divine revelation which Scripture attests contradicts a central tendency of post-modern thought[15].

2. Participation in Modern Scientific Culture

Another reason contemporary Catholic exegesis is scientific is that it exists in a scientific age and exegesis' presuppositions are inevitably molded by a scientific outlook. "Catholic exegetes approach the biblical text with a pre-understanding which holds closely together modern scientific culture and the religious tradition emanating from Israel and from the early Christian community" (III.b). Not only do Catholic exegetes receive the pre-understanding of modern scientific culture naturally by osmosis, they also deliberately embrace this pre-understanding in order to maintain dialogue with the culture in which they find themselves. One of the document's criticisms of fundamentalism's adherence to the cosmology of the Bible is that this unduly narrows faith's dialogue with culture (I.F.h). By insisting on a more open dialogue with the science of their time, Catholic exegesis identifies with a longstanding tradition that includes figures such as Origen, Augustine, and Aquinas[16].

3. Results of Scientific Approaches

For over two centuries scientific methods, and particularly the historical-critical method, have been adopted for the study of texts of the ancient world (Intro A.b; I.A.a). The use of these procedures, including textual criticism, literary criticism, and philological, linguistic and semantic analysis, has proven useful for history and literature. Although the Church was initially hesitant about their application to the study of Scripture due to the problematic philosophical commitments of their early advocates, those difficulties were eventually overcome (Intro A.b).

---

[15] Adam, *Postmodern Biblical Criticism*, 5-25. Although it is unlikely that the challenge of post-modern philosophy will fundamentally alter Catholic exegesis' essential principles, so far the Biblical Commission has not given consideration to this challenge. Vanhoozer's *Is There a Meaning?* provides a useful consideration of post-modernism's implications for exegesis from a Reformed point of view.

[16] This does not mean that Catholicism simply accepts all the claims made in the name of science. In fact a critical approach is vital, since, obviously, not all claims are valid, and it has been common for opponents of Christian faith to assume the mantle of science, while smuggling into their findings arbitrary and unscientific presuppositions. But at least since *Providentissimus Deus* (1893), the recommended defense against fraudulent scientific claims has been sound scholarship and the use of critical reason: "The first means [of defense against attacks on Christian truth in the Bible] is the study of the Oriental languages and of the art of criticism" (*EB* §118).

On the whole, Catholic exegetes today are pleased with the results of scientific means of Scripture study. Methods have progressed, and the historical-critical method has "led to a more precise understanding of the truth of Sacred Scripture" (I.A.4.c). This applies not only to the historical-critical method, but also to other kinds of scientific analysis of biblical texts and their interpretation, especially literary methods and philosophical hermeneutics (e.g., I.B.c; II.B.a). According to the *IBC*,

> Biblical studies have made great progress in the Catholic Church and the academic value of these studies has been acknowledged more and more in the scholarly world and among the faithful. This has greatly smoothed the path of ecumenical dialogue. The deepening of the Bible's influence upon theology has contributed to theological renewal. Interest in the Bible has grown among Catholics, with resultant progress in the Christian life. All those who have acquired a solid formation in this area consider it quite impossible to return to a precritical level of interpretation, a level which they now rightly judge to be quite inadequate. (Intro c)

Although the Biblical Commission acknowledges problems due to the improper use of scientific methods (Intro A.e-f), these do not justify rejecting a scientific approach to the study of Scripture.

4. *Presuppositions and Competencies of Disciplines*

On the other hand, the Biblical Commission insists that the usefulness of scientific methods and approaches for interpretation of the Bible depends on methodological rigor regarding their *presuppositions* and the limits of their competencies. Presuppositions must correspond to, or at least not contradict, the religious and revelatory message of inspired Scripture. The Biblical Commission says that the positive results from the historical-critical method occurred "once it was freed from external prejudices" (I.A.4.c). Rationalist historical interpretation, for instance, offered ingenious explanations of the miraculous in the Bible. But a supposedly scientific explanation of the miracles of Jesus or of predictive prophecies in the Old Testament loses its force when it becomes clear that the presuppositions of the method employed exclude from the outset the possibility of divine intervention in history. This kind of argument is circular.

The Commission articulates the need for methodological rigor which respects the limits of each discipline in its discussion of the use of psychological and psychoanalytical science for understanding the Bible:

> The dialogue between exegesis and psychology or psychoanalysis, begun with a view to a better understanding of the Bible, should clearly be

conducted in a critical manner, respecting the boundaries of each discipline. Whatever the circumstances, a psychology or psychoanalysis of an atheistic nature disqualifies itself from giving proper consideration to the data of faith. Useful as they may be to determine more exactly the extent of human responsibility, psychology and psychoanalysis should not serve to eliminate the reality of sin and of salvation. (I.D.3.d)

When psychology or psychoanalysis makes theological affirmations or denials, they exceed their proper competency. A similar point is made about cultural anthropology. While it offers useful information to help distinguish the universal and permanent from what is contingent and culturally determined in Scripture, cultural anthropology "is not qualified simply by itself to determine what is specifically the content of Revelation" (I.D.2.c).

5. *Two Ways of Being "Scientific"*

Although Catholic exegesis employs "secular" sciences, it is not one of them, since it recognizes Scripture as the word of God. Instead exegesis is a science of faith, a branch of theology[17].

Thus Catholic exegesis is scientific in two distinct senses. First, it is scientific in that it makes full and unprejudiced use of the secular sciences to understand the Scriptures (requiring that those sciences also be unprejudiced in their presuppositions regarding Christian faith). That has been the theme of this section. Second, Catholic exegesis is scientific in the same way that theology as a whole is a science[18], since exegesis, with the rest of Christian theology, accepts the data of revelation. What makes exegesis scientific in this second sense is its consideration of its object—the meaning of Scripture—in a critical and rational manner.

---

[17] This theme will be treated in part III, "Catholic Exegesis and Christian Faith".

[18] See Congregation for the Doctrine of the Faith, *Ecclesial Vocation of the Theologian* §9: "Through the course of centuries, theology has progressively developed into a true and proper science. The theologian must therefore be attentive to the epistemological requirements of his discipline, to the demands of rigorous critical standards, and thus to a rational verification of each stage of his research".

CHAPTER 3

Catholic Exegesis and History

Because the Bible is a collection of ancient writings, the two branches of human knowledge most relevant for interpreting it are quite naturally history and literary studies. Exegetes studying the Bible employ the same procedures other scholars use when interpreting ancient texts, a set of procedures commonly referred to as the historical-critical method. This method combines historical and literary modes of investigation and Catholic exegesis' use of the historical-critical method constitutes one of its basic principles (principle #15)[1]. The present principle, however, explains *why* Catholic exegesis is interested in history.

Principle #3

Catholic exegesis is concerned with history because of the historical character of biblical revelation. Although the Bible is not a history book in the modern sense and although it includes literary genres that are poetic, symbolic and imaginative, Scripture bears witness to a historical reality, i.e., the saving actions of God in the past which have implications for the present.

Interpretation of a biblical text must be consistent with the meaning expressed by the human authors. (II.B.1.g)

Historical study places biblical texts in their ancient contexts, helping to clarify the meaning of the biblical authors' message for their original readers and for us.

---

[1] Nevertheless, the PBC carefully defines and qualifies what it means by its embrace of the "historical-critical method"; the meaning of the term is not univocal.

Although Catholic exegesis employs a historical method it is not historicist or positivist, confining its view of truth to what can be demonstrated by supposedly objective historical analysis[2].

Explanation

This principle points to three reasons why Catholic exegetes must "pay due account to the *historical character* of biblical revelation" in fulfilling their task (III.C.1.a, emphasis original). The first and most important reason is that the Bible is "the written testimony to a series of interventions in which God reveals himself in human history" (Conclusion c). Second, faithfulness to God's message in Scripture requires that it must be interpreted in a manner that is consistent with the meaning expressed by the inspired human author (II.B.1). Third, historical circumstances shaped what is written, and this historical context must be taken into account in order to determine the meaning of a text then and now (Conclusion c). Finally, this principle makes clear what the historical character of Catholic exegesis does *not* mean.

1. Historical Reality

Although the Bible is not a history book in the modern sense and although it includes literary genres that are poetic, symbolic and imaginative, Scripture bears witness to a historical reality, i.e., the saving actions of God in the past which have implications for the present.

Christianity is a historical religion. That is, it speaks of a God who has revealed himself by acts of salvation in the course of human events. In this it resembles Judaism and Islam and differs from Bhuddism and Hinduism. Christian faith, and therefore Catholic exegesis, recognizes the Bible as not just a philosophy, not just a myth, and not just a moral lesson, although all of these elements may be found in the Bible. Rather, Scripture recounts real events that occurred in the past which have implications for human existence in the present. These saving acts begin in the history of Israel and reach their climax in the life, death and resurrection of Jesus Christ[3]. Explaining the

---

[2] Catholic interpretation's concern for history is dealt with in the *IBC* discussions of the historical-critical method (I.A), fundamentalist interpretation (I.F), and the literal sense (II.B.1). It also receives attention in the discussions of literary methods (I.B.3.l) and the canonical approach to Scripture (I.C.1.i). Finally, the *IBC*'s conclusion underscores this principle.

[3] Francis Martin points out that "in Christian antiquity, the events of the life of Christ were considered as the primary locus of revelation without much consideration being given to the verbal process by which those events reached the audience.... We can see the accent on event rather than the configuration in the fact that, in the written Gospel tradition, many events received successive interpretations by being narrated several times.... We may also see this in

reason for the use of the historical-critical method, Biblical Commission put it this way: "The Bible...does not present itself as a direct revelation of timeless truths but as the written testimony to a series of interventions in which God reveals himself in human history" (Conclusion c).

This does not mean that the Bible is a history book, much less that every statement in the Bible written in the past tense is historical as some fundamentalists may assume (I.F.e). Catholic exegesis is fully aware of the presence of non-historical genres and fictional stories in the Bible (II.B.1.b), as well as the fact that ancient authors wrote history differently than modern historians do, often for the purpose of conveying moral or religious lessons and without the same concern for exactitude[4]. For this reason the preoccupation of some authors with the accuracy of historical details misses the point. Nevertheless for Catholic interpretation, "ostensive reference", i.e., the relation between the narrated events and extra-textual reality, is important because human history is the stage on which the drama of salvation unfolds[5]. This perspective contrasts with that of some contemporary approaches which concern themselves exclusively with literary or theological meaning, with a seeming indifference to the historical reality to which the text refers.

2. Consistent Meaning

Interpretation of a biblical text must be consistent with the meaning expressed by the human authors. (II.B.1.g)

Another reason why Catholic exegesis is concerned with history is its conviction that God inspired the words of the human authors and editors of

---

the list of events found in the creeds, both in the NT (e.g., 1 Cor 15:3-5) and in later texts" ("Literary Theory, Philosophy of History", 601-602). The same pattern may be noted in the OT treatments of the deliverance from Egypt.

[4] George Montague says it well: "Unlike modern scientific research into history, the purpose of studying history, even secular history, was not the determination of facts in their particularity, not even the interrelation of events. History was studied for the lessons it contained. If this was true of the study of secular history, it was all the more true of biblical history. The events of history were more for *formation* than for information. For this reason there was little interest in verifying historical details... [emphasis original]" (*Understanding the Bible*, 53).

[5] According to the *IBC*, even the spiritual sense of Scripture has a realistic historical basis. "The spiritual sense results from setting the text in relation to *real facts* which are not foreign to it: the paschal event, in all its inexhaustible richness...[emphasis added]"(II.B.2.f). Jesus' resurrection "has established a radically new *historical* context, which sheds fresh light upon the ancient texts and causes them to undergo a change in meaning [emphasis added]" (II.B.2.a). Nevertheless, christological interpretation of the Old Testament is not granted the right "to empty out of the Old Testament its own proper meaning" lest it "deprive the New of its roots in history" (I.C.1.i). See principle #13.

the Bible, and that valid interpretation must respect the authors' historical communication. The Biblical Commission's definition of the literal sense (see principle #12) expresses this link between the human language and the divine meaning: "The literal sense of Scripture is that which has been expressed directly by the inspired human authors. Since it is the fruit of inspiration, this sense is also intended by God, as principal author" (II.B.1.c)[6]. It follows that later interpretation must be consistent with what the inspired authors wrote:

> One must reject as unauthentic every interpretation alien to the meaning expressed by the human authors in their written text. To admit the possibility of such alien meanings would be equivalent to cutting off the biblical message from its root, which is the Word of God in its historical communication; it would also mean opening the door to interpretations of a wildly subjective nature. (II.B.1.g, emphasis added)

In the next paragraph, however, the *IBC* qualifies this statement to make clear that a text's meaning is not imprisoned in a single historical context: "There are reasons...for not taking 'alien' in so strict a sense as to exclude all possibility of higher fulfillment" (II.B.2.a). Rather, the Commission says, the radically new historical context brought about by the death and resurrection of Jesus can expand a text's meaning.

Catholic exegesis' insistence on interpretation being consistent with the meaning expressed by the biblical authors is due, at least in part, to Christianity's fundamental value of faithfulness to the original message (see *DV* 8, 10)[7]. Paul exhorts the Thessalonians to hold fast to the traditions they have received (2 Thess 2:15), and warns the Galatians not to yield to another gospel even if he himself or an angel from heaven should proclaim it (Gal 1:8). Likewise, Jude 3 exhorts readers to contend "for the faith that was *once for all* entrusted to the saints", and the letters to Timothy urge him to guard what has been entrusted to him (1 Tim 6:20, 2 Tim 1:14). What holds true for the gospel holds true for the Christian understanding of the Bible, if not for individual texts, at least for Scripture's meaning as a whole[8]. The Bible

---

[6] See p. 165ff in principle #12 on the author's intention and the literal sense.

[7] Fitzmyer defends critical interpretation on this basis: "What ultimately lies behind the critical approach to the study of the Bible in the Church is the conviction that God's revelation in Christ took place in the past, and the ancient record of that self-manifestation of God in him is disclosed to the Church above all in the Bible, in the Word of God couched in ancient human wording.... Thus historical criticism assists the Church in its ongoing life by helping it to uncover the essence of the revelation once given to it—the meaning of the Word of God in ancient human words" ("Historical Criticism", 257-258).

[8] Christian tradition has tolerated the accommodation of individual texts, for example, in preaching or the liturgy, so long as the interpretation conformed to the "rule of faith". The

received as sacred Scripture is not a book which can validly be interpreted to say whatever one wants, no matter how edifying, interesting, or relevant the new interpretation may seem. It communicates a definite content bound by what the canonical authors and editors expressed in the final text. Even though interpretation of the Bible in new circumstances inevitably brings new dimensions of meaning, Catholic interpretation's responsibility to the original content remains[9].

The means to deriving the meaning expressed by the authors in their written texts is through "a careful analysis of the text, within its literary and *historical* context" (II.B.1.c, emphasis added). In this light the *IBC* commends the historical-critical method because it makes it possible "to understand far more accurately the intention of the authors and editors of the Bible, as well as the message they addressed to their first readers" (I.A.1.c).

3. Historical Context

The third reason for Catholic interpretation's concern for history is that historical study enables the interpreter to understand the text according to the culture and literary conventions of the period (II.B.1.b) and to understand the social conditions, the institutions, and the cultural and religious practices to which the biblical authors refer.

> Historical study places biblical texts in their historical contexts, helping to clarify the meaning of the biblical authors' message for their original readers and for us.

Pope Pius XII devoted several paragraphs to the importance of historical study in *Divino afflante Spiritu* (31-42, *EB* §555-561). He speaks of information lacking to commentators of past ages, now available, that can enhance interpretation. He states that the meaning of the "rules of grammar and philology alone" together with the literary context are insufficient to understand the biblical authors' meaning. Rather,

> the interpreter must, as it were, go back wholly in spirit to those remote centuries of the East and with the aid of history, archaeology, ethnology, and other sciences, accurately determine what modes of writing... the authors of that ancient period would be likely to use, and in fact did use. (*EB* §558)

Fathers of the Church welcomed allegorical interpretation on this basis (III.B.2.j). The Biblical Commission, however, mentions no exceptions to the standard of "not alien to the meaning expressed by the human authors", at least as far as exegesis is concerned.

[9] See principle #5 on philosophical hermeneutics, principle #12 on the literal sense, and principle #18 on actualization.

Vatican II's *Dei Verbum* also stressed the necessity of history to understand Scripture:

> For the correct understanding of what the sacred author wanted to assert, due attention must be paid to the customary and characteristic styles of perceiving, speaking, and narrating which prevailed at the time of the sacred writer, and to the customs men normally followed at that period in their everyday dealings with one another. (*DV* 12)

Everyone recognizes the value of understanding elements of culture such as covenant relationships, legal codes, and the practice of hospitality in the ancient Near East for the sake of interpreting the Bible. The *IBC* specifically mentions the importance of understanding the Jewish background to the New Testament[10] and the relation between the New Testament texts and the communities that gave rise to them[11]. Although the meaning of the biblical text for later generations is not confined to what the text meant in its original setting, history plays an important role in helping subsequent interpretation to remain faithful to the original message[12].

4. Rejection of Historicism and Historical Positivism

Despite Catholic exegesis' commitment to history, there are two tendencies of historical criticism that it seeks to avoid: historicism and historical positivism. The view that the meaning of a biblical text is precisely what it meant in its original setting and nothing more typifies historicism. Examples might include interpreting the story of Cain and Abel exclusively as the memory of an ancient conflict between shepherds and farmers or viewing the Epistle to the Galatians exclusively as a monument to conflict regarding circumcision in the early Church. The Biblical Commission rejects the "historicizing tendency" of "the older historical-critical exegesis" (I.A.4.f). In another place the Commission contrasts their christological interpretation of Nathan's prophecy to David (about God establishing his throne "forever", 2 Sam 7:12-13) to the views of "exegetes who have a narrow 'historicist' idea about the literal sense" (II.B.2.a). More will be said about historicism in the

---

[10] The *IBC* specifically recommends the study of Jewish traditions of interpretation in order to shed light on the intertestamental period and first century Judaism (I.C.2.c) and the study of ancient methods of exegesis to understand how biblical authors themselves interpreted prior biblical texts (III.A.2.f).

[11] "The task incumbent upon the exegete, to gain a better understanding of the early Church's witness to faith, cannot be achieved in a fully rigorous way without the scientific research which studies the strict relationship that exists between the texts of the New Testament and life as actually lived by the early Church" (I.D.1.e).

[12] See the discussion of the Scripture as human language above, p. 35ff.

discussion of Catholic exegesis' use of the historical-critical method (see principle #15, especially p. 243ff)[13]. In a word, historicism is belief in the sufficiency of historical explanation for interpreting Scripture.

Catholic interpretation likewise rejects "historical positivism". In its classic form, historical positivism "aims to produce [and thinks it can produce] an accurate and complete picture of the past on the basis of 'historically pure' sources"[14], discounting or reinterpreting sources "biased" by faith. The nineteenth-century attempts at reconstructing the life of Jesus (and some of the late twentieth century attempts) adopted this attitude[15]. The *IBC* says, "Contemporary hermeneutics is a healthy reaction to historical positivism and to the temptation to apply to the study of the Bible the purely objective criteria used in the natural sciences" (II.A.2.c). Historical positivism fails to see that history, exegesis, and the biblical texts themselves are all works of interpretation, and that historical facts untainted by interpretation do not exist[16]. Philosophical hermeneutics corrects this misperception[17].

Discussion

Catholic exegesis' relation with history is unfortunately more complex than the preceding explanation—which limits itself to what the *IBC* affirms— indicates. The discussion which follows attempts to clarify further the relation of Catholic interpretation to history.

5. Meanings of "History"

The terms "history" and "historical" bear a variety of senses, at least three of which occur in the *IBC*.

1) The first sense of "historical" refers to past reality, that is, to what existed or to what occurred. When the Commission says that the Bible bears "written testimony to a series of interventions in which God reveals himself in human history" (Conclusion c), it intends this first sense. The

---

[13] See also the discussion of the dynamic aspect of the literal sense, beginning p. 169.

[14] Latourelle, "Positivism, Historical", 785. See p. 82n for a summary of what the PBC said about positivist history in an earlier document. See Bartholomew, *Reading Ecclesiastes: Old Testament Exegesis and Hermeneutical Theory*, for a discussion of positivism in philosophy and literature, pp. 108-110.

[15] See Green, "Quest of the Historical", 550-553. Schneiders maintains that the "third quest" also works out of a basically historical-positivist model (Schneiders, *Revelatory Text*, xxiii). See also p. 106.

[16] See the enlightening discussion in Noble, *The Canonical Approach*, 99-107.

[17] See principle #5.

opposite of this first sense of historical is non-historical, "what did not occur".

2) The second sense of "historical" found in the document emphasizes the human, conditioned or limited nature of what occurred in the past. It is a way of characterizing the first sense of "history". The Biblical Commission intends this sense when it says that the historical-critical method is historical "above all because it seeks to shed light upon the historical processes which gave rise to biblical texts" (I.A.2.b). The opposite of "historical" in this second sense is "eternal" or "absolute". "Historical" in this sense does not exclude divine presence or activity, although the term emphasizes the finitude of the circumstances[18].

3) The third sense of "history" used in the document refers to the study of what happened in the past. Thus "history" is a branch of human knowledge which investigates the past to discover what happened and why. "Historiography", writing an account of the past, is history in this sense. Similarly, the adjective, "historical", in the term "historical-critical method" indicates it is a method that seeks to give an account of the past. A problem arises in deciding how to refer to past events which are beyond the empirical methods of historical research to verify or for which too little evidence is available[19]. Should they be referred to as "not historical"? To do so lends itself to the impression that their reality is being denied[20].

---

[18] An example of this use contrasted with its opposite occurs in Ratzinger's preface to the *IBC*: "Accordingly, the text of the document inquires into how the meaning of Scripture might become known—this meaning in which the human word and God's word work together in the singularity of *historical* events and the eternity of the everlasting Word which is contemporary in every age. The biblical word comes from a real past. It comes not only from the past, however, but at the same time from the eternity of God and it leads us into God's eternity..." (Preface c, emphasis added).

[19] It is easy for scholars to exaggerate the amount or certainty of the information history can provide about events recounted in the Bible. See Johnson, *The Real Jesus*, 81-140, for a useful description of history's limits in providing information about the early Church or the earthly life of Jesus.

[20] The classic instance of this is the resurrection of Christ. Because this event is beyond the capacity of historical (third sense) research to verify, some scholars who affirm the historical (first sense) reality of Jesus' resurrection think it better not to refer to the resurrection as historical (Johnson, *The Real Jesus*, 133-136; Schneiders, *Revelatory Text*, 101-116). Raymond Brown, however, while granting the inadequacy of historical methods to verify the resurrection itself, holds that the term "historical" should be used for the event itself, lest it be interpreted as a denial of its reality (*Virginal Conception, Bodily Resurrection*, 82-92).

Here is an application of the various meanings of "history" and "historical" to the use of those terms in principle #3 (using Arabic numerals to distinguish the three meanings distinguished above).

Catholic exegesis is concerned with *history* (3) because of the *historical* (1&2) character of revelation. Although the Bible is not a *history* (3) book in the modern sense..., Scripture bears witness to a *historical* (1) reality....

Historical (3) study places biblical texts in their ancient contexts, helping to clarify the meaning....

Although Catholic exegesis employs a *historical* (3) method...[it does not confine] its view of truth to what can be demonstrated by supposedly objective *historical* (3) analysis.

6.   *The Instrumental Role of History*

Despite its concern for history, exegesis itself is not a historical discipline whose task is to give an account of the past. Rather the task of exegesis is to explain the meaning of the text. In carrying out its work Catholic exegesis *makes use of* history and historical methods (third sense) to shed light on the biblical text[21]. This is important to affirm, because many biblical scholars have understood their primary role to be to study the history of Israel or of the early Church using biblical texts as a sources, or to ascertain the historicity of events narrated in the Bible[22], or to explain the text's redactional history[23].

---

[21] Martin distinguishes between historical and philological study that facilitates the communication of the text—exegesis' true task—and historical study that gets "behind a text in order to use it as a source for the history of early Christianity and as a norm for judging the meaning of a text" ("Literary Theory, Philosophy of History", 593).

[22] Vanhoye, "Catholicism and the Bible", 38: "Exegesis...seeks to illumine the total content of the text, not just which details are historical or non-historical. Exegesis emphasizes the content of faith, divine revelation, and the invitation to a renewed existence that is at the heart of the biblical text. The larger picture that the biblical text seeks to communicate concerns a religious message and not historical facticity. Naturally, for the essential facts, such as the crucifixion of Jesus, the texts render testimony that is very strong, and they intend to affirm the facticity of this event.... But for many other details—one sees, for example, the minor differences among the Gospels—historicity is not really the important thing. The important thing is the overall picture and the message it communicates".

[23] Vittorio Fusco states some of the uses of history in biblical study ("Un secolo di metodo storico", 83): "The *historian* can utilize the texts as sources for the reconstruction of certain events. Also in exegesis, as Betori notes, 'the reconstruction of the traditional and redactional development of a text can be a useful element for the determination of the text's meaning' (Betori, "Modelli interpretativi", 327). The research into historicity can respond to theological needs, although the historiographic reconstruction could never take the place of the text as a norm of faith. In *exegesis*, however, the text may never be reduced to only a means, a 'source', or 'document' from which to reconstruct events or derive doctrine [emphasis added]".

While these historical efforts make a valuable contribution to exegesis, they are not its fundamental task, nor does historical information drawn from biblical texts constitute biblical meaning. This is not to deny the value of specialized studies which are strictly historical. Historical research fulfills an indispensable role in exegesis, but as a means rather than an end.

7. Rejection of Historical Literalism and Non-Historical Approaches

Catholic exegesis' concern for history is important since it helps Catholic interpretation avoid two extremes. On the one hand, a historical concern distinguishes Catholic interpretation from fundamentalist interpretation. According to the Biblical Commission, fundamentalism errs by employing a

> naively literalist interpretation, one, that is to say, which excludes every effort at understanding the Bible that takes account of its historical origins and development (I.F.a).

> It fails to recognize that the Word of God has been formulated in language and expression conditioned by various periods...(I.F.d).

> Fundamentalism also places undue stress upon the inerrancy of certain details in the biblical texts, especially in what concerns historical events or supposedly scientific truth. It often historicizes material which from the start never claimed to be historical. It considers everything that is reported or recounted with verbs in the past tense...(I.F.e) [24].

Fundamentalism and Catholic interpretation agree that Scripture bears witness to a historical reality. But Catholic interpretation takes a more nuanced approach to history, distinguishes among literary forms, allows greater scope for historical knowledge to enlighten interpretation, acknowledges historical

---

In a footnote on the contribution of history to theology, Fusco observes that research on historicity can serve fundamental theology, and can also shed light on revelation's "historical trajectory" (83).

[24] The Biblical Commission makes some harsh generalizations about fundamentalist interpretation. This pleased some reviewers (Bergant, "Fundamentalism and the Biblical Commission"; Collins, "Methods of Biblical Interpretation"; Larraín, "El valor hermenéutico de la eclesialidad"), but seemed excessive to others (Ayres and Fowl, "(Mis)Reading the Face of God", 517; Marshall, "Review: IBC"; and especially, Shea, "Catholic Reaction to Fundamentalism"—see quote on p. 260n). It is perhaps indicative of the lack of dialogue between Catholicism and Fundamentalism that no fundamentalist review of the IBC has appeared. It may be questioned whether there are many fundamentalists who would identify with the approach to Scripture attributed to them by this document. But even if the IBC does not accurately describes the beliefs of many fundamentalists, it does define tendencies and a point of view from which Catholic interpretation may legitimately distinguish itself.

conditioning in the biblical word, and is not preoccupied with the accuracy of narrative details[25].

The other extreme, however, is to stand apart from history as do some literary and theological approaches which ignore or deny the reference of biblical texts to historical reality. The Biblical Commission addresses this tendency in its evaluation of semiotics:

> Semiotics can be usefully employed...only in so far as the method is separated from certain assumptions developed in structuralist philosophy, namely the refusal to accept individual personal identity within the text and extra-textual reference beyond it. The Bible is a Word that bears upon reality, a Word which God has spoken in a historical context and which God addresses to us today through the mediation of human authors. The semiotic approach must be open to history: first of all to the history of those who play a part in the texts; then to that of the authors and readers. (I.B.3.l)

Similarly, Bultmann's demythologizing interpretation is rejected because it empties the Bible "of its objective reality" and tends to reduce it "to an anthropological message only" (II.A.2.d). Bultmann was content to embrace and proclaim a Christ of faith detached from the Jesus of history.

8. Faith and History

If Catholic interpretation must distinguish itself from both fundamentalist literalism and from an indifference to history on the part of some literary or theological approaches, it must also distinguish itself from a third error. Given Catholic exegesis' respect for historical research, there exists a danger of reducing history (in the first sense described above) to what scientific history (third sense) can demonstrate, and to substitute historical reconstructions (whether of the life of Jesus or of the gospel message) for the depiction of these realities which the biblical texts themselves propose. This, in fact, is what some of the recent studies of the historical Jesus urge their readers to do. For example, Burton L. Mack presents Jesus as a Cynic philosopher[26] and Marcus Borg discovers that eschatology was not an

---

[25] While the Biblical Commission does well to distinguish Catholic interpretation from the two extremes regarding historical reference, there remains a need for greater clarity. On what basis does one determine which narrative "details" are unimportant and which are essential to the biblical message? Does the essential historicity of the Exodus matter? A similar tension exists in *Dei Verbum* 19 (following the 1964 PBC Instruction, *Sancta Mater Ecclesia*) which simultaneously affirms the historicity of the four Gospels, saying that they "faithfully hand on what Jesus...really did and taught for [our] eternal salvation", yet acknowledges the lack of historical exactitude by describing the retrospective, selective, kerygmatic, pastoral and synthetic manner in which the truth has been recorded for us.

[26] See Mack, *Myth of Innocence*.

important part of his message[27]. Rather than enrich the understanding of Jesus communicated by the gospels through additional historical insight, these approaches claim to offer more historically reliable depictions of Jesus and his message on the basis of critical methods and evidence from the apocryphal gospels.

In addition to problems in the historical methodology employed to produce these alternative depictions of Jesus (apparent in the diversity of results obtained from applying the same scientific methods to the same data)[28], Catholic interpretation has its own methodological basis for rejecting such proposals, a theological criterion. While it is open to considering new historical data and learning from it, Christian faith is governed by the presentation of Jesus and his message expressed in the canonical texts[29]. Catholic exegesis *grounds* its understanding of God's action in human history in Jesus Christ on the *testimony* of Scripture and Tradition which it has accepted, rather than on historical research. This is because in the last analysis, Christian exegesis is a theological rather than a historical discipline, whose ultimate foundation is revelation and faith rather than historical reasoning.

Does this mean that historical research is unimportant for Catholic exegesis' understanding of the life of Jesus or of history? By no means. Historical research can purify the Church's understanding of what the revealed content of Scripture really is. Just as the growth of scientific understanding about the cosmos led to the clear realization that Scripture does not claim to give a scientific account of the solar system, historical research has also shown that traditional understandings of Scripture's relation to history were mistaken in a variety of ways[30]. Many biblical books are the

---

[27] See Borg, "Non-Eschatological Jesus".

[28] See Evans, "Third Quest: A Bibliographical Essay", 540-542; Schneiders, *Revelatory Text*, xxiv, citing Powell, *Introduction to the Gospels*, 13-14.

[29] See principle #6, "A Hermeneutic of Faith", both for an explanation of this pre-understanding of Catholic interpretation, and for a discussion of whether this constitutes unscientific prejudice.

[30] In *Providentissimus Deus* (§120-122), Pope Leo XIII commented on the relation between Scripture and the natural sciences and suggested that the same principles apply to historical questions: "There can never, indeed, be any real discrepancy between the theologian [he is speaking of professors of Scripture] and the physicist, as long as each confines himself within his own lines, and both are careful, as St. Augustine warns us, 'not to make rash assertions, or to assert what is not known as known' [*De Gen. ad litt. imperfectus liber*, IX, 30]. If dissension should arise between them, here is the rule also laid down by St. Augustine for the theologian: 'Whatever they can really demonstrate to be true of physical nature we must show to be capable of reconciliation with our Scriptures; and whatever they assert in their treatises, which is contrary to these Scriptures of ours, that is to Catholic faith, we must either prove it as

fruit of a long editorial process, rather than the work of the famous individuals in Israel's history whose names they bear, as was commonly assumed. In general the authorship of biblical books is far from certain. Historically-sensitive research has discovered minor contradictions and apparent errors of fact. Historical study makes clear that although the Bible contains extraordinarily valuable historical information, it is not to be taken as a divinely inspired and inerrant history text. According to the *IBC*, the historical research of exegetes provides a perspective

> which systematic theologians should take into account as they seek to explain more clearly the theology of scriptural inspiration.... Exegesis creates, in particular, a more lively and precise awareness of the historical character of biblical inspiration. It shows that the process of inspiration is historical, not only because it took place over the course of the history of Israel and of the early Church, but also because it came about through the agency of human beings.... (III.D.1.b)

Like faith and reason, the testimony of Scripture and historical research are complementary sources of truth. Each has information the other lacks. From time to time tensions may arise when scientific history appears to contradict the testimony of Scripture regarding its essential message. But Christian faith, holding to the unity of truth, expects to resolve such apparent contradictions eventually, either by a deeper understanding of the biblical witness or by a more exact historical judgment.

---

well as we can to be entirely false, or at all events we must, without the smallest hesitation, believe it to be so' [Augustine, *De Gen. ad litt.*, I, 21, 41].

"To understand how just is the rule here formulated we must remember, first, that the sacred writers, or, to speak more accurately, the Holy Spirit 'who spoke by them, did not intend to teach men these things (that is to say, the essential nature of the things of the visible universe), things in no way profitable unto salvation' [*De Gen. ad litt.*, I, 9, 20]".

Pope Leo adds: "The principles laid down here will apply to cognate sciences, and especially history" (*PD* §123).

CHAPTER 4

The Use of Philological and Literary Analysis

Principle #4

Because Scripture is the word of God that has been expressed in writing, philological and literary analysis are necessary in order to understand all the means biblical authors employed to communicate their message.

Philological and literary analysis contributes to determining authentic readings, understanding vocabulary and syntax, distinguishing textual units, identifying genres, analyzing sources, and recognizing internal coherence in texts (I.A.3.c). Often they make clear what the human author intended to communicate.

Literary analysis underscores the importance of reading the Bible synchronically (I.A.3.c; Conclusion c-d), of reading texts in their literary contexts, and of recognizing plurality of meaning in written texts (II.B.d)[1].

Just as it makes use of history, Catholic exegesis makes use of the literary disciplines normally employed in the interpretation of written texts. This study refers to the totality of these disciplines under the heading, "philological

---

[1] The *IBC* indicates the importance of philological and literary analysis in its section on the historical-critical method (I.A), in a section devoted to literary methods (I.B), and in its discussion of the meanings of Scripture (II.B).

and literary analysis". Philological and literary analysis include morphology, syntax, historical philology, semantic analysis, and literary criticism[2].

Explanation

Philological and literary analysis is absolutely necessary for exegesis due to the simple fact that the Bible consists of human words which have been written down, and is, therefore, subject to the rules and conventions that make written communication possible. Philological and literary analysis considers the elements of language, whether oral or written, which convey meaning, including words, syntax, idioms metaphors, literary forms, genres, and structure.

1. The Contribution of Philological and Literary Analysis

Philological and literary analysis contributes to determining authentic readings, understanding vocabulary and syntax, distinguishing textual units, identifying genres, analyzing sources, and recognizing internal coherence in texts (I.A.3.c). Often they make clear what the human author intended to communicate.

From the beginning Jewish and Christian exegesis paid close attention to the use of words and syntax in the biblical text. Renewed appreciation for the study of the biblical text in its original languages began to take hold among Christian interpreters during the Renaissance. The recognition of various literary genres present in the Bible gained widespread acceptance over the last century and a half. Today sophisticated philological and literary analysis inform the historical-critical method and have given birth to new literary methods.

a) The Historical-Critical Method

Philological and literary analysis form an essential part of the historical-critical method[3]. First, they play a role in textual criticism, the process of determining the authentic text from the hundreds of ancient manuscripts that have come down to us. Although textual criticism depends primarily on

---

[2] Here "literary criticism" is intended in the sense that term conveys in the study of "secular" literature; it now also describes an aspect of the literary analysis of the Bible. The problem is that in biblical studies "literary criticism" has referred to what is better named "source criticism". This study will try to make clear by the context which of the two senses is intended.

[3] While it is possible to emphasize the historical aspect of the historical-critical method, Fitzmyer (and others) point out that the method "applies to the Bible all the critical techniques of classical philology" (Fitzmyer, *Scripture, the Soul of Theology*, 19). His description of the historical-critical method includes many philological and literary elements (19-24).

"external evidence" (that is, the comparison of manuscripts and manuscript traditions), it also employs "internal evidence" including the analysis of an author's style and vocabulary to help establish the most accurate text[4]. In addition, literary and philological analysis help the exegete understand the words in a text and the manner in which their context shapes their meaning; they help the exegete to know where to subdivide the text, to recognize possible sources, and to identify the proper literary genre. The *IBC*'s description of the historical-critical method shows the essential role of literary and philological disciplines:

> The text is then submitted to a linguistic (morphology and syntax) and semantic analysis, using the knowledge derived from historical philology. It is the role of literary criticism to determine the beginning and end of textual units, large and small, and to establish the internal coherence of the text. The existence of doublets, or irreconcilable differences, and of other indicators is a clue to the composite character of certain texts. These can then be divided into small units, the next step being to see whether these in turn can be assigned to different sources. Genre criticism seeks to identify literary genres, the social milieu that give rise to them, their particular features and the history of their development. (I.A.3.c)

In order to understand what the biblical authors intended it is necessary to understand as much as possible the literary conventions of the time. For instance,

> When a text is metaphorical, its literal sense is not that which flows immediately from a word to word translation (e.g., "Let your loins be girt": Luke 12:35), but that which corresponds to the metaphorical use of these terms ("Be ready for action"). When it is a question of a story, the literal sense does not necessarily imply belief that the facts recounted actually took place, for a story need not belong to the genre of history but be [sic] instead a work of imaginative fiction (II.B.1.b)

For example, the story of Job recounted at the beginning and end of the book of Job gives its protagonist no reference in time and only the far-off city of Uz (in Edom or Arabia) to locate him geographically. The heart of the book consists of Job's anguished speeches about his innocent suffering, the advice of his friends, and the word the Lord addresses to Job at the end. These literary indicators suggest that we are not dealing with the genres of history or biography, but with a story used as the vehicle for a message. Whether or not there was a Job, and, if so, what precisely happened to him, is not the point of this biblical book. Its literary genre is different from the historical books of the Old Testament.

---

[4] Metzger, *Textual Commentary*, 13-14.

b) New Literary Methods

In addition to the crucial role philological and literary analysis plays in the historical-critical method, new literary methods have arisen in the last forty years which exegetes have applied to the study of Scripture. The Biblical Commission singles out three for comment: rhetorical analysis, narrative analysis and semiotic analysis (I.B)[5]. Rhetorical analysis (I.B.1) reflects on the way in which biblical texts are intended to be persuasive and the means by which this effect is achieved. Narrative analysis (I.B.2) studies how the Bible uses the form of story to communicate its message. Semiotic analysis (I.B.3) studies the typical linguistic structures underlying biblical texts. The Biblical Commission commends each of these literary methods for their respective advantages (I.B.1.i-j; I.B.2.h; I.B.3.k,m) and for their attention to the internal unity of biblical texts and books, which is greater than the classical historical-critical method has recognized (I.C.a)[6].

2. Synchronic Reading, Literary Context and Plurality of Meaning

Literary analysis underscores the importance of reading the Bible synchronically (I.A.3.c; Conclusion c-d), of reading texts in their literary contexts, and of recognizing plurality of meaning in written texts (II.B.d).

Contemporary literary methods emphasize the finished literary work and take a *synchronic* approach to the biblical text. In a synchronic reading "the text is explained as it stands, on the basis of the mutual relationships between its diverse elements" (I.A.3.c). Rather than considering the text's development through time (diachronic analysis), synchronic study considers the text as the reader encounters it in its completed form. Literary analysis stresses interpreting texts as a whole, and thus the reading of every text in its literary context. This is in contrast to the tendency of some historical-critical analysis to pay excessive regard to small portions of texts, designated as earlier strata by source criticism. In its interest in the final text, contemporary literary analysis shares a common perspective with Catholic interpretation which affirms "it is the text in its final stage, rather than in its earlier editions, which is the expression of the Word of God" (I.A.3.f). Although the *IBC* insists that diachronic study is necessary and that its results should be

---

[5] As stated in the introduction, this study will not treat any of these methods in detail since its concern is not methods but principles of Catholic interpretation. Some additional discussion and bibliography on these methods appears in principle #16, "A Plurality of Methods and Approaches".

[6] Yet even this broadening of perspective is insufficient in the eyes of the Biblical Commission, since biblical books should be read in relationship to the whole of Scripture and the Great Tradition to which they belong (I.C.a), as later principles (#8, #10) state.

accepted by practitioners of literary methods (Conclusion c), the Biblical Commission affirms that "the synchronic approaches (the rhetorical, narrative, semiotic and others) are capable, to some extent at least, of bringing about a renewal of exegesis and making a very useful contribution" (Conclusion d).

Philological and literary analysis affirm yet another fact about interpretation which differs from the classical historical-critical approach, but which coincides with the Catholic tradition of interpretation, namely the openness of written texts to a plurality of meaning (II.B.b-d)[7]. Linguistics insists that words signify a range or field of meaning, and their meaning in any particular sentence is indicated by the context. Even then the meaning may intentionally be ambiguous. Irony functions by means of communicating at two levels of meaning. Poetry capitalizes on the capacity of language to convey a wealth of meaning. Biblical prophecy often exploits the multi-leveled potential of language. For instance, the "fire" of judgment which the LORD through the prophet promises to send (Amos 1-2) is a metaphor for God's wrath expressed in military defeat which Israel and the surrounding nations will experience. Yet in the ancient near east the literal destruction of one's city by fire was a terrifying possible consequence of military defeat. Prose narratives, i.e., stories, can bear a wealth of meaning that defies reduction to univocal interpretation. Furthermore, the process of reading, which some modern methods have emphasized and is, indeed, an essential aspect of literary communication, makes a plurality of meaning inevitable. For example, the story of the Prodigal Son (Lk 15) conveys various meanings depending on whether one approaches it from the perspective of the Prodigal, the Father, or the Elder Brother.

3. Example of Literary Contribution

Tremper Longman's interpretation of 1 Kings 22:1-38 illustrates the usefulness of insights from literary analysis for biblical exegesis[8]. His analysis of plot, genre, and narration help make clear what the author intended to communicate. First Longman discusses the narrative's plot:

> The plot may be traced by means of the conflict between characters in the story.... At least three clashes occur in 1 Kings 22. The first is the war between Israel and Aram, the conflict that provides the setting.... The second conflict is between Micaiah and Zedekiah, the latter representing all of the false prophets and the former representing Yahweh's chosen

---

[7] The study of philosophical hermeneutics also gives reason to recognize plural meanings. See p. 84.

[8] Longman, *Literary Approaches*, 101-111. (The *IBC* does not use this example.)

messenger. The third and most important conflict is between Ahab and Michaiah. Ahab, as in the earlier narratives concerning his reign, represents the apostate people of God. Micaiah represents Yahweh....

The plot finds its resolution as the arrow finds its target in the gaps of Ahab's armor and he eventually dies. The conflict between Ahab and God is thus the only one that finds explicit resolution in the story. The narrator is not concerned to inform us about the outcome of the struggle with Aram. Furthermore, ... we hear nothing from the true prophet after he is dragged off to prison.[9]

Longman holds that genre is a "fluid concept", i.e., that there is not a single genre with unchanging properties to which a text may be assigned, but a continuum of possible genres which express the similarities and dissimilarities of the text to other texts. Nevertheless, identifying the genres to which a text belongs is helpful since the reader's perception of genre guides his expectations. According to Longman the narrative about Ahab and Micaiah may be categorized along with most of the historical books of the Old Testament as *didactic history*: "1 Kings 22 is didactic in two ways. First it fits into the overall purpose of the Deuteronomic History to explain why Israel is now in exile. Second, it teaches the reader to avoid evil behavior...as it is embodied in Ahab"[10].

According to Longman, the narrator often holds the key to understanding the message of a biblical narrative[11]. In the Bible third-person "omniscient" narrative dominates, and the narrator renders an authoritative interpretation of the events which occur. 1 Kings 22 conforms to this pattern.

We come to know the narrator...not only from his intrusive comments but also from his management of the dialogue. Nevertheless, he guides our attitudes toward the events and the characters of the story primarily through explicit comments. The narrator is unnamed and not a character. He speaks of all the characters in the third person.... The narrator is omnipresent. He is a presence hovering in the king's council chambers (1 Kings 22:3), in the gate in Samaria (vv. 10-12), and in the Aramean camp (vv. 31-33). He is also with the messenger who summons Micaiah (v.13)....

The narrator's omniscience, though restrained, becomes manifest only in verse 34 in the comment that the arrow that killed Ahab was drawn at random. This comment assumes knowledge on the part of the narrator of the thought processes of the archer....

---

[9] Longman, *Literary Approaches*, 103-104.

[10] Longman, *Literary Approaches*, 104.

[11] "The message of a prose narrative in Scripture may be better understood by closely questioning the text concerning the narrator and his point of view" (Longman, *Literary Approaches*, 88).

Since the narrator is the literary device by which readers are guided in their interpretation of the events of the story, the analysis of the ideology of the narrator leads to a determination of the theological *Tendenz* of the passage, one of the goals of redaction criticism[12].

Discussion

4. *Literary Criticism and Biblical Studies*

Over the last sixty years literary criticism has witnessed the rise of various schools of thought which in turn have influenced biblical studies[13]. Early in the century traditional literary theory sought the meaning of a literary work in the record of the activities and thought life of the author in much the same way that the historical-critical method in biblical studies has sought the historical setting and author's intention. Thus to understand a poem or novel, the critic familiarized himself or herself with all the information available on the author's life circumstances and state of mind at the time by means of letters, diaries, the testimony of friends and family, etc.   In both traditional literary criticism and the historical-critical method, discovering the author's intentional meaning was the goal.

But beginning in 1940 a reaction set in taking the form of a movement called the New Criticism[14].   New Criticism stressed the impossibility of knowing an author's intention, since even authors sometimes do not know their intentions themselves. Furthermore, the author's intention is irrelevant, since meaning resides within the text of the free standing and public literary work itself. New Criticism described the older view as "the intentional fallacy"[15], and turned the attention of criticism to the text itself, urging that its

---

[12] Longman, *Literary Approaches*, 105-106.

[13] For a historical survey of these developments, see Longman, *Literary Approaches*, 13-46, whose account this section follows. For a more in-depth study of literary theory, see Lentricchia, *After the New Criticism*.

[14] See Fitzmyer, *The Biblical Commission's Document*, 50-52, for a brief description and a bibliography of the seminal works. See Bartholomew, *Reading Ecclesiastes: Old Testament Exegesis and Hermeneutical Theory*, 110-122, for more on New Criticism and its implications for biblical interpretation.

[15] Wimsatt and Beardsley, "Intentional Fallacy". Bartholomew notes that a second group of New Critics did not reject authorial intention so completely, wanting rather to put the emphasis on the intrinsic study of the "embodied intentionality" manifest in the text without totally excluding extrinsic evidence of what the author had in mind (*Reading Ecclesiastes*, 113-114).

meaning could be discovered by a close reading and an analysis of the text as a whole[16].

In the 1960's structuralism emerged as a major school of literary criticism[17]. It sought to establish a science or grammar of literature, to set out the "conditions of meaning"[18]. It explored the sign nature of language and language as a system of communication, a set of norms and rules which govern interpersonal communication. Structuralists locate the meaning of a work in the narrative conventions employed by its author in the text. The conventional code which authors use has a public meaning and, therefore, does not reside merely in the author's intention or the reader's pre-understanding. Writers use the devices or conventions of those who preceded them. There is an *intertextuality* between a text and the writings which precede it. "Every text takes shape as a mosaic of citations, every text is the absorbtion and transformation of other texts. The notion of intertextuality comes to take the place of the notion of intersubjectivity"[19]. Under the influence of Russian formalism[20] prose narrative came to be analyzed in terms of conventional roles and functions.

Still later came scholars who emphasized the role of the reader and the pre-understanding he brings to literary texts, which accounts for the diversity of interpretations of the same poem or the same novel. The reader creates his own meaning, or, at least, the perspectives he brings to his reading heavily condition the meaning the text has for him.

It was natural that the genuine insights found in each of these schools would influence biblical studies[21]. In addition, several prominent literary scholars conducted their own studies of the Bible as literature[22], bringing to

---

[16] E.D. Hirsch, Jr., however, argued that to lose sight of the author's intention in writing a text would result in the loss of any fixed meaning to a text. For that reason Hirsch identified the meaning of a text with the author's intended purpose (Longman, *Literary Approaches*, 20-21). Yet Hirsch sought to discover the author's intention through a study of the text itself, in comparison with similar texts, rather than by looking to extrinsic biographical or historical data. See *Validity in Interpretation*; *Aims of Interpretation*; and "Meaning and Significance Reinterpreted".

[17] See Culler, *Structuralist Poetics*.

[18] Longman, *Literary Approaches*, 30. See also Bartholomew, *Reading Ecclesiastes*, pp. 122-134.

[19] Longman, *Literary Approaches*, 32, citing Kristeva, *Semiotikè*, 146.

[20] Propp, *Morphology of the Folktale*.

[21] For a substantial bibliography on the application of new literary criticism to the Bible, see Fitzmyer, *The Biblical Commission's Document*, 52-53n.

[22] For example, Alter, *Art of Biblical Narrative*; and, *The Art of Biblical Poetry*; Frye, *The Great Code*; and Ryken, *Bible as Literature*. There has been ambivalence on the part of many Christian scholars about referring to the Bible as literature (see Longman, *Literary Approaches*, 8-10 for discussion and brief comments by Krister Stendhal, C.S. Lewis, J.G. Herder, T.S.

light aspects of the biblical writings, particularly their literary unity, which had not been adequately recognized by historical-criticism. When applied to Scripture, literary approaches deriving from New Criticism or structuralism often denied or did not concern themselves with the referentiality of the biblical text, i.e., with its claims regarding historical events and persons[23]. This was a natural consequence of applying to the Bible approaches used for literature which is usually fictive in character.

Biblical scholars themselves felt the need to balance historical-critical approaches which had become one-sided. In his 1968 Presidential Address to the Society for Biblical Literature, "Form Criticism and Beyond," James Muilenburg invited his colleagues to go beyond the form-critical study of "typical" pericopes and consider texts holistically, with attention to their individuality. He invited his colleagues to take up a broadened concept of rhetorical criticism[24]. Twenty-five years later the Pontifical Biblical Commission described and evaluated the use of three forms of rhetorical criticism in biblical studies: one with its roots in Aristotle's analysis of persuasive discourse, one with its roots in the study of Semitic literary composition, and the "New Rhetoric" which unites literary insight with historical and sociological analysis.

John R. Donahue traces origin of the literary turn in New Testament studies to the rise of redaction criticism in the 1960's[25]. Redaction criticism went in both a historical and a literary direction. German scholars "stressed

---

Eliot, and Northrop Frye). In the end the question turns both on one's definition of literature and on what one believes about the Bible. Secular universities offer courses on "The Bible as Literature." But the goals of an exclusively literary approach to the Bible differ considerably from the goals of Christian interpretation. The study of the Bible as literature concerns itself with the beauty of biblical narratives and poetry and seeks to classify the literary forms and techniques used by biblical authors. Christian exegesis, on the other hand, is primarily interested in understanding the message of the biblical authors, and, through that, the word of God. In doing so it makes use of literary science to help achieve this goal. Catholic exegesis appreciates the aesthetic wealth of the Bible (III.D.3.b) and assiduously studies its genres, forms and structures, but fixes its eye on the goal of understanding the communication of both the human authors and the divine Author, careful not to remain merely at the formal level (I.B.3.l).

[23] See Longman, *Literary Approaches*, 54-58. According to Donahue ("Literary Turn and New Testament Theology", 264), "The formalism and emphasis on the inner textual world of the biblical material itself, a legacy of the New Criticism, did not seem adequate for ancient texts, especially those at the foundation of Christian faith and theology".

[24] Muilenburg, "Form Criticism and Beyond".

[25] See Donahue, "Literary Turn and New Testament Theology". Donahue evaluates the implications for NT theology of the exegesis' borrowings from literary studies. He briefly analyzes the rise in biblical studies of narrative criticism, structuralism, reader-response criticism, deconstruction, and new historicism.

the difference between tradition and redaction and the need to write a careful history of the tradition. In North America...the method soon developed into full-scale literary criticism..."[26] In its literary development, redaction criticism perceived the Gospels as coherent wholes, self-consciously crafted narratives, resulting from literary imagination. This tendency in turn evolved in two directions: composition criticism, which emphasized the text's theological content; and narrative criticism, which took a formalist approach, locating the meaning of the biblical text in the details of its structure.

The Biblical Commission's response to these literary movements is open, but critical. A greater emphasis on studying the text itself in its entirety is evident in the welcome given to synchronic readings. A nuancing of the classical historical-critical search for the author's intention appears in the definition of the literal sense[27]. Yet New Criticism's extreme denial of the author and of the historical setting is rejected. The historical setting of composition is still valuable for interpretation because of the light it sheds on the human author's meaning. Catholic interpretation's concern for history rejects the excising of referentiality from Scripture. Scripture renders testimony to the real actions of God in the history of Israel and the Church, even if the line between history and non-historical story is not everywhere clearly drawn in Scripture. On the other hand, some acceptance is given to reader-oriented approaches, not to the point of granting that readers merely create meaning, but recognizing that pre-understanding must influence interpretation and can enrich it (e.g., II.A.1.d, II.A.2.f). The *IBC* sections on philosophical hermeneutics (II.A) and on contextual approaches (I.E.) manifest a qualified acceptance of reader-oriented interpretation.

Conspicuously absent from the Biblical Commission's list of contemporary literary methods and approaches for the interpreting of Scripture is "deconstruction". Perhaps this is due to the fact that in 1989, when the Biblical Commission drew up its list of methods and approaches to include, the influence of Jacques Derrida and deconstruction on biblical studies was still slight. But it is not hard to imagine that the Biblical Commission intentionally left it out, finding too little in common between Catholic principles of interpretation and the principles of deconstruction[28].

---

[26] Donahue, "Literary Turn and New Testament Theology", 254-255.

[27] See principle #12, especially p. 165ff.

[28] Klauk comments that the absence of deconstruction, post-structuralism and post-modernism is understandable, since these methods so far inspire little confidence ("Das neue Dokument: Darstellung und Würdigung", 77-78). Donahue concurs, considering deconstruction the least favorable partner of all the literary approaches for NT theology ("Literary Turn and New Testament Theology", 273n). However, Michael Edwards, evaluating deconstruction from a Christian perspective, seeks to point out the truth which

By denying the foundational belief of Western thought in "presence," i.e., the referentiality of words to realities, by its skepticism about the possibility of an act of literary communication, by the finding of *aporia* everywhere in the Bible and the slippage between signifier and signified, it was, perhaps, more difficult to see how deconstruction could contribute to Catholic interpretation.

5.   Catholic Exegesis and Literary Analysis

Principle #4 expresses Catholic exegesis' intention to avail itself of the philological and literary means normally employed in interpreting written texts. This kind of analysis has always played a part in Christian exegesis and in the historical-critical method; it has also contributed new methods to biblical studies.   In recent years literary studies have served to balance historical-critical exegesis which sometimes failed to recognize the literary coherence of texts and the wealth of meaning available.

The interests of Catholic exegesis, of course, go beyond the appreciation of literary beauty, the classification of literary techniques, and the enjoyment of a superlative story, although it includes all these.   Catholic exegesis' conviction regarding the historical revelation recounted by Scripture and its goal of explaining that religious message informs its use of literary approaches.

---

deconstruction contains, namely the extreme difficulties in human communication consequent to the Fall (*Christian Poetics*). Kevin J. Vanhoozer is another who appreciates some of the arguments of deconstruction, while proposing a carefully nuanced defense of the author and of determinacy of meaning (*Is There a Meaning?*).

CHAPTER 5

The Contribution of Philosophical Hermeneutics

The fact that Scripture comes to us from the past makes the study of history necessary. The fact that it comes in the form of written texts makes philological and literary analysis necessary. And the fact that it must be understood by human beings makes hermeneutics necessary, since hermeneutics is the science of interpretation. The *IBC* discusses the contribution of "philosophical" hermeneutics, which reflects upon human communication and interpretation in general, in the service of biblical hermeneutics. Philosophical hermeneutics shares many concerns with philosophy, often taking up questions of epistemology, metaphysics, and the quest for truth in human existence[1].

Principle #5

> *Because interpreting the Bible entails an act of human understanding like the act of understanding any other ancient writing, it is fitting that philosophical hermeneutics inform Catholic interpretation.*
>
> *It is not possible to understand any written text without "pre-understanding," i.e., presuppositions which guide comprehension (II.A.1.a). The act of understanding involves a dialectic between the pre-understanding of the interpreter and the perspective of the text*

---

[1] For more on philosophical hermeneutics in the context of biblical hermeneutics, see Bartholomew, *Reading Ecclesiastes: Old Testament Exegesis and Hermeneutical Theory*, Grech, *Ermeneutica e teologia biblica* and "Hermeneutics"; Lategan, "Hermeneutics"; Montague, *Understanding the Bible*; Palmer, *Interpretation Theory*; Thiselton, *Two Horizons* and *New Horizons in Hermeneutics*.

(II.A.1.c). Nevertheless, this pre-understanding must be open to correction in its dialogue with the reality of the text (II.A.1.a).

Since interpretation of the Bible involves the subjectivity of the interpreter, understanding is only possible if there is a fundamental affinity between the interpreter and his object. (II.A.2.c)

Some hermeneutical theories are inadequate due to presuppositions which are incompatible with the message of the Bible. (II.A.2.d)

Philosophical hermeneutics corrects some tendencies of historical-criticism, showing the inadequacy of historical positivism (II.B.2.c), the role of the reader in interpretation, possibilities of meaning beyond of a text's historical setting, and the openness of texts to a plurality of meaning (II.B.c; Conclusion d).

Because in the Bible Christians seek the meaning of ancient writings for the present, literary and historical criticism must be incorporated in a model of interpretation which overcomes the distance in time between the origin of the text and our contemporary age (II.A.2.a). Both the Bible itself and the history of its interpretation demonstrate a pattern of re-reading texts in the light of new circumstances (II.A.2.b) [2].

Explanation

Although it is the shortest major division of a chapter in the *IBC*, section II.A on philosophical hermeneutics is dense and crucial for the Commission's entire presentation of Catholic interpretation[3]. First the *IBC* succinctly summarizes certain key ideas from the hermeneutical writings of Rudolf Bultmann[4], Hans Georg Gadamer[5] and Paul Ricoeur[6]. Then an evaluation

---

[2] The Biblical Commission treats philosophical hermeneutics in part A of the chapter entitled "Hermeneutical Questions". However, allusions to philosophical hermeneutics are sprinkled throughout the document, and most of those references will be cited in the discussion that follows.

Although the *IBC* includes consideration of the special nature of the Bible as the word of God in its discussion of philosophical hermeneutics (II.A.2.a, d-f), this study will attempt to keep the two dimensions distinct. Principle #5 (above) summarizes the main implications of philosophical hermeneutics for the interpretation of the Bible as a human writing. Part III and especially principle #6 will consider the implications of philosophical hermeneutics for interpreting the Bible as the word of God.

[3] For a thoughtful commentary and substantial bibliography in the footnotes, see Vignolo, "Questioni di ermeneutica [*Commento*]".

[4] See Bultmann, *Theology of the New Testament, Jesus and the Word*, and "New Testament and Mythology".

section follows which highlights elements the Biblical Commission considers useful for exegesis. With the exception of Bultmann's existentialist philosophy and "excessive demythologization", which are criticized (II.A.2.d), the Biblical Commission's attitude toward the hermeneutical insights mentioned in the descriptive part is positive. Hermeneutical reflection is not merely optional, and the Commission challenges exegetes to take up the hermeneutical task: "All exegesis of texts is thus summoned to make itself fully complete through a 'hermeneutics' understood in this modern sense" (II.A.2.a).

1. Understanding and Pre-understanding

It is not possible to understand any written text without "pre-understanding," i.e., presuppositions which guide comprehension (II.A.1.a). The act of understanding involves a dialectic between the pre-understanding of the interpreter and the perspective of the text (II.A.1.c). Nevertheless, this pre-understanding must be open to correction in its dialogue with the reality of the text (II.A.1.a).

Whenever anyone attempts to understand a written text, he or she begins with some understanding of the words, the concepts, and the realities to which the words refer, or no understanding[7] is possible. This is what the term "pre-

---

[5] See Gadamer, *Truth and Method* and *Philosophical Hermeneutics*.

[6] See Ricoeur, *Conflict of Interpretations, Interpretation Theory* and *Essays on Biblical Interpretation*.

[7] The Biblical Commission's necessarily brief and simplified presentation of philosophical hermeneutics obscures the different uses authors make of different terms. The proper object of *understanding* and the relation between understanding and interpretation are among the matters viewed differently. The early theorists of hermeneutics (Friedrich Schleiermacher and Wilhelm Dilthey) view understanding as a psychological understanding of the author, a sharing of his experience and point of view. Heidegger and Bultmann interpret understanding as a decision which determines personal existence in response to the message of the text. Structuralists view the "grammar" of the text, grasping the relationship of the various typical elements of the text to one another, as the object of understanding. Gadamer and Ricoeur consider the reality to which the text refers as the object of understanding, while continuing to be concerned with its implications for human existence.

The Biblical Commission denies that the proper object of understanding in interpretation can be merely linguistic or cognitive: "Biblical knowledge should not stop short at language; it must seek to arrive at the reality of which the language speaks.... The religious language of the Bible...points to a transcendent reality and...awakens human beings to the deepest dimensions of personal existence" (II.A.1.d).

What is the relationship of understanding to interpretation? Gadamer distinguishes between *understanding*, which he values highly and views as an inner grasping of truth, with *explanation*, which he sees as the product of an extrinsic rational process (method) and considers much inferior. But interpretation would seem to entail both understanding and explanation. This is Ricoeur's view, who sees hermeneutics as a double-edged instrument,

understanding" (French, *"precompréhension"*; German, *"Vorverständnis"*) means. According to Bultmann, an individual's pre-understanding is based on his or her life-relationship (*Lebensverhältnis*) with the reality of which the text speaks (II.A.1.a). If an American reads a history of the American Revolution in 1776, he approaches it one way; if an Englishman reads it, he interprets what he reads in an entirely different way. Gadamer develops the notion of pre-understanding and relates it to the tradition or culture to which an individual belongs. He refers to this pre-understanding as the individual's "horizon of understanding". The *IBC* explains its origin:

> Anticipations and preconceptions affecting our understanding stem from the tradition which carries us. This tradition consists in a mass of historical and cultural data which constitute our life context and our horizon of understanding(II.A.1.c).

A person who was raised a Jew, for example, will approach the New Testament with quite a different pre-understanding than will a person who was raised a Christian.

Understanding a written text entails an encounter between an individual's pre-understanding and what the text says. If the individual keeps himself or herself closed to the world and message of the text, no understanding occurs. But if the reader allows his perspective to be altered in any way, if he takes into account more information provided by the text, or questions the text on the basis of what he already knows and questions what he knows on the basis of what he has read, understanding begins. According to Gadamer, "Understanding is reached in the fusion of the differing horizons of text and reader.... Hermeneutics is a dialectical process..." (II.A.1.c). Bultmann, like Schleiermacher and Dilthey, described the process of understanding as a hermeneutical circle: in order to understand something, a person must already have some understanding of it. Gadamer improves on the metaphor, making the process of understanding more like a spiral. A person must understand something already to understand the text, but the dialogue between his or her pre-understanding and the text will confirm what he knows or may contradict it, but in either case, it will add to his or her understanding, raising it to a higher level.

Thus, human understanding never begins with a *tabula rasa*, a completely blank page[8]. No one comes to the Bible (or any other book bearing truth claims which could affect the life of the reader) with complete objectivity—he or she will carry some preconceptions and be inclined toward

---

entailing a critical and a "listening" dimension (Thiselton, *New Horizons in Hermeneutics*, 347-348, 371-372). The *IBC* notion of interpretation entails both understanding and explanation.

[8] For a popular presentation of this idea, see Carson, "Tabula Rasa".

one position or another. However, human understanding is not necessarily constrained by the pre-understanding with which it begins. Human beings are capable of modifying the perspective with which they begin; they can progress in their understanding of what they read and even reach a conclusion opposite to the pre-understanding with which they started.

2. Affinity between Subject and Object

Since interpretation of the Bible involves the subjectivity of the interpreter, understanding is only possible if there is a fundamental affinity between the interpreter and his object. (II.A.2.c)

The *IBC* presents some of Gadamer's ideas on the relationship of subject and object in interpretation. Gadamer's description of understanding as a "fusion of the differing horizons" suggests a transforming union between the pre-understanding of the interpreter and the content of the text. Therefore, it is not surprising that true understanding requires a profound relationship between the reader and the reality to which the text refers. According to Gadamer, understanding "is possible only to the extent that there is a 'belonging' ('Zugehörigkeit'), that is, a fundamental affinity, between the interpreter and his or her object" (II.A.1.c). If there is not mutual "belonging" or affinity between the reader and the text, if there is hostility or skepticism or indifference in the reader, the reader remains outside, alienated from the meaning of the text, rather than comprehending it. Gadamer's notion of understanding goes beyond merely "objective", external understanding, to an inner understanding entailing a sympathy with the reality comprehended[9].

The Biblical Commission applies these insights to the interpretation of Scripture: "Access to a proper understanding of biblical texts is only granted to the person who has an affinity with what the text is saying on the basis of life experience" (II.A.2.c). And what does "belonging" and "affinity…on the basis of life experience" entail in relationship to Sacred Scripture? "An authentic interpretation of Scripture, then, involves in the first place a welcoming of the meaning that is given in the events and, in a supreme way, in the person of Jesus Christ" (II.A.2.d). However, the interpretive role of Christian faith belongs to the next chapter.

---

[9] Gadamer has been criticized by E. Betti and Hirsch for opening the door to an excessively subjective reading of the text and failing to provide an adequate means by which the voice of the text may be heard (Grech, "Hermeneutics", 422). Anthony C. Thiselton comments that Gadamer "lands firmly on the border between modern and post-modern thought" (*New Horizons in Hermeneutics*, 316). The Biblical Commission does not take up the controversial aspects of Gadamer's hermeneutic, and interprets Gadamer in light of Ricoeur—a move that was not appreciated by all (see below, 88n).

3.   Rejection of Incompatible Presuppositions

Some hermeneutical theories are inadequate due to presuppositions which are incompatible with the message of the Bible. (II.A.2.d)

The commentary on principle #2 (Catholic exegesis is scientific) already mentioned the necessity that scientific disciplines applied to biblical study not smuggle in presuppositions that contradict Scripture's message. But attentiveness to appropriate presuppositions applies to every interpretive effort, not only the use of scientific methods. After describing with approval Bultmann's desire to make the Bible speak to his contemporaries, the Biblical Commission points out the problematic presuppositions of the approach he adopted:

> Bultmann's existentialist interpretation tends to enclose the Christian message within the constraints of a particular [Heideggerian] philosophy. Moreover, by virtue of the presuppositions insisted upon in this hermeneutic, the religious message of the Bible is for the most part emptied of its objective reality (by means of an excessive "demythologization") and tends to be reduced to an anthropological message only. Philosophy becomes the norm of interpretation.... (II.A.2.d)[10]

Social bias may also furnish problematic presuppositions:

> Clearly to be rejected also is every attempt at actualization set in a direction contrary to evangelical justice and charity, such as, for example, the use of the Bible to justify racial segregation, anti-semitism or sexism whether on the part of men or of women (IV.A.3.d).

Elsewhere the *IBC* points out the unsuitability of presuppositions deriving from Marxist class struggle, rationalism, and atheistic materialism for interpreting the Bible (I.E.1.l; IV.A.3.c).

---

[10] Bultmann was arguably the most influential NT exegete of the 20th century. While recognizing his contribution, Ratzinger had focused his public criticisms of contemporary exegesis on the continuing influence of certain elements in Bultmann's hermeneutic ("Biblical Interpretation in Crisis" and *Schriftauslegung im Widerstreit*). For its part, the PBC acknowledged Bultmann's contributions to form criticism (I.A.1.c) and hermeneutics (the inevitability of pre-understanding, the attempt to make Scripture speak to his contemporaries, II.A.1), but criticized his presuppositions in two respects. First, Bultmann interpreted the Christian message entirely through the optic of Heideggerian existentialism, thus subjecting the gospel to philosophy. Second, he removed its transcendent dimension by means of "excessive demythologization". According to Grech, Bultmann's program of demythologization, his rejection of the historicity of the Gospels and his separation of the historical Jesus from faith in the Christ of the *kerygma* had a "harmful" effect on Christian hermeneutics ("Hermeneutics", 421, 424).

What is the standard by which presuppositions for interpreting the Bible may justly be evaluated? The content of Scripture itself provides the primary control: To avoid subjecting the Bible to contrary philosophies or tendentious premises, "interpretation will constantly submit its presuppositions to verification by the text" (II.A.2.e).

4. Correction of Historical-Critical Tendencies

Philosophical hermeneutics corrects some tendencies of historical-criticism, showing the inadequacy of historical positivism (II.B.2.c), the role of the reader in interpretation, possibilities of meaning beyond a text's historical setting, and the openness of texts to a plurality of meaning (II.B.c; Conclusion d).

Despite its overall positive evaluation of the historical-critical method, the Biblical Commission believes that philosophical hermeneutics has "shed light upon many aspects of the problem of interpretation that the historical-critical method has tended to ignore" (Conclusion d).

Historical positivism attempted to apply to history the objective criteria of the natural sciences. But contemporary philosophical hermeneutics has demonstrated "the involvement of the knowing subject in human understanding, especially as regards historical knowledge" (II.A.a). History is not reported and cannot be reported with the kind of objectivity possible in chemistry or physics: "On the one hand, all events reported in the Bible are interpreted events. On the other, all exegesis of the accounts of these events necessarily involves the exegete's own subjectivity" (II.A.2.c)[11].

It is obvious that philosophical hermeneutics thus recognizes the role of the reader in the process of interpretation. But the reader's inescapable subjectivity need not be regarded negatively. The reader's questions and interests permit the discovery of new dimensions to a text's meaning. Commenting on contextual approaches to interpretation, the *IBC* states,

---

[11] This is a subject the Biblical Commission treated in greater depth in a previous document (Fitzmyer, *Scripture and Christology*, 6-7; [*EB* §922-923]). Briefly summarized, the objectivity of the historical method is not the same as that of the natural sciences since it concerns itself with human experience, which cannot be verified by experimentation that produces repeatable results. Experience, *qua* experience, can only be understood "from within". Investigating human experience confronts the historian both with the subjectivity of the authors of the sources under consideration, but also with the researcher's own subjectivity as he or she inquires into the "truth" of history and brings his or her own questions and interests. The historical study of Jesus is an obvious example: it is never neutral because Jesus' life and message requires a decision on the part of anyone who studies it. On historical positivism, see also p. 57ff.

"Thus it is inevitable that some exegetes bring to their work points of view that are new and responsive to contemporary currents of thought which have not up till now been taken sufficiently into consideration" (I.E.a). Specifically the document recognizes the fresh insights discovered by those seeking social justice (I.E.1.i), by women exegetes (I.E.2.j-k), and by the poor (IV.C.3.m). Over time, the light which new questions and circumstances bring to the understanding of a text enriches its meaning.

The historical-critical method has tended to insist that a given text means only what the author intended in the particular historical circumstances in which the text was composed. However, the Biblical Commission thinks this is too narrow a perspective. First, this view is inadequate because the Bible itself demonstrates a pattern of re-reading texts at a later time in different circumstances in a manner that extends the original meaning (II.A.2.b). Grech describes this biblical pattern:

> For the Jews, the Torah and the prophets always speak to the generation that reads them. They recount their history in this way, not merely for purely historical interest, but as a living history with a message for their contemporaries. The authors' historical sense has value only insofar as it also speaks to the present....

> [In the New Testament] the literary technique adopted in re-reading the OT is similar, but the content is completely different, although in line with the traditional pattern of reinterpretation found in the Bible, which rereads the texts with the understanding offered by the most recent events in the history of salvation.... Consequently the Christ-event sheds light on the meaning of the biblical text, which thereby receives its full significance[12].

Second, those who selected the biblical texts and handed them on to posterity understood them to contain meaning beyond what was present in the human author's original historical communication.

> Indeed, what encouraged the believing community to preserve these texts was the conviction that they would continue to be bearers of light and life for generations of believers to come. The literal sense is, from the start, open to further developments, which are produced through the "re-reading" ("*relectures*") of texts in new contexts.... (II.B.1f)

Third, it is a mistake to restrict the meaning of a biblical text to what can be found in its historical setting because this is contrary to the nature of written texts.

---

[12] Grech, "Hermeneutics", 416-417.

One branch of modern hermeneutics has stressed that human speech gains an altogether fresh status when put in writing. A written text has the capacity to be placed in new circumstances, which will illuminate it in different ways, adding new meanings to the original sense. This capacity of written texts is especially operative in the case of the biblical writings.... (II.B.1.f)

In its descriptive section on philosophical hermeneutics the *IBC* states with apparent approval Ricoeur's view that a distance exists between a text and its author: "...once produced, the text takes on a certain autonomy in relation to its author; it begins its own career of meaning" (II.A.1.d)[13]. In their conclusion the Biblical Commission explicitly criticizes a tendency in the historical-critical method for its neglect of "the dynamic aspect of meaning":

> Concerned above all to establish the meaning of texts by situating them in their original historical context, this [historical-critical] method has at times shown itself insufficiently attentive to the dynamic aspect of meaning and to the possibility that meaning can continue to develop" (Conclusion d).

Finally, philosophical hermeneutics affirms that written texts are open to a plurality of meaning. In reaction to the four senses of medieval exegesis, historical-critical exegesis adopted the thesis that a text cannot have more than one meaning (II.B.b). "But this thesis has now run aground on the conclusions of theories of language and philosophical hermeneutics, both of which affirm that written texts are open to a plurality of meaning" (II.B.c)[14]. The Biblical Commission does not state which theories of philosophical hermeneutics it refers to, but two possibilities seem likely. Gadamer sees an endless chain of interpretations as successive individuals encounter and understand a text over time. This series of interpretations, this effective history of the text (*Wirkungsgeschichte*), constitutes tradition and manifests a plurality of meaning. Ricoeur emphasizes the symbolic and metaphorical language of the Bible which contains a "surplus of meaning" which gives rise to endless interpretation[15].

5. Bridge between the Past and Present

Because in the Bible Christians seek the meaning of ancient writings for the present, literary and historical criticism must be incorporated in a model of

---

[13] Ruppert clearly thinks that the Commission has made its own the notion of "career of meaning" ("Kommentierende Einführung", 41-42). Fitzmyer, however, says that he does not accept Ricoeur's notion of "career of meaning" (personal conversation at CBA meeting, 9 August 1999).

[14] See also the recognition of plurality in meaning deriving from literary studies, principle #4, p. 69.

[15] Montague, *Understanding the Bible*, 133-134.

interpretation which overcomes the distance in time between the origin of the text and our contemporary age (II.A.2.a). Both the Bible itself and the history of its interpretation demonstrate a pattern of re-reading texts in the light of new circumstances (II.A.2.b).

Literary methods can only explain what is in a text. Historical methods can only recount what a text meant in the past. But for Christians,

> the Bible is the Word of God for all succeeding ages. Hence the absolute necessity of a hermeneutical theory which allows for the incorporation of the *methods of literary and historical criticism within a broader model of interpretation* (II.A.2.a, emphasis added)

A hermeneutical theory is necessary to explain the relation of a text to reality and of past meaning to present meaning. In the case of Scripture received as the word of God, it must explain how these human writings are God's word to his people[16]. The failure to incorporate historical and literary methods within a "broader model of interpretation" led Schneiders to the conclusion that "contemporary New Testament scholarship…does not really 'know what it is doing' in the theoretical sense of that expression", and to develop her hermeneutic model[17]. The Biblical Commission tackled the same problem in the *IBC*.

It is not possible to understand or apply any document from the past without an interpretive step which bridges past and present. For example, if someone reads Aristotle's *Rhetoric* to deepen his or her understanding of any persuasive communication besides Greek oratory, the reader selects the elements that pertain to the oral or written communication under consideration and leaves aside the rest. When the U.S. Supreme Court is called upon to interpret the Constitution regarding the exercise of "free speech" on the Internet, it considers arguments regarding the founders'

---

[16] This aspect will receive treatment in part III of this study on Scripture as the word of God and in part IV, on the meaning of inspired Scripture.

[17] Schneiders, *Revelatory Text*, 21. Schneiders attempts to lessen the sting of her criticism by sandwiching it between encomiums of contemporary exegesis' achievements: "Against a background of profound respect, indeed admiration, for the prodigious accomplishments of modern historical critical biblical scholarship, this conclusion is nevertheless critical, even harsh: contemporary New Testament scholarship actually lacks a developed hermeneutical theory. To that extent, it does not really 'know what it is doing' in the theoretical sense of that expression. It knows *how* to do what it is doing, but has uncritically taken for granted that *what* it is doing is exactly and only what needs to be done for this text…to be truly understood. It is this unexamined presupposition, hidden beneath an impressive array of exegetical methods and an even more impressive array of exegetical results, that I want to bring out into the light for investigation". In the pages that follow, 21-25, Schneiders continues her critique of biblical scholarship's fascination with method(s), especially (but not only) historical criticism, and its consequent limited contribution to the spiritual life of Christians.

intentions, legal precedent subsequent to the writing of the Constitution and the new reality of the Internet in order to apply a 200-year-old document to the present. Both Aristotle's *Rhetoric* and the U.S. Constitution have something to say to modern readers. But to understand them they must be interpreted differently than a contemporary writing.

The *IBC* briefly traces the developing hermeneutical awareness in Bultmann, Gadamer, and Ricoeur. Bultmann emphasized the necessity of a path from past to present meaning because of the cultural and historical distance between the first and twentieth century. Gadamer stressed the interaction between the horizon of the interpreter and the horizon of the text which occurs in every generation of readers, inevitably resulting in new dimensions of meaning. Ricoeur emphasized the need for balance between the objective and subjective dimensions in interpretation. Because of the distance between a text and its readers, historical and literary methods are necessary for interpretation, to respect the otherness of the text. Nevertheless,

> the meaning of a text can be fully grasped only as it is actualized in the lives of readers who appropriate it. Beginning with their situation, they are summoned to uncover new meanings, along the fundamental line of meaning indicated by the text. Biblical knowledge should not stop short at language; it must seek to arrive at the reality of which the language speaks. (II.A.1.d) [18]

The Biblical Commission reports Ricoeur's view that a text is only fully understood when it is "actualized in the lives of readers who *appropriate* it". Understanding Scripture is not merely a matter of understanding words or concepts but of *engaging the reality to which the words refer*. The idea that interpretation must concern itself with the reality to which Scripture bears witness will be taken up in the next chapter.

In their evaluation of the hermeneutics of Bultmann, Gadamer and Ricoeur, the Biblical Commission concludes that the hermeneutical step of bridging the past and present is not merely optional. Rather, the *IBC* speaks of

> the *absolute necessity* of a hermeneutical theory which allows for the incorporation of the methods of literary and historical criticism within a broader model of interpretation. It is a question of overcoming the distance between the time of the authors and first addressees of the biblical texts and our own contemporary age, and of doing so in a way that permits a correct *actualization* of the scriptural message so that the Christian life of faith may find nourishment. *All exegesis of texts is thus summoned to make itself fully*

---

[18] Although it cannot be said that the Biblical Commission offers unqualified endorsement to everything in the descriptive section "Modern Perspectives" (II.A.1), it is obviously sympathetic to most of the insights of contemporary hermeneutics it chooses to recount.

complete through a "hermeneutics" understood in this modern sense. (II.A.2.a, emphasis added)[19]

The word "actualization" in this quotation sums up the bridging of past and present which is necessary for Christian exegesis. In its usage in the *IBC*, "actualize" means to bring into the present (from the French word for "present", *actuel*)[20]. This becomes an important concept for the first time in a church document on Scripture. The *IBC* uses the term frequently and devotes a major section of a chapter to it (IV.A). This study takes actualization to be a principle of Catholic interpretation (see principle #18).

The pattern of biblical interpretation present in both Scripture and tradition shows the necessity of closing the gap between what the text meant in the past and what it means in the present:

> The whole complex of the Old and New Testament writings show themselves to be the product of a long process where founding events constantly find reinterpretation through connection with the life of communities of faith. In Church tradition, the Fathers, as first interpreters of Scripture, considered that their exegesis of texts was complete only when it had found a meaning relevant to the situation of Christians in their own day. (II.A.2.b)

This has definite implications for contemporary exegesis. According to the Biblical Commission, "Exegesis is truly faithful to proper intention of biblical texts when it goes not only to the heart of their formulation to find the reality of faith there expressed but also seeks to link this reality to the experience of faith in our present world" (II.A.2.b).

Discussion

6. Evaluation

The *IBC* is the first official Church document which explicitly embraces and utilizes the science of philosophical hermeneutics. Church documents since *Providentissimus Deus* (1893) have gradually accepted historical and literary methods, but this is a new step. It is notable in light of the diverse positions that exist in contemporary hermeneutics that reviewers have

---

[19] Roberto Vignolo considers the last sentence of this quotation to be a valid warning in the present situation of biblical studies, too often content with an archaeological and formal reconstruction of the text. On the other hand, hermeneutics must not be viewed as the last step of interpretation, like the dessert offered after a *menu fisso*, a meal pre-determined by the application of a supposedly autonomous methodology. Exegesis must be aware of itself as a hermeneutic process precisely in the modern sense from the outset, in the choice and in the carrying out of its methods ("Questioni di ermeneutica [*Commento*]", 295n).

[20] For more on the meaning of actualization, see note, p. 290.

responded to the *IBC* section on philosophical hermeneutics very positively. On the whole the Biblical Commission has succeeded in harvesting useful insights from contemporary philosophical hermeneutics without entangling itself in disputed questions or defining Catholic interpretation in terms of a particular theory of interpretation[21].

An interesting feature of the Biblical Commission's treatment of philosophical hermeneutics is a matter that the Commission does not discuss, namely, the role in interpretation of the author's intention. The hermeneutics of Gadamer and Ricoeur as presented in the *IBC* are text-centered (and to some degree, reader-oriented), rather than oriented to the author's meaning. Although he recommends the use of historical criticism to respect the otherness of the text, Ricoeur declares,

> Not the intention of the author, which is supposed to be hidden behind the text; not the historical situation common to the author and his original readers; not the expectations or feelings of these original readers; not even their understanding of themselves as historical and cultural phenomena. What has to be appropriated is the meaning of the text itself, conceived in a dynamic way as the direction of thought opened up by a text. In other words, what has to be appropriated is nothing other than the power of disclosing a world that constitutes the reference of the text[22].

But the historical-critical method and Catholic exegesis since *Divino afflante Spiritu* (1943) have placed the primary stress on understanding the *mens auctoris*, the mind of the author. How are these differing perspectives to be held together? This matter will be taken up in the discussion of the literal sense (principle #12, especially p. 165ff).

The insights of philosophical hermeneutics prove to be extremely important for relating Catholic exegesis' use of scientific knowledge to its use of faith and theological principles[23]. Hermeneutics is the hinge which joins

---

[21] See, however, the criticism of Ayres and Fowl, "(Mis)Reading the Face of God". Ayres and Fowl point out that the *IBC* fails to do justice to Gadamer's rejection of "any general hermeneutical method for 'decoding' texts" and his promotion instead of "phronesis within a tradition-constituted process of inquiry" (517-518). They say, with some justification, that the *IBC* adopts Ricoeur's reading of Gadamer, which counters Gadamer's anti-methodological stance by stressing the distance between the text and readers and the need for literary and historical analysis to protect the text from subjective interpretation. It must be acknowledged that the *IBC*'s brief presentation of philosophical hermeneutics is a selective and harmonized reading. On the point in question, Ayres and Fowl agree with Gadamer over Ricoeur: they favor interpretation that develops from within the tradition of the community and that is oriented to its needs (see also Fowl, *Engaging Scripture*). They maintain that historical-critical concerns "are not foundational or determinative for Christians reading their Scripture" (528).

[22] Ricoeur, *Interpretation Theory*, 92.

[23] See part III, "Catholic Exegesis and Christian Faith".

faith and reason in the exegetical enterprise.   Several points may be mentioned.

First, the recognition of "pre-understanding" shows the legitimacy of approaching the Scriptures from a standpoint of Christian faith. Without this concept it might seem that a Christian could only approach a scientific study of the Bible by the systematic exclusion of insights, questions or concerns arising from his faith. The awareness that everyone comes to the biblical text with pre-understanding that conditions interpretation is more realistic. It moves the discussion to a consideration of the various pre-understandings that exist among interpreters and the consequences they have for interpretation. Hermeneutical awareness can enable interpreters to articulate their presuppositions and can aid dialogue among interpreters who begin from different pre-understandings.

Second, the insight that "belonging" or "affinity" between text and interpreter is a condition for an authentic understanding of a text argues for the advantage of Christian faith for interpreting the Christian Scriptures. Furthermore, it opens the door to recognizing the interpretive role of the Christian community.

Third, although it does not resolve every question, the principle that hermeneutical theories and their presuppositions must not contradict the Bible's message (or else constitute an *a priori* judgment against it) is useful for eliminating some unsuitable approaches to the biblical text.

Fourth, the recognition that the meaning of the text is not be confined to the meaning that was present in its original historical setting liberates interpretation from a narrow historicism. Furthermore, it suggests the value of a tradition of interpretation and opens the door to actualization.

Fifth, the possibility of plurality of meaning accords well with a long tradition of multiple senses in Scripture.

Finally, the recognition of the need for a hermeneutic which makes the step from what it meant *then*, to what it means *now*, summons exegesis to move beyond an archeological conception of its task. It also confirms the hermeneutical legitimacy of preaching and teaching which applies Scripture to new circumstances and questions.

7. Conclusion to Part II

There is no question that Catholic exegesis today shows respect for the human dimension of Sacred Scripture. In contrast to the period of anti-Modernist reaction at the beginning of this century, Catholic exegesis has embraced a scientific approach. History, literary and philological analysis, philosophical hermeneutics, psychoanalysis, cultural anthropology—every field of critical study is welcome to make a contribution to understanding the human words through which the word of God comes. Pope John Paul II has confirmed this direction and the progress that has taken place in this century (Address 8, 16). Despite real difficulties along the path which at times have impeded progress and have led some to oppose scientific exegesis, the Biblical Commission insists on the necessity of careful attention to the human dimension of Sacred Scripture. Nevertheless, scientific methods must be approached with care regarding their presuppositions, in order that no prejudice contrary to the message of Scripture compromise their results. If this rule is observed, Christian faith has nothing to fear from science and much to gain.

PART III

"THE WORD OF GOD": CATHOLIC EXEGESIS AND CHRISTIAN FAITH

Just as the fact that the Scripture comes to us in "human language" requires that it be interpreted in the light of history, literary analysis and other sciences, so also the fact that the Bible is the word of God requires that it be interpreted "theologically", by principles and methods suited to the understanding of divine revelation. Pope John Paul II puts it this way:

> In order to respect the coherence of the Church's faith and of scriptural inspiration, Catholic exegesis must be careful not to limit itself to the human aspects of the biblical texts. First and foremost, it must help the Christian people more clearly perceive the word of God in these texts so that they can better accept them in order to live in full communion with God. (Address 9)

In the application of "scientific" methods—the theme of chapter I of the *IBC* and part II of this work—there is no difference between the exegesis of a Catholic, Protestant, Jewish or even an unbelieving exegete, provided that one distinguishes between conclusions proceeding from scientific methods and those proceeding from the interpreter's presuppositions. So what distinguishes Catholic interpretation from all other interpretation of the Bible? Chapter III of the *IBC*, entitled "Characteristics of Catholic Interpretation", devotes itself to this theme[1].   In an introductory paragraph the Biblical Commission explains:

> What characterizes Catholic exegesis is that it deliberately places itself within the living tradition of the Church, whose first concern is fidelity to the revelation attested by the Bible. Modern hermeneutics has made clear, as we have noted, the impossibility of interpreting a text without starting from a "pre-understanding" of one type or another. Catholic exegetes approach the biblical text with a pre-understanding which holds closely together modern scientific culture and the religious tradition emanating from Israel and from the early Christian community. Their interpretation thereby stands in continuity with a dynamic pattern of interpretation that is found within the Bible itself and continues in the life of the Church. This dynamic pattern corresponds to the requirement that there be a lived affinity between the interpreter and the object, an affinity which constitutes, in fact, one of the conditions that makes the entire exegetical enterprise possible. (III.b)

In a time in which Catholic exegetes are seeking to understand more clearly their distinctive identity and task, the distinguishing characteristics of Catholic exegesis proposed by the Biblical Commission in chapter III of the *IBC* are extremely useful. They offer guidance which has value for the shape of Catholic interpretation everywhere it occurs: preaching, catechesis, and the biblical apostolate; Catholic theology and ecumenical dialogue; exegetical instruction in Catholic seminaries and universities; and publications of Catholic biblical scholarship[2].

Part III of this study, entitled, "'The Word of God': Catholic Exegesis and Christian Faith", treats these distinguishing characteristics of Catholic interpretation under six principles. Principle #6 introduces the "hermeneutic of faith" which distinguishes Catholic exegesis. Principle #7 regards the subject, i.e., the actor, in the interpretation of Scripture, namely, "the

---

[1] Ruppert contrasts the discussion of scientific methods and approaches (*IBC*, chapter 1) shared by exegetes of every persuasion, and the distinguishing traits of Catholic exegesis explained in chapter III ("Kommentierende Einführung", 44). So do Francesco Lambiasi ("Dimensioni caratteristiche [*Commento*]", 299) and Fitzmyer (*The Biblical Commission's Document*, 132-133). This recognition of what is specific to Catholic interpretation provides an important hermeneutical key for understanding the entire document. Many reviewers of the document failed to grasp the significance of this chapter and devoted most of their attention to the Commission's description of contemporary methods and approaches.

[2] These "Characteristics of Catholic Interpretation" are also important for Catholic exegetes who labor in interconfessional settings or secular universities, although obviously the expression of their Catholic perspective will assume a different form in dialogue with those who approach Scripture from different presuppositions. See Vanhoye, "Catholicism and the Bible", 38.

community of faith".   Principles #8 through #11 specify the Catholic hermeneutic of faith more precisely. It is interpretation in light of the biblical tradition and the canon of Scripture (#8), in light of the death and resurrection of Jesus (#9), and in light of the living Tradition of the Church (#10). Its aim is to explain Sacred Scripture's religious message (#11), and its ultimate goal is to nourish the body of Christ with the word of God.

CHAPTER 6

A Hermeneutic of Faith

Principle #6

Biblical knowledge cannot stop short at an understanding of words, concepts and events. It must seek to arrive at the reality of which the language speaks, a transcendent reality, communication with God. (II.A.1.d)

Reason alone is not able to fully comprehend the events and the message recounted in the Bible. In order to truly understand the Bible one must welcome the meaning given in the events, above all, in the person of Jesus Christ (II.A.2.d). Because the Bible is the word of God, it must be approached in the light of faith in order to be properly understood. Therefore, exegesis is a theological discipline.

The light of the Holy Spirit is needed to interpret Scripture correctly. As someone grows in the life of the Spirit, his or her capacity to understand the realities of which the Bible speaks also grows[1]. (II.A.2.f)

---

[1] Although the full flowering of the *IBC*'s teaching on the relation between Catholic exegesis and Christian faith occurs in chapter III, the elements of this principle which state its foundation are found in the section of chapter II which evaluates the usefulness of philosophical hermeneutics for exegesis (II.A.2). The three introductory paragraphs to chapter III apply these to Catholic interpretation (III.a-c). References to exegesis as a branch of theology appear in several places (e.g., III.D.a; III.D.1.a; Conclusion e).

Explanation

1. Language and Reality

> Biblical knowledge cannot stop short at an understanding of words, concepts and events. It must seek to arrive at the reality of which the language speaks, a transcendent reality, communication with God. (II.A.1.d)

Understanding a writing that claims to disclose life truths entails more than a word game or detached speculation about long past historical events. Authentic understanding requires engagement with the reality of which the text speaks. Bultmann spoke of the life-relationship (*Lebensverhältnis*) of the reader to the reality to which the text refers (II.A.1.a), while Gadamer spoke of the necessary belonging (*Zugehörigkeit*) or fundamental affinity between the object and its interpreter (II.A.1.c). Ricoeur insists that meaning is fully grasped only when it is actualized in the lives of readers who appropriate it (II.A.1.d). This holds true whether one reads Plato, Virgil, Dante, or the Bible.

However, biblical hermeneutics constitutes a unique instance of general hermeneutics by virtue of its object (II.A.2.f)[2]. The reality to which the Bible refers is God himself and his saving action in history accomplished above all in Jesus Christ. As Christian Sacred Scripture, it comes with the claim of being not only a record of past events, but a present communication of God to every human being, an "abiding means of communication and communion" between God and his believing people (Address 6). In the case of the Bible, to go beyond the words to understand the reality to which the text refers means to arrive at a transcendent reality, communication with God[3].

---

[2] Schneiders says it particularly well: "From one point of view the biblical text is a human text, and one can develop a hermeneutical theory that will ground its interpretation as a human text. Such a theory would be substantially identical with the hermeneutical theory developed for the interpretation of any classical religious text. From another point of view...this text is sacred scripture, and an adequate hermeneutical theory is one that takes full account of the Bible's reality as a human text that is a privileged mediation of the divine-human encounter. This amounts to a claim that biblical hermeneutics as such...encompasses the general canons of interpretation but is not simply identical with them, because the object of interpretation governs the theory of interpretation, and in the case of the Bible there is more here than a text" (*Revelatory Text*, 61). See also Vignolo, "Questioni di ermeneutica [*Commento*]", 278-279.

[3] Childs remarks along the same lines, "Exegesis [should] not confine itself to registering only the verbal sense of the text, but presses forward through the text to the subject matter (*res*) to which it points. Thus *erklären* and *verstehen* belong integrally together in the one enterprise and cannot be separated for long" ("Recovering Theological Exegesis", 19).

2. A Pre-understanding of Faith

Reason alone is not able to fully comprehend the events and the message recounted in the Bible. In order to truly understand the Bible one must welcome the meaning given in the events, above all, in the person of Jesus Christ (II.A.2.d). Because the Bible is the word of God, it must be approached in the light of faith in order to be properly understood. Therefore, exegesis is a theological discipline.

Because of its very special content, reason alone is insufficient to understand the Bible and its message. According to the *IBC*, "Particular presuppositions, such as the faith lived in ecclesial community and the light of the Spirit, control its interpretation" (II.A.2.f)[4]. This is only logical. If a person does not believe in God or in his saving action in Christ, his or her understanding remains limited to that of an outside observer, unable to fully engage or penetrate the reality to which the text refers. But if a person becomes a believer, the possibility of understanding at an entirely new level arises. Then he or she begins to perceive the reality of which the language speaks. The Commission puts it this way: "An authentic interpretation of Scripture...involves in the first place a welcoming of the meaning that is given in the events and, in a supreme way, in the person of Jesus Christ" (II.A.2.d). This is not far from what St. Paul says in an analogous discussion: "When one turns to the Lord, the veil is removed" (2 Cor 3:14-16).

In hermeneutical terms, faith in Christ is the *pre-understanding* suited to interpreting the Christian Bible. This pre-understanding faith is not an "unthematized" faith or a vague trust in Jesus Christ. Rather Catholic exegesis "deliberately places itself within the living tradition of the Church, whose first concern is fidelity to the revelation attested by the Bible" (III.b). In other words, Catholic exegesis accepts as its foundational presupposition the revelation mediated through Sacred Scripture and Sacred Tradition as the Church understands it[5]. This pre-understanding, shared with their predecessors in faith permits Catholic exegetes to stand "in continuity with a dynamic pattern of interpretation that is found within the Bible itself and continues in the life of the Church" (III.b).

---

[4] Paul Blowers is one of the reviewers who grasped the significance of the Biblical Commission's decision for a hermeneutic of faith, a community of interpretation and the guidance of a common rule of faith as the appropriate context for interpretation (Blowers, Levenson and Wilken, "Three Views").

[5] Cf. *DV* 2-10. Craig G. Bartholomew, an Anglican, likewise recommends a "Christian hermeneutic" in *Reading Ecclesiastes: Old Testament Exegesis and Hermeneutical Theory*, 207-212.

What is the precise content of Catholic exegesis' pre-understanding of faith? Fitzmyer articulates the presupposition of faith that he believes Christian interpreters must bring to the use of the historical-critical method in studying Scripture:

> Such a presupposition... include[s] the belief that the book being critically interpreted is the Word of God couched in human language of long ago; that the Bible is an inspired text, having authority for people of the Jewish-Christian heritage; that it represents a restricted canon of authoritative writings; that it has been given by God to his people for their edification and salvation; that the Spirit who inspired its human authors is the same Spirit that guides the community of interpreters and believers (the Church) to understand its text; that through the Bible God continues to speak to readers of every generation; and that it is properly expounded only in relation to the Tradition that has grown out of it[6].

This is an attempt to state the presuppositions of Christian exegesis regarding Scripture, its nature, purpose and interpretation. The totality of Catholic exegesis' pre-understanding of faith is as broad as the living Tradition in which Catholic interpretation deliberately places itself. The Biblical Commission describes the presuppositions of Catholic exegetes regarding biblical texts more briefly, and then adds, "These certainties of faith do not come to an exegete in an unrefined, raw state, but only as developed in the ecclesial community through the process of theological reflection" (III.D.1.a). In other words, the Church's understanding of the Gospel and its implications furnishes the pre-understanding of Catholic exegesis.

Christian faith thus constitutes the subjective qualification, the relationship of "belonging" between interpreter and the reality of the text, which "corresponds to the requirement that there be a lived affinity between the interpreter and the object, an affinity which constitutes, in fact, one of the conditions that makes the entire exegetical enterprise possible" (III.b) [7].

---

[6] Fitzmyer, *The Biblical Commission's Document*, 47-48. Fitzmyer offers more or less the same description of the presupposition of faith proper to Christian use of the historical-critical method in "Historical Criticism", 254-255.

[7] The concrete implications of this subjective qualification of the exegete will be developed under principle #17, "The Task of the Exegete". Here the PBC accepts one of the exhortations to exegesis which Ratzinger had offered in his New York address: "The exegete must realize he does not stand in some neutral area, above or outside history and church.... If [exegesis] wishes to be theology it must take a further step. It must recognize that the faith of the church is that form of "sympathia" without which the Bible remains a *closed* book. It must come to acknowledge this faith as a hermeneutic, the space for understanding, which does not do dogmatic violence to the Bible, but precisely allows the solitary possibility for the Bible to be itself" ("Biblical Interpretation in Crisis", 22-23).

Because it depends on faith in revealed truth and not reason alone, Catholic exegesis is "a theological discipline, *fides quaerens intellectum*" (III.D.a). Catholic exegetes bring to their task "presuppositions based on the certainties of faith: the Bible is a text inspired by God, entrusted to the Church for the nurturing of faith and guidance of the Christian life" (III.D.1.a). In its conclusion the Biblical Commission cautions exegetes against confining their efforts to a professional scrutiny of the historical and literary dimensions of Scripture. The Commission stresses the importance of Catholic exegesis maintaining "its identity as a theological discipline, the principal aim of which is the deepening of faith" (Conclusion e)[8].

3. The Role of the Spirit

The light of the Holy Spirit is needed to interpret Scripture correctly. As someone grows in the life of the Spirit, his or her capacity to understand the realities of which the Bible speaks also grows. (II.A.2.f)

Christians believe they enjoy a resource for understanding Scripture beyond that provided by an appropriate pre-understanding and an affinity to the text, namely, the help of the Holy Spirit[9]. According to the Biblical Commission, "As the reader matures in the life of the Spirit, so there grows also his or her capacity to understand the realities of which the Bible speaks" (II.A.2.f).

The *IBC* speaks of how the Spirit (in fulfillment of Christ's promise, cf. Jn 16:12-13; 14:26) helped Jesus' disciples progressively understand the revelation they had received (III.B.a) and inspired the writing of the Sacred Books. The Spirit guided the Church in discerning which writings should constitute the canon of Sacred Scripture (III.B.1.a). The same Holy Spirit "provided the Church with continual assistance for the interpretation of its inspired writings" (III.B.2.a). This help from the Spirit in understanding the Scriptures continues today (III.B.a) [10]. The Biblical Commission's statements

---

[8] For more on exegesis as a theological discipline, see principle #17, especially p. 280ff.

[9] Commission member Armando Levoratti comments on Origen's and *DV* 12's rule that Scripture is to be read and interpreted "by the same Spirit by which it was written": "This kind of reading requires going beyond a simplistic confidence in the possibility of disclosing the full meaning of the inspired texts from a purely historical, descriptive, or scientific standpoint, for the word of God finds no acceptance until it is sealed by the inward witness of the Holy Spirit, and the heart finds its rest in Scripture only through this inward testimony. The Spirit does not give new and hitherto unheard revelations. What the Spirit does is to confirm the teaching of the gospel in our hearts…" ("How to Interpret", 11).

[10] In response to an interview question, Vanhoye offered the following on the role of the Spirit in reading and interpreting the Bible: "I would say that the Spirit's part is to put us into personal and living contact with God by means of the written word. A scholar who simply

on the role of the Holy Spirit in interpreting Scripture echo St. Paul's insistence on the necessity of the Spirit to understand spiritual things (1 Cor 2:11-16). Pope John Paul II stresses the role of the Spirit in the life and work of the exegete and links it to personal prayer (Address 9.d)[11].

Discussion

4. Objections to a Hermeneutic of Faith

A variety of objections can be lodged against the idea that exegesis should begin with a pre-understanding of Christian faith, and some reviewers of the *IBC* have challenged this principle of Catholic interpretation. At first sight it seems as though an *a priori* commitment to faith would contradict the critical nature of exegesis. Does not this limit or short-circuit the possibilities for new discovery or of correcting false prior understandings? Does not a hermeneutic of faith lead to eisegesis—a reading of theological conclusions into the text—rather than reading theology out of the text?

Also, it seems illogical to say that a person who is not a believer, or who does not have the "Spirit", cannot understand the Bible. Robert P. Carroll objects to the *IBC*'s statement: "A psychology or psychoanalysis of an atheistic nature disqualifies itself from giving proper consideration to the data of faith" (I.D.3.e). Carroll answers: "Unless the document writers also assent to the proposition that theistic positions cannot give proper consideration to atheistic matters I cannot see the logic of this claim"[12].

5. Exegesis Apart from Faith Presuppositions

In fact many Catholic exegetes reject a hermeneutic of faith in interpreting the Bible, perhaps believing that the interests of objective research are better served by prescinding from faith perspectives. In a 1990 article, J. M. Sevrin sought to explain to theologians how exegesis is commonly understood and practiced today[13]. Sevrin draws a contrast between

---

analyzes the text might discover its meaning but lack the contact with God that renders the biblical word truly present, truly efficacious. But the Holy Spirit opens our eyes to see the deeper meaning, the religious message, that is found in the text.... The Spirit makes us realize that this biblical text forms part of a continuing dialogue between Christ and His Church, and we are involved in that dialogue.... The text ceases to be an object, but becomes a living mediation that deepens and sheds light on our relationship with God...("Catholicism and the Bible", 39).

[11] See principle #17, "The Task of the Exegete", especially p. 276ff.

[12] Carroll, "Cracks in the Soul of Theology", 145-146.

[13] Sevrin, "L' exégèse critique". This section will follow Vanhoye's presentation of Sevrin's article and his critique in Vanhoye, "Esegesi biblica e teologia", 274-277. Vanhoye

"critical exegesis", which, he says, "considers the text by itself, in the moment of its writing and prior to the tradition—biblical or ecclesiastical—which will receive it", and what he calls a "believing hermeneutic"[14]. The latter "receives the text in the totality of the biblical and ecclesiastical tradition and in the light of faith"[15], and belongs *not* to the task of the Catholic exegete, but to the theologian. According to Sevrin, the critical exegete seeks "to set aside his own subjective position, to suspend his faith and his doubts.... *Since exegesis is an autonomous exercise of human reason, it cannot give place to faith in its operations or criteria* [emphasis added]"[16]. Sevrin holds that the exegete must concern himself only with the human sense of the text and only with the resources of human reason: "Once the exegete arrives at a representation of the human and contingent meaning of the text, he passes on the baton to the theologian, the integral interpreter, whose responsibility it is to show how the human meaning is effectively the word of God"[17]. Sevrin considers this concept of critical exegesis to be in accord with the role the Second Vatican Council grants to the exegete in *Dei Verbum* 12. Sevrin argues that critical exegesis thus defined should be viewed as a theological discipline, even though it excludes faith presuppositions, since its object of study is Scripture which Christian faith recognizes as the word of God[18].

6. Inadequacy of Exegesis Apart from Faith

However, in an article published in 1991, Vanhoye takes sharp exception to Sevrin's description of the exegete's role[19]. At that time the Biblical Commission was working on the *IBC* and on this topic Vanhoye's article anticipates the position of the *IBC*. After its publication, Vanhoye renewed his criticism of exegesis that seeks to separate presuppositions of faith from biblical exegesis in an address published in 1994[20].

---

makes very clear that he agrees with Sevrin on many points. The matter he objects to, however, is the way Sevrin conceives of the role of exegesis in the theological enterprise, which *de facto* reduces it to an ancillary historical and literary discipline, rather than being its vital "soul".

[14] Sevrin, "L' exégèse critique", 147.

[15] Sevrin, "L' exégèse critique", 147.

[16] Sevrin, "L' exégèse critique", 152, 157.

[17] Sevrin, "L' exégèse critique", 159.

[18] Another Catholic exegete who offers theoretical objection to faith presuppositions is John J. Collins. Collins urges the exclusion of faith presuppositions for the sake of a "critical" biblical theology ("Critical Biblical Theology"). See the discussion in this work, p. 238ff.

[19] Vanhoye, "Esegesi biblica e teologia".

[20] Vanhoye, "Dopo la *Divino afflante Spiritu*". The second article organizes the material somewhat differently and adds the following point: Critical exegesis which attempts to prescind from faith considerations follows from an inadequate concept of science modeled on the

Acknowledging that the general tendency among exegetes lies in the direction of applying only the resources of human reason, Vanhoye argues that the result of this neutrality in regard to Christian faith removes exegesis from the realm of theology and reduces it to the scientific study of ancient texts[21]. "This is a very sharp division of tasks, indeed excessively so, since it establishes a complete heterogeneity between exegesis and theology"[22]. Vanhoye cites Childs who has argued that exegesis done outside a framework of faith cannot be useful to theology, since "it is logically impossible to construct a bridge from a neutral descriptive content to a theological reality"[23].

Furthermore, Sevrin has misunderstood what *Dei Verbum* actually said about the role of the exegete. *Dei Verbum* 12 stresses that both the historico-literary and theological dimensions belong to the exegete's task. After speaking of the necessity of a literary and historical approach to the Scriptures, the Council continues,

> No less serious attention must be given to the content and unity of the whole of Scripture, if the meaning of the sacred texts is to be correctly brought to light. The living tradition of the whole Church must be taken into account along with [the analogy of faith][24]. It is the task of *exegetes* to work according to these rules toward a better understanding and explanation of the meaning of sacred Scripture...[emphasis added]. (*DV* 12)

According to Vanhoye the error of exegesis apart from faith presuppositions lies in failing to think deeply enough about the issue of pre-

---

experimental and physical sciences which strives to achieve complete objectivity in its procedures. But this approach fails to take into account the differences appropriate to the humanities and to theological disciplines. Objectivity in the humanities cannot be the same as it is in the physical sciences, since the object of study is radically different (p. 45).

[21] Vanhoye, "Esegesi biblica e teologia", 274,

[22] Vanhoye, "Dopo la *Divino afflante Spiritu*", 45.

[23] Childs, "Interpretation in Faith", 438, cited by Vanhoye, "Esegesi biblica e teologia", 275. Ruppert makes a similar observation ("Kommentierende Einführung", 45-46). According to Ruppert, a purely literary-scientific exegesis can certainly make excellent literary-scientific and literary-historical discoveries, but the claim of the text to be Sacred Scripture remains hidden on the grounds of the method's self-limitation. Canonical interpretation seeks to remedy this problem.

[24] Abbott's translation does not provide the literal reading, "the analogy of faith", but, instead, paraphrases it as "the harmony which exists between elements of the faith". The *Concise Dictionary of Theology* (O'Collins and Farrugia, p. 10) defines the analogy of faith as "an expression drawn from Romans 12:6 and used in Catholic theology to recall that a passage of scripture or an aspect of faith should be interpreted in the context of the one, whole and indivisible faith of the church (DS 3016, 3283)". The *Catechism of the Catholic Church* defines the analogy of faith as "the coherence of the truths of faith among themselves and within the whole plan of Revelation" (§ 114).

understanding.   After observing that everyone agrees that some pre-understanding is necessary to understand a text or message, he writes[25],

> It is evident, on the other hand, that not every pre-understanding is equally valid as the point of departure for the interpretation of a given text. Now when one considers the Bible, which reports religious experiences and appeals to the religious capacity of human beings, which will be the most appropriate pre-understanding? A neutral pre-understanding, which has no other criteria than those of reason? Or the pre-understanding given by an experience of faith?... To interpret the Bible, the most valid point of departure is the experience of faith, transmitted by the same Tradition which gave origin to the biblical texts.... Whoever does not have this correct pre-comprehension can still study the texts from other points of view and achieve very interesting results of a philological, literary, historical, or psychological nature. But the essence escapes him![26]

But what about the objection that a pre-understanding of faith leads to reading into the biblical text later doctrinal traditions? Vanhoye replies by distinguishing between the content of Christian faith expressed in Scripture and the historical development of doctrine. The paragraph which follows summarizes Vanhoye's argument[27].

It is true that a pre-understanding brings with it the risk of excessively influencing the interpretation of a text [III.b][28]. Indeed, a rigorous effort must be made to define the meaning of the text at the moment of its writing. But this does not mean an effort to get behind biblical or ecclesiastical tradition, *since texts are themselves the fruit of the tradition which preceded them* [III.A.a]. The goal is not to prescind from tradition altogether, but only to clarify the status of the tradition at the time the text came into being, prescinding from the elements which entered the tradition later[29]. *The exegete must distinguish the pre-understanding of faith from the historical development of the doctrine of faith* [III.a]. To interpret biblical texts there is absolutely no reason to "suspend one's faith", but it is necessary to suspend one's ideas on the subsequent conceptualization of faith so as not to be guilty

---

[25] Elsewhere in the article Vanhoye, speaking of the role of pre-understanding even in textual criticism, gives the example of the importance to internal criticism of the critic's conception of the whole of a work to make decisions about particular readings.

[26] Vanhoye, "Esegesi biblica e teologia", 276.

[27] Vanhoye, "Esegesi biblica e teologia", 277-278. Most of the same affirmations are found in the *IBC*, but the argument is clearer in Vanhoye's article.

[28] Where the *IBC* echoes points made in Vanhoye's argument, the references will be indicated within brackets.

[29] Two examples are given: one must not attribute to the original meaning of pre-exilic texts elements which derive from the post-exilic tradition; one must not attribute to NT texts the christological precision of later councils.

of interpreting texts anachronistically. The Bible never contradicts the Great Tradition of faith, but it can very well contradict traditions which are the fruit of an evolution not sufficiently faithful to the Word of God. The discernment in question is often very difficult, but it constitutes a condition for the authentic progress of theology. If exegesis is practiced as a theological discipline, with a pre-understanding of faith and with scientific rigor, it will both nourish faith and purify it. It nourishes faith with a more accurate understanding of faith's original expressions, and it purifies it, by leading it to renounce certain ways of idealizing revelation according to merely human ways of thinking.

In other words, both exegesis which excludes faith presuppositions and exegesis characterized by a pre-understanding of faith will use scientific methods and will seek to identify the meaning of the text on the occasion of its writing. Both will refuse to attribute a later doctrinal development to the literal sense of the text. The difference is that exegesis which excludes faith presuppositions is limited to recognizing a human communication in the text, while exegesis beginning from a hermeneutic of faith can perceive both a human communication and the word of God. The task of faith-neutral exegesis is complete when the philosophical, historical or literary significance of the text has been explained. However, the task of exegesis characterized by a pre-understanding of Christian faith is not finished until the religious or theological significance of the text as God's word has been explained [III.C.1.b-f]. Sevrin reserves this last procedure to the theologian as "integral interpreter". Vanhoye and the Biblical Commission insist with *Dei Verbum* 12 that this "integral" interpretation is an inalienable responsibility of the exegete[30].

7. Non-believers and Interpretation

But what about Carroll's objection to the notion that faith is necessary to understand the Bible, and arguing that this is analogous to saying that "theistic positions cannot give proper consideration to atheistic matters"? In the end, this discussion turns on what it means "to understand". If "to understand" simply means an intellectual comprehension of the words, the concepts they represent, the relations among them, and the ability to explain those ideas, faith is clearly not necessary or even the most important requirement for understanding. Philological, literary, historical and analytical skills are more

---

[30] See Gilbert, "Exegesis, Integral" for a view of exegesis which coincides with Vanhoye's and the Commission's. A fuller treatment of the respective roles of exegetes and theologians appears in principle #17. The *IBC* treats the relationship of exegesis with "other theological disciplines" in section III.D.

important. But if "to understand" entails engagement with the reality to which a text refers, and if the essential message of the Bible is religious and its primary referent is God, then it becomes clear why atheistic presuppositions could be problematic for understanding. The *IBC* draws its stronger view of the nature of understanding from its reflection upon modern hermeneutics (II.A).

Schneiders distinguishes three levels of understanding which various relations to the Christian tradition make possible[31]. First, in light of the historic relationship between the New Testament and the Christian tradition, at least an extrinsic relationship with the tradition is necessary for valid interpretation. The interpreter requires some acquaintance with the Christian tradition to understand, for instance, the New Testament presentation of Jesus as Messiah. Second, Schneiders argues that in order for someone to understand the New Testament as a whole, he or she would need to

> be open to the invitation that the text addresses to the reader… [namely,] to full participation in the tradition ([e.g.,] John 20:31).… Interpretation in the full sense of the word cannot terminate in a phenomenology of textual sense but must proceed to the referent. To foreclose *a priori* the engagement of these truth claims is to vitiate the work of interpretation[32].

Here Schneiders follows Gadamer's principle that the interpretation of a classic requires a loyal engagement of its truth claims "even if such engagement leads eventually to the establishment of their falsity"[33]. (According to Schneiders, this applies to a Christian interpreter's reading of the Koran or of the Bhagavad Gita, and would presumably, also apply to a Christian interpreter's reading of atheistic writings.) Finally,

> the optimal position from which to engage the meaning of the NT is that of full participation in the tradition that produced this book, canonized it as its authentic and normative self-expression, and constitutes its integral and authoritative context of interpretation.… Just as living experience as an American is not only not a hindrance to the constitutional jurist [seeking to interpret the U.S. Constitution] but a primary advantage, so living within the Christian tradition of faith is not only not a threat to scholarly objectivity in interpretation of the biblical text but provides a privileged thematic and intuitive access to its meaning[34].

---

[31] Schneiders, *Revelatory Text*, 89-90 (see also pp. xxxiv-xxxviii [in the second edition only] and 59-61).

[32] Schneiders, *Revelatory Text*, 89-90.

[33] Schneiders, *Revelatory Text*, 60, citing Gadamer, *Truth and Method*, 362-379].

[34] Schneiders, *Revelatory Text*, 90.

8. The Bible in Critical Historical Study

It might appear that the Biblical Commission's insistence on a presupposition of faith in Catholic exegesis would exclude Catholic biblical scholars studying the Bible in the same way that historians study other ancient texts. But that would be an erroneous conclusion. Although the *IBC* does not discuss it, the previous document of the Biblical Commission, *Scripture and Christology* (1984)[35], insists that the historical study of Jesus "*is quite necessary* that two dangers may be avoided, viz. that Jesus not be regarded as a mere mythological hero, or that the recognition of him as Messiah and Son of God not be reduced to some irrational fideism [emphasis original]"[36]. Similarly, despite his criticisms of the historical-critical method, Ratzinger insists on a historical study of Scripture, since faith must be ready to give a reason for its hope[37]. Nevertheless, historical study by itself does not suffice as a foundation for theology[38].

Vanhoye distinguishes "between exegesis, properly speaking, and the use of biblical texts for historical purposes"[39]. Responding to a question about John Meier's *The Marginal Jew*, which adopts a methodology that prescinds from religious faith, the Secretary of the Commission describes Meier's book as

> not an exegetical work but a work of historical research...that conforms to the current requirements of historical science. Exegesis, on the other hand, seeks to illumine the total content of the text, not just which details are historical or nonhistorical.... The larger picture that the biblical text seeks to communicate concerns a religious message...[40].

9. Pre-understanding and the Reader's Obligation to the Truth

Vanhoye and the *IBC* have shown how a hermeneutic of faith need not lead to eisegesis and can and should correct defective interpretations in light

---

[35] Commission Biblique Pontificale, *Bible et Christologie*; Fitzmyer, *Scripture and Christology*.

[36] Fitzmyer, *Scripture and Christology*, 7 (§1.1.3). The Biblical Commission recalls the history of the 19th century quest for the historical Jesus with all its shortcomings and describes enhancements to the historical-critical method that permit more fruitful historical research: the recognition of the difference between objectivity in the natural sciences and human sciences, of the role of the historian's own subjectivity, and of the impossibility of neutrality and complete objectivity in the historical study of the life of Jesus (5-7).

[37] Neuhaus, *Biblical Interpretation in Crisis*, 118.

[38] Fitzmyer, *Scripture and Christology*, pp. 21, 24, 26-27 (§1.2.3.1-2; 1.2.6.1-2; 1.2.7.3-4). See also the discussion on "Faith and History" earlier in this study, p. 62.

[39] Vanhoye, "Catholicism and the Bible", 38.

[40] Vanhoye, "Catholicism and the Bible", 38.

of the original meaning of the text. A pre-understanding of faith does not impose a particular exegetical result, but rather makes a reading of Scripture as the word of God possible.

However, even if a pre-understanding of faith does not impose subsequent doctrinal developments on earlier expressions of the Christian tradition, it has important consequences for interpretation. Like every pre-understanding, a hermeneutic of faith will be inclined toward some interpretations and be disinclined toward others. For instance, a pre-understanding of Christian faith will not easily accept the notion that the biblical writers were liars or charlatans, and will incline to regard them instead as conscientious and honest. A pre-understanding of faith will incline a reader to interpret the Bible as consistent with itself, and will disincline him or her from viewing it as a mass of contradictions.

But these predispositions due to a pre-understanding of faith are not cast in concrete. There is a hermeneutical circle. If a reader is truly open to the text, a change can occur and should occur. The reader's ultimate obligation is to the truth[41]. A careful consideration of contradictory details in the text may modify a reader's pre-understanding about the extent or nature of biblical inerrancy, as it has for Catholic exegesis as a whole over the last century. One can begin with a certain notion of scriptural inspiration and modify that notion by deeper recognition of the human and contingent aspects one discovers in the text.

Theoretically and psychologically speaking, a pre-understanding that remains open to the truth claims of the text imposes no limit on the interpretive outcomes for any individual interpreter. One may begin as Christian, with a pre-understanding of faith, and finish as an unbeliever. One may begin as an atheist, with a pre-understanding of skepticism, and finish as a believer. Both paths have been trod. An individual's understanding of Scripture can change radically as he or she honestly engages the text. The understanding of communities of interpretation also may change, although, these communities have their boundaries. Christian interpretation, for instance, holds to the divine sonship of Jesus while both rabbinic and Islamic interpretation exclude it. The boundaries recognized by particular

---

[41] See Neuhaus, *Biblical Interpretation in Crisis*, 133-137, for an account of an interesting discussion among the participants at the conference at which Cardinal Ratzinger offered his critique of the historical-critical method. Neuhaus posed the question to the Cardinal about what a Catholic exegete must do if he finds convincing proof in the NT that *contradicts* the teaching of the Church. For such a dilemma Ratzinger counseled patience, humility, and a reconsideration of all aspects of the question. Ultimately, however, "If you cannot find anything supportive of the church's doctrine, and if you find absolute evidence for your idea, then you must convert" (p. 136).

communities do not determine for individual interpreters the outcome of interpretations of texts, but they do impose some limits on interpretation for those who wish to identify with those communities of faith.

So far the content of the Catholic pre-understanding of faith has only been described in general terms—it is faith in Christ, it is faith in the revelation mediated through Scripture and Tradition. The next principle discusses the Church as the community of interpretation suited to the interpretation of the Christian Scriptures. The remaining principles in part III will specify other distinguishing characteristics of the pre-understanding of faith coherent with the revelation attested by the Bible and the Church's living Tradition (IIIb).

CHAPTER 7

The Role of the Community of Faith

Principle #7

The believing community, the People of God, provides the truly adequate context for interpreting Scripture (I.C.1.g). Scripture took shape within the traditions of faith of Israel and the early Church, and contributed in turn to the development of their traditions (III.A.3.f).

The Scriptures belong to the entire Church (III.B.3.i) and all of the members of the Church have a role in the interpretation of Scripture (III.B.3.b). People of lowly status, according to Scripture itself, are privileged hearers of the word of God (III.B.3.f).

Various special roles in interpretation belong to clergy, catechists, exegetes and others (III.B.3.i). Church authority is responsible to see that interpretation remains faithful to the Gospel and the Great Tradition, and the Magisterium exercises a role of final authority if occasion requires it (I.C.1.g)[1].

---

[1] The role of the community of faith in interpreting Scripture, while present throughout the *IBC*, receives special mention in the discussion of the canonical approach (I.C.1). It also appears in chapter III, entitled "Characteristics of Catholic Interpretation", where it speaks of interpretation in the biblical tradition (especially, III.A.3.f) and in the tradition of the Church (especially III.B.a).

Explanation

1. The Church and Interpretation

This principle responds to the important question, who is qualified to interpret Scripture?

> The believing community, the Church, provides a truly adequate context for interpreting Scripture (I.C.1.g). Scripture comes from the traditions of faith of believing communities, and has in turn contributed to the development of their traditions (III.A.3.f).

If faith is the pre-understanding most suited to understand Scripture as the word of God, it is only logical that community of those who believe is the group which enjoys a special advantage in Scripture's interpretation[2].

But there is more to it than that. The stronger reason for the Church's privileged role in interpreting Scripture is the unique relationship between Scripture and the Church. The Christian Bible grew out of the life of faith of Israel[3] and the Church:

> Its texts were recognized by the communities of the Former Covenant and by those of the apostolic age as the genuine expression of the common faith. It is in accordance with the interpretative work of these communities and together with it that the texts were accepted as Sacred Scripture.... (III.A.3.a.)

The development of the canon entailed a judgment about which writings corresponded with God's saving words and deeds among them. "Guided by the Holy Spirit and in the light of the living Tradition which it has received, the *Church has discerned* the writings which should be regarded as Sacred Scripture..." (III.B.1.a, emphasis added). Although the processes by which the canon emerged are not fully known and continue as a matter of scholarly discussion, the *IBC* affirms that "Sacred Scripture has come into existence on the basis of a consensus in the believing communities recognizing in the texts the expression of revealed faith" (III.A.3.c).

---

[2] For a review of the *IBC* that particularly attends to the relation of Church and Scripture, see Senior, "Church and the Word".

[3] The *IBC* acknowledges the Church's dependence on Israel for the books of the OT: "The communities of the Old Covenant... received these texts as a patrimony to be preserved and handed on" (III.B.1.b). Although their concern is with the Christian Bible consisting of the Old and New Testaments, the Biblical Commission does not wish to diminish Israel's interpretation of their Scriptures. While affirming that the Church reads the Old Testament in light of the death and resurrection of Jesus, this understanding "ought not, however, mean doing away with all attempt to be consistent with that earlier canonical interpretation which preceded the Christian Passover" (I.C.1.i).

Nevertheless, Scripture is not merely the product of ecclesial decision or Spirit-led Tradition. Throughout her history, Scripture has shaped and continues to shape the Church. Catholics recognize a reciprocal relationship between Scripture and Church by which biblical texts "have contributed...to the development of traditions" (III.A.3.f).

> In discerning the canon of Scripture, the Church was also discerning and defining her own identity. Henceforth Scripture was to function as a mirror in which the Church could continually rediscover her identity and assess, century after century, the way in which she constantly responds to the gospel and equips herself to be an apt vehicle of its transmission (cf. *Dei Verbum*, 7). (III.B.1.e)

> Scripture has been at the forefront of all the important moments of renewal in the life of the Church, from the Monastic movement of the early centuries to the recent era of the Second Vatican Council. (III.B.3.a)

> The Bible is the privileged means which God uses yet again in our own day to shape the building up and the growth of the Church as the People of God. (III.C.1.f)

As the last text suggests, Scripture is a means through which God speaks to the Church. According to *Dei Verbum* 21, "In the sacred books, the Father who is in heaven meets His children with great love and speaks with them".

The *IBC* calls upon exegetes to explain the "ecclesial meaning" of the text (III.C.1.c), referring to "the relationship that exists between the Bible and the Church" (III.C.1.f). Vanhoye comments on the "ecclesial meaning" of Scripture, saying,

> The Spirit makes us realize that this biblical text forms part of a continuing dialogue between Christ and his Church, and we are involved in that dialogue.... The text ceases to be an object, but becomes a living mediation that deepens and sheds light on our relationship with God, which even communicates to us the power of doing what the text proposes[4].

The consequence of this intimate relation between Scripture and Church is that "the interpretation of Scripture takes place in the heart of the Church: in its plurality and its unity, and within its tradition of faith (III.A.3.f)[5].

---

[4] Vanhoye, "Catholicism and the Bible", 39.

[5] Neither in this section nor in the document as a whole does the Biblical Commission intend to treat the differences between Catholic and Protestant principles of interpretation. But the issues are not easy to avoid. In the discussion of fundamentalism (I.F), critical reference is made to fundamentalists' adherence to the principle of *sola scriptura*. When some German Evangelicals reacted to this as a criticism of themselves, Ruppert hastened to explain that the Commission did not intend to equate their position with that of the (mostly North American) fundamentalists whom the PBC had in mind, nor did it intend a polemic against the Protestant

2. The Role of Every Christian in Interpretation

The Scriptures belong to the entire Church (III.B.3.i) and all of the members of the Church have a role in the interpretation of Scripture (III.B.3.c). People of lowly status, according to Scripture itself, are privileged hearers of the word of God (III.B.3.f).

Citing the documents of the Second Vatican Council, the Biblical Commission lays stress on the Bible as belonging to all Christians. It is the "communal treasure of the *entire* body of believers" (III.B.3.a, emphasis added). With Sacred Tradition, Sacred Scripture has been "entrusted to the Church" (*DV* 10), not to her pastors only. "*All the baptized,* when they bring their faith to the celebration of the Eucharist, recognize the presence of Christ also in his word, 'for it is he himself who speaks when the holy scriptures are read in the Church' (*SC* 7)" (III.B.3.b, emphasis added). The "sense of the faith" (*sensus fidei*), which comes from the Holy Spirit, enables the people of God to accept, hold fast, and penetrate more deeply the word of God when they hear it (III.B.3.b, with reference to *Lumen Gentium*, 12). The "*local church* as a whole" (III.B.3.d, emphasis original) knows that God is speaking to her when she hears the word of God. "The Spirit is, assuredly, also given to *individual Christians*, so that their hearts can 'burn within them' (Luke 24:32), as they pray and prayerfully study the Scripture within the context of their personal lives" (III.B.3.e, emphasis original)." Yet such a reading, the *IBC* tells us, is never completely private, since the believer reads within the faith of the Church[6].

Hearing the word of God in Scripture is not something confined to a powerful elite in the Church. On the contrary,

> The entire biblical tradition and in a particular way, the teaching of Jesus in the Gospels indicates as privileged hearers of the Word of God those whom the world considers *people of lowly status*.[emphasis original]... Those who, in their powerlessness and lack of human resources, find themselves forced to put their trust in God alone and in his justice have *a capacity for*

---

principle of *sola scriptura* (Ruppert, "Kommentierende Einführung", 37n). The *IBC* represents a statement of Catholic interpretation considered in relation to modern methods and approaches, rather than in relation to traditional Protestant interpretation. Nevertheless, the differences between Catholic and classical Protestant interpretation appear, especially in this principle (#7) which discusses the role of the Church, and in principle #10, which discusses the role of Tradition.

[6] Martin Stowasser regards the *IBC* as clearly establishing the competence of the laity for biblical interpretation and sees in this a rediscovery of the *sensus fidelium* in Roman documents ("'...damit das Urteil der Kirche reife'", 212-214). It is a striking contrast to *Providentissimus Deus* in which the laity appeared more as wards to be protected and taught.

hearing and interpreting [emphasis added] the Word of God which should be taken into account by the whole Church.... (III.B.3.f-g)

There is reason to rejoice in seeing the Bible in the hands of people of lowly condition and of the poor; *they can bring to its interpretation and to its actualization a light more penetrating* [emphasis added], from the spiritual and existential point of view, than that which comes from a learning that relies upon its own resources alone (cf. Matt 11:25). (IV.C.3.m)

It is striking that despite all the Biblical Commission's regard for the value of scientific methods and approaches and sophisticated hermeneutics, it is able to affirm forcefully the competence of believers unskilled in these matters to read and interpret Scripture. How? First, it is not to be imagined that the Biblical Commission envisions learned exegetical articles to emerge from the uneducated poor. Rather, the Commission has in mind a grasp and actualization of Scripture's essential message. Second, the means by which "people of lowly status" can interpret Scripture include their pre-understanding of faith, their lived affinity with the text, and the help of the Holy Spirit. Ultimately these qualifications are the most important for understanding Scripture.

3. *Special Roles in Interpretation*

Various special roles in interpretation belong to clergy, catechists, exegetes and others. Church authority is responsible to see that interpretation remains faithful to the Gospel and the Great Tradition, and the Magisterium exercises a role of final authority if occasion requires it. (III.B.3.i; I.C.1.g)

Alongside the interpretation of the local church and individual Christians, *various special roles in interpretation belong to clergy, exegetes and others.* Bishops are "the first witnesses and guarantors of the living tradition within which Scripture is interpreted" (III.B.3.c). Priests "have as their primary duty the proclamation of the Word" (III.B.3.c, citing *Presbyterorum Ordinis, 4*). The *IBC* elaborates on the role of priests and deacons, as ministers of the Word (Acts 6:4). The clergy have not been called to preach "their own ideas" but the word of God (III.B.3.c). Indeed, "they are gifted with a particular charism for the interpretation of Scripture when they *apply* the eternal truths of the Gospel to the concrete circumstances of daily life" (III.B.3.c, emphasis added). They should explain the unity of word and sacrament. Nor is it enough that the clergy simply impart instruction. Rather they are to "assist the faithful to understand and discern what the Word of God is saying to them in their hearts when they hear and reflect up on the Scriptures" (III.B.3.d)[7].

Exegetes exercise the charism of teaching (the *IBC* refers to 1 Cor 12:28-30, Rom 12:6-7, and Eph 4:11-16) with a particular ability to build up the body of Christ through expertise in interpreting Scripture (III.B.3.h). Their expertise in ancient languages, history and culture, textual criticism, and literary studies helps them to explain the literal sense of Scripture. Beyond their scientific endeavors, "animated by the same Spirit that inspired the Scriptures", they also serve the Church by teaching and raising up other servants of the word of God, who themselves feed the people of God from the Scriptures (III.B.3.h)[8].

In the context of diverse gifts and functions in regard to Scripture's interpretation, the unique role of the Church's teaching office emerges[9]. The *IBC* quotes *Dei Verbum* 10 on the Magisterium's responsibility for authoritative interpretation of the word of God, and then comments:

> Thus, in the last resort it is the Magisterium which has the responsibility of guaranteeing the authenticity of interpretation and, should the occasion arise, of pointing out instances where any particular interpretation is not compatible with the authentic Gospel. It discharges this function within the *koinonia* of the Body...; to this end it consults theologians, exegetes, and other experts whose legitimate liberty it recognizes...in the common goal of "preserving the people of God in the truth which sets them free" (CDF, *Instruction concerning the Ecclesial Vocation of the Theologian,* 21). (III.B.3.i)

This citation is virtually all the *IBC* says about the role of Church authority in exegesis[10]. Although early in this century in reaction to modernism, Church authority exercised a somewhat heavy-handed approach towards exegesis, this

---

[7] Biblical interpretation in pastoral ministry will be considered in the discussion of principle #20, "The Use of the Bible in the Church".

[8] A fuller treatment of the role of the exegete occurs in principle #17.

[9] For an account of the development in the relationship between exegesis and the Magisterium according to magisterial documents, beginning with *Providentissimus Deus* through the *IBC*, see Stowasser, "'...damit das Urteil der Kirche reife'", 207-212.

[10] Besides a short statement quoted later in this paragraph, the only other reference to magisterial authority is IV.A.3.e: "False paths will be avoided if actualization of the biblical message begins with a correct interpretation of the text and continues within the stream of the living Tradition, under the guidance of the Church's Magisterium". Nevertheless, Robert P. Carroll considers the Biblical Commission's document a ploy by Church authorities: "I detect here that ancient game of Jacob dressing up in the clothes of Esau.... The clothes may be the clothes of historical-critical methodology, but the voice is still that of the crafty, scheming Jacob seeking to acquire all the power for himself. The magisterium may dress in modernist clothes, the old authoritarian voice remains its own" ("Cracks in the Soul of Theology", 143).

text better represents the Catholic approach. The final authority in scriptural interpretation, as in doctrine, belongs to the Church's pastors. Yet this use of authority is a "last resort"; it is carried out in a spirit of communion (*koinonia*) and entails consulting the opinion of experts. Its purpose is not control but fidelity to the Gospel: "Church authority, exercised as a service of the community, must see to it that this interpretation remains faithful to the great Tradition which has produced the texts" (I.C.g). In fact over the centuries only a handful of texts have been subject to authoritative interpretation by the Magisterium[11]. Nevertheless, the treatment of exegetes prior to Vatican II rankles the generation that remembers these events and makes this a sensitive subject still[12].

Discussion

4. Rejection of Reserving Interpretation to Scripture Scholars

While some have accused the Catholic hierarchy of exercising a monopoly in interpreting the Bible, others have criticized the exegetical guild for excluding non-professionals. The introduction to the *IBC* repeats one such charge:

> Instead of making for easier and more secure access to the living sources of God's Word, [scientific exegesis] makes of the Bible a closed book. Interpretation may always have been something of a problem, but now it requires such technical requirements as to render it a domain reserved for a few specialists alone. To the latter some apply the phrase of the gospel: "You have taken away the key of knowledge; you have not entered in yourselves, and you have hindered those who sought to enter" (Lk 11:52; cf. Mt 23:13). (Intro f)

The Biblical Commission makes a strenuous effort to eliminate the basis for this accusation. The repeated emphasis on the Scriptures belonging to entire Church and interpretation to all the baptized certainly helps. So does the recognition of the hermeneutical advantage of "people of lowly status" (III.B.3.f), which implicitly gives priority to the religious over academic prerequisites for valid interpretation.

---

[11] See Brown and Schneiders, "Hermeneutics [*NJBC*]", §80-89.

[12] Hans-Josef Klauck ("Das neue Dokument: Darstellung und Würdigung", 63-64) expressed satisfaction that despite Ratzinger's criticisms of historical-critical exegesis, the Prefect of the CDF judged a consideration of the problem by the Biblical Commission to have been a more appropriate response to the problem than a magisterial intervention would have been (see Ratzinger, "Modernità atea", 67-68).

Chapter IV of the *IBC*, entitled "Interpretation of the Bible in the Life of the Church", concretely envisions interpretation taking place at every level: individually in *lectio divina*, in groups—whether Bible studies or "basic Christian communities"—and by catechists, clergy and all those engaged in pastoral ministry. The Commission encourages actualization and inculturation of the biblical word. A tone of confident openness predominates. Even when cautions are given regarding interpretation by untrained lay people, they are mild: "Exegetes can render useful assistance in avoiding actualizations of the biblical message that are not well grounded in the text" (IV.C.3.m); "Persons engaged in the work of actualization who do not themselves have training in exegetical procedures should have recourse to good introductions to Scripture..." (IV.A.2.e).

CHAPTER 8

Interpretation in Light of the Biblical Tradition, the Unity of Scripture, and the Canon

Principle #8

Catholic exegesis seeks to interpret the Sacred Scripture in continuity with the dynamic pattern of interpretation found within the Bible itself. In the Bible later writings often depend on earlier texts when their authors re-read what had been written before in light of new questions and circumstances (III.A.1.a). Catholic exegesis seeks both to be faithful to the understanding of faith expressed in the Bible and to maintain dialogue with the generation of today (III.A.3.h).

Catholic exegesis recognizes the essential unity of Scripture, which encompasses differing perspectives (III.A.2.g), yet presents an array of witnesses to one great Tradition (I.C.a, III.A.a).

Catholic exegesis interprets individual texts in the light of the whole canon of Scripture[1]. (I.C.b; III.D.4.b)

---

[1] This important principle of Catholic interpretation appears in the *IBC* in the subsection of the chapter entitled "Characteristics of Catholic Interpretation" devoted to "Interpretation in the Biblical Tradition" (III.A). Along with the section that follows it, "Interpretation in the Tradition of the Church" (III.B), this section consists of observations about interpretation in the past which shape the essential character of Catholic interpretation. Additional commentary on interpreting Scripture in light of the canon appears in the section of the first chapter devoted to the canonical approach (I.C.1).

Explanation

The pre-understanding of faith which Catholic exegetes share with their predecessors in faith leads to continuity with the "pattern of interpretation that is found within the Bible itself and continues in the life of the Church" (III.b; see also IV.A.1.e). The *IBC* singles out two features of the biblical tradition of interpretation for comment: first, the fact that biblical authors frequently re-read earlier texts in the light of new questions and circumstances, and, second, the way the New Testament interprets the "Old Testament". The first will be treated here as principle #8; the second provides a principle of Catholic interpretation in its own right, which this study will take up next as #9.

1. Continuity with Biblical Interpretation

> *Catholic exegesis seeks to interpret the Sacred Scripture in continuity with the dynamic pattern of interpretation found within the Bible itself. In the Bible later writings often depend on earlier texts when their authors re-read what had been written before in light of new questions and circumstances (III.A.1.a). Catholic exegesis seeks both to be faithful to the understanding of faith expressed in the Bible and to maintain dialogue with the generation of today (III.A.3.h).*

In recent years scholars have become more conscious of the way the Scripture interprets itself through re-readings[2]. The Commission explains,

> More recent writings allude to older ones, creat[ing] "re-readings" (*relectures*) which develop new aspects of meaning, sometimes quite different from the original sense. A text may also make explicit reference to older passages, whether it is to deepen their meaning or to make known their fulfillment. (III.A.1.a)

The *IBC* then provides four examples of texts and the re-readings they receive throughout the Bible (III.A.1.b-e): 1) the promise of inheriting the land (Gen 15:7,18), eventually re-read as "the eternal inheritance" (Heb 9:15); 2) the prophecy of Nathan to David promising a "house secure forever", re-read as the universal reign of Christ (e.g., Mk 11:10; Mt 28:18); 3) Jeremiah's prophecy of 70 years of chastisement, re-read by the author of Daniel many years later (Dan 9:24-27); and 4) the basic affirmation that God rewards the good and punishes the evil (e.g., Ps 1, 112), challenged and re-read many

---

[2] Ruppert gives credit to French scholars, especially A. Gelin ("La question des 'relectures'", 303-315), for drawing attention to this feature of biblical writings (Ruppert, "Kommentierende Einführung", 44-45). For an enlightening analysis of the concept of re-reading and its possible significance for understanding inspiration, the canon and reception, see Scholtissek, "Relecture".

times until "it plumbs more profoundly the full depths of the mystery" (Job; Isa 53, etc.)[3].

Various lessons about biblical interpretation follow from the way in which "Scripture reveals its own interpretation of texts" (III.A.3.b).

Re-readings within Scripture reveal that interpretation is inescapable and even constitutive of the Bible itself. This fact simultaneously contradicts fundamentalism, which sometimes claims to avoid interpretation, and historical positivism, which claims an analogous objectivity[4].

Re-readings such as these reveal the inadequacy of biblical interpretation which confines itself to explaining what a text meant in its original historical setting. Such a procedure, which is the proper task of historical-critical exegesis, may succeed at ascertaining the literal sense, but falls short of explaining the full biblical meaning[5]. Instead, to ascertain the biblical meaning requires an interpretive process which takes into account the "possibility that meaning can continue to develop" (Conclusion d).

Furthermore, the biblical pattern of re-readings shows the hermeneutical legitimacy of contemporary re-readings, i.e., actualizations of the biblical text. Believers, whether in Israel or in the Church, have *always* re-read the Scriptures in the light of their contemporary circumstances to discover God's word to them in the present. According to the Biblical Commission,

> Granted that the expression of faith, such as it is found in the Sacred Scripture,... has had to renew itself continually in order to meet new situations,... the interpretation of the Bible should likewise involve an aspect of creativity; it ought also to confront new questions, so as to respond to them out of the Bible (III.A.3.d).

Indeed, "dialogue with the understanding of faith prevailing in earlier times...must be matched by a dialogue with the generation of today" (III.A.3.h).

There are limits, however, to the ways in which contemporary interpretation should follow biblical precedents. Although the exegete must understand the ancient techniques of exegesis so as to correctly interpret the biblical authors, "it remains true that the exegete need not put absolute value

---

[3] This summary of the *IBC* text compresses four already dense paragraphs (III.A.1.b-e) which describe the process of re-reading with references to texts from various moments in the re-reading process. The Biblical Commission's examples of biblical re-readings merit careful reading.

[4] Vignolo, "Questioni di ermeneutica [*Commento*]", 276.

[5] Ruppert, "Kommentierende Einführung", 45. Brown agrees and goes further, insisting that "biblical" meaning must also take into account "what the passage means today in the context of the Christian Church" (*Critical Meaning*, 20; see also 30-32). In the opinion of this writer, Brown takes this too far, eliminating the specificity of "biblical meaning".

in something which simply reflects limited human understanding" (III.A.2.f). Modern Catholic interpreters need not be bound to the exegetical methods of the past, even those used by biblical authors.

It is significant that, in the babel of voices offering ideas about interpreting the Bible, the Pontifical Biblical Commission looks to Scripture itself for guidance about the defining characteristics of Catholic interpretation. Biblical revelation includes patterns for interpreting the Scripture which are normative. The Biblical Commission treats as paradigmatic for Christian interpretation the Scripture's re-readings of earlier writings in the light of new circumstances and the New Testament's interpretation of the Old Testament in light of the paschal mystery, without absolutizing the interpretive methods of the first century. In looking to Scripture itself for guidance about biblical interpretation, the Biblical Commission points to a promising path out of the confusion surrounding contemporary interpretation[6].

2. Recognition of Scripture's Essential Unity

Catholic exegesis recognizes the essential unity of Scripture, which encompasses differing perspectives (III.A.2.g), yet presents an array of witnesses to one great Tradition (I.C.a, III.A.a).

Reflecting the tradition of interpretation in the Church, *Dei Verbum* 12 insists that "no less serious attention [than is given to historical and literary analysis] must be given to the *content and unity of the whole of Scripture*, if the meaning of the sacred texts is to be correctly brought to light [emphasis added]". The *IBC* makes the same point, but it employs different language and it explicitly acknowledges the diversity found in the biblical text. After praising the various literary methods for their stress on the internal unity of the texts, the Biblical Commission speaks of the insufficiency of these methods, since they consider each of the biblical writings in isolation:

> But the Bible is not a compilation of texts unrelated to each other; rather, it is a gathering together of a whole array of witnesses from one great Tradition. To be fully adequate to the object of its study, biblical exegesis must keep this truth firmly in mind. (I.C.a)

In another place the Commission says, "multiple traditions have flowed together little by little to form one great common tradition. The Bible is a privileged expression of this process" (III.A.a). Recognition of the essential unity of Scripture clearly derives from a Catholic pre-understanding of faith in the divine inspiration of Sacred Scripture. Yet the unity of the Bible is also a literary fact deriving from its intertextuality: "One thing that gives the Bible

---

[6] See Ellis, "Interpretation of the Bible Within the Bible".

an inner unity, unique of its kind, is the fact that later biblical writings often depend upon earlier ones" (III.A.1.a). The *IBC* then describes the successive re-readings, mentioned earlier in this chapter, which knit the Bible together.

Nevertheless, as well trained exegetes, the Commission members are not unaware of the diversity in the Bible[7]:

> Within the New Testament, as already within the Old, one can see the juxtaposing of different perspectives that sit sometimes in tension with one another: for example, regarding the status of Jesus (John 8:29; 16:32 and Mark 15:34) or the value of the Mosaic Law (Matt 5:17-19 and Rom 6:14) or the necessity of works for justification (James 2:24 and Rom 3:28; Eph 2:8-9). One of the characteristics of the Bible is precisely the absence of a sense of systematization and the presence, on the contrary, of things held in dynamic tension. The Bible is a repository of many ways of interpreting the same events and reflecting upon the same problems. (III.A.2.g)

According to the Biblical Commission, this diversity has implications for interpretation:

> In itself it urges us to avoid excessive simplification and narrowness of spirit. (III.A.2.g)

> Interpretation must necessarily show a certain *pluralism*. No single interpretation can exhaust the meaning of the whole which is a symphony of voices. Thus the interpretation of one text has to avoid seeking to dominate at the expense of others. (III.A.3.e, emphasis added)

3. Interpretation in the Light of the Canon

Catholic exegesis interprets individual texts in the light of the whole canon of Scripture. (I.C.b; III.D.4.b)

Catholic exegesis' adherence to the canon of Scripture follows from faith in the activity of the Holy Spirit in the selection, transmission, and composition of the these writings:

> Guided by the Holy Spirit and in the light of the living Tradition which it has received, the Church has discerned the writings which should be regarded as Sacred Scripture in the sense that, "having been written under the inspiration of the Holy Spirit, they have God as their author and have been handed on as such to the Church" (*Dei Verbum* 11) and contain "that truth which God wanted put into the Sacred Writings for the sake of our salvation" (ibid.). (III.B.1.a)

---

[7] See Levoratti's discussion of unity and diversity in the Bible in "How to Interpret", 11-15.

The *IBC* describes the relationship between the Church and the canon in the strongest terms[8]:

> In discerning the canon of Scripture, the Church was also discerning and defining her own identity. Henceforth Scripture was to function as a mirror in which the Church could continually rediscover her identity and assess, century after century, the way in which she constantly responds to the gospel and equips herself to be an apt vehicle of its transmission (cf. *Dei Verbum* 7). This confers on the canonical writings a salvific and theological value completely different from that attaching to other ancient texts. (III.B.1.e)

These writings have a unique authority and are "fundamental for the understanding of the Christian faith": "Inspired Scripture is precisely Scripture in that it has been recognized by the Church as the rule of faith" (III.B.1.f).

The canonical status of the biblical writings has implications for their interpretation:

> Hence the significance , in this light [i.e., of their recognition by the Church], of both *the final form* in which each of the books of the Bible appears and of *the complete whole* which all together make up as Canon. Each individual book only becomes biblical in the light of the Canon as a whole. (I.C.1.f, emphasis added)

First, the object of interpretation is the final, i.e., the canonical, form of the biblical writings—not the sources that lie behind it or a historical reconstruction of its original content[9]. This is an important interpretive decision reflecting Christian faith about the Sacred Scripture that has been handed on by the Church. Second, it is not sufficient to interpret each biblical writing on its own. The canon creates a *new context* which conditions the meaning of each part: "Although each book of the Bible was written with its own particular end in view and has its own specific meaning, it takes on a deeper meaning when it becomes part of the canon as a whole" (III.C.1.e; see also II.B.3.c). To interpret a text in its context means to address both the particular and canonical dimension of context:

> The primary task of the exegete is to determine as accurately as possible the meaning of biblical texts in their own proper context, that is, first of all, in

---

[8] The link between Scripture and Tradition is equally strong. In its section on "Interpretation in the Tradition of the Church" (III.B) the Commission chose to treat only two topics, the "Formation of the Canon" (III.B.1) and "Patristic Interpretation" (III.B.2). The canon of Scripture is one of the most important expressions of Tradition.

[9] This point receives fuller treatment in principle #1. See also Costacurta, "Esegesi e lettura credente", for a good discussion of this point.

their particular literary and historical context *and then in the context of the wider canon of Scripture*". (III.D.4.b, emphasis added)

Concretely, what does it mean to interpret individual texts in light of the whole canon? The *IBC* offers one possibility when it states of canonical interpretation that "the exegetical task includes bringing out the truth of Augustine's dictum: '*Novum Testamentum in Vetere latet, et in Novo Vetus patet*'"[10] (III.C.1.e). Both Old Testament and New Testament texts benefit from being understood in light of texts from the other Testament[11].

Vanhoye gives an example of the canonical sense which also sheds light on Scripture's unity amid diversity:

An example would be the justification apart from works in St. Paul and the justification with works in St. James. This, in appearance, is a contradiction. But if we look at the texts more closely we see there is no contradiction, since St. James speaks of justification by works of faith. On this point Paul is in complete agreement with James, even if he does not express himself the same way. For St. Paul, the faith that counts is the faith that works through love. This example illustrates apparent contradictions in the Bible which can stimulate theological reflection and are important because they help us avoid perspectives which might otherwise be one-sided[12].

Other examples may be given. A canonical interpretation of Job begins with the final canonical text including the conclusion, which many scholars think was added later (the canonical Job is also the one which Jas 5:11 interprets). When a Christian interprets Job in the light of the whole canon of Scripture, its meaning changes. Job's ignorance of the afterlife "is modified when Job is included in an OT canon that contains affirmations of resurrection or other forms of afterlife (Isa 26; Dan; Wis; 2 Mac) and is modified even more when joined to a NT canon that is unanimous in its affirmation of an afterlife"[13]. Christian belief in the resurrection offers new hope to Job's depiction of innocent suffering, but it does not make it irrelevant, nor should it "silence Job's protest against resorting to an afterlife

---

[10] "The New Testament lies hidden in the Old, and the Old becomes clear in the New" (cf. *Quaest. in Hept.*, 2, 73: CSEL 28, III, 3, p.141, as translated and cited in the *IBC*).

[11] See Senior, "Church and the Word": "The interpreter takes seriously the entire canon of the Scriptures so that no single biblical text can be taken in isolation from the entirety of the biblical word. And the Catholic interpreter views the entire message of scripture from a strong christological perspective, that is, with the realization that ultimately all of the Bible relates to the paschal mystery of Christ's death and resurrection" (580).

[12] Vanhoye, "Catholicism and the Bible", 37.

[13] Brown, *Critical Meaning*, 31.

as a solution for all the problems of justice"[14].   According to Brown, a Mary/Eve parallelism in the individual writings of the New Testament is hard to verify. But according the ecumenical study, *Mary in the New Testament*, "When John and Revelation are put in the same canon, a catalytic action may occur, so that the two women are brought together and the parallelism to Eve becomes more probable"[15].

Discussion

4. The Canon, the Unity of Scripture and Progress in Theology

The decision to interpret particular Scriptural writings in light of the canon of Scripture presupposes a belief in Scripture's unity, which in turn presupposes a belief in its divine inspiration and authorship. Awareness of apparent contradictions, tensions and diversity in the biblical writings affords scope for theological creativity and discovery.

The affirmation of the unity of the Bible proceeds from a pre-understanding of Christian faith which accepts it as divinely inspired, "having God as its primary author". This unity does not imply the unanimity in point of view of all the biblical writers. Indeed, it proceeds from an understanding that there has been progress and development in biblical revelation. This gradually unfolding revelation explains why later biblical authors know more, for instance, about life after death, and why moral progress is evident in the biblical record (e.g., the evolution from polygamy to monogamous marriage). Of course the fullness of revelation occurs in the Person of Jesus and in his incarnation, and death and resurrection. The Holy Spirit continued (and continues) to make known the implications of this wonderful revelation.

Still, the unity of the Bible was easier to affirm in pre-critical times. The historical-critical study of the Bible has systematically examined the Bible in its most minute units and has found differing or contradictory accounts of events, and not infrequently, differing viewpoints among biblical authors.

At times an emphasis on differences and contradictions in the text has trivialized interpretation. In biblical writings which bear signs of redaction over the ages scholars have sometimes been too ready to interpret difficult texts as later additions that simply disagree with earlier strata. Three problems characterize such interpretations. First, they are hypothetical and often are contradicted by subsequent scholarship (especially literary studies). Second, they excuse the exegete from the task of explaining the meaning of

---

[14] Brown, *Critical Meaning*, 20.
[15] Brown, *Mary in the New Testament*, 30-31.

biblical writings in their final stage. Third, by stressing difficulties in the text or by urging complicated redactional hypotheses they deny, implicitly or explicitly, that coherent meaning exists in those biblical writings. Yet this contradicts the experience of generations of Jews and Christians. Similar consequences follow from viewing the Bible as a diverse library of ancient writings, composed by many authors over the course of a millennium, collected on who-knows-what basis[16]. The result is a loss of meaning and authority for the message of the Bible as a whole. On this point post-modern thought with its suspicion of claims to objective meaning makes common cause with the older rationalist historical criticism, proclaiming the heterogeneity of the biblical writings.

In this context the Biblical Commission shows itself courageous in affirming the traditional Christian interpretive principles of the unity of Scripture and of interpreting particular texts in light of the canon of Scripture. First, despite being fully aware of the tensions and apparent contradictions found by modern research, they confidently affirm in the light of Christian faith that "the Bible is not a compilation of texts unrelated to each other; rather, it is a gathering together of a whole array of witnesses from one great Tradition" (I.C.a). Second, by saying that exegetes should study each text *both* in its particular literary and historical context (which almost everyone does) *and* in its *canonical* context (which is much less common), the Biblical Commission is urging Catholic exegetes to avoid banal and shallow solutions to tensions in the text and, instead, to accept the exegetical and theological challenge of hearing the "symphony of voices" (III.A.3.e) present in the Bible.

On the other hand, the Biblical Commission does not promote the facile harmonization of which interpreters in the past have sometimes been guilty. It recognizes that "one of the characteristics of the Bible is precisely the absence of a sense of systematization and the presence, on the contrary, of things held in dynamic tension" (III.A.2.g). For example, in the face of the basic affirmation of retributive justice, "Scripture allows strong voices of protestation and argument to be heard...as little by little it plumbs more profoundly the full depths of the mystery" (III.A.1.f). Literary scholars have helped exegetes to appreciate the advantages of non-systematic speech for communicating ideas[17]. Stories, parables, proverbs, paradoxes, and aporias in the text and the cognitive dissonance they provoke compel the reader to think more deeply and permit him or her to penetrate the contradictions and

---

[16] E.g., Philip R. Davies argues that the canonization of the Hebrew Scriptures was primarily a function of archiving by Temple scribes (see *Scribes and Schools*).

[17] See Weber, "Making the Biblical Account Relevant".

nuances of the reality under consideration. Scripture as a whole offers this kind of advantage—it is a blessing, rather than a curse, that the written word of God did not come in the form of a theological *summa*!

Theological progress in the history of the Church has always required a struggle with tensions in Scripture to understand and articulate the paradoxical unity of revealed truth. In the past the path to progress in theology has been impeded both by fideist harmonization and by critical fragmentation of Scripture's testimony. Now, however, critical awareness of the tensions and diversity of perspective present in the Bible, when combined with a pre-understanding of faith in the one great Tradition manifest in the canon of Sacred Scripture, holds out the promise of a new and more profound grasp of biblical revelation.

5. *Catholic Exegesis and the Canonical Approach*

Although only the historical-critical method is identified as "indispensable", a close reading of the *IBC*'s description of the canonical approach (I.C) reveals a close correlation between the canonical approach and the fundamental principles which the Biblical Commission espouses. The canonical approach is described as "beginning from within an explicit framework of faith" (I.C.1.a, principle #6), as attempting to remedy a weakness of the historical-critical method, completing it, rather than claiming to be a substitute for it (I.A.1.b, principle #15), and as desiring to make the results of exegesis useful to theology (I.A.1.a, principle #6, #17). "To achieve this, [the canonical approach] interprets each biblical text in the light of the Canon of Scriptures, ...the Bible as received as the norm of faith by a community of believers" (I.C.1.b, principle #8). The goal of arriving at a presentation of Scripture "valid for our time", i.e., actualization, is also mentioned (I.C.1.b, principle #18). The *IBC* notes Childs' concentration on the final canonical form of the text (I.C.1.d, principle #1). In its evaluative comments, the Biblical Commission specifically endorses the canonical approach's reaction "against placing an exaggerated value upon what is supposed to be original and early, as if this alone were authentic" (I.C.1.f, principles #5, #8, #13, #14). These are all major themes of the *IBC* and principles of Catholic interpretation.

Nevertheless some differences between canonical criticism and Catholic interpretation may be noted. The Biblical Commission does not agree that the "canonical process", which James Sanders makes the object of his study, should be recognized "as the guiding principle for the interpretation of

Scripture today" (I.C.1.h)[18]. Likewise, the Commission is more cautious than the advocates of the canonical approach regarding the degree of agreement possible between Jewish and Christian canonical interpretation of the writings of the Old Testament. It points out that the differences between the Jewish and Christian[19] canonical collections necessarily lead to differences in canonical interpretation (I.A.1.i). Also, the fact that "the Church reads the Old Testament in the light of the paschal mystery" inevitably distinguishes Christian and Jewish interpretation of these books.

---

[18] "Whereas the final and definitive form is certainly canonical and authoritative, it is far from certain that earlier forms in the process would have been so recognized by the entire community of faith or that the earlier forms are valid criteria of interpretation, despite the light that they may shed on the genesis or development of the text concerned" (Fitzmyer, *The Biblical Commission's Document*, 69-70).

[19] Here it would be more accurate if the *IBC* said "Catholic and Orthodox" canons, since most Protestants follow the Jewish Hebrew canon.

CHAPTER 9

Interpretation of the Old Testament in Light of the Paschal Mystery

Principle #9

The Church regards the Old Testament as inspired Scripture, faithfully conveying God's revelation (III.A.2.a; III.B.1.b).

The New Testament interprets the Old Testament in the light of the paschal mystery (I.C.1.i). Jesus' life, death and resurrection fulfill the Old Testament Scriptures (III.A.2.a). Jesus' own interpretation of the Old Testament and that of the Apostles expressed in the New Testament under the inspiration of the Spirit are authoritative, even if some of the interpretive procedures employed by New Testament authors reflect the ways of thinking of a particular time period (III.A.2.f).

Christians do not limit the meaning of the Old Testament to the ways in which it prepares for the coming of Christ. Rather the Church esteems the canonical interpretation of the Old Testament before the Christian Passover as a stage in the history of salvation (I.C.1.i). Christians continue to draw sustenance from the inspired message of the Old Testament (III.A.2.e)[1].

---

[1] The primary exposition of this principle appears in a sub-section of the treatment of "Interpretation in the Biblical Tradition" (III.A) devoted to "Relationships between the Old Testament and the New" (III.A.2). Yet the relation between the two testaments also receives mention in the discussions of the formation of the canon (III.B.b-d), the canonical approach (I.C.1.i), the approach through recourse to Jewish interpretation (I.C.2.e), the spiritual sense (II.B.2), and the task of the exegete (III.C.1.c-d).

Explanation

1. The Old Testament As Inspired Scripture

The Church regards the Old Testament as inspired Scripture, faithfully conveying God's revelation (III.A.2.a; III.B.1.b).

The Church's regard for and interpretation of the writings which Christians call the Old Testament finds expression in the New Testament. To begin with, the New Testament authors "accorded to the Old Testament the value of divine revelation" (III.A.2.a). They regarded these texts as "'Sacred Scripture' (Rom 1:2), 'inspired' by the Spirit of God (2 Tim 3:16; cf. 2 Pet 1:20-21), which 'can never be annulled'" (III.B.1.b). Furthermore, they attribute this view to Jesus himself (e.g., Mt 5:17; Jn 10:35). The rejection or deprecation of the Old Testament by ancient and modern writers[2] has no foundation in Scripture nor any place in Catholic interpretation.

2. Christian Interpretation of the Old Testament

Yet the fact must not be denied or minimized that the New Testament's interpretation of the Jewish Scriptures radically altered the interpretation which had dominated until that point.

The New Testament interprets the Old Testament in the light of the paschal mystery (I.C.1.i). Jesus' life, death and resurrection fulfill the Old Testament Scriptures (III.A.2.a). Jesus' own interpretation of the Old Testament and that of the Apostles expressed in the New Testament under the inspiration of the Spirit are authoritative, even if some of the interpretive procedures employed by New Testament authors reflect the ways of thinking of a particular time period (III.A.2.f).

The authors of the New Testament believed that the revelation expressed in the sacred writings of the Old Covenant "found *fulfillment* in the life, in the teaching and above all in the death and resurrection of Jesus" (III.A.2.a,

---

[2] Commenting on the *IBC*'s treatment of this theme, Francesco Lambiasi describes three contrasting stances of scholars in this century toward the status of the OT. In the position of those who do not consider the OT to be the true word of God for Christians, he places Bultmann and Friedrich Baumgärtel, who regard it merely as the history of Israel and the "law" which prepare the way for the Gospel of universal grace revealed in the NT. At the opposite extreme stands Wilhelm Vischer, who sees an "identity" between the OT and the NT, since Jesus Christ has fulfilled the OT promises. According to Lambiasi, Vischer fails to do justice to the differences between OT expectations and NT fulfillment. Finally, the majority of scholars accept the OT as the word of God for Christians and concern themselves with defining the mutual relations between the OT and NT; Lambiasi names Henri de Lubac and Pierre Grelot as examples. See Lambiasi, "Dimensioni caratteristiche [*Commento*]", 311-315.

emphasis added), which all occurred "according to the Scriptures" (1 Cor 15:3-5)[3]. This fulfillment was not one of merely material correspondence, but of mutual illumination between Scripture and events: "What becomes clear is that Scripture reveals the meaning of events and that events reveal the meaning of Scripture, that is, they require that certain aspects of the received interpretation be set aside and a new interpretation adopted" (III.A.2.b).

A christological reading of the Old Testament lies at the heart of the biblical interpretation expressed in the New Testament[4]:

> Although Christ established the New Covenant in his blood, the books of the First Covenant have not lost their value. Assumed into the proclamation of the Gospel, they *acquire and display their full meaning in the "mystery of Christ"* (Eph 3:4); they shed light upon multiple aspects of this mystery, while in turn being illuminated by it themselves. (III.C.1.d, emphasis added)

Jesus' death and resurrection provided a new historical context in which to interpret many things expressed in the Jewish Scriptures:

> The death of the Messiah, "king of the Jews" (Mark 15:26 and parallels), prompted a transformation of the purely earthly interpretation of the royal psalms and messianic prophecies. The resurrection and heavenly glorification of Jesus as Son of God lent these texts a fullness of meaning previously unimaginable. The result was that some expressions which had seemed to be hyperbole had now to be taken literally. They came to be seen as divine preparations to express the glory of Christ Jesus, for Jesus is truly "Lord" (Ps 110:1), in the fullest sense of the word (Acts 2:3-6; Phil 2:10-11; Heb 1:10-12); he is Son of God (Ps 2:7; Mk 14:62; Rom 1:3-4), God with God (Ps 45:7; Heb 1:8; Jn 1:1, 20:28); "his reign will have no end" (Lk 1:32-33; cf. 1 Chron 17:11-14; Ps 45:7; Heb 1:8) and he is at the same time "priest forever" (Ps 110:4; Heb 5:6-10; 7:23-24). (III.A.2.d)

Jesus himself had initiated a new interpretation of Israel's Scriptures (III.A.2.c), distinct from that of the "scribes and Pharisees" in regard to the demands of righteousness (Matt 5:17-48), the observance of the Sabbath (Mark 2:27-28 and parallels), the precepts of ritual purity (Mark 7:1-23 and

---

[3] Lambiasi proposes a methodology for re-reading the OT in the light of the NT under three headings: the *factors* which required it (Jesus' example of interpretation and the Easter event); the *foundations* on which it is established (the doctrine of inspiration and the validity and particularity of the OT); and the *criteria* for recognizing in the NT a real fulfillment of the OT (continuity with the ancient promise, discontinuity and a qualitative leap to a higher level). He follows his theoretical presentation with a number of examples. See Lambiasi, "Dimensioni caratteristiche [*Commento*]", 316-325.

[4] See Jensen, "Old Testament in the New Testament" and Simian-Yofre, "Old and New Testament", especially 291-292.

parallels), and the attitude toward tax collectors and sinners (Mark 2:15-17 and parallels)[5].

The Easter events and the glorified Christ's gift of the Holy Spirit led the authors of New Testament to perceive the "spiritual sense" of the Old Testament[6]. "While this meant that they came to stress more than ever the prophetic value of the Old Testament, it also had the effect of relativizing very considerably its value as a system of salvation" (III.A.2.e). The prophetic character of the Old Testament was important for explaining Jesus Christ to Israel (e.g., Acts 2:14-36; 3:17-26; 13:16-41) and for showing the coherence of the plan of God to all (1 Cor 15:3-5; Eph 1:3-14). The "relativizing" of the law as a system of salvation "already appears in the Gospels (cf. Matt 11:11-13 and parallels; 12:41-42 and parallels; John 4:12-14; 5:37; 6:32), emerges strongly in certain Pauline letters [Gal 2:15-5:1; Rom 3:20-21; 6:14] as well as in the Letter to the Hebrews [7:11-19; 10:8-9]"[7] (III.A.2.e). As a result of this re-interpretation of the Old Testament, Gentile members of the people of God are not bound by the law of Moses, now "reduced in its entirety to the status of a legal code of a particular people" (III.A.2.e). Nevertheless, Gentile Christians gain "spiritual sustenance" from the Scriptures of the Old Covenant which help them "discover the full dimension of the paschal mystery which now governs their lives" (III.A.2.e).

According to the Biblical Commission, the New Testament's interpretation of the Jewish Scriptures is fundamental to Christian faith: "The Church reads the Old Testament in the light of the paschal mystery", and "This new determination of meaning has become an integral element of Christian faith" (I.C.1.i).

---

[5] Levenson criticizes the *IBC* for being insufficiently critical in its attribution of these positions to Jesus, rather than to later controversies between the Church and Judaism. However, it seems to this writer that the Commission has chosen historically probable examples of Jesus' differences with currents in first-century Judaism. Levenson's underlying concern appears a couple of paragraphs later: "So long as the figure of Jesus is protected from rigorous historical-critical analysis, the danger of anti-Semitic interpretation will survive.... There is no substitute for the cauterization through historical criticism of the virulent anti-Semitic statements that have been put in the mouth of Jesus. Without this the Church's denunciations of anti-Semitism ring hollow" (Blowers, Levenson and Wilken, "Three Views", 44). But not even a determined rejection of anti-Semitic interpretation should bias exegesis. Properly understood, the statements attributed to Jesus by NT authors (all of whom, probably, were Jewish) are not anti-Semitic (see, for example, Girard, "Anti-Semitism in the Gospels?"; Mejía, "Antisemitism in the Bible"; Motyer, "John's Gospel Anti-Semitic?").

[6] See principle #13.

[7] The references in brackets come from a sentence in the *IBC* that follows the quotation.

3. The Old Testament's Pre-Christian Canonical Meaning

Christians do not limit the meaning of the Old Testament to the ways in which it prepares for the coming of Christ. Rather the Church esteems the canonical interpretation of the Old Testament before the Christian Passover as a stage in the history of salvation (I.C.1.i). She continues to draw sustenance from the inspired message of the Old Testament (I.A.2.e).

Although the Church interprets the Old Testament in light of the life, death and resurrection of Jesus, this does not mean "doing away with all attempt to be consistent with that earlier canonical interpretation which preceded the Christian Passover" (I.C.1.i). Two reasons justify this restraint. First, as the *IBC* puts it, "One must respect each stage of the history of salvation. To empty out of the Old Testament its own proper meaning would be to deprive the New of its roots in history" (I.C.1.i). Some patristic and medieval allegorizing interpretation had this tendency, which, among other problems, sometimes caused Christians to forget their roots in Judaism.

Second, the literal sense of many Old Testament texts provides important instruction for Christian life[8]. This is what the author of 2 Timothy had in mind when he wrote, "All Scripture", referring at that time only to what Christians today call the Old Testament, "is inspired by God and is useful for teaching, for reproof, for correction, and for training in righteousness" (2 Tim 3:16). Perhaps[9] this is what the Biblical Commission was referring to when they wrote, "Already in the Old Testament, there are many instances where texts have a religious or spiritual sense as their literal sense. Christian faith recognizes in such cases an anticipatory relationship to the new life brought by Christ "(II.B.2.d).

Discussion

Several reviewers criticized the *IBC*'s presentation of the relations between the Old Testament and the New Testament. Some felt that the Biblical Commission oversimplified the relations between the two Testaments and tried to avoid the inevitable tension between the Scriptures of Israel and the kerygma of the Church. Some, while positive about the document as a whole, objected to its openness to "christocentric" and typological readings of

---

[8] See discussion on p. 193.

[9] I say, "perhaps", because the Biblical Commission does not explicitly state the benefits of the OT for Christians apart from the light of its relationship to Christ and the paschal mystery. This omission leaves its document vulnerable to some of the criticisms it receives (see discussion section below). The use of the term "spiritual sense" in this context is also unclear. See the note discussing the statement of the Commission under principle #13 on the spiritual sense, p. 193.

the Old Testament, not denying the historic role of this kind of interpretation, but calling into question its value for today. The following section will examine the issues raised by Roland Murphy and Erich Zenger, both of whom liked the *IBC* overall, but took exception to its handling of the Old Testament.

4. The Criticisms of Roland Murphy and Erich Zenger

a) Distortion of Old Testament Voices

Murphy points out that traditional exegesis often distorted the message of Old Testament authors. Sometimes this occurred by reading Christian eschatology into the interpretation of the Old Testament. For example, he cites Jerome's misreading of Job 19:25-27 to encompass the doctrine of the resurrection, and the *Imitation of Christ*'s use of Eccles 1:1, "Vanity of vanities...," to teach Christian asceticism and an orientation to the eternal life. Murphy also objects to typological interpretation, which, he says, overwhelms the literal sense, "forcing the earlier Testament into the mold of the later"[10].

b) Need Today Different from Early Church

Murphy acknowledges that typology is a biblical way of thinking, both in the Old Testament and the New Testament, and that New Testament exegesis of the Old Testament is christocentric. Although this type of interpretation is part of the Catholic tradition, he believes it cannot be identified as *the* Catholic approach:

> A rather rare taste is required for a modern reader to appreciate those time-honored approaches.... Indeed, they play a relatively insignificant role outside the liturgy, which keeps their memory alive. They are hardly a vivid part of the current "living tradition".... Unlike the situation in the first century..., it is easier today to learn the reality of Christ from the Gospels and Epistles without belaboring the text of the Hebrew Bible with strained associations that are no longer needed. The major point is acquired: typology is a biblical mind-set.... Now what does the Hebrew Bible say on its own?[11]

Murphy's point about the first century situation is that the early Christians had no other recourse to understand Jesus than in the light of the Jewish Scriptures: "The role of the Hebrew Bible *after* Christ, however, is different from the one it had in explaining Christ to the first believers.... More avenues

---

[10] Murphy, "What Is Catholic? Revisited",114.

[11] Murphy, "What Is Catholic? Revisited",114.

than the christological have become available—indeed fruitful and necessary"[12].

Murphy recalls the Biblical Commission's statement that "to empty out of the Old Testament its own proper meaning would be to deprive the New of its roots in history" (I.C.1.i), but Murphy concludes that when the Biblical Commission speaks of reading the Old Testament in the light of the paschal mystery, "It does not seem to be meant as an hermeneutical principle", but rather "the ultimate truth and goal" by which Christians should measure "their total understanding of the biblical message"[13].

c) Value of the Literal Sense for Christians

Instead of a "christocentric" reading of the Old Testament, Murphy advocates a "christian" reading, which is rigorous about attending to the literal meaning of texts and does not refer directly to Christ[14]. Instead it may center on the Father of Jesus Christ, or God's relationship with his people, or the experience of biblical characters. Christians need not pray Psalm 23 in reference to Jesus; we can pray it in reference to YHWH as the shepherd of his people as it was originally understood. Many of the lines of the psalms are timeless and open-ended, permitting direct actualization without a christological reinterpretation[15].

Zenger also advocates the value of the literal sense of the Old Testament for Christians[16]. Some books of the Old Testament, such as Qoheleth, Job, Ruth, Esther, and Judith, do not yield so readily to a "fulfillment" approach. Amos and Jonah do not need the New Testament for their message to be complete and important. In addition, the Old Testament continues to have value as a book of promise. The eschatology which Jesus proclaimed and taught in the "Our Father" is the fulfillment of Old Testament promises. The Old Testament teaches how to live with failed expectations and with promises which are as yet unfulfilled. Finally, for some aspects of life, the "First Testament" has an original divine message which is not repeated in the same way in the New Testament. In this respect, the Old Testament serves as a completion and correction of a one-sided reading of the New Testament.

---

[12] Murphy, "What Is Catholic? Revisited",114.

[13] Murphy, "What Is Catholic? Revisited",114.

[14] Murphy, "What Is Catholic? Revisited",114-115.

[15] Murphy also urges this possibility in "Reflections on 'Actualization'", 80-81. As a hermeneutical theory that works with the literal sense, Murphy recommends Sean McEvenue's application of Bernard Lonergan's insights to interpretation for personal transformation (McEvenue, *Truth in Literature*, 7-73, 158-167).

[16] Zenger, "Weisse Flecken im neuen Dokument", 173-176.

d) Relationship to Judaism

Zenger is particularly concerned about the implications of Christian interpretation of the Old Testament for relations between Christianity and Judaism[17]. He points out that the early Church accepted the Bible of Israel, implicitly recognizing the validity of a pre-Christian reading, even as it expressed a christological re-reading in the New Testament writings. This reminds us that the Jews were the first addressees of the Bible, and that the Church continues to have a special relationship with Israel and with Judaism (the Church has a Jewish-Christian identity). Zenger expresses concern about the *IBC*'s openness to allegory[18] and typology in light of the problems they produced over the centuries, sometimes including anti-Jewish interpretation and the hermeneutical dispossession of the Jews. Zenger concedes that these methods can uncover a deeper dimension to the biblical text in a canonical reading of the whole Bible, yet he cautions against using these methods in a way that produces an unhealthy dominance of the "First Testament" by the "Second".

e) Evaluation of criticism

Murphy and Zenger make valid points about the value of the literal sense of the Old Testament for Christian life, even if some parts of the Old Testament do not lend themselves to a literal reading for Christians. While this affirmation contradicts nothing said by the Biblical Commission, it does highlight a vagueness on the topic in the *IBC* which could be misunderstood to imply that the only Christian use of the Old Testament is by means of an explicitly christological re-reading. On the other hand, Murphy clearly misreads the document when he denies the paschal mystery is intended to function as a hermeneutical principle[19]. The Biblical Commission asserts the

---

[17] Zenger prefers to speak of the First and Second Testament. See his *Der Erste Testament*.

[18] Zenger is mistaken on this point ("Weisse Flecken im neuen Dokument", 176): nowhere does the *IBC* recommend allegory.

[19] Ayres and Fowl also fault Murphy for this interpretation of the *IBC* and argue themselves that the paschal mystery is the *primary* hermeneutical principle for the reading of Scripture ("[Mis]reading the Face of God, 521n). Murphy defends his rejection of the paschal mystery as a hermeneutical principle in *Theological Studies* ("Primary Hermeneutical Principle?") for essentially the same reasons indicated above. Murphy is concerned to preserve the literal sense of the OT for Christians (particularly the OT's revelation of the Father of Jesus Christ) and to resist exclusive christological interpretation. He prefers to describe the paschal mystery as the "*telos*", "context", or "presupposition" of Christian interpretation, insisting, that "this Christian orientation does not dictate methods of literary interpretation" (pp. 144, 146n). At this point the issue turns on one's definition of "hermeneutical principle".

principle of interpretation of the Old Testament in light of the death and resurrection of Jesus several times in the *IBC*, as the first part of this chapter indicates.

Again, Murphy makes a valid point that the need of modern Christians to know Christ through the Old Testament is different from that of Christians in the first century[20]. However, the proper conclusion is that more avenues have been opened to modern Christian interpreters of the Old Testament—not that the original path of the Christian interpretation of the Old Testament should be closed or shunned! On the contrary, the avenue of Old Testament interpretation followed by the New Testament authors and attributed to Jesus himself (Lk 18:31; 24:27, 44) must remain normative and central for Christians. What higher authority exists for defining Christian interpretation of the Old Testament than the New Testament? Furthermore, the liturgy's preservation of this pattern of interpretation should be considered more than a mere vestige left by a particular moment in the Church's history, but rather a strong argument for its continuance and renewal in accord with the venerable principle, *lex orandi, lex credendi*. If abuses in typological interpretation have tarnished its image, let a more sober Christian typology take its place. If heavy-handed traditional Christian interpretation has domesticated some of the Old Testament's distinctive testimony to the truth, let it be reformed. As Murphy himself says in answer to criticisms of the historical-critical method, "the method itself is not to be identified with abuses" (113).

Probably both Murphy's and Zenger's criticisms should be taken as a warning not to return to the excesses of patristic and medieval christological interpretation which often dominated the Old Testament at the expense of its rich and multi-faceted teaching. However, the Biblical Commission's reaffirmation of interpretation of the Old Testament in light of the death and resurrection of Christ and their careful definitions of the spiritual and fuller senses (see principles #13 and #14) correct an excess in the opposite direction. A hermeneutically naïve use of the historical-critical method has suppressed the Christian pattern of Old Testament interpretation found in the New Testament and the liturgy. In the opinion of this writer, Christian interpretation of the Old Testament must not be a case of either/or: either exclusively christological or exclusively literal. Rather both approaches are necessary and complementary if the full riches of the Old Testament are to be enjoyed by Christians.

---

[20] De Lubac makes an analogous point (*Sources of Revelation*, 4-5).

CHAPTER 10

Interpretation in Light of the Living Tradition of the Church

Principle #10

Catholic exegesis deliberately places itself within the stream of the living Tradition of the Church (III.b) and seeks to be faithful to the revelation handed on by the great Tradition, of which the Bible is itself a witness (Conclusion e).

Within this living Tradition, the Fathers of the Church have a foundational place, having drawn from the whole of Scripture the basic orientations which shaped the doctrinal tradition of the Church, and having provided a rich theological teaching for the instruction and spiritual sustenance of the faithful (III.B.2.b). However, Catholic exegesis is not bound by the Fathers' exegetical methods (II.B.2.h; III.B.2.k)[1].

---

[1] This principle, like the others we are considering in part III of this study, appears in the important chapter of the *IBC* devoted to "Characteristics of Catholic Interpretation", particularly the second section which describes "Interpretation In The Tradition Of The Church" (III.B). It also appears in the sections of the document devoted to the canonical approach (I.C.1) and to actualization (IV.A), and in Pope John Paul II's Address to the Biblical Commission (§10).

Explanation

1. Catholic Exegesis and Tradition

Catholic exegesis deliberately places itself within the stream of the living Tradition of the Church (III.b) and seeks to be faithful to the revelation handed on by the great Tradition, of which the Bible is itself a witness (Conclusion e).

This paragraph of principle #10 combines the two statements from the *IBC* regarding the relation of Catholic interpretation to Tradition[2]:

What characterizes Catholic exegesis is that it deliberately places itself within the living tradition[3] of the Church, whose first concern is fidelity to the revelation attested by the Bible. (III.b)

Through fidelity to the great Tradition, of which the Bible itself is a witness, Catholic exegesis should...maintain its identity as a *theological discipline*, the principal aim of which is the deepening of faith.   (Conclusion e, emphasis original)

To understand this principle it is necessary to briefly recall the Catholic understanding of "Tradition", although a thorough discussion of that topic is beyond the scope of this study[4].

a)   Catholic Understanding of Tradition

Tradition may be defined as the living presence of the word of God in the life of the Church through time. As the communication of divine revelation, Tradition must be distinguished from various theological, disciplinary, liturgical or devotional *traditions* that have arisen that seek to give expression

---

[2] The statement of principle #10 uses the expression "stream of Tradition" which is found in Address 10, I.A.3.c, and IV.A.3.e.

[3] The *IBC* is inconsistent in its capitalization of "Tradition", which has led to some confusion. On five occasions when it appears the Biblical Commission intends to refer to Tradition as the authentic bearer of divine revelation it does not capitalize the term (III.b,III.B.2.b, III.B.3.c; IV.A.1.e—twice). On other occasions the *IBC* does capitalize it (e.g., I.C.a, I.E.1.n, III.B.2.b *et passim*). This pattern of capitalization occurs both in the French original and in the English translation. According to Vanhoye, this inconsistency was purely accidental, reflecting no intention on the part of the Biblical Commission (Fax to author in response to query, 31 January 2000).

[4] What follows is drawn from *DV* 7-10; CCC 74-100; O'Collins and Farrugia, *Concise Dictionary of Theology*; Pottmeyer, "Tradition"; and Wicks, *Introduction to Theological Method*, 68-94.

to it[5]. Tradition entails both the *content* of divine revelation and the *process* of its communication in the life of the Church. The *content* of Tradition is everything Christ revealed to the apostles and what the Holy Spirit enabled them to understand later. It is the apostolic preaching, teaching, legislation, practice, and example which finds normative but not exhaustive expression in the writings of the New Testament. The *process* of handing on Tradition's content occurs in the life of the Church by the activity of her members as the Church "in her teaching, life and worship, perpetuates and hands on to all generations all that she herself is, all that she believes" (*DV* 8). In this process bishops, as the successors to the apostles, have a special role in handing on and authoritatively interpreting the Tradition. Through the process of Tradition, the content of the "tradition which comes from the apostles *develops* in the Church with the help of the Holy Spirit" as there is "growth in the understanding of the realities and the words which have been handed down [emphasis added]" (*DV* 8).

The word "Tradition" is often modified in the *IBC* by the adjectives "living" (8x) and "great" (5x). When the *IBC* describes Tradition as "living", it emphasizes its contemporary and vital presence in the Church, and that it consists of more than "a mere communication of individual truths but as the life-bestowing presence of God's word"[6]. When the *IBC* describes Tradition as "great", it contrasts it with lesser traditions and emphasizes the antiquity and universality of the Church's Tradition.

Scripture and Tradition flow "from the same divine wellspring" (*DV* 9) and "form one sacred deposit of the word of God, which is committed to the Church" (*DV* 10). The relationship between Scripture and Tradition is reciprocal; each acts upon the other. The notion that Scripture should be interpreted in light of Tradition follows from the fact that the canon of Scripture itself is a fruit of Tradition. The *IBC* recounts how the Church, guided by the Holy Spirit and in the light of the living Tradition, "discerned the writings which should be regarded as Sacred Scripture" (III.B.1.a). At the same time, meditation on Scripture has nourished and formed the development of Tradition in the Church. The "rule of faith", the element of Tradition by which teaching was measured in the early Church, consisted of

---

[5] This study will capitalize "Tradition" as the channel of divine revelation except in quotations of sources which do not distinguish the word by capitalization, including the *IBC* itself and the Abbott—Gallagher translation of the documents of Vatican II used in this study.

[6] Pottmeyer, "Tradition", 1123. *Dei Verbum* introduced a broader and more dynamic understanding of Tradition than post-Tridentine theology had taught.

"the clearer passages in Holy Scripture"[7]. Likewise, the Creed is derived from Scripture and serves its interpretation. The mutual influence of Scripture and Tradition continues to the present:

> United to the living Tradition which preceded it, which accompanies it and *is nourished by it* (cf. *Dei Verbum*, 21), the Bible is the privileged means which God uses yet again in our own day to shape the building up and the growth of the Church as the People of God" (III.C.1.f, emphasis added).

How does one ascertain what accords with the living Tradition? Simple participation in the life of the Church brings a sharing in Tradition, a connatural familiarity. Besides Scripture itself, the writings of the Fathers of the Church bear witness to Tradition. So do the Church's creeds, her liturgy, the writings of the saints, and the dogmatic definitions of Councils and Popes. The contemporary teaching of the Pope and bishops witnesses to Tradition, since "bishops, as successors of the apostles, are the first witnesses and guarantors of the living tradition within which Scripture is interpreted..." (III.B.3.c, cf. I.C.g).

b) Exegesis

When *Catholic exegesis deliberately places itself within the stream of the living Tradition of the Church and seeks to be faithful to the revelation handed on by the great Tradition* (principle #10), Catholic exegesis embraces Tradition both as content and process. Exegesis receives the content of Tradition handed on to it in the life of the Church, and exegesis participates in the transmission of Tradition through its service of biblical interpretation.

The Biblical Commission sees Tradition contributing to the process of interpretation differently, depending on the nature of the interpretive task. For all Catholic interpretation, Tradition provides the pre-understanding and the "lived affinity" which makes interpretation possible (III.b, see principle #6). This entails more than the cognitive aspects of a presupposition of faith:

> Faith traditions formed the living context for the literary activity of the authors of Sacred Scripture.... In like manner, the interpretation of Sacred Scripture requires full participation on the part of exegetes in the life and faith of the believing community of their own time. (III.A.3.g)

---

[7] Thus, Pottmeyer, "Tradition", 1122, citing Augustine, "*de scripturarum planioribus locis et ecclesiae auctoritate*" (*Doct. chr.* 3.2.2). For more on the "rule of faith", see Wicks, "Rule of Faith [*DFT*]", 959-961: "The rule was not applied to the genuine prophetic and apostolic books as an ecclesiastical principle external to them. Instead the rule was the very meaning of the Scriptures themselves..." (960).

Participation in the life of the Church and its Tradition of faith provides the matrix for Catholic interpretation.

For *scientific exegesis*, however, a pre-understanding of faith received from Tradition, like every other presupposition, brings to exegesis the risk of prejudicing its results[8]. According to the *IBC*, the exegete must be careful to avoid the danger of "attributing to biblical texts a meaning which they do not contain but which is the product of a later development within the tradition" (III.c).

When it comes to *actualizing Scripture*, i.e., explaining the Bible's meaning for the present and applying it pastorally in the community of faith, Tradition guides interpretation more directly:

> The living tradition of the community of faith stimulates the task of actualization. This community places itself in explicit continuity with the communities which gave rise to Scripture and which preserved and handed it on. In the process of actualization, tradition plays a double role: on the one hand it provides protection against deviant interpretations; on the other hand, it ensures the transmission of the original dynamism (IV.A.1.e).

When the *IBC* discusses the use of the Bible in pastoral ministry, catechesis and preaching in particular, it says that Scripture should be "explained in the context of the Tradition" (IV.C.3.b). In other words, in pastoral ministry Tradition not only provides a pre-understanding of faith, it guides the explanation of texts.

So, for example, when an exegete studies John 14 which speaks of Jesus' relationship to his Father and the Spirit, he needs to be careful to distinguish between what the text itself affirms and the fullness of Trinitarian doctrine that developed later. However, when a preacher or catechist explains the same text, or when an exegete goes to actualize the text, he or she should explain the text in the light of Tradition, in view of what the Church has come to understand under the Spirit's influence about the realities of which the text speaks.

2. Exegesis and the Fathers of the Church

The Catholic and Orthodox Churches have long given great weight to the interpretation of the Fathers of the Church, at times virtually identified with Tradition, as a guide and control to Christian interpretation of the Bible. Yet the nature and extent of patristic authority for Catholic biblical interpretation

---

[8] See the discussion of this problem in the discussion of a hermeneutic of faith on p. 103ff.

has not been clear[9]. Critical exegesis has recognized that the extreme allegorical interpretation of some of the Fathers is eisegesis, and therefore does not truly render the meaning of the text. For this reason, historical-critical exegesis has ignored and sometimes derogated patristic interpretation. Critics of the historical-critical method, on the other hand, have found in patristic exegesis the theological and spiritual approach to Scripture lacking in much contemporary exegesis and have advocated its rehabilitation[10]. The paragraph of principle #10 printed below synthesizes the balanced conclusion of the Biblical Commission:

> *Within this living Tradition, the Fathers of the Church have a foundational place, having drawn from the whole of Scripture the basic orientations which shaped the doctrinal tradition of the Church, and having provided a rich theological teaching for the instruction and spiritual sustenance of the faithful (III.B.2.b).*

> *However, Catholic exegesis is not bound by the Fathers' exegetical methods. (II.B.2.h; III.B.2.k)*

According to the Biblical Commission, just as the Fathers had an important role in the development of the canon of Scripture, they "likewise have a foundational role in relation to the living tradition which unceasingly accompanies and guides the Church's reading and interpretation of Scripture" (III.B.2.b). The *IBC* identifies a two-fold contribution of the Fathers which

---

[9] The injunction of the Fourth Session of the Council of Trent that "no one dare to interpret the Scripture in a way contrary to the unanimous consensus of the Fathers" (DS 1507, Neuner and Dupuis, *The Christian Faith*, 97-98, §215) was often repeated (DS 1863, 3007). This oft-repeated formula was significantly qualified by Pope Pius XII's statement, "There are but few texts whose sense has been defined by the authority of the Church; nor are those more numerous about which the teaching of the Holy Fathers is unanimous" (*DAS* 47, *DS* 3831, *EB* §565). See Fitzmyer, *The Biblical Commission's Document*, 150n. For a fuller account of the authority accorded to the Church Fathers in magisterial documents beginning with *Providentissimus Deus*, see Stowasser, "'...damit das Urteil der Kirche reife'", 206-207.

[10] Some the advocates of patristic exegesis have also been advocates of the "spiritual sense". For more about this controversy, see the "Discussion" on the Spiritual Sense (principle #13). However, the concern to recover the benefits of patristic exegesis is by no means confined to opponents of the historical-critical method. Maurice Gilbert, for instance, disagrees with scientific criticism's break with the exegesis of the Fathers: "However, such a break with this great exegetical tradition can be seen all the more clearly as an error that must be corrected if Catholic exegesis intends—as it certainly should, if it is to be true to its nature and ecclesial function—to remain an exegesis that is truly carried out within and by the Church. The Fathers, the medieval Doctors, and the humanist exegetes approached and commented on the Scriptures within the faith of the Church. Their exegesis was often to a greater extent than ours ecclesial, theological, spiritual, and pastoral, and many people feel strongly that it is vital for modern exegesis to recover these values and orientations" ("New Horizons and Present Needs", 335-336).

accounts for their foundational role. First, Church Fathers "have drawn out from the totality of Scripture the basic orientations which shaped the doctrinal tradition of the Church" (III.B.2.b). By this the Biblical Commission seems to refer to the patristic biblical interpretation which shaped the doctrinal decisions of the early centuries of the Church expressed in the great Councils, doctrinal decisions which remain valid and which guide Catholic interpretation today. Second, the Fathers "have provided a rich theological teaching for the instruction and spiritual sustenance of the faithful" (III.B.2.b). Here the Commission refers to the continuing fruitfulness of the writings of the Fathers of the Church, which play a part in theological reflection and spiritual reading (e.g., the Office of Readings)[11].

The *IBC* calls attention to something about the Fathers' approach to Scripture which they want to recommend. After describing various traits of patristic exegesis without explicit evaluation (see "Discussion" below), the Biblical Commission concludes its presentation this way: "The Fathers of the Church teach [us] to read the Bible theologically, within the heart of a living Tradition, with an authentic Christian spirit" (III.B.2.k). In other words, the Fathers' strong point was interpreting Scripture from within a hermeneutic of faith, seeking to hear and understand the word of God in it, and with a commitment to the Gospel as the Church has always understood it. Fitzmyer puts it this way:

> What the Fathers thus strove to accomplish by their allegorical interpretation is still a legitimate goal of all biblical interpretation. If the sophisticated historical-critical method of interpretation is "indispensable" and actually required today [cf. I.A.a], it *still has to be practised with the same goal and motivation as characterized the patristic method just described* [emphasis added][12].

Nevertheless, respect for the Fathers—the doctrinal results of their interpretation and their theological approach to Scripture—does not commend all their exegetical methods which at times reflect the limitations of their age. On the contrary, "the allegorical interpretation of Scripture so characteristic of patristic exegesis runs the risk of being something of an embarrassment to people today" (III.B.2.k). And in another place, referring to the patristic use

---

[11] A helpful summary of the approach of the Church Fathers to each of the books of the Bible along with a bibliography of patristic writings on each book may be found in Balás and Bingham, "Patristic Exegesis of the Books of the Bible [IBCom]".

[12] Fitzmyer, *The Biblical Commission's Document*, 149-150. Despite this statement, Fitzmyer has generally expressed strong resistance toward the revival of patristic exegesis, particularly allegory: "When it comes to the allegorical interpretation of Scripture that the Fathers used, I have only one comment: *admirandum sed non imitandum*, 'to be marveled at but not imitated'" (Fitzmyer and Stahel, "Interview", 11).

of rabbinic methods and Hellenistic allegorical interpretation, the *IBC* says, "Modern exegesis cannot ascribe true interpretative value to this kind of procedure" (II.B.2.h)[13].

Discussion

3.   Evaluation of Patristic Exegesis

The Biblical Commission had some difficulty making up its mind about what to say about patristic exegesis. According to Lambiasi, the provisional outline of their document (January 1991) did not treat this subject[14].   The October 1991 outline included it in chapter I as one of the "approaches based on tradition" (I.C in the final version). At the end of 1991 the first draft of the document included a section on patristic exegesis in the chapter on characteristics of Catholic interpretation (its present location).   That draft included the statement that the Fathers "provide a model which is always valid of effective interpretation and of proclamation of the Scriptures in situations and cultures remote from those in which the Bible was formed". That statement was liable to misinterpretation, so a more nuanced presentation of the Fathers' contribution (summarized above) appeared in July of 1992 which remained more or less intact through the final redaction.

Although the *IBC*'s two-page account of patristic exegesis is almost entirely descriptive rather than overtly evaluative, one can infer a certain sympathy on the part of the Biblical Commission toward patristic interpretation by means of subtle signs.   First, in some cases the Commission evaluates positively elsewhere in the document traits which it attributes to patristic interpretation.   Second, sometimes the Biblical Commission's choice of vocabulary suggests a positive or negative stance, as when it says that the Fathers' use of allegory "transcends" the method employed by pagan authors (III.B.2.h).   Third, in some instances the trait attributed to patristic exegesis accords with traditional Church teaching about Scripture.

Below is a summary of the implicit evaluation, based on such indicators, which the Commission gives to various features of patristic exegesis.   Each of

---

[13] Klauck feel this statement is a little too strong in light of the positive things the Biblical Commission says about rabbinic and patristic interpretation ("Das neue Dokument: Darstellung und Würdigung", 80). According to Klauck, no one pleads for a restoration of allegory as of old.   Nevertheless, a positive reevaluation of allegory and its hermeneutic potential is unmistakably underway (see p. 80, footnote 48 of Klauck's article for a brief bibliography), even if it does not find an adequate reflection in the Biblical Commission's document.

[14] The information on the development of the text given in this paragraph comes from Lambiasi, "Dimensioni caratteristiche [*Commento*]", 338.

the descriptive statements of the Biblical Commission regarding patristic exegesis found in the *IBC* is categorized under the headings, "Admirable," "Not-to-be-imitated", and "No Comment"[15].

Admirable Features of Patristic Exegesis

1. High value on the reading of Scripture and its interpretation (c)[16]

2. Priority on reading the Bible in Church, in the liturgy (d)

3. Interpretations of a theological and pastoral nature aimed at promoting relationship with God (d)

4. Treatment of the Bible as the Book of God, of inexhaustible meaning (j), without reducing human authors to passive instruments or homogenizing the whole (e)

5. Chief concern to live from the Bible in communion with brothers and sisters (g)

6. Conviction that the Bible as God's book was given by God to the Church (i)

7. Despite frequent recourse to allegorical interpretation [viewed negatively], rare abandonment of the literalness and historicity of texts [viewed positively] (h)

8. Fathers' recourse to allegory transcends simple adaptation of method employed by pagan authors (h)

9. View that God is constantly speaking to his Christian people a message that is ever relevant for their time (i)

10. Motivation behind questionable methods (allegory, prooftexting) was pastoral and pedagogical, convinced all was written for our instruction (i)

Not-To-Be-Imitated Features of Patristic Exegesis

1. Scant attention to the historical development of revelation (e)

2. Use of a sentence out of context to bring out some revealed truth they found expressed within it (f)

---

[15] Readers are invited to consult section III.B.2 to ascertain if their reading supports the interpretation proposed.

[16] Letters in parentheses refer to paragraph numbers in section III.B.2 in which the statements are located.

3. Use of texts out of context in apologetics (vs. Jewish positions) and in theological disputes (f)

4. Use of the text of the Bible current in their own context rather than determination of the best text possible (g)

5. Frequent recourse to allegory (h) to avoid the scandal to which some texts give rise

6. Mixing of typological and allegorical interpretations in an inextricable way (i)

7. View that "any particular passage is open to any particular interpretation on an allegorical basis [sic]" (j)

Other Traits of Patristic Exegesis ("No comment")

1. Presentation of the *Logos* as author of the Old Testament and insistence that all Scripture has a christological meaning (e)

2. Nothing to be set aside as out of date or completely lacking meaning in the Bible (i)

3. View that other interpreters are free to offer any other interpretation, provided they respect the analogy of faith (j)

In general, reviewers of the *IBC* consider its treatment of patristic exegesis to be positive, yet appropriately critical of the Fathers' allegorical extremes. Thus Klauck is pleased with the Commission's "tribute" to the Fathers and credits it to a rediscovery of patristic exegesis that is taking place[17]. However, Basil Studer, a patristics scholar, complains that the *IBC*

---

[17] Klauck, "Das neue Dokument: Darstellung und Würdigung", 83. As recently as 1990 in the *NJBC*, Brown relegated interest in patristic exegesis to the past rather than the present discussion of interpretation (Brown and Schneiders, "Hermeneutics [*NJBC*]", §48). However, a steady stream of articles and books on patristic interpretation of Scripture support Klauck's view that a "rediscovery" is underway. See, for example, Studer's review of seven recent publications, "Neuerscheinungen zur Exegese der Kirchenväter" and the reviews of twelve other works on patristic exegesis in the same issue of *Theologische Revue* (93:2, 1997), pp. 95-116. In the English-speaking world older works on patristic exegesis are being translated and published (e.g., de Lubac, *Medieval Exegesis* and Simonetti, *Biblical Interpretation in the Early Church*). In addition, an American publisher has launched a twenty-seven volume patristic commentary on the entire Bible (six volumes have appeared so far) under the editorial direction of T.C. Oden and an international ecumenical team of scholars (the Ancient Christian Commentary on Scripture series, Intervarsity Press).

shows that Catholic exegetes have not yet taken note of the results of patristic research conducted over the last thirty years.[18] Specifically, Studer objects to the Commission's highlighting (critically) the Fathers' allegorical methods, and, presumably, failing to adequately express the positive features of patristic exegesis. As the foregoing analysis shows, this writer reads the Biblical Commission's attitude toward patristic interpretation more positively than Studer does[19].

---

[18] Studer, "Die patristische Exegese, eine Aktualisierung".

[19] Studer's article, written, he explains, before he saw the *IBC*, is a learned overview of patristic exegesis, which analyzes its distinctive characteristics sympathetically. It seems to this writer that on a number of points the *IBC* agrees with Studer: the Fathers' priority on pastoral actualization, the fact that their use of allegory cannot simply be reduced to hellenistic patterns, and the actualizing reading of the Bible in the liturgy. To these points Studer adds the origin of patristic models of interpretation in the teaching of Jesus and Paul, the differing characteristics of patristic interpretation in commentaries and homilies, the concern of the Fathers for the reality which the Scripture referred to over its literary presentation, and the way ancient education shaped the interpretation of the Fathers and their audiences.

CHAPTER 11

The Aim of Interpretation: To Explain Scripture's Religious Message

After the preceding chapters it should be clear that the goal of Catholic interpretation is to explain the religious meaning of Scripture. While it is true that any interpreter who works according to the principles of faith described above could hardly fail to explain the Bible's religious message, it is nevertheless useful to define exegesis' *raison d'être*, which can serve as a criterion by which its results are measured. Furthermore, there is considerable evidence of confusion about exegesis' purpose. Vanhoye observes,

> In the legitimate desire to be scientific there is a tendency among scholars to study the Bible without paying attention to its religious message, seeking only to clarify, for instance, the historical context or the stages of the formation of a text. The Biblical Commission was concerned about this situation. There exist enormous exegetical studies in which the religious content is practically absent. But the Bible is a collection of religious writings. If one does not explain the religious meaning of a biblical writing, one has not exegeted the text adequately[1].

Principle #11

The primary aim of Catholic exegesis is to explain the religious message of the Bible, i.e., its meaning as the word which God continues to address to the Church and to the entire world (IV.a,

---

[1] Vanhoye, "Catholicism and the Bible", 36.

III.C.1.b).   The ultimate purpose of Catholic exegesis is to nourish and build up the body of Christ with the word of God[2].

Explanation

Although the idea that exegesis' purpose is religious is assumed everywhere in the *IBC*, it is not expressed in this language[3]. Other words convey the same idea. For instance, in the Conclusion it states,

> Catholic exegesis should…maintain its identity as a *theological discipline*, the principal aim of which is the deepening of faith…. Its task is to fulfill, in the Church and in the world, a vital function, that of contributing to an ever more authentic transmission of the content of the inspired Scriptures. (Conclusion e, emphasis original)

Thus exegesis' principal aim is the *deepening of faith* by transmitting Scripture's *inspired content[4]*.

1.   Scripture's Religious Meaning

The logic behind this principle of Catholic interpretation is simple. The purpose of Scripture itself is to communicate a religious message. It follows that the goal of the exegesis of Scripture is to relay that same message. The Pope explains exegesis' task in these terms:

> Indeed, [the true meaning of the Scriptures] is inseparable from their goal, which is to put believers into a personal relationship with God. (Address 11)

> These texts have not been given to individual researchers "to satisfy their curiosity or provide them with subjects for study and research" (*Divino afflante Spiritu*: EB, n. 566); they have been entrusted to the community of believers, to the Church of Christ, in order to nourish faith and guide the life of charity. Respect for this purpose conditions the validity of the interpretation. (Address 10)

To explain the Bible's "religious message" means to uncover the meaning that Scripture has as the word of God, as a divine communication. One could refer to Scripture's religious message as its theological meaning,

---

[2] Some of the places where the *IBC* indicates that exegesis' purpose is to explain the Bible's religious meaning include the Introduction (B.b), Conclusion (e-f), II.A.2.a; III.B.3.h; III.C.b; III.D.2.a, and the Address of Pope John Paul II (1, 9, 10, 14).

[3] The *IBC* does refer to Scripture's "religious content" in III.D.2.a and its "religious message" in II.A.2.d.

[4] See Costacurta, "Esegesi e lettura credente" on this topic and other aspects of a hermeneutic of faith touched on in the *IBC*.

provided that theological meaning is understood broadly enough. Scripture's religious meaning includes everything it says about God's relationship with the human race: what it reveals about the Trinitarian God and his plan of salvation (doctrine); the guidance it offers for human life (wisdom and morals), the means it provides of encountering God (texts for worship, prayer and meditation). Exegesis, whose work is the study of Scripture, can only be the "soul of theology" (*DV* 24) if it "pays particular attention to the religious content of the biblical writings" (III.D.2.a).

An important dimension of the "religious message" of the Bible is that it is concerned with the present religious significance of the text for Christian faith. This must be distinguished from its original religious meaning to its author or first readers, even though that past meaning bears an essential relation to its religious meaning for Christian faith today. Exegesis properly begins with the study of a text in its original historical setting. But if it stops there, it has only done the preliminary historical spadework to its real task, to explain the religious significance of the text for Christian faith in the present. After describing the necessity of historical-critical study of a text, the Biblical Commission goes on to say,

> In their work of interpretation, Catholic exegetes must never forget that what they are interpreting is the Word of God. Their common task is not finished when they have simply determined sources, defined forms or explained literary procedures. They arrive at the true goal of their work only when they have explained the meaning of the biblical text as God's word for today. (III.C.1.b-c)

Because Scripture is the word of God for all time, its explanation cannot be limited to its meaning at a moment in the past[5].

A final distinguishing characteristic of the religious message of Scripture is that it is not subjective, reducible to whatever religious or spiritual or philosophical ideas someone might find in the Bible, or merely "religious" in a generic sense. Of course, interpreters beginning from diverse presuppositions are free to find meanings in the Bible that strike them as "religious". However, the religious meaning of the Bible which Catholic exegesis sets out to explain is what Scripture says as the foundational written expression of the Gospel, of Christian revelation. Just as the religious meaning of the Koran may be reasonably defined as its meaning to the Muslim tradition, and the religious meaning of the Veda to Hindu tradition, so

---

[5] Nevertheless, a distinction can be made between the role of the exegete and the role of the pastor or preacher in explaining the meaning of the text for the present. See "Actualization and Exegesis", p. 298ff.

the religious meaning of the Christian Bible is the meaning that corresponds to the religious tradition which produced and preserved it[6].

2. Pastoral Orientation of Exegesis in the Church

The ultimate purpose of Catholic exegesis is to nourish and build up the body of Christ with the word of God.

The Biblical Commission says that exegesis is both a work of scholarship and an ecclesial task (III.C.a).   However, it is important to understand the relationship between these two aspects. Exegesis is a work of scholarship *for the sake of* rendering an ecclesial service. The Biblical Commission is well aware of the tendency to lose the ordering of these two aspects, so in their conclusion to the *IBC* they offer a clear and balanced statement of the proper relationship between exegesis' scholarly character and its ultimate purpose:

> Catholic exegesis should avoid as much as possible this kind of professional bias [that of remaining "absorbed solely in the issues of sources"] and maintain its identity as a theological discipline, the principal aim of which is the deepening of faith. This does not mean a lesser involvement in scholarly research of the most rigorous kind, nor should it provide excuse for abuse of methodology out of apologetic concern. Each sector of research (textual criticism, linguistic study, literary analysis, etc.) has its own proper rules, which it ought follow with full autonomy. But no one of these specializations is an end in itself. *In the organization of the exegetical task as a whole, the orientation toward the principal goal should remain paramount* and thereby serve to obviate any waste of energy. Catholic exegesis does not have the right to become lost, like a stream of water, in the sands of a hypercritical analysis. *Its task is to fulfill, in the Church and in the world, a vital function, that of contributing to an ever more authentic transmission of the content of the inspired Scriptures.* (Conclusion e; emphasis added)

The *IBC* and other Church documents on Scripture associate exegesis with the pastoral role of feeding or nourishing.   This follows from the orientation of Scripture itself: "These texts…have been entrusted to the community of believers…in order to nourish faith and guide the life of

---

[6] This argument is more complicated in the case of the writings which Jews regard as the *Tanakh* and Christians as the Old Testament.   Both Jews and Christians identify with the religious heritage of Israel despite their parting of the ways in the first century over the identity of Jesus.   Christians interpret the Old Testament in light of the death and resurrection of Jesus and the New Testament, and Jews interpret the Hebrew Bible in the light of rabbinic tradition. Between these two interpretations there are both important shared perspectives and important differences.

charity" (Address 10). Words such as "nourish" and "build up" occur again and again in the *IBC*[7].

Discussion

3. Usefulness of the Principle

The only meaning which is the business of the Church, *qua* Church, is the Bible's religious meaning, the Bible as a divine communication.   The Church's interest in the Bible's contribution to history, literature or science in themselves is minor in comparison.   Even in the past when the Church attempted to defend the historical or scientific positions based on the Bible, biblical cosmology, for example, her underlying interest was to defend the truthfulness and reliability of the Bible's religious message.

Once the concept of the "religious message" of the Bible becomes clear, this principle becomes useful. In the face of the abundance and diversity of resources that confront the student of Scripture, it enables the reader to pose a simple discriminating question: What value does this article, book, course or commentary have for ascertaining the religious meaning of the Bible? Or, to phrase it differently, how does this resource help Christians understand God's word to them in Scripture?

This does not mean that all resources need directly explain the religious meaning. On the contrary, some books offering only historical background will be more useful for Catholics understanding God's word to them in Scripture than mountains of devotional or homiletic books. The question, however, invites the student of Scripture to seek the connection between the resource and interpretation's aim.

Posing the question about the relevance of a resource to Scripture's religious meaning not only helps to evaluate materials, it can help all who study or teach Scripture to keep the end in view. Without keeping an eye on the goal, everyone, not only exegetes, runs the risk of becoming lost "in the sands of hypercritical analysis" (Conclusion e), of being confused before a panoply of approaches, or of drowning in the vast ocean of literature about the Bible. Rather, bearing in mind Scripture's religious purpose reminds readers always to query their methods, their commentaries, their teachers and themselves, what is the religious meaning? How is this text the word of God?

---

[7] For instance, we read that the aim of interpretation is "spiritual nourishment" for the people of God so that Scripture may be "the source for them of a life of faith hope and of love" (Intro B.b); that a hermeneutic theory is needed "so that the Christian life of faith may find nourishment" (II.A.2.a); and that the Church esteems exegetes for "building up the body of Christ" through their expertise (III.B.3.h).

4. Exegesis in the Academy

Undoubtedly, the most significant contemporary challenge to exegesis explaining Scripture's religious meaning and attaining its pastoral goal is its setting in the academy. Charles Conroy, commenting on the occasion of the centenary of the *Revue Biblique*, contrasted the social location of Old Testament studies today to what it was one hundred years ago. At that time, the Hebrew Scriptures were studied primarily within the religious contexts of Christian or Jewish institutions of sacred learning. Today these studies are vigorously pursued in the faculties of secular universities. This change of setting has influenced the content of exegetical studies.

> This may help to explain why many exegetical writings do not seem to be very theological in character. It is not that all exegetes are necessarily insensitive to theology; it is simply that they often write in the first place for their colleagues in the international, interconfessional, and inter-religious community of Old Testament scholars[8].

Not only does exegesis' social location affect what Christian scholars write, it has influenced the way they think about their task. Schneiders, writing about New Testament exegetes, comments, "Even among believing biblical scholars there are those who acknowledge the relationship between faith and the Bible but do not think that that relationship has any practical bearing on the scholarly task of exegeting the text"[9].

Scholars of various confessions have identified a few particular consequences of this state of affairs. Some have pointed out that the academy's exclusively literary and historical approach fails to do justice to the religious nature of the texts. Luke Timothy Johnson points out the inadequacy of a secular approach to a religious text:

> Members of a religious movement produced these compositions for other members of that movement. More than that, specifically religious experiences and convictions generated the writings. To read these

---

[8] Conroy, "Present State of Old Testament Studies", 598-599. Conroy is describing rather than criticizing this phenomenon. He accepts the fact of exegesis' social location and the consequence that this shifts the focus of discussion from Christian or Jewish theological concerns and requires that its discourse be subject to the same "rigorous intersubjective control" that other academic disciplines demand (p. 599). One may question, however, whether the situation that has developed is really healthy. While it is clear that academic exegesis should not limit itself to confessional in-house theological concerns, theological interest should not be marginalized and "intersubjective control" should not mean expecting a false neutrality about the Bible on the part of believing scholars.

[9] Schneiders, *Revelatory Text*, 12.

compositions in terms simply of the historical information they provide is to miss the most important and explicit information they offer the reader...[10].

The *IBC* makes the same argument: "Faith traditions formed the living context for the literary context of the authors of Scripture", and that has implications for valid interpretation (III.A.3.f-g).

Other scholars object to the academy's past and present practice of studying Scripture beginning from philosophically hostile presuppositions. According to Levenson, a "desacralization" of Scripture occurs in the biblical studies programs in universities and even seminaries when the historical-critical method of modern academic scholarship is granted exclusive authority[11]. Karl P. Donfried, speaking to an ecumenical conference of exegetes and theologians[12] concerned about the shift in the context in which Scripture is interpreted, outlines the problem this way:

> This social shift has...[resulted in] a new alliance with the academy in opposition to the classical expressions of the Christian faith. In the name of history, which often is a pretense for an ideological theology, classical and normative expressions of Christian theology are frequently attacked[13].

The *IBC* for its part stresses the necessity of excluding presuppositions incompatible with Scripture's religious message, although in regard to the historical-critical method, it regards problematic presuppositions as distinct from the method itself, and as a past rather than a present problem (Intro A.b, I.A.4.b, I.A.4.e)[14].

Others have noted negative pastoral consequences to exegesis' setting in the academy. The problem received classic expression in 1975 in F. Dreyfus' "Exégèse en Sorbonne, exégèse en église"[15]. According to Dreyfus, pastors and faithful were finding that scholarly exegesis was not helping them to hear and live the word of God found in Scripture. Rather than opening the path to Scripture, it erected barriers to ordinary believers being able to understand it. Academic exegesis sought an archaeological knowledge of the historical and

---

[10] Johnson, "Academy vs. the Gospels", 13.

[11] Blowers, Levenson and Wilken, "Three Views", 42. See also Levenson, "Unexamined Commitments of Criticism", and *The Hebrew Bible, the Old Testament*, 106-126.

[12] The conference resulted in a book, Braaten, *Reclaiming the Bible for the Church*. Contributors include Brevard S. Childs, Karl P. Donfried, Roy A. Harrisville, Alister E. McGrath, Robert W. Jenson, Thomas Hopko, Elizabeth Achtemeier, and Aidan Kavanaugh.

[13] Donfried, "Alien Hermeneutics", 19.

[14] See the discussion regarding principle #15 on the historical-critical method.

[15] Dreyfus, "Exégèse en Sorbonne". This article was published in Italian in 1992 in a collection of articles by Dreyfus and Refoulé with a preface by Vanhoye (Refoulé and Dreyfus, *Quale esegesi oggi?*). These articles anticipate many of the conclusions of the Biblical Commission.

cultural roots of Scripture and was unable to bring the Bible's meaning into the present. It set narrow limits to the meaning of Scripture, rejecting the plurality of meaning which traditionally enabled believers to apply Scripture to their lives. It functioned as a literary discipline according to the canons of contemporary research, rather than as a service in the Church aiming at leading the faithful toward salvation[16].

An orientation toward the academy, whose presuppositions and interests differ from those of the Church, influences how Catholic exegetes teach Scripture. Here the evidence is only anecdotal, but significant nevertheless. During the course of his studies over the last ten years, this writer has had the opportunity to ask students from Catholic seminaries and universities in many places about their Scripture courses. Although there are some impressive exceptions, he has found that—except for individuals who take a special interest in history, literature or languages—the general experience is disappointment with Scripture courses. Most students approach Scripture courses with an interest in learning about God from the book which they regard as the primary written testimony to revelation. They often leave with their thirst unquenched by an approach which studies Scripture "just like any other ancient writing". Students need to learn about the human dimensions of the text, but their desire to understand the divine dimension of the text must not be mistaken for fundamentalism.

Sometimes the problem is an academic professionalism, especially in introductory courses. Sr. Macrina Scott, OSF, director of the highly successful Biblical School of the Archdiocese of Denver explained why she normally avoids hiring instructors with doctoral degrees:

> Our experience shows that devoting their energies to the scholarly issues currently being debated interferes with a scholar's ability to help ordinary people relate Scripture to their lives, especially in the first few years after getting their doctorates. Though some scholars communicate about the Bible with ordinary people exceptionally well, for many who get their doctorates, it's hard to come back...[17].

It is obvious that a variety of problems have been associated with exegesis' location in the academy, and the Biblical Commission attempts to

---

[16] Curtin provides a useful summary in English of Dreyfus' article ("Historical Criticism and Theological Interpretation", 177-182; see also Simian-Yofre, "Esegesi, Fede e Teologia", 9-14).

[17] Williamson, "Actualization: A New Emphasis", 19.

respond to many of them[18]. But is the Biblical Commission's response adequate? Levenson doubts that it is:

> The fact remains, however, that unless the Catholic Church (re)ghettoizes itself, as I think to be logistically impossible, its exegetes will continue to be integral members of communities of interpretation that are religiously diverse and whose *lingua franca* has long been historicism and naturalism.... Means will have to be found to prosecute biblical scholarship on genuinely public grounds—that is , on grounds that are pluralistic and not simply historicistic and naturalistic. How this can be done is an issue as vexing as it is pressing and one on which the Commission offers no help. A schizoid solution—the Catholic exegete as Catholic in church but historicist in the academy—will not effectively redress the recession of the divine dimension of the text...[19].

Asked to respond to Levenson, Vanhoye agreed on the importance of finding a way to pursue biblical scholarship in a pluralistic setting without succumbing to "historicism and naturalism", and said that the Commission was not able to take up the question of Catholic exegesis' participation in the academy[20]. When asked whether exegesis in the Church and the academy ought to be conducted on different bases, Vanhoye again agreed with Levenson that the two ought not be separated. Catholic exegesis must retain its pre-understanding of faith in the academy and its scholarly rigor in the Church as it seeks to explain the meaning of the biblical texts. The extremes to avoid seem to be ghettoization, on the one hand—i.e., carrying out Catholic biblical interpretation in its own world according to Catholic principles—and, on the other hand, assimilation—allowing Catholic interpretation to lose its religious character and pastoral orientation in order to fit into the discourse of the secular academy.

The two extremes could be viewed as analogous to two periods of Catholic Scripture scholarship in this century, before and after Pope Pius XII's *Divino afflante Spiritu*[21]. Before *Divino afflante Spiritu* Catholic

---

[18] See principle #15 on the historical-critical method for some of the ways the *IBC* has attempted to respond to criticisms of contemporary exegesis.

[19] Blowers, Levenson and Wilken, "Three Views", 42. The specific concerns Levenson mentions here are the problematic presuppositions of historicism and naturalism. However, desacralization of the text in the academy also occurs when aesthetic, ideological or political interests dominate at the expense of the essentially religious message of the text.

[20] Vanhoye, "Catholicism and the Bible", 36.

[21] See Johnson, "What's Catholic About It?" for a periodization like this. In 1981 Brown divided the twentieth century in three periods in regard to its acceptance of critical methods: 1900-1940 was characterized by the rejection of modern biblical criticism out of fear of its consequences for doctrine; 1940 until the end of Vatican II saw "the introduction of biblical criticism and the gradual but reluctant acceptance of its initial results"; and 1970-2000

Church authorities mistrusted scientific biblical criticism and rejected many of its conclusions. Even up until the Second Vatican Council, some excellent and loyal Catholic exegetes were silenced on account of their critical exegetical work. The result was that apart from a few exceptional individuals, Catholic biblical scholarship remained isolated from the wider world of academic biblical study and stagnated. After the Council there was an understandable desire for Catholic scholars to "catch up" in the use of modern methods and to end their isolation from the broader world of biblical scholarship. The result was a tendency for Catholic exegesis to downplay Catholic hermeneutical distinctives and to participate in the broader exegetical enterprise, often exclusively at the level of results obtainable from shared scientific methods[22].

How much does Catholic exegesis today aim at explaining the religious meaning of Sacred Scripture? If one considers the content of commentaries by Catholic scholars, or of Catholic contributions to journals or biblical association meetings, one sees both some excellent contributions and ample room for improvement[23]. In many issues of Catholic exegetical journals, for instance, a relatively small percentage of the articles explain the religious message of a text or relate exegetical content to theology, worship, or Christian life[24]. This is not to say that every article in exegetical journals

---

"involved the painful assimilation of those implications for Catholic doctrine, theology, and practice" (*Critical Meaning*, ix). In hindsight it appears that Brown's expectations for the third period were overly optimistic. It appears instead that an intermediate stage of Catholic acquisition of critical methods needed to take place before Catholic doctrine, theology and practice could assimilate those methods in the life of the Church. It may be hoped that the first part of the twenty-first century will see that integration.

[22] Johnson comments, "Indeed, the indistinguishability of Catholic scholarship has been a matter of some pride as pioneering figures moved from the margins to the heart of academic respectability..." ("What's Catholic About It?", 12).

[23] Gilbert sees a more theological exegesis as the direction of the future: "Although historical and literary analysis of biblical texts has become necessary and indeed indispensable, such work is seen less and less as the last word of exegesis for today. If the exegete is not able to show how his technical analyses throw real light on the actual message of the Scriptures—which, when all is said and done, belongs to the theological and even theologal order—he disappoints his readers and listeners, who expect much more from him" (Gilbert, "New Horizons and Present Needs", 336).

[24] To test this impression, this writer examined seven issues of the *Catholic Biblical Quarterly*, dating from July 1998 through January 2000, to determine how many articles "explain the religious message of a text or relate exegetical content to theology, worship or Christian life". He found that only 11 of the 44 articles published during this period met this criterion. (Readers who wish to see how this criterion was applied may do so. Below are the names of the authors whose articles considered a text's religious message: Volume 60—

should have direct religious relevance—it is fitting that a certain percentage of articles should address historical, literary or methodological questions that serve the interpretive enterprise. But unless Catholic exegesis normally explains or somehow relates its findings to the text's religious message it cannot avoid giving credence to the notion that exegesis is irrelevant to Christian faith and life[25]. Put more positively, the principle regarding exegesis' religious aim (principle #11) invites Catholic exegetes to serve as salt and light in the world of academic biblical scholarship.

Often what has been lacking is a bridge between scholarly reflection on biblical interpretation and the life of faith. In the *IBC* the Biblical Commission sought to provide such a bridge, but they are not the only ones. Many believing exegetes have been arriving at the conclusion that exegesis is inadequate when it confines its attention to scientific methods and an examination of biblical writings in their human dimensions. This realization coincides with deeper hermeneutical awareness in the academy that challenges the possibility of purely neutral "objective" interpretation, and which invites open consideration of the exegete's commitments and pre-understanding.

In recent years several substantial works by exegetes and theologians have sought to relate scholarly exegesis to Scripture's religious message. Schneiders' *The Revelatory Text* presents a hermeneutic model that she believes enables Scripture to be approached as the word of God and read for personal transformation. At the same time she insists that faith must play an explicit part in the public sphere of academic discourse, and that for the Christian interpreter, faith is not a detachable accessory that can be checked at the door[26]. Some authors, notably Sean E. McEvenue and Ben F. Meyer, have

---

Michaels, Giblin, Dillon; Volume 61—Carpinelli, Longenecker, van der Watt, McIlraith, Goldingay, Wagner; Volume 62—Gagnon, Plevnik.)

[25] It is the author's impression that the gap between exegesis and the religious meaning of Scripture among Catholics is most pronounced in North American scholarship. Paging through recent volumes of *New Testament Abstracts*, he finds that proportionately much more attention is given to theological and religious implications of texts in French, Italian, Spanish, Portuguese, Polish and even German language scholarly biblical publications.

[26] Schneiders, *Revelatory Text*, xxxiv-xxxviii, 121-122. In the course of her remarks, Schneiders names inerrancy as an example of "faith presupposition or dogmatic affirmations" excluded by the need to speak a public language in the academic forum. At the same time she maintains that "faith as an existential coordinate of life and as a tradition involving truth claims can be represented in the public forum in non-distorting and non-oppressive ways.... The biblical interpreter needs and has a right to the explicit functioning of her or his faith in the task of interpretation" (xxxvii). These views are inconsistent. It is clear that Schneiders regards her belief in Jesus and her feminist commitment as belonging to the category of "faith as an existential coordinate of life and as a tradition involving truth claims that can be represented in

sought to overcome the philosophical challenges to interpretation by following Bernard Lonergan's insights in what they call "critical realist hermeneutics"[27]. Stephen Fowl's *Engaging Scripture* seeks to return biblical interpretation to the service of the Christian community by advocating a theological interpretation controlled by its interpretive interest, namely, an "ever deeper communion with the triune God and with each other"[28]. Kevin J. Vanhoozer tackles the challenge to Christian interpretation raised by deconstruction in *Is There Meaning in This Text?*[29]. In a quest for the application of *fides quaerens intellectum* to hermeneutics, Vanhoozer offers a new account of the author's intention and literal sense, and calls for Christian interpretation which communicates the meaning *and* significance of the text. Francis Watson and Werner Jeanrond, from their respective perspectives as exegete and systematic theologian, argue for theological interpretation of Scripture[30]. Finally, from a perspective which is at once Orthodox and fully aware of the critical issues, Theodore G. Stylianopoulos offers a hermeneutic that unites critical scholarship and faith in a transformational model of interpretation[31]. Although all these works differ among themselves in various ways, and although none can be said to offer a definitive solution, their existence is a sign of hope to those who desire to see a scholarly exegesis which explains Scripture's religious message.

It is not entirely clear how the secular academy will respond to more scholars whose exegesis explicitly reflects a pre-understanding rooted in Christian faith, who concern themselves with the religious meaning of the text, and whose ultimate interest is the pastoral application of Scripture to life.

---

the public forum...". Schneiders' confuses the legitimacy of interpreting from the perspective of one's pre-understanding of faith, social location and ideological commitments, with the futility of grounding arguments on beliefs or values which one's dialogue partners do not share. In interpreting Scripture in the public forum Schneiders is in the same position as the inerrantist. She may choose either to explain her perspective to an interlocutor who does not share it but is willing to make the effort to understand her interpretation of a text, or she may bracket her Christian or feminist presuppositions to attempt to persuade her interlocutor of her interpretation on the basis of presuppositions they do share.

[27] See McEvenue and Meyer, *Lonergan's Hermeneutics*; McEvenue, *Truth in Literature*; and Meyer, *Reality and Illusion*. For a brief introduction to critical realist hermeneutics, see Montague, *Understanding the Bible*, 152-158.

[28] See Fowl, *Engaging Scripture*, vii. Fowl's attitude toward the pursuit of objective meaning as that is commonly conceived in the academy, however, is distinctly cool. For a critical evaluation of Fowl, see Vanhoozer, "Realism, Reading and Reformation", 26-28.

[29] Vanhoozer, *Is There a Meaning?*

[30] Jeanrond, *Text and Interpretation* and "After Hermeneutics"; and Watson, *Text, Church and World*.

[31] Stylianopoulos, *New Testament: An Orthodox Perspective*.

There remain heirs to the Enlightenment who want their believing colleagues to keep their faith out of interpreting the Bible and who wish to strictly exclude theology from the exegetical enterprise. Philip R. Davies advocates this view in *Whose Bible Is It Anyway?*[32]. Other scholars of a post-modern mentality welcome all pre-understandings and all interpretations, but at the expense of refusing the possibility of objective truth to any of them. Nevertheless, one may hope that the academic community as a whole will consider on their merits works of scholarship explicitly reflecting various Christian, Jewish, and non-believing pre-understandings in an openminded search for the truth about the meaning of the Bible.

Whatever the response in the academy, it is important that Catholic exegetes find ways of doing exegesis in a manner that reflects their faith and that fulfills the Church's vital need for interpretation of the Bible that explains its religious message.

---

[32] Davies, *Whose Bible?*   Watson offers a persuasive response in Watson, "Bible, Theology and the University".

PART IV

THE MEANING OF INSPIRED SCRIPTURE

Ancient exegesis recognized more than one level of meaning in Sacred Scripture. Among the Fathers of the Church, the distinction between the literal and the spiritual senses was the most common. Medieval exegesis accepted Cassian's four-fold sense of Scripture, the literal (or historical), the allegorical, the moral (or tropological), and the anagogical. The last three were recognized as spiritual senses. Historical criticism reacted to this exegesis which sometimes seemed arbitrary or subjective. The classic historical-critical method admitted the possibility of only a single meaning, that of the author's intention present within the circumstances which produced the text.

According to the Biblical Commission, the thesis of only one meaning has "run aground" (II.B.c) on developments both in philosophical hermeneutics and in theories of language. The Commission insists on the presence of a wealth of meaning, affirming the existence of two primary senses of inspired Scripture, the literal and the spiritual sense. A third sense of Scripture, the fuller sense, is categorized as a particular sub-type of the spiritual sense.

CHAPTER 12

The Literal Sense

Principle #12

The literal sense of Scripture is that which has been expressed directly by the inspired human authors. Since it is the fruit of inspiration, this sense is also intended by God, as principal author. One arrives at this sense by means of a careful analysis of the text, within its literary and historical context (II.B.1.c).

The literal meanings of many texts possess a dynamic aspect that enables them to be re-read later in new circumstances (II.B.1.e) [1].

Explanation

Principle #12, which defines the literal sense of Scripture, is one of the most important of Catholic principles of interpretation. The *IBC* says that the principal task of exegesis is discovering the literal sense of the text (II.B.1.c), so it is not surprising that the Pontifical Biblical Commission's definition is worded with care. Despite, or perhaps, on account of this care, the *IBC*'s discussion of the literal sense leaves a number of questions unanswered. The exposition that follows will explain what the Biblical Commission says about the literal sense and point out some of the unanswered questions.

---

[1] The definition which constitutes this principle of Catholic interpretation is a direct quote from the *IBC* (II.B.1.c). Most of what the document says about the literal meaning of Scripture is found in the first part of section II.B entitled, "The Meaning of Inspired Scripture." In addition brief references to the literal sense are found in section I.A on the Historical-Critical Method and in section III.C on "The Role of the Exegete".

1. Definition

The literal sense of Scripture is that which has been expressed directly by the inspired human authors.

✳ The Biblical Commission defines the literal sense of Scripture as the meaning "which has been expressed directly by the inspired human authors"(II.B.1.c).

The focus of the literal sense is the meaning of the *human authors*, not a meaning unknown to them because it was in God's mind, nor a meaning unknown to them because subsequent human interpreters would read it into their writings. These may indeed be viewed as meanings of Scripture (and the former constitutes the "fuller sense") but they do not conform to the literal sense of Scripture as the *IBC* defines it.

The phrase "which has been expressed" stresses that the meaning of these human authors is to be sought in the words of the text, rather than in anything that may stand "behind" or "in front of" what has been written down.

According to Fitzmyer, the word "directly" is included in the definition to distinguish what the author(s) of the text said from a quotation of the words by a later scriptural author or as interpreted in a *sensus plenior* or canonical interpretation[2]. So for instance, the *literal* sense of Isa 7:14, "the *almah* will conceive," refers to the young woman in the seventh century BC who would shortly give birth, notwithstanding Matthew's quotation of this text in reference to the conception of Christ in Mt 1:23.

The *IBC* does not specify what it means by the "*inspired human authors*", and this does raise a question. The fact that critical study has shown some of the biblical writings to be compositions in which many individuals have had a hand raises the question, who are the inspired authors of the Bible? Are they Moses and the prophets in whose names the writings have been passed on to us, or are they the secretaries, chroniclers, and redactors through whose efforts we have received the writings in our possession[3]? Fitzmyer says that the "inspired human authors" of the Commission's definition refer to "the

---

[2] Fitzmyer, "Literal and Spiritual Senses", 135. According to Fitzmyer, Avery Dulles misinterprets "directly" in the definition of the literal sense to refer to the author's intention, "which was not in the minds of the members of the Commission: in fact, it was excluded" (p. 136n; Fitzmyer refers to Dulles, "A Theological Appraisal", 31).

[3] Traditionally the inspiration and authority of the Scriptures has often been explained on the basis that they were written by prophets and apostles. *Dei Verbum* 18 handles this problem regarding the Gospels by affirming they are of "apostolic origin," in that they originated with the apostles' preaching, but were handed on to us in written form by the apostles and "apostolic men". Thus inspiration is attributed not only to the apostles, but to those who entrusted their message to writing who are seen as "apostolic" in some sense.

last one responsible for the final form of the words in a given statement or story"[4]. He attributes no special "apostolic" or "prophetic" quality to these individuals: they are "the inspired human authors," whoever they may have been, because they wrote what Christians recognize as the inspired Scriptures.

2. *Authorial Intention*

What is striking about this definition of the literal sense is that there is no explicit reference to the intention of the human author. As recently as 1990, Raymond Brown, writing in the *New Jerome Biblical Commentary* (*NJBC*), described most exegetes as understanding the literal sense to be "The sense which the human author directly *intended* and which the written words conveyed [emphasis added]"[5]. Since the *IBC*'s publication several Commission members have explicitly contrasted its definition of the literal sense with this earlier scholarly definition[6]. Fitzmyer explains what the shift means:

> This [definition of the *IBC*] may seem at first sight to be as comprehensive as what Pius XII means when he stated that the foremost endeavor of the Catholic exegete was to "define clearly that sense of the biblical words which is called literal...so that the mind of the author may be made abundantly clear" (§23). More recent hermeneutical studies, however, have made it clear that the authorial intention of a text is not always so apparent. Hence the Commission does not state that the literal sense is that which has been *intended* by the inspired human author; it is rather that which has been *expressed* by him. Some of his intention may be gauged by what he has expressed, but that scarcely leads to a full manifestation of his intention, especially when one is dealing with such ancient texts as those in the Old and New Testament, written in languages of long ago [emphasis original][7].

Nevertheless, the omission of explicit reference to the author's intention does not signal a radical change in the definition of the literal sense. According to

---

[4] Fitzmyer, "Literal and Spiritual Senses", 135.

[5] Brown and Schneiders, "Hermeneutics [*NJBC*]", 1148, §9.

[6] Dumais, "Sens de l'Écriture", 311; Fitzmyer, "Literal and Spiritual Senses", 35; and Levoratti, "How to Interpret", 22.

[7] Fitzmyer, *The Biblical Commission's Document*, 120-121. The citation from Pius XII may be found in *EB* §550 (*DAS* 23). Fitzmyer treats this point at greater length in two articles ("Senses of Scripture" and "Literal and Spiritual Senses"). While agreeing that there are problems with determining the author's intention which merit this reformulation of the definition of the literal sense, Fitzmyer does not accept the notion that authorial intention is a fallacy and holds that an autonomous meaning for the text in relation to its author is problematic from a theological point of view. The Bible's status as the primary source for divine revelation "demands that there be a basic homogeneity between what it meant and what it means" ("Literal and Spiritual Senses", 138).

Fitzmyer, the Commission's definition "seemed to convey sufficiently what has always been meant by the definition of the literal sense"[8]. Commission member Ruppert confirms that the Commission still has the author's intention in mind[9]. These explanations make clear that the *IBC* does not redefine the literal sense as textual meaning, i.e., the meaning of the words without regard to the human authors who wrote with the intention of communicating something. Vignolo describes the new definition of the literal sense not as an elimination of the traditional doctrine of *intentio auctoris*, but a better formulation of it as an *expressio auctoris*, thus freeing the literal sense from intellectual or psychological speculation about the author[10].

The Biblical Commission goes on to affirm that the literal sense—that which the author has expressed—corresponds to the divine intention:

> *Since it is the fruit of inspiration, this sense is also intended by God, as principal author (II.B.1.c).*

The logic of this statement (a direct quotation from the *IBC*) is beyond doubt—what is inspired by God must be willed by him. This is not an exclusive prerogative of the literal sense; the point is that the literal sense is no less intended by God than the spiritual or fuller senses. Vignolo makes an interesting observation about the Biblical Commission's retreat from speaking

---

[8] Fitzmyer, "Literal and Spiritual Senses", 137. Fitzmyer's reference to what has "always been meant" by the literal sense fails to do justice to the immense changes this concept has undergone (see the "Discussion" section of this chapter). Presumably what Fitzmyer means is that the Commission's definition of the literal sense does not differ substantially from the definition of Pius XII in *DAS*, and from a definition that is widely accepted in critical scholarship today.

[9] "The PBC understands the literal sense in dependence on the encyclical of Pius XII, as that meaning which the human author intended" (Ruppert, "Kommentierende Einführung", 41). Ruppert adds that when a biblical text presents itself in the form of redacted material, the question of authorial intention arises in a new form. Ruppert says that he and a minority of the Commission maintain that the charism of inspiration and the literal sense should be considered to belong to the biblical text itself, rather than to the intention of an inspired author. The Commission did not attempt to reach a decision on this matter. Nevertheless, a tendency may be noted. While a continued affirmation of the inspiration of biblical authors can be expected, scientific exegesis, with its awareness of the complex redactional processes which produced the biblical texts, may lead to a greater stress on the inspiration and meaning of the text itself, independent of the historical circumstances of who wrote and under what circumstances. It is natural and reasonable for interest and emphasis to shift from the process of biblical composition, which on account of our limited data often remains unknowable or uncertain, to the product which we tranquilly possess, the biblical text itself.

[10] The new formulation integrates the literal sense "within a wider conception of the text as objective communication of meanings not all of which are necessarily, always, and completely tied to the conscious awareness" of the author (Vignolo, "Questioni di ermeneutica [*Commento*]", 282-283).

about the human author's intention and its strong affirmation regarding the divine authorial intention: "The center of gravity of the doctrine of inspiration, which traditionally has led to investigating the subjectivity of the sacred writer in order to reconstruct the mental act of producing the text, shifts rather to the literary product, the text itself"[11].

3. Determination of the Literal Sense

How does one derive the literal sense of a given text? "One arrives at this sense by means of a careful analysis of the text, within its literary and historical context" (II.B.1.c). Following *Divino afflante Spiritu* (EB §550, 560), the Biblical Commission affirms, "The principal task of exegesis is to carry out this analysis, making use of all the resources of literary and historical research.... To this end, the study of ancient literary genres is particularly necessary" (II.B.1.c). So the text itself is the object of careful study, and literary and historical sciences provide the tools for this task. It may be noted that the consultation of other theological sources does not play a role in the determining the literal sense.

However, *determining the "literary and historical context"* of a text sounds simpler than it is, especially in the case of books that seem have undergone considerable editing over the centuries. What is the proper literary and historical context in which a text from Isaiah should be interpreted? Many scholars hold that Isaiah consists of three (or four) distinct units, composed over two or three centuries in vastly different historical circumstances, and that it achieved its final form a century or two later still. Obviously, one can reap benefits by considering a text from Isaiah in light of all its literary and historical contexts. But to determine *the* literal sense, should one determine a text's meaning in the light of the whole book of Isaiah, or in the light of Second Isaiah, for example? Although the *IBC* does not address this specifically in its discussion of the literal sense, it would appear that the final form of the biblical book (principle #1), rather than a critically reconstructed Second Isaiah, provides the proper *literary* context for determining the literal sense of a text[12].

The *historical context* in which the literal sense should be determined is also challenging. Should the literal sense of a text from First Isaiah which

---

[11] Vignolo, "Questioni di ermeneutica [*Commento*]", 283.

[12] Raymond Brown maintains that the final form of a biblical book (he mentions Isaiah, in particular) provides the proper context for determining the literal sense of a text (*Critical Meaning*, 30, text and footnote). Interestingly, the *NJBC* takes the opposite route, offering separate commentaries on First and Second Isaiah which interpret texts in light of the respective probable historical contexts.

has undergone significant redaction be determined in light of the original historical context, the historical circumstance of its modifications during the Babylonian exile, or in the circumstances of its final redaction a century or two later? To be consistent with privileging the final form of a biblical book, it might seem that the historical circumstances of the final redaction would provide the most unified view of the meaning of its parts. On the other hand, the biblical text provides much less information about the historical setting of final editing than it does about the events the text records. However, the Biblical Commission does not discuss this problem.

4. Literal Sense and Literalistic Interpretation

The Biblical Commission takes care to distinguish the literal sense from literalistic interpretation of Scripture sometimes called "literal". Two kinds of literalism are noted. First, the term, "literal sense", has sometimes designated the meaning of the words themselves without interpretation of metaphors employed by the author (e.g., thus Origen and many patristic and medieval authors before Aquinas). However, the *IBC* points out that the literal and inspired sense of Luke 12:35, "Let your loins be girt", should not be understood to be, "Put your belt on", but, "Get ready for action" (II.B.1.b). The second kind of literalism which the *IBC* rejects is that which takes everything in the past tense as history, and was earlier mentioned as characteristic of fundamentalism (I.F.e). According to the *IBC*, "When it is a question of a story, the literal sense does not necessarily imply belief that the facts recounted actually took place, for a story need not belong to the genre of history but be instead [sic] a work of imaginative fiction" (II.B.1.b).

5. Plural Meanings

The Biblical Commission offers further clarifications of the literal sense. A text can have more than one literal sense for two reasons. First, sometimes a human author intends to refer to more than one level of reality at the same time. This is especially true in poetry, but also in other kinds of writing especially when symbolism or irony is employed. The *IBC* mentions the Fourth Gospel, and Fitzmyer lists a few good examples: "the meaning of a;nwqen in John 3:3,4,7; of 'living water' in 4:10-14; of going up' in 7:8"[13].

Second, divine inspiration can cause a human utterance with only one intended meaning to have another meaning. The Commission cites an example it acknowledges as "extreme": When the high priest Caiaphas says in John 11:50 that, "It is expedient for you that one man should die for the

---

[13] Fitzmyer, *The Biblical Commission's Document*, 122n.

people, and that the whole nation should not perish", he is advocating Jesus' execution. But the Evangelist informs us, that, at the same time, God was speaking through Caiaphas about his redemptive plan. Both meanings to Caiaphas' words are literal senses, because they are both made clear by the context, in this case, by the direct explanation of the evangelist[14].

6. "Dynamic Aspect"

The literal meanings of many texts possess a dynamic aspect that enables them to be re-read later in new circumstances (II.B.1.e).

Perhaps the most interesting and significant insight into the meaning of the literal sense offered by the Biblical Commission is what it calls the *"dynamic aspect"* of the literal meaning of many texts. By this the Commission refers to a "direction of thought"[15], or potential extension of meaning ("more or less foreseeable") present in some texts (II.B.1.e). This "dynamic aspect" provides the capacity for these texts to be re-read later in new circumstances. Commission member Brendan Byrne uses the analogy of a flashlight beam, which is conical in shape and becomes wider the farther it shines from its point of origin[16].

The Commission illustrates the dynamic aspect with the example of the royal psalms: "In speaking of the king, the psalmist evokes at one and the same time both the institution as it actually was and an idealized vision of kingship as God intended it to be" (II.B.1.e). Psalm 72, a prayer for the king, provides a good example (not given in the *IBC*). The words of the psalmist, while written for the king of his own time, express the longing that Israel's king be always triumphant over oppressors, the just defender of the poor and needy, and that his reign be universal and endure for ever. The ability to be re-read in new contexts and to take on new meanings belongs perhaps to all written texts, as Gadamer and especially Ricoeur have stressed. Yet this is especially true of biblical texts recognized as the word of God, which were preserved and collected precisely on account of the belief that they would speak to future generations. This dynamic aspect, this openendedness, is an extremely important characteristic of the literal sense, because it provides the opening which all re-readings, including the spiritual sense, make use of.

---

[14] According to Vanhoye, the purpose of the example was merely to illustrate how distinct the meaning on the human and divine levels can be. Even words of human malice can be directed by God to have another meaning. In fact, all the human actions that contributed to the passion had a malicious human intention, but a salvific divine intention (conversation with author, 22 February 1999).

[15] This phrase comes directly from Ricoeur, e.g., *Interpretation Theory*, 92.

[16] Conversation with the author, 9 August 1999.

Is there a control on or limit to the "dynamic aspect" of texts? Yes. While insisting that the literal meaning of texts must not be limited by "tying [it] in too rigidly to precise historical circumstances" as historical-critical exegesis has tended to do (II.B.1.e), the Biblical Commission insists that one cannot "attribute to a biblical text whatever meaning we like, interpreting it in a wholly subjective way.... One must reject as inauthentic every interpretation *alien* to the meaning expressed by the human authors in their written text" (II.B.1.g, emphasis added). Thus, the "dynamic aspect" of the literal sense, its "direction of thought", the "extension" of its meaning, must remain homogeneous with what the human author expressed in the text. "To admit...alien meanings would be equivalent to cutting off the biblical message from its root, which is the Word of God in its historical communication..." (II.B.1.g).

Having said this, it must be acknowledged that in practice it may not always be easy to distinguish between an interpretation based on the "dynamic aspect" of the literal sense which follows the text's "line of thought, from an interpretation that is "alien" to what the human author expressed in the text".

Discussion

7. The History of the Literal Sense

The various ways in which the literal sense has been defined have shaped interpretation at least since the priority of the literal sense became widely accepted. Whenever the term "literal" or "spiritual" is used, it is necessary to know what the interpreter intends by the term, and under what other terms the interpreter categorizes other dimensions of scriptural meaning. Each combination of the senses represents a system, intending to express the fullness of Scriptural meaning. The meanings of the various senses of Scripture change in relation to one another. The significance of the Biblical Commission's definition of the literal sense emerges with greater clarity against the backdrop of the history of the senses[17].

---

[17] See Brown, *The Sensus Plenior*; Grant and Tracy, *Short History of Interpretation*; Grech, "Hermeneutics"; Montague, *Understanding the Bible*, 29-104; Prior, *Historical Critical Method in Catholic Exegesis*, 43-55, 174-182, 269-275; Rogerson and Jeanrond, "Interpretation, History of"; Smalley, *Study of the Bible in the Middle Ages*. In addition to these general accounts, the discussion between Childs and James Barr, as interpreted by Paul R. Noble, yields some important insights into the differences between Reformation and modern critical conceptions of the literal sense (Barr, "Jowett and the 'Original Meaning'", "Jowett and the Reading of the Bible" and "The Literal, the Allegorical, and Scholarship"; Childs, "The *Sensus Literalis*" and "Critical Reflections"; Noble, "The *Sensus Literalis*"). Also, see Tábet,

a) Patristic and Medieval Interpretation

Origen (185-253) was the first to speak of the senses of Scripture. He identifies three levels of understanding Scripture—the literal, moral, and spiritual—which correspond to the Pauline tri-partite division of man as body, soul and spirit (1 Thess 5:23). For Origen the literal sense was the most superficial, an understanding confined to the "letter" of what was written. The literal sense included the narration of events or the plain meaning of the words of Scripture, for instance, the verbal meaning of the law or of the instructions of Paul. Like many other patristic and medieval interpreters, Origen did not include the metaphorical sense in his understanding of the literal meaning. Therefore, the literal sense of Jesus' parables were the stories themselves; the interpretation of the parables belonged to the spiritual or allegorical sense. Origen considered the literal sense to be the sense accessible to uninstructed Christians or to human reason alone. He found it inadequate because by itself it fails to reveal the unity of the Old Testament and New Testament, because it contains contradictions to common sense and reason, and because it portrays some Old Testament heroes and God himself acting in ways which are morally objectionable. The literal sense alone fails to present a coherent picture of the Christian mystery, which Origen instead found revealed at a deeper level. The true meaning of Scripture was the spiritual or mystical meaning, which required Christian faith, prayer, and the help of the Spirit to penetrate. Like St. Paul in Gal 4:24, Origen used allegory to explain Scripture's spiritual meaning.

The school of Antioch reacted to the allegorical interpretation of Origen and the Alexandrians for several reasons. Often allegorical interpretation was so excessive that it failed to render the meaning of the biblical text, but instead read into it whatever it pleased. Furthermore, gnostics used allegorical interpretation to attribute only symbolic meaning to biblical events which orthodox Christianity considered foundational history. So Diodore of Tarsus (c. 330-390), St. Chrysostom (c. 347-407), Theodore of Mopsuestia (c. 350-428) and Theodoret (c. 393-460) emphasized the literal sense and exercised caution in determining which Old Testament texts referred to Christ or the Christian dispensation. It must not be thought that the Antiochenes rejected typology or more-than-literal interpretation, since they clearly did not. They taught a kind of deeper understanding of biblical texts which they called *theoria*, which has been variously translated, "insight", "vision", or

---

"Il senso litterale e il senso spirituale" for a history of the senses in documents of the magisterium.

"contemplation"[18]. Yet they were more circumspect in their assertions about deeper meanings and, above all, insisted that the spiritual meanings of *theoria* be grounded in and related to the literal sense. The Antiochenes also began to incorporate the notion of the author's intention into their understanding of the literal sense.

Augustine (354-430) did not have a consistent manner of referring to the senses of Scripture, but he did show more concern than Origen, for instance, that the interpreter seek to discover the author's intention[19]. According to Henry Chadwick, "He is normally content with two—literal-'carnal'-historical and allegorical-mystical-spiritual"[20]. In *On Genesis* Augustine describes four kinds of objective meaning in biblical texts: the eternal realities, the facts narrated, future realities, and what we are commanded or warned[21]. These four, redefined by Cassian as the allegorical, literal, anagogical and moral, became the paradigm for medieval interpretation. It is important to note that the sense called "literal" usually did not refer to the author's intention—which in Augustine, might be reflected in any of the four kinds of meaning depending on the text—but instead to facts which are narrated. Indeed, it was often called the *sensus historicus*, the historical sense. Thus in the 13th century when Augustine of Denmark coined his famous couplet,

> *Littera gesta docet, quid credas allegoria,*
> *moralis quid agas, quid speres anagogia*[22],

---

[18] Montague (*Understanding the Bible*, 42), following J.N.D. Kelly, uses "insight"; Grech speaks of "vision" ("Hermeneutics", 418).

[19] "Whoever understands in Sacred Scriptures something other than *what the writer had in mind* is deceived, although he does not lie. Yet as I began to say, if he is deceived in an interpretation by which, however, he builds up charity (which is the end of the precept), he is deceived in the same way as is someone who leaves the road through error, but makes his way through the field to the place where the road also leads. Nevertheless, he must be corrected and must be shown how it is more advantageous not to leave the road, lest by a habit of deviating he may be drawn into a crossroads or even go the wrong way. By rashly asserting something *which the author did not intend*, he frequently runs into other passages which he cannot reconcile to that interpretation [emphasis added]" (Augustine, *De doctrina Christiana*, I.36-37; *PL* 34, 34-35; translated in *FOC* 4, 57-58; cited in Prior, *Historical Critical Method in Catholic Exegesis*, 49-50). Augustine is referring to the intention of the *human* author.

[20] Chadwick, "Augustine", 66. Chadwick adds, "One isolated text (*Util. Cred* 5-8) has a four-fold sense (historical, aetiological, analogical, allegorical)…".

[21] *On Genesis*, I, c.i, n.1 (*PL* xxxiv, 247), cited in Montague, *Understanding the Bible*, 50.

[22] "The letter teaches deeds; allegory, what you should believe; the moral sense, what you should do; and the anagogical sense, what to hope for."

the literal sense (*littera*) is confined to teaching *gesta*, events, i.e., what has been said and done.

b) Thomas Aquinas

A tendency to define the literal sense as what the author intended and to privilege this sense reached its authoritative expression in St. Thomas Aquinas[23]. Although he sometimes employs the traditional term "*sensus historicus*" (used interchangeably with *sensus litteralis*), the literal sense for St. Thomas no longer meant merely *gesta*, what was narrated, but the author's intention. Because it is the author's intention that counts, the things signified by metaphors and other figures of speech belong to the literal sense.

However, St. Thomas' view must not be confused with the modern critical notion of authorial intention, which concerns itself exclusively with the intention of the *human* author. In the same sentence in which Thomas affirms that "the literal sense is that which the author intends [*quem auctor intendit*]," he continues, "and the author of Holy Scripture is God who comprehends everything" (*ST* 1.q.1.a 10)[24]. Elsewhere Thomas refers to what the human author intended as the *sensus principalis* or *sensus proprius*[25]. It seems that Thomas did not attempt to distinguish the intentions of the divine and human authors, perhaps considering that divine inspiration caused the sacred writers to share in the mind of God regarding what they wrote in Scripture. The literal sense of a text was determined by determining its meaning in its immediate context and in the whole of Scripture (especially parallel passages). In the case of Old Testament texts[26] which subsequent events revealed referred to Christ, their christological meaning was understood as their literal sense, since that was the meaning which God, the author of Scripture, clearly intended.

---

[23] "The literal sense is what the author intends" (*ST* 1.q.1,a.10). Gregory the Great, Alexander Hales, and Albert the Great preceded Thomas Aquinas in this way of thinking. This thesis will give special attention to Thomas's view of the senses, not because the views he expressed originated with him, but because of the importance of Thomas' definitions in subsequent Christian tradition. For a fuller presentation of Thomas' approach to the senses, see Tábet, "Il senso litterale e il senso spirituale", 26-29.

[24] Aquinas, *Summa Theologica*, 39.

[25] See IV *Sent. dist.* 21, q.1, a.2,ql. 1 ad 3 and *Qdlb.* VII, q.y, a.14, obj.5. Differences existed among precritical interpreters of Scripture regarding the attention they devoted to understanding the biblical authors' historical circumstances and intention and Thomas was among those ancient interpreters who manifested a concern for the intention of the human authors.

[26] OT *types*, however, formed a separate category, the spiritual sense (see below).

In explaining the senses of Scripture St. Thomas distinguishes between signification by words (*voces*) and signification by the things (or realities, *res*) to which the words refer. The meaning of the words comprises the literal sense. The meaning of the "things"—events, persons, and objects—represented by the words of Scripture comprises the spiritual sense (and Thomas includes the allegorical, moral and anagogical meanings under this heading)[27]. These "things" (like the words of Scripture) convey meanings intended by God, who has the power of conveying meaning through things (including events), as well as words. For instance, Old Testament types—the flood and new beginning of the human race through Noah, the Passover sacrifice, the passage through the Red Sea, individuals who point to Christ such as Adam, Abel, Isaac, Moses, Solomon—illustrate Scripture's spiritual sense. The spiritual sense is based on and presupposes the literal (or historical) sense, since the "things" of Scripture are themselves communicated by means of words. St. Thomas insists that only the literal sense provides a legitimate basis for theological argument, "for nothing necessary for faith is contained under the spiritual sense that is not openly conveyed through the literal sense elsewhere" (ST 1,q.1,a 10 ad 1)[28].

c) The Reformation

The Reformers went further than Aquinas, rejecting the notion of a distinct spiritual or allegorical sense, and insisted on the exclusive authority of the literal sense (which they also referred to as the "simple" or "grammatical" sense). They particularly opposed "allegory"[29]. Calvin sought to gain access to the mind of the biblical writer (*mens auctoris*), by studying the original languages, the forms of expression, the historical circumstances and the literary context[30]. Nevertheless, their opposition to allegory did not mean that

---

[27] "Well then, the allegorical sense is brought into play when the things of the Old Law signify the things of the New Law; the moral sense when the things done in Christ and in those who prefigured him are signs of what we should carry out; and the anagogical sense when the things that lie ahead in eternal glory are signified" (*ST* I, q. 1, a. 10; translation from Aquinas, *Summa Theologica*, 39). Thomas uses the term "allegorical" here in a different sense that the *IBC* does when it alludes to the allegorical excesses of some of the Church Fathers (II.B.2.h).

[28] Aquinas, *Summa Theologica*, 39.

[29] Calvin is consistent in this position (Schwöbel, "Calvin", 98-100), while Luther shows considerable fluctuation. In some writings Luther follows the traditional four-fold interpretation, distinguishing between the "literal" and the "prophetic" senses (McGrath, "Luther", 414-415). Luther's position against the allegorical method hardened in time (Childs, "The *Sensus Literalis*"; Ramm, *Protestant Biblical Interpretation*).

[30] Schwöbel, "Calvin", 100. Before him, the school of St. Victor in Paris (Hugo, Richard, and Andrew of the Abbey at St. Victor) had already stressed the role of the liberal arts, history, and geography as necessary for literal exegesis.

the Reformers rejected typology or figural interpretation[31]. Rather, they considered the *literal* sense of Old Testament prophecies and types to embrace the meaning that the New Testament accords them in keeping with the principle, Scripture interprets Scripture. The Reformers held to an "organic theological unity"[32] of the word of God and their concept of the literal sense encompassed a canonical sense as well[33]. Although there is a distinctively "Protestant" flavor to the way the Reformers articulated their hermeneutical principles, they shared in what George Lindbeck refers to as the classic pre-modern Christian hermeneutic, "reading Scripture as a Christ-centered narrationally and typologically unified whole in conformity to a Trinitarian rule of faith" typologically (if not allegorically) applicable to the present[34].

Precritical Christian interpretation, including that of the Reformers, did not distinguish between the meaning of the text and its religious application to the life of the believer. Exegesis and application comprised a single act of interpretation. Likewise, no distinction was made between the literal-historical sense of a text and the events which the Bible narrated. It was assumed that what was narrated was precisely what occurred. Noble explains:

> The Reformers believed a historical event was rendered to the reader by the literal meaning of the text. Accepting this, figural interpretation made the further point that this could be done in such a way that the event not only "signified itself" but signified some other event also, through the "patterned" way in which the event was presented. These patterns were not imposed upon the text by the reader, but discovered in the text itself; thus figural interpretation sought to bring together temporally separated events into a unified whole, through their literary presentation[35].

---

[31] According to Hans Frei (*Eclipse of Biblical Narrative*, 2), "[For precritical scholars] figuration or typology was a natural extension of literal interpretation. It was literalism at the level of the whole biblical story and thus of the depiction of the whole of historical reality. Figuration was at once a literary and historical procedure, an interpretation of stories and their meanings by weaving them together into a common narrative referring to a single history and its patterns of meaning". For example, the Reformers did not simply take the facts narrated in the succession of David in a literalistic historical sense, as so many wars. Rather, they understood the literal sense of those events to include a prefiguring of Christ. According to Noble, the Reformers had a *literary* understanding of the literal sense ("The *Sensus Literalis*", 16).

[32] Ramm, *Protestant Biblical Interpretation*, 55-56.

[33] Noble, "The *Sensus Literalis*", 1.

[34] Lindbeck, "Scripture, Consensus and Community", 77, cf. 75.

[35] Noble, "The *Sensus Literalis*", 14. This approach of the Reformers has something in common with Thomas Aquinas' understanding of the spiritual sense, God communicating through events (*res*) as well as words.

d)   Critical Scholarship

The rise of critical scholarship introduced profound changes in the understanding of the literal sense. Enlightenment biblical scholarship sought to approach Scripture on the basis of reason alone and denied an interpretive role to dogma, tradition, and the Church. Obviously, Aquinas' definition of the literal sense as the *divine* author's intention no longer pertained. Similarly, the Enlightenment's separation of the Bible from the communities of faith (Israel and the Church) which produced it, and its rejection of the divine inspiration and intrinsic unity of the Scripture, meant that the literal sense of a text was not defined in relation to the canon as a whole. This latter had been the ordinary practice up through the Reformation. According to Childs, "During the pre-critical period the literal sense had always been defined in relation to [the] canonical writings"[36]. Historical interests and methods replaced theological interests and methods in defining the literal sense. The human author's intention and the historical circumstances of a text's writing monopolized the attention of interpreters. Superficially the critical exegesis of the Enlightenment period might appear to resemble the exegesis of the Renaissance and Reformation, but in fact it marked a decisive parting of the ways between theological exegesis that was historically and literarily aware, and exegesis that was primarily historical and literary, even if it permitted subsequent theological reflection.

Childs has isolated another important change in the definition of the literal sense introduced by critical scholarship in comparison with that of the Reformers and the earlier Christian tradition. Critical scholarship redefined the literal sense as the original sense, i.e., the meaning the text had on the occasion in which it was produced by the author or editor:

> Among the Reformers the identity of the literal and the historical sense had been assumed and the terms *sensus literalis* and *sensus historicus* were often interchanged. In the new [i.e., critical] approach the identity of the terms was also continued, but the historical sense now determined its content. The historical sense of the text was construed as being the *original* meaning of the text as it emerged in its pristine situation. Therefore, the aim of the interpreter was to reconstruct the original occasion of the historical references on the basis of which the truth of the biblical text could be determined. In sum, the *sensus literalis* had become the *sensus originalis*[37].

Previously the term *sensus historicus* referred to the literal sense's function of recounting events. Although some earlier authors (e.g., Augustine, Aquinas,

---

[36] Childs, "The *Sensus Literalis*", 90-91.

[37] See Noble, "The *Sensus Literalis*", 10-13, Childs, "The *Sensus Literalis*", 89.

Calvin) had concerned themselves with the circumstances of a biblical text's composition as important clues to its meaning, traditional Catholic and Reformation authors did not restrict the literal sense to the original meaning of the text as expressed by its author in its historical context. Rather, the traditional understanding of the literal sense united, without distinguishing among them, the human author's original meaning, the meaning of the text in light of the canon[38], its theological meaning and sometimes its contemporary application. It was this broader concept of the literal sense which was capable of providing the sole basis for theological argument. Critical scholarship, however, grew increasingly aware of these distinctions, and increasingly rigid in limiting the literal sense to a text's original meaning in its original historical context. The process reached its clearest expression in the 1960's in Krister Stendahl's distinction between what Scripture *meant* and what the text *means*, and his proposal that exegesis and biblical theology confine themselves to the first of these[39].

e)   Catholic Magisterium on the Senses

How did developments in magisterial teaching over the last century affect Catholic understanding of the senses of Scripture?   Leo XIII's *Providentissimus Deus* (1893) touches on the literal sense twice[40].   Pope Leo upheld Thomas Aquinas' perspective that the literal sense is primary. Like Thomas, he maintained that allegorical or figurative senses are legitimate (and derive from the Apostles), although they may not be used in proof of doctrines. Leo XIII emphasized the wealth of meaning present in the inspired text which strains the capacities of the literal sense to express[41].

Pius XII's *Divino afflante Spiritu* (1943) emphasizes that "the greatest endeavor [of interpreters] should be to discern and define clearly" the literal sense (*DAS* 23), by which he means "the literal meaning of the words

---

[38] The clearest instance of this was the identification of the literal sense of many OT texts in reference to Christ, especially when NT texts interpreted them that way and thus made their literal sense clear. Another classic instance was the general understanding that the literal sense of the Song of Songs was its reference to the spousal relation between Christ and the Church. Commission member Domingo Muñoz León retains that the *IBC* continues to consider this as the literal sense of the Song ("Los sentidos", 102-103).

[39] Stendahl, "Biblical Theology".

[40] *EB* §108, 112.

[41] "For the language of the Bible is employed to express, under the inspiration of the Holy Spirit, many things which are beyond the power and scope of the reason of man—that is to say, divine mysteries and all that is related to them. There is sometimes in such passages a fullness and a hidden depth of meaning which the letter hardly expresses and which the laws of interpretation hardly warrant. Moreover, the literal sense itself frequently admits other senses, adapted to illustrate dogma or to confirm morality" (*EB* §108).

intended and expressed by the sacred writer" (*DAS* 26) [42]. While in some respects Pius XII's view of the senses of Scripture follows St. Thomas Aquinas, Pius defines the literal sense to refer to the human author's intention (*DAS* 23, 26, 34, 35; *EB* §550, 552, 557, 558), while Thomas had defined it as the divine Author's intention. This is not an insignificant change[43]. Presumably Pope Pius wished to secure a more objective approach to articulating Scripture' message than that which characterized the advocates of "mystical" or "spiritual" interpretation[44]. Pius' definition of the literal sense protected the ability of the biblical authors to speak for themselves, rather than allow their voices to be drowned out by subsequent interpretation or pious eisegesis. Pope Pius' definition of the literal sense as the author's intention set Catholic exegesis on a path that coincided in many respects with the direction of contemporary scientific exegesis.

Nevertheless, Pius' approach to the senses differed from that of critical exegesis in two crucial ways. First, Pius also taught that the Catholic exegete must "search out and expound" the spiritual sense as well as the literal. While for Aquinas the spiritual sense consisted of the meaning conveyed by the "things" recounted in the words of Scripture, for Pope Pius, the spiritual sense consists in the way "what was said and done in the Old Testament was ordained and disposed by God [to prefigure what was] to come under the new

---

[42] Pius XII stresses the necessity of mastering the languages, attending to the context, entering as much as possible into the spirit of the ancient near east with the aid of history and related disciplines, familiarizing oneself with the modes of expression of the time, endeavoring to determine the author's circumstances and the sources available to him (*DAS* 33-37, *EB* §556-559).

Pius XII holds the line against improperly expanded notions of the spiritual sense: "Let [exegetes] scrupulously refrain from proposing as the genuine meaning of Sacred Scripture other figurative senses. It may indeed be useful, especially in preaching, to illustrate and present the matters of faith and morals by a broader use of the Sacred Text in the figurative sense, provided this be done with moderation and restraint; it should, however, not be forgotten that this use of the Sacred Scripture is, as it were, extrinsic to it and accidental, and that…it is not free from danger, since the faithful…wish to know what God has told us in the Sacred Letters rather than what an ingenious orator or writer may suggest by a clever use of the words of Scripture". (*DAS* 27, *EB* §553).

[43] It seems to this writer that Tábet excessively harmonizes the approaches to the literal sense of St. Thomas and Pius XII, stressing Thomas' interest in the human author's intention and downplaying the novelty of Pius' emphasis on the historical circumstances and the mind of the author ("Il senso litterale e il senso spirituale", 47-48). However, Tábet is quite justified in affirming that Pius like Thomas is primarily interested in theological meaning of the text, a point that many who cite *DAS* in defense of critical methods overlook.

[44] *Divino afflante Spiritu* defended scientific Catholic exegesis from the attacks of those who opposed it and wished to substitute "mystical" or "spiritual" exegesis" (*DAS* 25, *EB* §552). Pope John Paul II recalls these circumstances surrounding *DAS* in his Address, 3-5.

dispensation of grace" (*DAS* 26, *EB* §552). The specific content of this spiritual sense, Pius taught, has been divinely revealed:

> Now Our Divine Savior Himself points out to us and teaches us this same sense in the Holy Gospel; the Apostles also, following the example of the Master, profess it in their spoken and written words; the unchanging tradition of the Church approves it; and finally, the most ancient usage of the liturgy proclaims it, wherever may be rightly applied the well-known principle: "The rule of prayer is the rule of faith". (*DAS* 26)[45]

The second way Pope Pius' approach to the senses distinguished itself from that of critical exegesis was his insistence that exegesis communicate the theological meaning of Scripture[46]:

> With special zeal should they apply themselves, not only to expounding exclusively these matters which belong to the historical, archaeological, philological and other auxiliary sciences—as, to Our regret, is done in certain commentaries,—but, having duly referred to these, in so far as they may aid the exegesis, they should set forth in particular the theological doctrine in faith and morals of the individual books and texts.... (*DAS* 24, *EB* §551)[47]

The notion that in explaining the literal sense, exegesis or biblical theology should confine itself to historical description and prescind from explaining the theological (i.e., doctrinal) significance of Scripture, is utterly foreign to *Divino afflante Spiritu*. In summary, in *Divino afflante Spiritu* Pope Pius XII accepted critical scholarship's definition of the literal sense as the meaning intended by the author in his historical circumstances, yet taught the spiritual sense to be an essential aspect of Scripture's meaning; in addition, he insisted that the role of the exegete entailed explaining the theological meaning of Scripture.

---

[45] Pius XII continues: "Let Catholic exegetes then disclose and expound this spiritual significance, intended and ordained by God, with that care which the dignity of the divine word demands; but let them scrupulously refrain from proposing as the genuine meaning of Sacred Scripture other figurative senses" (*DAS* 27, *EB* §553).

[46] Tábet distinguishes two aspects of the meaning of the literal sense in the teaching of Pius XII in *DAS*: "Therefore, the 'literal sense' actually embraces both the 'literal-historical' sense—which historical science studies—and the 'literal-theological sense, which interprets the texts in the wider context of revelation" (Tábet, "Il senso litterale e il senso spirituale", 23-24).

[47] Pius also says that exegetes teaching in seminaries should stress the literal and theological meaning of Scripture: "Hence their exegetical explanation should aim especially at the theological doctrine.... The literal sense and especially the theological let them propose with such definiteness, explain with such skill and inculcate with such ardor that in their students may be in a sense verified what happened to the disciples on the way to Emmaus, when, having heard the words of the Master, they exclaimed: 'Was not our heart burning within us, whilst He opened to us the Scriptures?'" (*DAS* 54, *EB* §567).

Although Vatican II's *Dei Verbum* does not discuss the senses of Scripture explicitly, it develops the approach of Pope Pius XII. The Council document emphasizes that God speaks through Scripture in a human manner and urges investigation of what the sacred writers "really intended", referring to the literal sense. At the same time the Council says that interpreters must search out what "God wanted to manifest by means of their words" (*DV 12*)[48]. The addition of the latter phrase suggests, first, that the Council Fathers did not simply equate the human authors' meaning with the divine intention, and, second, that they did not want to limit the work of exegetes to explaining the human authors' intentions in their historical circumstances[49]. A theological reading of Scripture and an openness to more-than-literal senses is suggested by the "rules" of interpretation that follow regarding interpreting Scripture "according to the same Spirit by whom it was written", attending "to the content and unity of the whole of Scripture", and taking into account "the living tradition of the whole Church" and the "analogy of faith" (*DV* 12). *Dei Verbum* 15 makes explicit mention of the way the Old Testament *types* indicate the meaning of the coming of Christ and his kingdom.

The reception of *Divino afflante Spiritu* (and *Dei Verbum*) followed history's law that one reaction engenders another. The defensive suppression of critical methods that preceded the publication of *Divino afflante Spiritu* and which continued to some degree up to the Second Vatican Council provoked an enthusiastic and often unreflective embrace of critical approaches on the part of many Catholic scholars after the Council. Pius XII's encyclical was subjected to a selective reading in which the elements which conformed to the views of the wider world of scientific exegesis (predominantly German and Protestant) were appropriated, and the elements that did not, often were ignored.

---

[48] The Abbot translation interprets *Dei Verbum* 12 this way, but goes beyond the Latin text: "the interpreter of sacred Scripture, in order to see clearly what God wanted to communicate to us, should carefully investigate what meaning the sacred writers really intended, and *what* God wanted to manifest by means of their words". The second "what" (here italicized) does not appear in the Latin original ("*interpres Sacrae Scripturae, ut perspiciat, quid Ipse nobiscum communicare voluerit, attente investigare debet, quid hagiographi reapse significare intenderint et eorum verbis manifestare Deo placuerit*"). Nevertheless, the content and structure of the section as a whole supports this interpretation.

[49] In an introduction to *Dei Verbum* Ratzinger affirmed that one of the three reasons which led the Second Vatican Council to elaborate the *Constitution on Divine Revelation* was the theological problem that had arisen due to the application of historical-critical methods for the interpretation of Scripture ("Dogmatische Konstitution: Einleitung", 498-503, as cited in de la Potterie, "Il Concilio Vaticano II e la Bibbia", 21). On *DV* 12 and author's intention, see Alonso Schökel, "Considerazioni sulla *Dei Verbum*".

f)   Problems Due to the Critical Definition of the Literal Sense

In an article published in 1977 Childs analyzed the difficulties which critical exegesis' approach to the literal sense introduced to a Christian reading of the Bible[50]. What follows is a brief listing of some of those difficulties, drawing for the most part on Childs' analysis:

1. The identification of the literal sense with the *sensus originalis*, when combined with the critical discovery that the biblical texts are the product of a lengthy process of redaction, led to separating texts from their present literary contexts, and re-constructing them according to hypotheses about their origins. However, both the reconstruction of texts and of historical circumstances are highly speculative enterprises, sometimes yielding as many diverse results as there are interpreters. Childs compares the new situation to the problem of the multiple sense of Scripture in the past:

    > Whereas during the medieval period the crucial issue lay in the usage made of the multiple layers of meaning *above* the text, the issue now turns on the multiple layers of meaning *below* the text. The parallel consists in the threat from both directions to undermine the literal sense [emphasis original]...[51].

2. The *historical* orientation of the new definition of the literal sense had another consequence. The meaning or truth of the biblical text began to be sought *behind* the text, in the historical events themselves, or in religious ideas they represented, or in a certain consciousness which the text expressed.

3. Both of the difficulties mentioned in the previous two paragraphs relativized the importance of the final form of the biblical books, turning attention away from the inspired text itself.

4. Exclusively considering the literal sense and defining it as a text's meaning in its original historical circumstances introduced a vast distance between the Old Testament and the New Testament, since it is apparent that Jesus' birth, life, death and resurrection exceeded the understanding of the Old Testament authors who prepared for his coming. (In *Divino afflante Spiritu* it was the spiritual sense that had provided the link between the Testaments.)

5. A similar distancing occurs between the literal sense of any biblical text and its contemporary meaning, between exegesis and theology or

---

[50] The idea for this list and some its points come from Childs, "The *Sensus Literalis*", 90-91.

[51] Childs, "The *Sensus Literalis*", 92.

actualization. No matter how appropriate later readings of a biblical text may be, they are not the literal sense of the text when it is equated with the author's intention in his original circumstances.

g)   The *IBC* on the Literal Sense

In the light of the history of the literal sense, some features of the *IBC*'s definition and approach stand out in clearer relief. The Biblical Commission, like Pius XII in *Divino afflante Spiritu*, has defined the literal sense in a manner similar to the definition employed by critical scholarship: the literal sense refers to what the author expressed in his own historical context, "directly", i.e., apart from canonical considerations.

Yet the Biblical Commission's approach to the literal sense differs from the approach taken by earlier generations of historical-critical scholars, and in doing so overcomes some of the difficulties that had arisen. First, the *IBC* rejects the idea of confining a text's meaning within the historical circumstances of its writing[52]. Rather the *IBC* seeks the "direction of thought" in a text, the "openness" inherent in many texts which enables them to be re-read in different circumstances. This "dynamic aspect" provides the opening for "fulfillment" of Old Testament texts by New Testament texts and validates actualization as an interpretive procedure[53]. Second, the *IBC*'s definition of the literal sense focuses attention on the text itself, rather than what lies behind it, since the literal sense is what has been "directly expressed by the inspired human authors" (II.B.1.c). Third, the *IBC*'s pre-understanding of faith recognizes the literal sense as intended by God, thus enabling it to be the basis of theological affirmation. Finally, the *IBC* does not consider that the literal sense divulges Scripture's complete meaning. Rather, the spiritual and fuller senses of Scripture must be taken into account. The insufficiency of the literal sense alone is indicated by the *IBC*'s understanding that after determining the literal sense, exegetes should determine the meaning of biblical texts "in the wider canon of Scripture" (III.D.4.b), since biblical meaning is found "in the light of the Canon as a whole" (I.C.1f; principle #8).

---

[52] "Historical-critical exegesis has too often tended to limit the meaning of texts by tying it too rigidly to precise historical circumstances. It should seek rather to determine the direction of thought expressed by the text; this direction, far from working towards a limitation of meaning, will on the contrary dispose the exegete to perceive extensions of it that are more or less foreseeable in advance" (II.B.1.e).

[53] Yet at the same time, the Biblical Commission's view of the literal sense rejects arbitrary or wholly subjective readings, insisting that "one must reject as unauthentic every interpretation alien to the meaning expressed by the human authors in their written text" (II.B.1.g).

8. *The Future of the Literal Sense*

The *IBC*'s approach to the literal sense frees it from a psychologizing notion of authorial intention and from a historicist view that confines meaning to what was understood in the original historical circumstances. It does so on the basis of literary and hermeneutical insights and on the basis of the pattern of re-readings found in Scripture itself. But the discussion regarding Scripture's literal meaning continues unabated with proposals coming from a variety of directions. Within the Biblical Commission itself clear differences of opinion are apparent. This chapter will conclude by briefly describing some of the proposals about conceptualizing Scripture's meaning likely to influence future formulations of the literal sense.

a) Giving Place to Texts and Readers

As has been noted, the insights of literary studies and philosophical hermeneutics led the Commission away from a narrow understanding of authorial intention toward a definition that can encompass, to some degree, re-readings of authorial meaning in new circumstances[54]. Some authors, however, would like to take this process further. Commission member Marcel Dumais maintains that interpretation seeks the intention of the text (produced by a historical author), rather than the intention of the author himself[55]. The literal or textual meaning is larger than the original historical meaning. Interpreters read the text in living continuity with the original meaning of the author but go beyond it. Dumais argues that the meaning of a work always remains potential; it does not attain real existence until it is actualized in a particular interpretation. The text itself determines a trajectory, a line of meaning which valid interpretations follow. He questions whether one can speak of objective meaning in view of the fact that a reading-subject is necessary for its explanation. A good interpretation, according to Dumais, can neither be purely objective nor purely subjective. Meaning is produced by the reader in the act of receiving from the text. Rather than speak of plural senses, Dumais prefers to speak of plural readings. To be valid all of these must align themselves with the direction indicated by the text[56]. The succession of good readings of the biblical text over the course of

---

[54] See Jensen, "Beyond the Literal Sense" for a defense of christological interpretation in the *Catechism of the Catholic Church* (*CCC*) on the basis of developments in hermeneutics.

[55] Dumais, "Sens de l'Écriture", 324-325.

[56] Dumais' approach is not far from Schneiders' view (which also relies on Ricoeur): a text's meaning should not be fixed in a single determination of authorial meaning, but rather is embodied in a variety of faithful interpretations. Schneiders proposes replacing authorial intention as the objective pole of interpretation with "ideal meaning" (*Revelatory Text*, xxx-

the centuries enriches the meaning of the text. The "history of the effects of the text" (*Wirkungsgeschichte*) in some sense is constitutive of the meaning of Scripture and forms part of the horizon of the interpreter.

b) Stressing the Inspiration of the Text Rather Than of the Author

Some scholars maintain that the theology of biblical inspiration should be re-formulated to stress the inspiration of the text rather than of the biblical authors. According to Dumais the romantic nineteenth century mentality which equated the author's original intention with the literal sense of Scripture led the theology of inspiration to emphasize the psychology of the inspired writer, his thoughts and his volitions, rather than to emphasize the inspired text as the ancient Fathers had[57]. Furthermore, critical awareness of the many hands that took part in the composition of the biblical books has introduced a serious difficulty to the link between inspiration and authorial intention. Which original intended meaning was inspired? That of the first author or of subsequent redactor(s)? Critical scholarship's discovery of the composite authorship of many of the biblical writings also inclines Lothar Ruppert to favor shifting the emphasis to the inspiration of the biblical text[58].

---

xxxiv; cf. 144-148): "By 'ideal meaning' I mean not a textual semantic content but a certain dynamic structure in the text that derives from the confluence of three factors: (a) the dialectic between sense and reference... by which the text says something intelligible about something (even if what it says is false); (b) the genre in which the intelligible utterance is expressed and by which it is shaped; (c) the personal style of the author" (xxxii). Applying this to the parable of the Good Samaritan, Schneiders explains, "The confluence of these factors gives the text of the Good Samaritan a dynamic structure that guides interpretation in a certain direction....There are numerous possible interpretations of this parable.... But the ideal meaning rules out certain lines of interpretation" (xxxiii). Schneiders suggests that a musical score provides an analogy to a text: all renditions of Beethoven's "Fifth Symphony", for instance, "should sound alike, that is, they should each realize the ideal structure inscribed in the score, but every rendition should also be unique and original because of the interpretation by a particular conductor and orchestra" (xxxiii).

[57] Dumais, "Sens de l'Écriture", 314. Catholic emphasis on inspiration's effect on the inner workings of the author's mind found expression in Leo XIII's *Providentissimus Deus*: "By his supernatural power He [the Holy Spirit] so stimulated them to write, so assisted them while they were writing that they properly conceived in their mind, wished to write down faithfully, and expressed aptly with infallible truth all those things, and only those things, which He himself ordered..." (DS 3293, *EB* §125). According to Jared Wicks, this formulation "closely follows the descriptive definition of inspiration given in J.B. Franzelin's *De Divina Traditione et Scriptura*" (Rome 1870, with new editions in 1875, 1882, and 1896)..." (*Introduction to Theological Method*, 56n). The Fathers of the Second Vatican Council chose not to reaffirm Leo XIII's description of the process of inspiration although it was proposed to them in the 1962 *Schema de fontibus, no. 8*. Rather, in *Dei Verbum* 11 the "Council is notably reserved in stating how the Holy Spirit interacts with human authors" (Wicks, 56).

[58] Ruppert, "Kommentierende Einführung", 41.

c) Respecting Authorial Intention and the Message-Character of Scripture

For several decades E.D. Hirsch, Jr., and others have argued against strong literary and philosophical currents for the necessity of distinguishing a text's *meaning* from its *significance*. A text's "meaning" is determinate, indicated by linguistic signs in the text and theoretically anchored in what the author intended to communicate. The "significance" of a text, however, is not determined; it is the relationship which an interpreter makes between the "meaning" given in the text and the rest of reality. In 1986 Hirsch modified his distinction to take into account the intention of authors to write for the future, to transcend the limitations of their own historical contexts[59]. More recently, Kevin J. Vanhoozer has argued persuasively on the basis of speech-act theory and legal hermeneutics that the meaning of a text should be identified with the author's communicative action[60]. Taking into account both its critics and its advocates, Vanhoozer concludes that Hirsch's meaning/significance distinction continues to be valid and important [61].

From a theological point of view, faithfulness to the original content of the gospel is extremely important[62]. Furthermore, ecumenical dialogues, such as the Lutheran-Catholic dialogue on Justification, have made progress by examining biblical texts to better understand the meaning intended by the authors. If the meaning of the text cannot be grounded in the author's meaning, but instead includes its subsequent interpretation, how can progress toward a common understanding of apostolic doctrine occur?

d) Taking Into Account the Intention of the Divine Author

Since the literal sense is defined as what the human authors expressed (implying that they basically understood what they expressed), the literal sense by itself only partially achieves the goal of Christian interpretation, namely, to understand the divine communication in Scripture. The *IBC*, much like *Divino afflante Spiritu*, supplies what is lacking in the literal sense by also teaching about the spiritual and the fuller senses of Scripture. This is because the understanding of the human authors of the Old Testament did not include important aspects of the divine Author's intention, above all, the ways in which the Old Testament prepares for and refers to Jesus Christ.

There could be another way of going about this. It would be possible to shift the focus of exegesis to make the communicative intent of Scripture's

---

[59] Hirsch, "Meaning and Significance Reinterpreted", and "Transhistorical Intentions and Allegory".

[60] Vanhoozer, *Is There a Meaning?*, 73-90 and 201-280, especially 240-265.

[61] Vanhoozer, *Is There a Meaning?*, 260.

[62] See the brief discussion of this point in the discussion of exegesis and history, p. 54ff.

divine Author the direct object of attention. Various scholars have proposed that the communicative intention of Scripture's divine Author is made clearest in the light of the canon of Scripture[63]. Childs has long argued for the canonical approach as the most fruitful path to theologically adequate exegesis, pointing to a "canonical intention" which determines biblical meaning. Recently Paul R. Noble, offering a critical reconstruction of Child's hermeneutic, has recognized that "Only *divine* authorship could account for the meaning that Childs wishes to find in the Bible"[64]. Noble proposes a formal model by which the divine and human intentionality can be related in the canon[65]. Kevin J. Vanhoozer, while arguing forcefully for the link between authorial intention and textual meaning, maintains that

> the fuller meaning" of Scripture—the meaning associated with divine authorship—emerges only at the level of the whole canon.... *If we are reading the Bible as the Word of God, therefore, I suggest that the context that yields this maximal sense is the canon, taken as a unified communicative act.* The books of Scripture, taken individually, may anticipate the whole, but the canon alone is its *instantiation*...[emphasis original][66].

---

[63] Thus Vanhoozer, *Is There a Meaning?*, 263-265; Noble, *The Canonical Approach*, 340-350; cf., Dohmen, "Was Gott sagen wollte...".

[64] Noble, *The Canonical Approach*, 206.

[65] "The formal model, then, which I am proposing is that the biblical canon be construed as analogous to the 'collected works' of a single author. This (divine) author wrote them (over a considerable period of time) by assuming a variety of authorial *personae*, each with its own distinctive character, historical situation, etc. As one moves, therefore, from one book to another one encounters a diversity of 'implied authors', each of whom must be understood on their own terms; yet behind them all is a single controlling intelligence, working to an overall plan. Because of this, these diverse works therefore can—and for a full understanding, must—be read as a unified canon. The point of this model is to suggest that there are significant parallels between the exegetical problems posed by a divine-human biblical canon and those which we already know how to handle in a secular context (e.g., in taking account of the respective roles of the implied author and real author in interpreting a modern novel)..." (Noble, *The Canonical Approach*, 341). Noble makes clear that this is intended as a *formal* model, "whose purpose is to suggest various interpretive procedures which might be fruitful", and not a *material* model intending to suggest *how* the Bible was inspired (341). He then sketches out how such a model might be used. His first principle is that exegesis must always begin with the understanding of a text in its original historical context, and subsequently discerning higher levels of canonical meaning (cf. 342-347).

[66] Yet Vanhoozer continues to respect the authorial intention of the individual biblical writings: "*The divine intention does not contravene the intention of the human author but rather supervenes upon it* [emphasis original]. In the same way, the canon does not change or contradict the meaning of Isaiah 53 but supervenes on it and specifies its referent. In speaking of the Suffering Servant, Isaiah was referring to Christ (viz., God's gracious provision for Israel and the World), just as Priestly, speaking of dephlogisticated air was referring to oxygen"

This re-orientation of the exegetical task toward the intention of the divine Author could suggest either redefining the literal sense as the canonical sense (which would resemble its definition by Aquinas and the Reformers), or retaining the definition of the literal sense as the human author's meaning but explicitly subordinating it to the canonical sense.

Nicholas Wolterstorff proposes another promising way of taking into account the divine Author[67]. Like the Biblical Commission, Wolterstorff concerns himself with what the human author actually said (rather than what he intended) which Wolterstorff refers to as "authorial-discourse" interpretation. He then introduces the concept of "double-agency discourse": a person's performance of an illocutionary act by means of another person performing a locutionary or illocutionary act[68]. Examples of double-agency discourse include someone deputizing another person or someone appropriating the discourse of another, for instance, by citing them in agreement. This concept provides a path for understanding how God speaks through Scripture—by deputizing the human authors, by appropriating their words, or perhaps by other means of understanding inspiration. It provides a way of seeing the unity of the canon, which comprises, in its totality, "God's book". Finally, it opens the way to interpreting Scripture for "divine discourse" through a double hermeneutic which begins by interpreting the human discourse (in the manner that scientific exegesis commonly does) and then by interpreting what God has said by way of this human discourse.

e) Accepting More-Than-Literal Meanings

There is considerable interest in interpretation that does not confine itself to what the human author expressed. This interest comes from a variety of quarters: from those re-appropriating patristic exegesis, from those interpreting from feminist or liberationist perspectives, from those urging pastoral readings of Scripture determined by their helpfulness "for building up the Christian community in faith and appropriate practice"[69]. Undoubtedly, a

---

(265). Vanhoozer had referred earlier (262) to Joseph Priestly's references to oxygen in 1772 as "dephlogisticated air". The point was that an author's intended meaning can be inadequately conceived, yet still really refer to a reality that can be better described later.

[67] Wolterstorff, *Divine Discourse*, "Promise of Speech Act Theory".

[68] These terms are drawn from speech act theory. Vanhoozer explains: "The locutionary act refers to the act of saying something.... The illocutionary act refers to what we do when we say something.... It is the illocution that makes a set of words into a particular type of communicative action (e.g., an assertion, a question, a warning, a command, etc.)" ("Language, Literature, Hermeneutics, and Biblical Theology", 33).

[69] Ayres and Fowl, "(Mis)Reading the Face of God", 528. For an explanation of this approach see Fowl, *Engaging Scripture*. See also Johnson's appeal for "responsible readings"

reaction has set in against historical-critical exegesis' sometimes historicist and overly rigid approach, exclusively valuing a critically-determined literal sense. The future understanding of the literal sense may depend to some degree on the place that other readings of Scripture are granted. If only a critically-determined literal sense counts, the pressure will increase to expand its definition or to deny its validity or relevance. For their part, the Biblical Commission has opened up the meaning of the literal sense, by recognizing its dynamic aspect and the legitimacy of re-readings (actualizations) in new circumstances (cf. IV.A.2.e). They have also opened the way to more-than-literal interpretation by re-presenting the spiritual sense and introducing the fuller sense (principles #13 and #14).

Will that be enough? And if not, how can arbitrary interpretation be avoided? The crucial question which non-literal readings raise is that of faithfulness to the message of Scripture. The *IBC* reports, without evaluative comment, that the patristic approach to diversity in interpretive procedures was to allow various interpretations, provided that they conformed to the analogy of faith (III.B.2.j), meaning the Christian message as a whole as understood in the Church. Perhaps this ancient rule could again provide the necessary safeguard for more-than-literal interpretation.

---

rather than methodologically-determined "right" interpretations ("What's Catholic About It?"), 16.

CHAPTER 13

The Spiritual Sense, Typology

Principle #13

The spiritual sense of Sacred Scripture is the meaning expressed by the biblical texts when read under the influence of the Holy Spirit in the context of the paschal mystery and of the new life which flows from it. (II.B.2.b)

The spiritual sense is always founded on the literal sense. A relationship of continuity and conformity between the literal and the spiritual sense is necessary in order for the literal sense of an Old Testament text to be fulfilled at a higher level in the New. (II.B.2.e)

Typology is an aspect of the spiritual sense[1]. (II.B.2.i)

Explanation

1. An Example of the Spiritual Sense

The Biblical Commission begins its explanation of the spiritual sense by giving an example. In the oracle of Nathan recounted in 2 Sam 7:12-13 (also 1 Chr 17:11-14), God promises David that he will raise up one of his sons to

---

[1] The *IBC* treats the spiritual sense of Scripture in section II.B.2, a part of the chapter devoted to hermeneutical questions. It also refers to the spiritual sense in its discussion of relationships between the Old Testament and the New Testament (III.A.2), and indirectly when it discusses the responsibility of exegetes to explain the christological, canonical and ecclesial meaning of Scripture of Scripture (III.C.1.c-e). Pope John Paul II comments on the spiritual sense in his Address (§5).

be king and will establish the throne of this son's kingdom forever. Viewed in its original context, this seems to be prophetic hyperbole, promising David an enduring dynasty. But now, in light of the fact that "Christ being raised from the dead, will never die again" (Rom 6:9), this text must be taken literally. The Commission anticipates the objection of "exegetes who have a narrow, 'historicist' idea about the literal sense", who might argue that the christological interpretation is "alien to the original" (II.B.2.a). But here is where recognition of the "dynamic aspect" that characterizes the literal sense of many texts shows its worth[2]. Interpreting this text in reference to Christ recognizes "a profound element of continuity as well as a move to a different level: Christ rules forever, but not on the earthly throne of David" (II.B.2.a).

The spiritual sense refers in large part (though not exclusively) to the ways in which Jesus *fulfilled* the Old Testament Scriptures. Fitzmyer equates the spiritual sense which the Commission describes with the christological sense of the Old Testament[3]. Vanhoye agrees, provided that christological is taken in a broad sense, to encompass ecclesiological and eschatological meanings[4]. It comprises the central core of what Lindbeck calls the "classic Christian hermeneutic" shared by all Christians up to the time of the Enlightenment[5]. Although the Commission gives it a new definition that locates it in terms of contemporary hermeneutics, it is the same spiritual sense to which Pius XII refers in *Divino afflante Spiritu*: "For what was said and done in the Old Testament was ordained and disposed by God with such consummate wisdom, that things past prefigured in a spiritual way those that were to come under the new dispensation of grace" (*DAS* 26, *EB* §552)[6].

---

[2] The fact that 2 Sam 7:12-13 has such an inherent "open-endedness" is evident in the frequent re-readings it receives in Israel's history before the coming of Christ.

[3] Fitzmyer, "Literal and Spiritual Senses", 141, and *The Biblical Commission's Document*, 125-126.

[4] Vanhoye, conversation with author, 22 February 1999.

[5] Lindbeck, "Scripture, Consensus, and Community".

[6] Below is a continuation of the quotation given in the text which indicates the seriousness with which Pope Pius XII regarded the spiritual sense: "Wherefore the exegete, just as he must search out and expound the literal meaning of the words, intended and expressed by the sacred writer, so also must he do likewise for the spiritual sense, provided it is clearly intended by God. For God alone could have known this spiritual meaning and have revealed it to us. Now Our Divine Savior Himself points out to us and teaches us this same sense in the Holy Gospel; the Apostles also, following the example of the Master, profess it in their spoken and written words; the unchanging tradition of the Church approves it; and finally the most ancient usage of the liturgy proclaims it, wherever may be rightly applied the well-known principle: 'The rule of prayer is the rule of faith'" (*DAS* 26, *EB* §552). For more on of Pope Pius XII's understanding of the spiritual sense, see p. 178ff. and the note on p. 200.

2. A "Real" Sense of Scripture

The spiritual sense of Sacred Scripture is the meaning expressed by the biblical texts when read under the influence of the Holy Spirit in the context of the paschal mystery and of the new life which flows from it. (II.B.2.b)

The definition of the spiritual sense given above comes directly from the words of the Biblical Commission:

As a general rule, we can define the spiritual sense, as understood by Christian faith, as *the meaning expressed by the biblical texts* when read under the influence of the Holy Spirit, in the contexts of the paschal mystery of Christ and of the new life which flows from it [emphasis added]. (II.B.2.b)

The spiritual sense is not simply a meaning read into the Bible, but a meaning the texts themselves express when read in the light of the realities which Christian faith attests. It is not a "soft" sense of meaning: "The spiritual sense is not to be confused with subjective interpretations stemming from the imagination or intellectual speculation. The spiritual sense results from setting the text in relation to real facts..." (II.B.2.f). In his Address, Pope John Paul II also stressed the objectivity of the spiritual sense:

The spiritual sense must offer proof of its authenticity. A merely subjective inspiration is insufficient. One must be able to show that it is a sense "willed by God himself", a spiritual meaning "given by God" to the inspired text (*EB* § 552-553). Determining the spiritual sense then, belongs itself to the realm of exegetical science. (Address 5)[7]

What are the foundations of the spiritual sense? First, comprehension of the spiritual sense of Scripture is clearly founded on Christian faith in the *historical fact* of the *death and resurrection of Jesus* and in the meaning revelation ascribes to that event. Here the Biblical Commission refers not to mere "intertextuality", a literary relation between texts in the Old Testament and texts in the New Testament, but a realistic relation between the meaning of (especially Old Testament) biblical texts and a "new historical context, which sheds fresh light upon the ancient texts and causes them to undergo a change in meaning" (II.B.2.a). Second, recognition of the spiritual sense of Old Testament Scripture is founded on the *New Testament's testimony that the Scriptures have been fulfilled* in the paschal mystery. "In it the New Testament recognizes the fulfillment of the Scriptures. It is therefore quite acceptable to re-read the Scripture in the light of this new context, which is that of life in the Spirit" (II.B.2.b). Finally, as the last words of the preceding

---

[7] Exegetical "science" in this case obviously refers to exegesis as a branch of theology which is a science of faith.

quotation indicate, it is the *action of the Holy Spirit* which reveals Scripture's spiritual meaning.

The Spirit's role is important in the recognition of the spiritual sense: "the spiritual sense…[is] the meaning expressed by the biblical texts when read, *under the influence of the Holy Spirit…*" (II.B.2.b, emphasis added). In addition, "Spiritual interpretation…will discover the authentic spiritual sense only to the extent that…[it] holds together three levels of reality: the biblical text, the paschal mystery, and *the present circumstances of life in the Spirit*" (II.B.2.g, emphasis added). One can distinguish two aspects of the Spirit's work in communicating the spiritual sense, one objective and located in the post-Easter past, and the other subjective and contemporary for every generation of believers. Objectively, the Spirit revealed in the light of the paschal event the deeper significance of what had been written previously. Thus, the apostolic Church's discovery of how both Old Testament prophecies and institutions (such as the Passover and Day of Atonement sacrifices) found their fulfillment in Jesus. Subjectively, the Spirit makes this real to the interpreter and enables him or her to understand the implications the word of God in his or her present circumstances[8]. Although the Commission document does not say so, it seems that the role of the Spirit in interpreting Scripture corresponds to what is promised of the Spirit in the Gospel of John: "But the Advocate, the Holy Spirit, whom the Father will send in my name, will teach you everything, and remind you of all that I have said to you" (14:26); "When the Spirit of truth comes, he will guide you into all the truth…"(16:13a). The necessity of the Spirit for an objectively correct interpretation of Old Testament prophecies is forcefully implied in 2 Pet 1:20-21: "First of all you must understand this, that no prophecy of scripture is a matter of one's own interpretation, because no prophecy ever came by human will, but men and women moved by the Holy Spirit spoke from God".

3. *The Spiritual Sense in the New Testament*

The *IBC* makes two interesting points about the relationship of the spiritual sense to the literal sense. First, they are not necessarily distinct: "When a biblical text relates directly to the paschal mystery of Christ or to the new life which results from it, its literal sense is already a spiritual sense. Such is regularly the case in the New Testament" (II.B.2.d). In other words, because the literal sense of the New Testament conveys a meaning "under the influence of the Holy Spirit in the context of the Paschal Mystery", the literal and spiritual sense of the New Testament are identical. Therefore it is not

---

[8] See the discussion of the Spirit's role in principle #6, p. 99ff.

appropriate to simply limit the spiritual sense to a Christian reading of the Old Testament, even if Christian exegesis most often refers to the Old Testament when it speaks of the spiritual sense.

Having said this, the Biblical Commission wanted to make very clear that the value of the Old Testament does not consist only in its pointing to New Testament realities[9]: "But already in the Old Testament, there are many instances where texts have a religious or spiritual sense as their literal sense" (II.B.2.d). Fitzmyer offers several good examples[10]: Christians can profitably pray the Shema or the 23rd Psalm in their literal senses, i.e., without christological interpretation. Similarly, the ethical injunctions of the Decalogue or of the prophets are capable of guiding Christians in how to live, just as they have guided and do guide observant Jews. It seems, however, that here the Biblical Commission would have done better simply to affirm the religious value for Christians of the literal sense of many Old Testament texts, rather than describe this benefit using the term "spiritual sense" (II.B.2.d). By doing so, the Biblical Commission uses the term in a different sense than their definition proposes[11].

4. Relationship of the Spiritual and Literal Senses

The spiritual sense is always founded on the literal sense. A relationship of continuity and conformity between the literal and the spiritual sense is

---

[9] According to Vanhoye, this was the intention of the Commission in including the last two sentences of II.B.2.d (Vanhoye, conversation with author, 22 February 1999).

[10] Fitzmyer, "Literal and Spiritual Senses", 144. See the discussion of OT interpretation in principle #9.

[11] Fitzmyer also maintains that this usage of the term "spiritual sense" in II.B.2.d means something different than the christological sense intended by the Commission's definition. He says that it would perhaps be better to refer to this meaning for Christians of the OT as "the 'religious' import of what has been literally expressed" ("Literal and Spiritual Senses", 144-145). But Fitzmyer feels prevented from referring to it as the literal sense on account of the traditional understanding of the senses summarized in Augustine of Denmark's couplet ("*Littera gesta docet, quid credas allegoria,/ moralis quid agas, quid speres anagogia*", quoted by the PBC in II.B.a) which grants only "*gesta*", i.e., deeds or events, to the *littera*, and instruction for faith and morals to *allegoria* and *moralis*. Fitzmyer is right not to want to refer to the non-christological religious meaning of the OT as the spiritual sense. To do so is to deprive the inspired literal sense of the OT of its religious meaning and to undermine the univocity of the Commission's helpful new definition of the spiritual sense. However, Fitzmyer need not be stopped by Augustine of Denmark's couplet. That division of the senses really only applies to narrative texts—not psalms, wisdom literature, or other OT genres. Likewise, the spirit-letter dichotomy which characterizes some patristic and medieval interpretation and which reserves all the important signification for Christian faith and life to the spiritual sense does not harmonize with the Biblical Commission's definitions of the literal and spiritual senses.

necessary in order for the literal sense of an Old Testament text to be fulfilled at a higher level in the New. (II.B.2.e)

The second comment of the Commission about the relationship of the literal and spiritual senses provides a control to spiritual interpretation: the spiritual sense is always based upon the literal sense, which is its "indispensable foundation" (II.B.2.d). An interesting argument is adduced, based on the spiritual meaning of the Old Testament: "Otherwise, one could not speak of the 'fulfillment' of Scripture. Indeed in order that there be a fulfillment, a relationship of continuity and of conformity is essential" (II.B.2.d).

The insistence on continuity between the literal and spiritual senses recalls what was said in the discussion of the literal sense about the "dynamic aspect" of certain texts. The *IBC* is saying that in many, if not all, cases, the spiritual sense is the dynamic aspect of the literal sense now understood in the light of subsequent events, i.e., the Paschal event, to have been "fulfilled" at a higher level than was originally apparent. Thus the royal psalms and Old Testament prophecies about a future Davidic king are fulfilled in Jesus. Likewise Old Testament prophecies of a glorious future for Israel that remain unfulfilled (e.g., Isa 2:1-5; 25:6-10; 61-62; Ezek 37; 47:1-12; Joel 3:17-21; Mic 6:8-20) may now be seen to refer to the fullness of the kingdom of God which Jesus will usher in at his second coming[12].

Not all cases are so clear. Can the Christian observance of Sunday as the Lord's Day be seen as fulfilling the Old Testament Sabbath legislation? By what criteria does one determine whether "a relationship of continuity and conformity" exists between the literal sense and a proposed spiritual sense? The Commission does not say. It does however reject the allegorical approach of ancient exegesis, which labored "to find a spiritual sense in the minutest details of the biblical text... making use of rabbinic methods or...Hellenistic allegorical exegesis.... Modern exegesis cannot ascribe true interpretive value to this kind of procedure" (II.B.2.h).

5. Typology

Although ancient and medieval exegesis did not distinguish between them, more recent scholarship draws a distinction between allegorical and typological interpretation[13]. The typical[14] sense has been understood as the

---

[12] This example and the texts cited are supplied by the author, not the Biblical Commission.

[13] For an overview of typology, see Brown, "Hermeneutics [*JBC*]", §71-78.

deeper meaning of the persons, places and events in the Bible when they are seen to have foreshadowed subsequent persons, places, and events in God's work of salvation[15]. The New Testament itself provides many examples of typological interpretation of Old Testament realities which foreshadow Christ or the realities of the New Covenant. These include Adam as a figure of Christ (Rom 5:14, 1 Cor 15:45-49), the flood and the crossing of the Red Sea as types of baptism (1 Pet 3:20-21; 1 Cor 10:1), Israel in the wilderness as a type of the Church's earthly pilgrimage (1 Cor 10:1-11), the Passover lamb as a type of Christ (John 1:29; 1 Cor 6:7), etc.. Along with messianic prophecy, the New Testament treats typology as one of the primary indicators of the profound unity between the saving action of God in the Old Covenant and that in Christ.

Most definitions of typology including that given above put the emphasis on the relationship between the realities—the persons, places and things—rather than the texts of the Old Testament and the corresponding realities in the New Testament. But the Commission refines this understanding, observing that it is not the realities themselves that the New Testament cites, but their *scriptural descriptions*, giving the example of the voice of Abel (Gen 4:10 and Heb 11:4 and 12:24). Therefore typology belongs under the heading of Scriptural meaning. The Biblical Commission sees typology as an instance of the spiritual sense, since it obviously satisfies the definition, "the meaning expressed by the biblical texts when read under the influence of the Holy Spirit in the context of the Paschal Mystery and of the new life which flows from it" (II.B.2.b).

Discussion

6. *Advocacy and Caution about the Spiritual Sense*

The Biblical Commission's explanation of the spiritual sense was not a lightly considered foray into an uncontested topic. Rather it was a carefully measured contribution to a longstanding discussion regarding the place of the spiritual sense in light of scientific exegesis. The discussion has been lively up until the present, and it has included both those who advocate spiritual exegesis, sometimes against historical-critical analysis, and those, especially critical exegetes, who are leery about exegesis concerning itself with anything but the literal sense established by the historical-critical method. Brown, who

---

[14] Both the words "typical" and "typological" can refer to biblical types, as they do in the usage noted and the sentence that precedes it. The term "typological" can also be used more generally to mean "figurative". In this study the context should make the meaning clear.

[15] Brown and Schneiders, "Hermeneutics [*NJBC*]", 1156-1157.

belongs to the latter group, summarizes the recent history of those advocating the spiritual sense:

> We may begin the discussion of recently advocated more-than-literal exegesis with attempts to draw from patristic spiritual exegesis its core-perceptions without embracing the exaggerations and without denigrating the contributions of modern historical-critical exegesis.... The movement found its strongest proponents in England and in France in the 1940's through the 1960's, partially in order to preserve a rich heritage, partially in reaction to theological sterility in some historical-critical exegesis. Studies of Origen mentioned above, such as those written by de Lubac, Daniélou, and Hanson, not only defended the sobriety of Alexandrian exegesis but also implicitly or explicitly pleaded for the continuing relevance of symbolic interpretations[16].

In his 1990 *NJBC* article on "Hermeneutics", Brown relegated this movement to the past rather than the present discussion of biblical hermeneutics[17]. However, the Biblical Commission's new definition of the spiritual sense draws upon insights gained from this movement.

De Lubac, a historical theologian[18], made the weightiest contribution in three major works. In *Histoire et Esprit* (1950) de Lubac seeks to rehabilitate the memory of Origen, who epitomizes spiritual interpretation and the methodology that sees theology as wisdom gained through meditation on Scripture. In *Exégèse médievale I-IV* (1959, 1961, 1964) and in *The Sources of Revelation* (1968)[19], de Lubac traces the history of the "spiritual interpretation" of the Bible (especially the Old Testament), beginning with the writings of St. Paul and the Letter to the Hebrews up to modern times.

---

[16] Brown and Schneiders, "Hermeneutics [*NJBC*]", 1156.

[17] Brown and Schneiders, "Hermeneutics [*NJBC*]", 1157, §48.

[18] See D'Ambrosio, "Henri de Lubac". Marcellino D'Ambrosio finds in de Lubac no rejection of the historical-critical method, but an awareness of its limits, and an anticipation of how those limits might be surpassed. Rather than being pre-critical, de Lubac is a precursor of post-critical interpretation. D'Ambrosio's points to the philosophy of Maurice Blondel ("Histoire et dogme") as the source of the presuppositions that underlie de Lubac's critique of scientific exegesis and his interest in the "spiritual meaning." Blondel insists on the "'radical insufficiency' of either the empirical, inductive sciences or the exact, deductive sciences to provide a complete picture of human reality" (73). Blondel applies this general critique of positive science specifically to biblical exegesis, contrasting the outer manifestations with *life's inner reality*. He considers tradition to perform an indispensable role in the interpretation of historical persons, events, and texts, because it passes on the life, the inner reality of those persons. For a summary of de Lubac's proposal for the spiritual sense, see Tábet, "Il senso litterale e il senso spirituale", 29-37.

[19] De Lubac, *Sources of Revelation* (French original, 1967, *L' Écriture dans la tradition* [Paris: Aubier]).

Drawing from *The Sources of Revelation*, which recapitulates the other two on the spiritual sense, one can sum up some of his central ideas as follows:

1. Spiritual interpretation was an essential aspect of the Christian understanding of the relationship of Christ to God's words and deeds in the Old Testament[20].

2. When one uses the term "spiritual meaning" to refer to what the ancients often called allegory, one highlights that one refers to what is interior, what is allied with truth, and the meaning that comes to us from the Spirit (as does also the literal meaning). One indicates that it is a meaning that leads to the realities of the spiritual life, and that can only be the fruit of a spiritual life.

3. The literal historical meaning and the spiritual meaning coincide, interpenetrate and need one another.

4. The spiritual meaning of the Old Testament is none other than the New Testament.

Although de Lubac describes spiritual exegesis and its role in tradition brilliantly, he does not systematize his conclusions or offer a clear proposal for how spiritual exegesis might be employed today and integrated with scientific exegesis.

During the late 1980's and 1990's the Belgian exegete, Ignace de la Potterie, advocated a recovery of the spiritual sense in a series of articles[21]. Alluding to the teaching of Jerome and citing the hermeneutical principle of *Dei Verbum* 12 that "holy Scripture must be read and interpreted according to the same Spirit by whom it was written", de la Potterie describes both a subjective and an objective aspect to the spiritual sense. The subjective aspect includes the light of faith and the exegete's "participation in the Church's movement of conversion" without which it is impossible to understand Scripture[22]. The objective aspect is an "interiority" in Scripture itself, "the presence of the Spirit in the letter", a deeper meaning, a "mystery" beneath the surface of Scripture due to its divine inspiration[23]. Scientific exegesis has

---

[20] De Lubac, *Sources of Revelation*, 5. Here de Lubac explains that Christians today "can behave like pure literalists without any great harm" because they inherit a ready-made Christianity with its spirituality and formulations already worked out, thanks in part to the Fathers' use of the spiritual sense.

[21] See de la Potterie, "Reading Holy Scripture 'in the Spirit'", "Interpretation in the Spirit (*Dei Verbum* 12c)", "The Spiritual Sense", *Storia e mistero*, and "Storia e mistero".

[22] De la Potterie, "Reading Holy Scripture 'in the Spirit'", 311.

[23] De la Potterie, "Reading Holy Scripture 'in the Spirit'", 312. It should be apparent that de la Potterie's distinction between the subjective and objective work of the Spirit in relation to the Bible is a different distinction from the objective-subjective aspects of the Spirit's role in interpretation described earlier in this chapter.

lost the deep meaning of the text, its marrow, its life, its character as divine revelation. The truth of Scripture is not truth in the positivist sense of modern science, but the grace of revealed truth, the Gospel that saves[24]. De la Potterie urges interpretation with a clearer awareness of the theology of inspiration, drawing upon the tradition of the Church, and the analogy of faith, which, along with the unity of Scripture, provide sufficient controls on spiritual interpretation. He advocates the spiritual sense as part of a broader concern that Catholic exegesis reject the historicist and positivist tendencies in the historical-critical method and embrace a hermeneutic of faith. De la Potterie is persuasive about most of what he affirms, but does not articulate how the "spiritual interpretation" which he is advocating can be successfully related to the critical methods which he also values.

Catholic scholars who have expressed reservations about the efforts to rediscover the spiritual sense of Scripture are concerned about several things. First, the term "spiritual meaning" or "spiritual sense" is vague, and is easily used to justify subjective or accommodated interpretations. Fitzmyer refers to the term "spiritual meaning" as a "weasel word" on account of its lack of precision and frequent abuse[25]. Second, advocates of the spiritual sense appear to their critics as nostalgic and uncritical regarding patristic and medieval allegorization[26]. Third, insofar as "spiritual interpretation" introduces subjective readings, eisegesis, or accommodated interpretations, it threatens the objectivity of the biblical message, undermining its authority and blunting its critical function in the Church. Finally, the critics of spiritual exegesis are themselves practitioners of the historical-critical method and perceive the advocacy of the spiritual sense as an attack on the method they consider essential to a reasonable, as opposed to a naïve, approach to Scripture.

The Biblical Commission's position addresses some of the central concerns of both sides without perhaps entirely satisfying either those advocating or those objecting to the spiritual interpretation of Scripture. As scholars versed in the historical-critical method, the members of the Commission insist on the necessity of this method, the priority of establishing the literal sense, and a concern to safeguard the objectivity of Scripture's content. While appreciating aspects of patristic exegesis, they explicitly reject

---

[24] De la Potterie, "L'esegesi biblica, scienza della fede", 163-165.

[25] Fitzmyer, "Literal and Spiritual Senses", 139-140; Fitzmyer and Stahel, "Interview", 10.

[26] Perhaps de Lubac and de la Potterie may be regarded as nostalgic, but their learned contributions to this discussion and their sophisticated understandings of Scripture cannot reasonably be considered "uncritical".

the allegorical extremes to which many Fathers resorted as lacking "true interpretative value" (II.B.2.h). They also give a precise definition to the spiritual sense which excludes mere accommodation or subjective or speculative interpretation, and which could prevent abuse of the term. On the other hand, those who have been urging the recovery of the spiritual sense should be pleased that despite its loyalty to both the historical-critical method and the priority of the literal sense, the Biblical Commission has reaffirmed the validity and importance of the spiritual sense of Scripture. Fitzmyer, an occasionally harsh critic of the spiritual meaning as it is commonly urged, explains the Commission's endorsement of the spiritual sense:

> This spiritual sense recognizes a unity in the written Word of God, i.e., in the Old and New Testaments together, which the Christian interpreter has to respect. It recognizes this as a theological unity that the Church has kept alive through its living Tradition, a unity which respects the two Testaments and does not try to confuse them.... It recognizes too that Old Testament themes are enriched by their New Testament counterparts and are progressively transformed by the New Testament's thrust.
>
> ...This traditional meaning is likewise the motivation for the use of the Old Testament in much of the Christian liturgy. In itself, this christological meaning of the Old Testament is not problematic, even if one has to recognize that it is a sense added to the literal sense of the Old Testament[27].

Furthermore, the Commission says that it is the *responsibility* of exegetes to "explain the christological, canonical, and ecclesial meanings of the biblical texts" (III.C.1c). The Biblical Commission's definition of the spiritual sense resembles, in some respects, de Lubac's description of this sense in the medieval tradition, for example. It has already been noted that the Commission insists that Catholic interpretation employs a hermeneutic of faith and agrees that the life of the Spirit is essential to understanding the Scriptures. These are points stressed by de la Potterie. Nevertheless, the Commission uses sober language, prescinding from mystical tones or maximizing theological language regarding Scripture's inner reality used by some Church Fathers and advocates of the spiritual sense[28].

---

[27] Fitzmyer, "Literal and Spiritual Senses", 141-142.

[28] This does not imply a rejection of these theological affirmations on the part of the Biblical Commission, but rather the desire to avoid entering into a discussion of the theology of inspiration (Intro B.b), and the desire to avoid imprecision or exaggeration about the meaning of the spiritual sense. Yet it may be debated whether a document attempting to give an overall account of interpretation in the Church should limit itself in this way.

7. The Spiritual Sense According to the Biblical Commission

a) A New Kind of Definition

The careful observer will note that the definition of the spiritual sense as "the meaning expressed by the biblical texts when read under the influence of the Holy Spirit in the context of the Paschal Mystery" (II.B.2.b) differs from previous definitions in the tradition. Before Thomas Aquinas the spiritual sense was rather loosely defined. But St. Thomas (*ST* I.a.I,10) defines the spiritual sense to be "things" or "realities" (*res*) recounted in Scripture which God uses to signify other realities. Thomas means primarily Old Testament events, individuals, institutions or objects which refer to Christ and the realities of the New Covenant, i.e., what is generally described as typology[29]. Rather than defining the spiritual sense in terms of the signification of realities by other realities, the Commission defines it as *texts re-contextualized by subsequent events*, namely, the death and resurrection of Christ and the new life that flows from it. This new context includes the light of revelation, since these texts are read "under the influence of the Holy Spirit". The Biblical Commission's re-definition of the spiritual sense is not opposed to the traditional definition, but it follows more closely upon modern hermeneutical insights referred to earlier in the same chapter of the *IBC*, recognizing that it is the nature of written texts to be re-read in the light of new circumstances. In addition, the new definition is capable of including a broader range of post-Paschal meanings to Old Testament texts which otherwise might escape categorization. For instance, the meaning in light of the paschal event of Nathan's prophecy (2 Sam 7), which promises that God will establish the throne of David's son "forever", would not satisfy St. Thomas' definition of the spiritual sense, since it is not "things" signifying other "things". However, the expanded meaning of Nathan's prophecy fits the Biblical Commission's definition of the spiritual sense nicely, as a meaning expressed by the text when read in the context of the paschal mystery under the illumination of the Spirit.

---

[29] While Thomas Aquinas understood the spiritual sense of Scripture as the typical sense, when "things signified by the words in their turn also signify other things" (*ST* Ia.I,10,3), Pope Pius XII modifies Thomas' definition. Instead of referring to the signifying role of "things [*res*]", Pius says that the spiritual sense consists of both "what was said and done [*dicta vel facta*]" in the OT that prefigured the new dispensation in Christ (*DAS* 26, *EB* §552). By mentioning *dicta*, some authors suggest that Pius XII was leaving room for the *sensus plenior*, a meaning to their words that the human authors did not fully realize (see Brown, *The Sensus Plenior*, 138-139). Tábet, however, citing other authorities, argues that Pius was simply intending to expand Thomas' definition of the spiritual sense to include OT "literary types" (see discussion in Tábet, "Il senso litterale e il senso spirituale", 24n).

b) Achievement

The Biblical Commission has rendered a real service in providing this new definition of the spiritual sense. Insofar as the spiritual sense reveals how Jesus fulfills the Old Testament, it belongs to Church doctrine and to the classical Christian hermeneutic which Catholics share with other Christians[30]. Besides being faithful to the theological tradition, the Commission's definition draws upon modern hermeneutical insights. In addition, the Commission's explanation of the spiritual sense provides a balanced response to the sometimes heated recent discussion of spiritual interpretation in the Church[31]. Although the *IBC* by no means has spoken the final word on the recovery of the spiritual sense, it does mark a step forward.

8. *Contemporary Neglect*

Although the Biblical Commission says that it is the responsibility of exegetes to explain the christological meaning of texts, contemporary scholarly explanation of the christological sense of Old Testament texts is conspicuous for its rarity. Instead, attention tends to rest on the literal sense, understood as the original meaning, even for the texts whose most obvious and profoundest meanings concern the paschal mystery or whose historical referents are obscure and irrelevant to Christian life today.

To illustrate tendencies in the current practice, this section will briefly contrast the *IBC*'s interpretation of Nathan's prophecy (2 Sam 7:12-13) with the interpretation given in two recent prominent single volume commentaries: the *New Jerome Biblical Commentary* (*NJBC*, 1990), and the *International Bible Commentary* (*IBCom*, 1999).

The Biblical Commission interprets 2 Sam 7:12-13 to possess a spiritual meaning when read in light of Christ's death and resurrection. The Old Testament text is read in light of the paschal mystery and "undergoe[s] a change in meaning" at the same time as it attains a "higher fulfillment" (II.B.2.a):

> Certain texts which in ancient times had to be thought of as hyperbole (e.g., the oracle where God, speaking of a son of David, promised to establish his throne "forever"): ...these texts must now be taken literally, because

---

[30] Ghiberti and Mosetto, *L'interpretazione: Commento*, 292n.

[31] Despite this progress there are some indications that the Biblical Commission did not discuss the spiritual sense enough to be completely clear on what they meant. Thus Fitzmyer and Dumais both attempt to clarify the confusing reference to the "religious or spiritual" (II.B.2.d) meaning of the OT (Fitzmyer, "Literal and Spiritual Senses", 139-145; Dumais, "Sens de l'Écriture", 329-330), and Levoratti ties the spiritual sense to spiritual reading and distances it from exegesis and theology ("How to Interpret", 23-24).

"Christ, having been raised from the dead, dies no more" (Rom 6:9)....
Those who are open to the dynamic aspect of a text will recognize a
profound element of continuity as well as a move to a different level: Christ
rules forever, but not on the earthly throne of David. (II.B.2.a)

Here is what the *NJBC* comment says about the same text:

The unit is fundamental in Israelite, Jewish and Christian royal messianism.
A highly nuanced playing on house, dynasty, and temple themes connects it
with narratives before and after. Deuteronomistic editors or earlier post-
Davidic redactors may be responsible for the unit's present location.... The
multivalent house theme connects with the story line in chap 6. Nathan
who is mentioned elsewhere only where Bathsheba and Solomon
appear...is part of the dynasty theme[32].

This interpretation represents the not-uncommon tendency to report on a
text's use elsewhere in Scripture, to comment on its literary context, its
redaction history and thematic elements, and to fail to explain its meaning.

The comment in the *IBCom*, while acknowledging that these words in 2
Sam 7 express the New Testament understanding of Jesus significance,
stresses discontinuity between the prophecy and Jesus' kingdom:

The words of prophetic hope (*unfulfilled unless radically re-understood*—
e.g., Isa 9:6-7; 11:1-9) were widely used to express the NT understanding of
Jesus' significance. Since Jesus' kingdom "is not of this world" it is *not a
direct application* of 2 Sam 7. The Davidic dynasty in 2 Sam 7 is of this
world. In the texts of prophetic hope it *moves toward the realm of
metaphor and symbol*. In the NT it has *entered the realm of theology*
[emphasis added][33].

The italicized phrases express the distancing of the Old Testament text from
its New Testament fulfillment. The effect of this exegesis is opposite to the
IBC, conveying the impression that the New Testament interpretation is an
imaginative construal, alien to the text's historical meaning (regarded as the
real meaning). It fits the *IBC*'s characterization of an inadequate approach:
"Exegetes who have a narrow, 'historicist' idea about the literal sense will
judge that here is an example of interpretation alien to the original" (II.B.2.a).

Besides its ability to recognize the continuity between this Old Testament
text and its New Testament fulfillment, what is refreshing about the *IBC*'s
interpretation is its *stance*. The Biblical Commission interprets the Old

---

[32] Campbell and Flanagan, "1-2 Samuel", 156.

[33] Campbell and O'Brien, "1-2 Samuel", 596. No special criticism is intended of the
authors of these comments on 2 Sam 7 in the *NJBC* and the *IBCom*. The approach taken in
each commentary is representative of common practice. The *IBC*'s re-presentation of the
spiritual and fuller senses challenges that practice.

Testament from within the tradition of faith expressed in the New Testament. The other commentators view the same facts, but as though studying them from outside, looking in at how believers understand the text.

A variety of factors may help to explain the contemporary absence of Catholic spiritual interpretation. The absence of a clear definition of the spiritual sense in modern times contributed to the impression that the "spiritual sense" belonged to eisegesis, or to devotional or homiletic interpretation. The tendency of the historical-critical method toward an exclusive interest in original meanings has already been mentioned. Also the association of the spiritual sense with anti-critical perspectives may have increased the reticence of scholars to explicate it. Finally, the social location of exegesis in secular university settings has tended to inhibit exegesis from within a faith perspective. Once scholarly neglect of the spiritual sense was established, it naturally perpetuated itself, since scholarly discussion tends to respond to what other scholars are already saying and doing.

It may be fervently hoped that Catholic scholars will accept the challenge and opportunity which the Biblical Commission's definition of the spiritual sense offers them. It is exegetes who can put flesh on, and, if necessary, refine the new definition of the spiritual sense by employing it especially in Old Testament studies. As Pope John Paul said, commenting on *Divino afflante Spiritu* in his "Address" to the Biblical Commission, "Determining the spiritual sense... belongs itself to the realm of exegetical science" (Address 5)[34]. If interpreters accept the challenge, the explication of the spiritual sense of Scripture holds potential benefits not only for enlightening exegesis but also for the nourishment of the people of God.

---

[34] For reference to *DAS*, see note on p. 179.

CHAPTER 14

The Fuller Sense (*Sensus Plenior*)

Principle #14

✳ *The fuller sense (sensus plenior) is a deeper meaning of the text, intended by God but not clearly expressed by the human author (II.B.3.a). It has its foundation in the fact that the Holy Spirit, principal author of the Bible, can guide human authors in the choice of expressions in such a way that the latter will express a truth, the fullest depths of which the authors do not perceive (II.B.3.c).*

The existence of a fuller sense to a biblical text can be recognized when one studies the text in the light of other biblical texts or authoritative doctrinal traditions which utilize it[1]. (II.B.3.a)

Explanation

1. Description

- *The fuller sense* (sensus plenior) *is a deeper meaning of the text, intended by God but not clearly expressed by the human author. (II.B.3.a)*

The Biblical Commission recognizes more-than-literal meanings which preserve a continuity with the literal sense, namely, the spiritual sense, which results from reading texts in the light of the new historical context of the

---

[1] Every reference to the fuller sense of Scripture in the *IBC* is found in a brief section (three paragraphs) devoted to it in the chapter dedicated to hermeneutical questions (II.B.3). The wording of this principle is taken almost verbatim from the Biblical Commission's document.

paschal event under the influence of the Spirit. Yet there remain other texts which are interpreted by later biblical texts or authoritative Church teaching to have meanings which appear to go beyond what the human author intended to express by his words. Either the subsequent biblical author takes up the text in a new context, "which confers upon it a new literal sense" (II.B.3.b) or an authoritative doctrinal tradition or conciliar definition gives a text a meaning which Christians recognize as authentic. The Biblical Commission identifies such meanings as the "fuller" sense, or *sensus plenior* of a biblical text. The *IBC* is the first church document to recognize this sense which scholars have discussed since the 1920's.

2. Foundations

> *It has its foundation in the fact that the Holy Spirit, principal author of the Bible, can guide human authors in the choice of expressions in such a way that the latter will express a truth the fullest depths of which the authors do not perceive (II.B.3.c).*

It would be a mistake to think that what is called the fuller sense is simply an officially sanctioned accommodation of a biblical text. The Commission gives both a theological and a philosophical explanation for the validity of the fuller sense. Theologically, its basis is the doctrine of inspiration:

> It has its foundation in the fact that the Holy Spirit, principal author of the Bible, can guide human authors in the choice of expressions in such a way that the latter will express a truth[,] the fullest depths of which the authors themselves do not perceive. This deeper truth will be more fully revealed in the course of time—on the one hand, through further divine interventions which clarify the meaning of texts and, on the other, through the insertion of texts into the canon of Scripture. (II.B.3.c)

Philosophically, as in the case of the spiritual sense, the hermeneutical principle which justifies an increase in meaning is a re-reading of the text in new context. The *IBC* quotation above finishes as follows: "In these ways there is created a new context, which brings out fresh possibilities of meaning that had lain hidden in the original context" (II.B.3.c).

3. Examples

The *IBC* offers three examples of the fuller sense. The Gospel of Matthew affirms that the virginal conception of Jesus took place in fulfillment of a prophecy in Isa 7:14: "All this took place to fulfill what had been spoken by the Lord through the prophet: 'Look, the virgin shall conceive and bear a son, and they shall name him Emmanuel', which means, 'God is with us'" (Mt 1:22-23). Matthew cites the Septuagint version of the prophecy which uses the word *parthenos*, "virgin", while the original Hebrew text uses the more general term, *almah*, meaning, "young woman". Furthermore, the context of Isa 7:14 suggests that the prophet was intending to refer to the birth of a child contemporaneous to the events then taking place. Matthew thus indicates that God had a deeper purpose in the words he spoke through Isaiah than the prophet himself realized.

The other two examples which the Biblical Commission gives us show that New Testament texts may bear a fuller sense which is confirmed in the doctrine of the Church. "Patristic and conciliar teaching about the Trinity expresses the fuller sense of the New Testament regarding God the Father, Son, and the Holy Spirit" (II.B.3.b). In other words, patristic and conciliar teaching on the Trinity shows a more developed and precise conception of the divinity of the Son and the Spirit and the relationship among the members of the Trinity ("three persons in one God") than it appears the Scriptural authors themselves expressed when they wrote[2]. Yet this later more precise understanding (not necessarily its particular formulations) is a true, divinely intended sense of the New Testament texts on the three Divine Persons. Similarly, "the definition of original sin by the Council of Trent provided the fuller sense of Paul's teaching in Rom 5:12-21 about the consequences of the sin of Adam for humanity" (II.B.3.b)[3]. While the Pauline text can be read as ambiguous about the transmission of original sin to the whole human race on account of Adam's sin, the subsequent conciliar dogmatic definition which cites Rom 5 enables us to recognize the transmission of original sin to humanity through Adam's sin as the fuller sense of Paul's words[4].

---

[2] Fitzmyer, *The Biblical Commission's Document*, 131.

[3] See the Council of Trent, Decree on Original Sin (17 June 1546), DS §1510-1516.

[4] This sentence is my interpretation of the *IBC*'s explanation, quoted in the previous sentence. The example remains a bit murky. Was the Biblical Commission referring to the famous evfV w- difficulty of Rom 5:12 (the text cited by the Council of Trent)? The Vulgate interprets the verse as follows: "Sin came into the world through one man, and death through sin, and so death spread to all men as all sinned *in him*." Yet most scholars are convinced that the evfV w- which Jerome translated as "in him"—referring to Adam (a grammatically possible translation)—should in its context rather be translated as a conjunction, "*because* all sinned". Is the Biblical Commission saying that the doctrine of the Vulgate translation of this verse is the fuller sense, even if it is a less probable translation of what the author intended by those words? Or is the Biblical Commission simply saying that the doctrine of Trent on original sin as a whole is a fuller sense of the whole section, 5:12-21, i.e., not clearly expressed in the text but attributed to it by later authority, and therefore to be accepted as its fuller meaning?

4. Relation to the Literal and Spiritual Senses

The part of the definition of the fuller sense which says that it is a deeper meaning "not clearly expressed by the human author" clearly distinguishes it from the literal sense, whose content is "that which has been expressed directly by the human authors" (II.B.2.c, principle #12).

However, the fact that the fuller sense is defined as a "deeper meaning of the text, intended by God" (II.B.3.b) raises the question of its relationship to the spiritual sense. The Biblical Commission links the two senses in one sentence: "In a word [Fr., *En définitive*, "finally"], one might think of the 'fuller sense' as another way of indicating the spiritual sense of a biblical text in the case where the spiritual sense is distinct from the literal sense." Thus, the fuller sense is a sub-category of the spiritual sense.

This statement that the fuller sense belongs to the spiritual sense sheds additional light on both senses. Unlike other claimed instances of the spiritual sense, an interpretation claiming to render the fuller sense of a text is not obliged to demonstrate its relationship of homogeneity or continuity with the literal sense of a text. However, the fact that the Biblical Commission sees the fuller sense as a spiritual sense demonstrates that it shares the fundamental characteristic of the spiritual sense, namely, it is a meaning expressed by the text "when read under the influence of the Holy Spirit, in the context of the paschal mystery of Christ and of the new life which flows from it" (II.B.2.b, principle #13).

The last two examples of the fuller sense of New Testament texts—regarding the relation of conciliar definitions of Trinitarian doctrine and original sin—indicate that the "context of the paschal mystery and of the new life which flows from it" does not end with New Testament interpretations of Old Testament realities or texts. Rather, the new context can encompass consideration of a text in light of "the internal development of revelation" in the Tradition of the Church (II.B.3.a).

5. Controls

. *The existence of a fuller sense to a biblical text can be recognized when one studies the text in the light of other biblical texts or authoritative doctrinal traditions which utilize it. (II.B.3.a)*

Obviously the introduction of a spiritual sense of Scripture distinct from the literal sense could open the door to a host of arbitrary or subjective interpretations. Fully aware of this the Biblical Commission insists on a criterion of control. To be accepted as a valid instance of the fuller sense, an interpretation must have the warrant of an explicit biblical text or an authentic doctrinal tradition or conciliar definition which attributes the meaning in question to another biblical text.

Discussion

6. History

The fuller sense is a relatively new way of classifying Scriptural meaning due to modern attention to the human author's intention. In the precritical past interpreters were generally not concerned about how much the human author understood his texts the way they were subsequently understood. The fact that the Bible expressed the word of God was sufficient, and the relationship between that written word of God and the intention of its human authors was not of great interest. The rise of historical consciousness changed that, and the fuller sense was an attempt to acknowledge a distinction between inspired meanings the human author did not perceive and those he did.

The concept of the *sensus plenior*, the "fuller sense", was first proposed by Andrea Fernández in 1925[5]. Fernández' reasons were apologetic: he sought a basis for theological exegesis in light of the rejection of the traditional four senses by the Reformation and critical scholarship. Later advocates included Joseph Coppens, Pierre Benoit and Raymond Brown[6]. The *sensus plenior* permitted interpreters to acknowledge the limited knowledge and intention of the human authors of Scripture, and, at the same time, to affirm the deeper meaning of texts, e.g., the fulfillment of the Old Testament in Christ, as a meaning placed in Scripture by its divine author. It also opened the way to the acceptance of other later applications of texts in the Fathers of the Church, the liturgy, and in theological authors. This deeper meaning was not seen as accessible through the historical-critical method, which derives the literal sense, but through consideration of later texts in the progression of revelation and theological reflection. The *NJBC* offers a standard definition:

> The *sensus plenior* is the deeper meaning, intended by God but not clearly intended by the human author, that is seen to exist in the words of Scripture when they are studied in the light of further revelation or of development in the understanding of revelation[7].

In his 1955 doctoral dissertation, Brown's argued that the *sensus plenior*, taken together with the typical sense, provided a more satisfactory way of

---

[5] Fernández, "Hermeneutica", 306-307.
[6] See Coppens, "Le problème d'un sens biblique plénier" and Brown, *The Sensus Plenior*.
[7] Brown and Schneiders, "Hermeneutics [*NJBC*]", 1157.

referring to the more-than-literal senses of Scripture than the "spiritual sense", which other authors proposed. He objected to the vagueness of the definitions of the spiritual sense proposed up until that time. Brown saw the *sensus plenior* standing between the literal sense and the typical sense, which at that time enjoyed wide acceptance: "Like the literal sense it is a meaning of the text; unlike it, it is not within the clear purview of the hagiographer. It shares this latter characteristic with the typical sense; but unlike the typical sense, it is not a sense of 'things' but of words"[8]. The fact that Brown's *sensus plenior* included all the "deeper" senses of the words of Scripture other than typology made it a broader category than the "fuller sense" under the *IBC*'s definition.

For a variety of reasons scholars lost interest in the *sensus plenior* in the years following the Second Vatican Council, so that, according to Brown, there has been virtually no discussion of it since 1970[9]. Brian McNeil credits this decline of the *sensus plenior* in part to its dependence on *a priori* theological principles[10]. Post-conciliar exegesis was more concerned with studying texts "in their historically conditioned individuality" and was reluctant to "subordinate" Old Testament texts to Christology and ecclesiology[11]. Furthermore,

> An academically neutral exegesis is reluctant to speak so readily about what God intended the authors of the OT texts to say; and in the *de facto* separation of exegesis and dogmatics as autonomous disciplines in Catholic Theology, theories like the *sensus plenior* which concern both disciplines at once are not likely to find persons sufficiently competent in both to be able to discuss them and defend them[12].

Brown himself came to believe that the *sensus plenior* was unlikely to gain acceptance due to its dependence on a scholastic instrumental understanding of inspiration which had been "in vogue among Catholics" at the time the theory of the *sensus plenior* was developed[13]:

> There are those who find difficulty with such a theory in which God intimately guides every step from thought to word, and they prefer to approach inspiration as a social charism or from the aspect of the post-factum role of Scripture in the community.... Perhaps the solution is to take the emphasis off the mechanics of the divine and human intentions and to concentrate rather on the close relationship between the idea of the *sensus plenior* and the modern interest in the hermeneutical value of language.

---

[8] Brown, *The Sensus Plenior*, 122.
[9] Brown and Schneiders, "Hermeneutics [*NJBC*]", 1157.
[10] McNeil, "*Sensus Plenior* [*DBI*]", 621-622.
[11] McNeil, "*Sensus Plenior* [*DBI*]", 622.
[12] McNeil, "*Sensus Plenior* [*DBI*]", 622.
[13] Brown and Schneiders, "Hermeneutics [*NJBC*]", 1157, §50.

> The language of Scripture may have had one meaning in the human author's situation; yet in a different situation (e.g., that of the Church today) it may make its point in a different way and to this extent mean something different.[14]

Brown came to think that the future of the *sensus plenior* and of the typical sense lay in the context of a broader treatment of more-than-literal meaning of the Bible. In 1992 he saw "its contemporary continuation as the 'fuller sense' or 'excess of meaning'... in literary criticism related to the new hermeneutic"[15].

7. *The Fuller Sense in the* IBC

The Biblical Commission has breathed new life into the concept of the *sensus plenior*, which they call the "fuller sense", choosing to express the concept in modern languages rather than in Latin. Although Brown may not have anticipated the conclusions of the Biblical Commission regarding more-than-literal senses of Scripture, he was right in thinking that "modern interest in the hermeneutical value of language" held a key. According to Brown, "The language of Scripture may have had one meaning in the human author's situation; yet in a different situation...it may...mean something different"[16]. This statement is not far from the Commission's explanation of the philosophical basis of the fuller sense, namely that "In these ways [i.e., through further divine interventions which clarify texts and through the insertion of texts into the canon] there is a created a new context, which brings out fresh possibilities of meaning that had lain hidden in the original context" (II.B.3.c).

The Biblical Commission does not attempt to speculate on "the mechanics of the divine and human intentions" of how God inspired a deeper meaning than the human author expressed in the text. Rather the Commission makes the simple theological affirmation that "the Holy Spirit, principal author of the Bible, can guide human authors in the choice of expressions in such a way that the latter will express a truth[,] the fullest depths of which the authors do not perceive. This deeper truth will be more fully revealed in the course of time" (II.B.3.c).

Christoph Dohmen maintains that the *IBC*'s section on the fuller sense lays hold of a central issue for the interpretation of the Christian Bible. He concludes his article,

---

[14] Brown, "Hermeneutics [*JBC*]", §68.

[15] Brown and Schneiders, "Hermeneutics [*NJBC*]", 1157, §51.

[16] Brown, "Hermeneutics [*JBC*]", §68.

At this point one senses that the *sensus plenior* is no longer a relic of exegetical history, mentioned in passing, but an important aspect of biblical hermeneutics to be safeguarded. It relates to the understanding of the Bible in its twofold unity, the basis of the "soul of theology"[17].

At first glance Dohmen seems to be overstating the point. In the *IBC* the role of the fuller sense remains limited, and the texts which satisfy its strict controls are not numerous. However, deeper reflection leads this author to agree with Dohmen, on account of the theological affirmation (stated above) which the explanation of the fuller sense elicits from the Biblical Commission. Except for what it says about the role of the Holy Spirit, the *IBC*'s explanations of both the literal sense and the spiritual sense can be justified by hermeneutical principles that characterize any other human document. The literal sense of Scripture is the author's meaning which, like other texts, can bear meaning that transcends the original circumstances. The spiritual sense, in the *IBC*'s explanation, is a re-reading of the literal sense in light of new circumstances, just as any other book, the *Diary of Anne Frank*, for instance, might take on new meaning in the light of subsequent events[18]. The *IBC*'s explanations of the literal and spiritual sense are made "from below", explaining them in familiar hermeneutical concepts. However, when the Commission speaks of the fuller sense it affirms that God guided the expression of the human authors to achieve a purpose which he had in mind but which they did not know. At this point ordinary hermeneutical concepts are transcended, and the discussion turns to what is unique to the hermeneutics of Sacred Scripture. Dohmen realizes that this same affirmation about God guiding the expression of Scripture also applies to interpretation in light of the canon, and he would like to see the relation between the fuller and the canonical sense of Scripture further explored. It is the acknowledgment of divine authorship that enables the Bible to be the soul of theology.

The affirmation that the Holy Spirit "can guide human authors in the choice of expressions" reflects back on the spiritual sense as well. While it is possible to explain the spiritual sense of 2 Sam 7:12-13 (Nathan's prophecy to David) "from below" as the *IBC* has done, in terms of a Christian re-reading of the text in light of the fact of Jesus' resurrection, it is also possible to explain it "from above", as the divinely guided expression of the Old Testament author to express a truth which God had in mind but which the human author did not fully perceive. Considered from this vantage point, the spiritual sense forms a sub-category of the fuller sense. Among all the Old

---

[17] Dohmen, "Was Gott sagen wollte...", 251-254.

[18] Of course the paschal event is of an entirely different order, and the Biblical Commission also speaks of the role of the Spirit in the re-reading process.

Testament texts which find fulfillment in the New, the spiritual sense describes those texts characterized by continuity between the literal sense and its fulfillment in light of the paschal event. These were the instances in which the words of the Old Testament suggest that divine inspiration granted the human authors some inkling, however vague, of a truth that would become more clear in light of the paschal mystery.

8. A Table of the Senses, Evaluation

The significance of each of the individual senses of Scripture can best be understood in the context of an overview of the senses and their interrelationships. To put the Biblical Commission's view of the senses in perspective, a schematic representation comparing it with other conceptions may be useful.

Aquinas' Division of the Senses on the Basis of the Material Object of Interpretation, 13th century (ST Ia. I, 10)

Sense of the words:

(1) Literal Sense. The intention of the divine author (with which, perhaps, the intention of the human author was presumed to coincide).

Sense of the "things" (res):

(2) Spiritual Sense. What the "things"—events, persons, institutions, objects—of Scripture signify according to God's intention. Includes the allegorical, moral, and anagogical senses. However, since this meaning is not in words, it is not suited for theological argument.

Pius XII's Division on the Basis of the Human Author's Intention and divinely ordered Old Testament realities that prefigure the New Covenant, 1943 (DAS)[19]

Sense of the words understood according to the mind of the human author:

---

[19] Tábet emphasizes the continuity between the approach to the senses of St. Thomas and Pope Pius XII and would therefore envision Pius' schema as a slight modification of Thomas' ("Il senso litterale e il senso spirituale", 46-48). Such a schema would indicate only a modest change in the spiritual sense to include literary types. However, Pius' stress on the human author's intention in the literal sense and his identifying the orientation of the spiritual sense toward the "new dispensation of grace" warrants the schema given above. As such, it marks a clear development on the way toward the position of the IBC.

(1) Literal Sense. What the human author intended which also manifested the divine intention on account of inspiration.

Sense of the "words and deeds" of the Old Testament divinely intended to prefigure the dispensation of grace:

(2) Spiritual Sense. Only those spiritual meanings which can be shown to be intended by God[20].

Brown's Division On The Basis Of The Human Author's Intention, 1955[21]

Meaning intended by the human author:

(1) Literal Sense. What the divine and human authors both clearly intended.

Meaning intended by God that goes beyond what the human author intended:

(2) *Sensus Plenior*. Flowing from the words of Scripture.

(3) Typical Sense. Flowing from the "things" described in Scripture.

Biblical Commission's Division On the Basis of the New Context of the Paschal Mystery and the Influence of the Holy Spirit, 1993

Meaning expressed (intended) by the human author:

(1) Literal Sense. Also a meaning intended by God.

Meaning of text in the context of the paschal mystery under the influence of the Holy Spirit:

(2) Spiritual sense. A meaning consistent with the meaning expressed by the human author (the literal sense), and willed by God (since elucidated by the Spirit). Typology belongs to this sense.

(3) Fuller sense: A deeper meaning NOT clearly expressed by the human author, but nevertheless, intended by God. A special case of the spiritual sense.

---

[20] To be admitted as a spiritual sense intended by God, confirmation must be found elsewhere in Scripture, tradition, or in ancient liturgical usage. This is a similar, but more inclusive criterion of authenticity, in comparison to the *IBC*'s "control" on the fuller sense (subsequent Scriptural interpretation or authoritative doctrinal tradition).

[21] Based on Brown, "Hermeneutics [*JBC*]", §79.

All are attempts at categorizing the classic pattern of Christian interpretation, especially of the Old Testament, which goes back to the New Testament and to Jesus himself. Aquinas, following Augustine, distinguishes figurative meaning and makes the material object of interpretation the basis of division. After the rise of historical consciousness and critical scholarship which concerned itself with the question of the human author's intention in a new way, Pius XII reconceives Aquinas' division, making the intention of the human author a defining characteristic of the literal sense and recognizing the christological orientation of the spiritual sense. Continuing the dialogue with scientific study of Scripture, Brown makes the human author's intention the basis for the fundamental division of the senses. Brown also brings greater clarity to more-than-literal meanings, distinguishing between the typological sense which refers to the meaning of "things" (*res*) and the *sensus plenior* which refers to the meaning of the words[22].

The Biblical Commission's division, based on the new context of the paschal event and the influence of the Spirit, marks a genuine advance[23]. First, it provides a weighty theological criterion of division between the literal and spiritual senses, rather than the philosophical criterion of "material object" or historical criterion of "author's intention". Second, the Biblical Commission's division of the senses corresponds to the historical unfolding of the Christian interpretation of the Old Testament—only after the death and resurrection of Christ were the minds of Christians "opened to understand the Scriptures" (Luke 24:45). Third, it recognizes the activity of the Spirit as the

---

[22] This depiction of various divisions of the senses helps one to see that Brown's 1955 proposal for the *sensus plenior* was a broader category than the fuller sense as defined by the Biblical Commission. In the *IBC* the primary division is between the literal and spiritual sense, with the fuller sense being one kind of spiritual sense. In Brown's proposal the *sensus plenior* included every genuine subsequent meaning the author did not clearly intend apart from typology.

[23] Despite his article's many useful contributions, Tábet misunderstands the *IBC*'s division of the literal and spiritual senses as a function of "what could be called the 'exterior sense' and the 'interior sense' of Scripture" ("Il senso litterale e il senso spirituale", 46). On the one hand, the Biblical Commission never speaks of either sense in terms of interiority or exteriority. On the other, the Commission calls upon exegetes to communicate the "religious content" and "theological meaning" of texts (III.D.2.a, 4.b), without limiting or identifying this with the spiritual sense. Christian faith draws nourishment both from the literal sense and the spiritual sense of Scripture. The *IBC*'s lead example of the spiritual sense, recognizing God's promise to David of a son who would sit on his throne "forever" (2 Sam 7:12-13) as fulfilled in Christ's eternal rule, appears as an open, public sense of the text in light of the new context of Jesus' resurrection, rather than as an interior dimension of meaning. It appears that the *IBC*'s confusing reference to the "religious or spiritual sense" in the OT (II.B.2.d—see discussion on p. 193n) has led Tábet to interpret the spiritual sense too generically as "the Christian-religious meaning of Scripture" ("Il senso litterale e il senso spirituale", 12).

source of the Christian hermeneutic. Fourth, it is grounded philosophically in modern hermeneutical insight about the capacity of written texts to yield new meanings in new contexts. Fifth, it corrects the traditional view that typology is exclusively a relationship between the "things" (*res*), recognizing that typology depends on Scripture's depiction of these "things", and it accepts typology as a subset of the spiritual sense. Sixth, respecting modern historical-consciousness, it distinguishes, within the spiritual sense, between subsequent meanings that bear a relationship to what the human author originally expressed, and those which do not. The improvement which this writer would recommend to what the Biblical Commission has done would be to explicitly state that the spiritual sense of Old Testament texts is not only a valid re-reading of their meaning in the light of the paschal mystery, but that it is also a divinely-intended meaning.

Of course, applying the Biblical Commission's definitions of the senses of Scripture will not be problem-free. The greatest difficulty in discerning the spiritual sense will be the determination of whether a subsequent meaning is "alien" to the literal sense, or whether it is consistent with it, perhaps due to some open or "dynamic" dimension present in the literal sense. If the subsequent meaning is judged to be "alien" from the original literal sense, it may only be considered a true sense of the text if adequate subsequent Scriptural texts or authoritative doctrinal traditions justify its being considered an instance of the fuller sense.

PART V

METHODS AND APPROACHES

The last two parts of this study have treated the principles that enable Catholics to interpret Scripture as the word of God. It is time to turn again to a consideration of the human dimension of the Bible, because the word of God comes to us in historically-conditioned human language, just as the divine Word once came in a human body. Part V will address the methods and approaches based on human knowledge and reason which make it possible to understand the historically-conditioned human language through which God speaks. Principle #15 concerns the method which the Biblical Commission calls "indispensable", namely the historical-critical method. Principle #16 concerns other methods and approaches which can yield insight into the meaning of the biblical word.

CHAPTER 15

The Use of the Historical-Critical Method

Principle #15

The historical-critical method is the indispensable tool of scientific exegesis to ascertain the literal sense in a diachronic manner. (I.A.4.g, I.A.a)

In order to complete this task, it must include a synchronic study of the final form of the text, which is the expression of the word of God. (I.A.4.f)

The historical-critical method can and must be used without philosophical presuppositions contrary to Christian faith. (I.A.4.b-c)

Despite its importance, the historical-critical method cannot be granted a monopoly, and exegetes must be conscious of its limits. Exegetes must recognize the dynamic aspect of meaning and the possibility that meaning can continue to develop (Conclusion d)[1].

---

[1] The treatment of the historical-critical method occurs in several locations in the *IBC*. Ratzinger touches on it in his preface as does Pope John Paul II in his "Address" (7, 13, 14). Then the Commission itself discusses the method in their introduction (Intro A), sections I.A and III.C.1.a, and their conclusion (c-d).

Explanation

1. Necessity

The historical-critical method is the indispensable tool of scientific exegesis to ascertain the literal sense in a diachronic manner (I.A.1.g, I.A.a).

Due to the fact that the biblical writings are ancient texts and that the historical-critical method is the standard scientific way of studying ancient texts, it follows that Catholic exegesis must make use of this method (I.A.a). Human authors and editors composed the biblical texts in human language, so it is appropriate and necessary that scientific historical and literary means be employed in their interpretation.

Chapter 3 discussed the reasons why Catholic exegesis is concerned with history. Christian revelation does not come primarily as propositions which reveal truth in an abstract manner detached from historical reference. Instead God reveals himself to human beings through powerful saving acts in particular times and places and through words which interpret and are interpreted by those events. Historical study is necessary to understand the historical contexts of the biblical authors and their audiences, as well as to understand the meaning of the words, literary conventions, and concepts the biblical writers employed. Here the historical-critical method has made a notable contribution. Previous generations of Jewish and Christian interpreters had far less knowledge of the "concrete and diverse circumstances in which the Word of God took root among the people" (I.A.4.c). Advances have also occurred in understanding the diverse literary genres employed by biblical authors, and in understanding the meaning of the Hebrew, Aramaic and Greek words they used[2].

The literal sense, as explained in principle #12, is the meaning that was expressed by the biblical authors and editors in the text. One ascertains the literal sense by a careful study of a text in its literary and historical context. This is precisely the task that the historical-critical method takes up (I.A.4.g).

---

[2] Fitzmyer mentions several archaeological discoveries which have greatly enhanced our understanding of biblical times and texts: the discovery and deciphering of the Rosetta Stone (1799, 1827) and of the Bisitun inscription of Darius the Great (1846) opened up comparisons with Egyptian, Assyrian and Babylonian literature; discoveries of thousands of Greek papyri in Egypt in the 19th century shed light on the Septuagint and the NT; in the 20th century the discovery of many Aramaic documents in Egypt, important Ugaritic literature in Syria, and the Dead Sea Scrolls at Qumran (1947-1956) "have contributed much to the critical study of the OT text and to the historical study of the Palestinian Jewish culture in which Christianity and its NT find their matrix" (*Scripture, the Soul of Theology*, 12-14; see also *The Biblical Commission's Document*, 33-36).

The historical-critical method takes a "diachronic" approach to the study of the Scripture, meaning that it seeks to understand the development of texts and traditions historically. Even though a synchronic reading of the text in its final stage is absolutely necessary, since the final stage "is the expression of the Word of God" (I.A.4.f), an exclusively synchronic reading, such as some literary methods have proposed, is rejected as an "excess", as "neglecting history" (I.A.4.f). The conclusions of diachronic study are to be accepted in their "main lines" (Conclusion c). For example, this means accepting that many of the biblical books now in our possession "are not the creation of a single author, but …have had a long prehistory…tied either to the history of Israel or to that of the early Church" (I.A.4.c). Diachronic study deepens our understanding of texts, making known, for instance,

> the historical dynamism which animates Sacred Scripture and… shedding light upon its rich complexity: for example, the Covenant Code (Exodus 21-23) reflects a political, social and religious situation of Israelite society different from that reflected in the other law codes preserved in Deuteronomy (chapters 12-26) and in Leviticus (the Holiness Code, chapters 17-26) (I.A.4.f).

The Biblical Commission stresses the necessity of a diachronic approach, calling it "indispensable" (Conclusion c). For the Biblical Commission, "diachronic" does not always imply a study of sources behind the text, although that is one dimension of a text's history to be considered[3].

---

[3] See the section of this work on the final text and source criticism, p .37, for an account of the Biblical Commission's nuanced attitude toward source criticism. Fusco objects to the IBC's emphasis on diachronic which he perceives as prioritizing pre-canonical sources ("Un secolo di metodo. storico", 388). However, the *IBC*'s use of the words *diachronic* and *synchronic* is interesting. This pair of words is used to refer to two overlapping oppositions (which are not distinguished in the *IBC*). Diachronic and synchronic may be used to mean, respectively, "historical" (from *dia* + *chronos*, "through time") and "without regard to historical considerations, simultaneous" (from *syn* + *chronos*). Or, they may be used in a narrower sense to contrast the study of sources that lie behind a text (diachronic) with the study of the text in its final form (synchronic). On nine out of ten occasions in which the Biblical Commission uses the term, "diachronic" (Intro A.d, twice; I.A.2.b; I.A.4.f; I.A.4.g; I.B.2.i; and Conclusion c, twice), the context suggests that the broader sense of "through time", or "in historical perspective", is the primary intended meaning. Only in I.A.3.c is the narrower sense of studying sources clearly implied. This analysis of its usage suggests that the Biblical Commission's primary concern is for the historical dimension of exegesis, rather than the study of pre-canonical sources (which they also value). The *IBC*'s uses of the word *synchronic* confirm this impression. Of the eleven times the Commission uses the word *synchronic*, three instances merely categorize some of the new approaches to Scripture (Intro A.d; I.B.3.a; and Conclusion c), six instances refer to non-historical approaches always with at least a hint of criticism indicating their incompleteness (Intro A.g; I.A.4.f, second instance; I.B.1.k; I.B.2.i; and Conclusion c, twice), and two instances refer approvingly to the study of the final form of

2. Definition

The *IBC* defines what it means by the historical-critical method by succinctly describing its essential principles and procedures. According to the Biblical Commission, the historical-critical method is *historical*

> above all because it seeks to shed light upon the historical processes which gave rise to biblical texts…. At the different stages of their production, the texts of the Bible were addressed to various categories of hearers or readers, living in different places at different times. (I.A.2.b)

The method is *critical* "because in each of its steps…it operates with the help of scientific criteria that seek to be as objective as possible" (I.A.2.c). The historical-critical method analyzes the biblical text in the same way it would study any other ancient writing, "as an expression of human discourse" (I.A.2.d). Yet in its final step, in the context of redaction criticism, the method helps the exegete "to gain a better grasp on the content of divine revelation" (I.A.2.d).

The historical-critical method has itself evolved over time, and the Biblical Commission briefly describes its principal procedures at its current stage of development. Paraphrasing from section I.A.3, the historical-critical method follows these steps[4]:

1. *Textual criticism* seeks to establish a text as close to the original as possible on the testimony of the oldest and best manuscripts, papyri, ancient translations and patristic citations.

2. *Linguistic and semantic analysis* proceeds with the resources of historical philology to examine the words and their syntax.

3. *Literary criticism* determines the beginning and end of textual units and the internal coherence of the text; it considers whether parts of the text can be assigned to different sources.

4. *Genre criticism* seeks to identify literary genres and the social milieu that gave rise to them.

5. *Tradition criticism* locates texts in the stream of a particular tradition and attempts to trace the development of this tradition over time.

---

the text (I.A.3.c and I.A.4.f). When Fitzmyer explains the meaning of "diachronic" and "synchronic", he also emphasizes a historical approach, rather than source criticism (*The Biblical Commission's Document*, 23n).

[4] See Prior, *Historical Critical Method in Catholic Exegesis*, 19-42, for a brief description of each of these steps. For more, see Hayes and Holladay, *Biblical Exegesis*, Stuart, "Exegesis", and their respective bibliographies.

6. *Redaction criticism* studies the modifications these traditions have undergone and analyzes the final text, trying to identify the characteristic tendencies of the concluding stage of the process.

7. If the text is of historical genre or if it contains historical information, *historical criticism* evaluates the historical significance of what the text reports.

3. Synchronic Analysis of the Final Text

In order to complete this task [of ascertaining the literal sense], it must include a synchronic study of the final form of the text, which is the expression of the word of God. (I.A.4.f)

The Biblical Commission attributes great importance to redaction criticism (step #6 in the preceding list) because it includes a synchronic analysis of the text as it now stands. According to the Biblical Commission, synchronic analysis examines a text in its present form "on the basis of the mutual relationships between its diverse elements, and with an eye to its character as a message communicated by the author to his contemporaries" (I.A.3.c). This, the Commission tells us, is "a legitimate operation, for it is the text in its final stage, rather than in its earlier editions, which is the expression of the Word of God" (I.A.4.f)[5]. Once the final text has been studied, the interpreter is ready to consider the implications of the text for Christian faith and life (I.A.3.c).

4. Exclusion of Prejudicial Presuppositions

The historical-critical method can and must be used without philosophical presuppositions contrary to Christian faith (I.A.4.b-c).

The Biblical Commission is well aware that the development and use of historical-critical methods for the study of the Bible has been problematic. In the Commission's Introduction, they acknowledge that "often the methods, despite their positive elements, have shown themselves to be wedded to positions hostile to the Christian faith" (Intro A.b). The Commission recalls this again in a section devoted to the history of the method where they state that "on the basis of certain philosophical ideas, some exegetes expressed negative judgements against the Bible" (I.A.1.b). The reference is to the fact that the historical-critical method developed in the atmosphere of the

---

[5] Here is an instance in which a hermeneutic of faith informs the use of a scientific method. Christian belief in the divine inspiration of the canonical Scriptures prioritizes Catholic exegesis' interest in the final form of the text.

Enlightenment and post-Enlightenment periods in the hands of rationalist and deist scholars. Fitzmyer illustrates this by recalling the historical Jesus research of H.S. Reimarus, F.C. Baur, H.E.G. Paulus, D.F. Strauss, B. Bauer and E. Renan, which stemmed from a desire to undermine traditional Christianity[6]. The prejudices of this earlier quest for the historical Jesus were exposed by Albert Schweitzer's classic, *The Quest of the Historical Jesus*[7].

The susceptibility of the historical-critical method to presuppositions which are contrary to Christian faith, however, is not confined to previous centuries. Bultmann's biblical hermeneutic based on the existential philosophy of Martin Heidegger and characterized by "excessive 'demythologization'" were also problematic, emptying the Bible's religious message of its objective reality and reducing it to a merely anthropological message (II.A.2.d). Atheistic psychological or psychoanalytic presuppositions (I.D.3.e), as well as materialist and one-sidedly immanentist (I.E.1.k-l) or ideological biases are also incompatible with the message of Scripture.

Nevertheless, the Commission affirms that the historical-critical method can be used "in an objective manner", without *a priori* presuppositions which govern its conclusions (I.A.4.b)[8]: "If its use is accompanied by *a priori* principles, that is not something pertaining to the method itself, but to certain hermeneutical choices..." (I.A.4.b). In other words, if there are presuppositions contrary to Christian faith, that is something the particular exegete brings to his or her work, and is not an intrinsic characteristic of the historical-critical method itself.

An analogy may help explain the Commission's meaning. The use of the historical-critical method in exegesis may be compared to the use of a pair of glasses in the act of seeing objects at a distance. In themselves a pair of glasses can see nothing; visual perception requires human eyes and a human

---

[6] Fitzmyer, *Scripture, the Soul of Theology*, 25-26, and *The Biblical Commission's Document*, 45-46.

[7] Schweitzer, *Quest of the Historical Jesus*

[8] Levenson comments, "The notion of a method without *a priori* suppositions is philosophically naïve", and offers the example of historical criticism's *a priori* denial of prophetic foreknowledge of the future (Blowers, Levenson and Wilken, "Three Views", 43). Vanhoye responds, "When the Commission says that the historical-critical method may be practiced without any *a priori* assumption, we meant that the method is not necessarily tied to the particular assumptions of the Bultmann school that reduce the content of Scripture to an anthropological message. But we do not deny that some position is necessary to understand the text, and we emphasize that the most appropriate pre-understanding is one that stands in continuity with the biblical text, namely the pre-understanding of the living tradition of the Church. If we attempt to read the Bible with materialistic presuppositions as our pre-understanding, we exclude in advance its primary message" ("Catholicism and the Bible", 38).

brain to interpret the images of light and color which pass through the lenses. Similarly, the historical-critical method by itself does not produce results; it is an instrument in a human act of interpretation. A second parallel may be drawn. Just as two elements determine the correctness of what is seen through eyeglasses—the glasses themselves and the eyesight of the individual—so it is in exegesis. Both the method and the presuppositions which the exegete brings to the task will determine the soundness of his or her interpretation.

The historical-critical method, like a pair of glasses, is an instrument. Just as good eyesight or poor eyesight and prior visual experiences and expectations may affect what someone is able to see through a pair of glasses, so the presuppositions which the exegete brings to his work condition the conclusions he or she will reach on the basis of the historical-critical method. For example, a rationalist, making use of the method, may look at a biblical miracle and will see either an event that never happened or an event that has a natural explanation. When the Christian interpreter examines a miracle account using the "glasses", he or she may evaluate the context and the literary form through which the miracle is reported to ascertain whether the author's intention was historical or fictional. If the intent was historical, the Christian interpreter is open to believe a miracle occurred, since his pre-understanding acknowledges divine intervention in history and the truthfulness of the biblical authors.

5. *Limits*

Despite its importance, the historical-critical method cannot be granted a monopoly, and exegetes must be conscious of its limits. Exegetes must recognize the dynamic aspect of meaning and the possibility that meaning can continue to develop (Conclusion d).

For awhile in Catholic circles the historical-critical exegesis did exercise a practical monopoly, especially during the twenty-year period following the Second Vatican Council. However, according to the Biblical Commission, "No scientific method...is fully adequate to comprehend the biblical texts in all their richness" (I.B.a). Every method is a tool which is suited to examine certain aspects of the text and necessarily neglects others. Other methods and approaches explore other dimensions of the text and make a complementary contribution (see principle #16). The historical-critical method must be viewed as a *necessary but not sufficient resource* for biblical interpretation[9].

---

[9] Prior provides a useful summary of the *IBC's* evaluation of the historical-critical method under three headings: Why is the historical-critical method necessary? Why is the historical-

Rather, it is important, says the Commission, to keep in mind the limitations of the historical-critical method which recent developments in philosophical hermeneutics have revealed and which the patterns of interpretation in the biblical tradition and the Tradition of the Church illustrate. The historical-critical method, in its search for meaning in original historical contexts, "has at times shown itself insufficiently attentive to the dynamic aspect of meaning and to the possibility that meaning can continue to develop" (Conclusion d)[10].

Discussion

More than any other factor, controversy regarding the historical-critical method led the Pontifical Biblical Commission to take up the topic of interpretation of the Bible in the Church and to produce the *IBC*[11]. It follows that the document's treatment of the historical-critical method is one of its most important features.

The "Discussion" of the use of the historical-critical method has four sections. The first briefly considers the criticisms brought against the historical-critical method and the defense offered by the Biblical Commission. The second details how the Biblical Commission has taken into account more of the criticisms of the historical-critical method than might first appear, proposing a particular approach to the historical-critical method that is compatible with the principles of Catholic interpretation. The last two sections identify weaknesses in the *IBC*'s treatment of the historical-critical method. The third section suggests that the *IBC* is insufficiently critical of the

---

critical method limited? What are the ways in which the limitations of the method are rectified? (See *Historical Critical Method in Catholic Exegesis*, 248-262). According to Prior, the *IBC* recognizes the following limits in the historical-critical method (summarizing pp. 253-259): 1) Its classical practice tended toward "hyper-criticism", restricting attention to historical meaning and dismantling the text into sources while neglecting the final form. 2) Its usefulness depends on the presuppositions of the exegete. 3) It tends toward a narrow interpretation of the text, having difficulty recognizing plural meanings and lacking a methodological basis to move beyond the work or corpus of an author [to recognize canonical meaning?]. 4) It is not able to discover the spiritual sense of texts when that sense goes beyond the literal sense (e.g., in the OT). 5) It does not provide a methodology to determine the christological, canonical and ecclesial aspects of texts, which are basic to Catholic exegesis. 6) It provides no methodology for taking into account the interaction between reader and text that is necessary for understanding. 7) It is unable to recognize Scripture as the word of God on account of its neutrality. 8) It fails to consider the dynamic aspect of the text. 9) Its sociological studies lack sufficient data to provide a comprehensive picture of ancient society.

[10] See principle #12 on the literal sense.

[11] See the discussion of the circumstances which occasioned the *IBC* in the "Introduction to the Document", p. 17ff.

presuppositions of the historical-critical method as it is commonly practiced today. The fourth section notes that the document gives too little attention to the relation between history and faith, in view of the challenges to that relation which historical-critical studies often raise.

6. Criticism and Defense of the Historical-Critical Method

The Biblical Commission's consideration of methods in interpretation in the Church, and the historical-critical method in particular, did not take place in a moment of detached reflection. Rather the Commission took up a topic that was still highly contested after thirty-five years of debate regarding the proper use of critical methods in Catholic exegesis[12]. Some of the Commission members had themselves been vigorous participants in that debate[13]. Cardinal Ratzinger and the Commission members hoped that they could make a contribution to overcoming the "crisis" regarding exegetical methods which had arisen[14].

The *IBC* mentions many of the criticisms that had been brought to bear on historical-critical exegesis, both by scholars and by lay readers of the Bible (Intro A.d-f). The Commission acknowledges the historic link between scientific methods and positions hostile to Christian faith (Intro A.b), and the fact that many of the faithful have judged it "deficient from the point of view of faith" (Intro A.d). They describe the rise of competing synchronic and other methods that seek to view texts in contemporary perspectives, because the historical-critical method tended to enclose the meaning of the Bible in the past. Some people concluded that "scientific exegesis... provoke[s]... doubt upon numerous points previously accepted without difficulty", and that "it impels some exegetes to adopt positions contrary to the faith of the Church on matters...such as the virginal conception of Jesus and his miracles, and even his resurrection and divinity" (Intro A.e). Some accuse scientific exegesis of

---

[12] For a thorough account of the scholarly discussion from 1958 to 1983, see Curtin, "Historical Criticism and Theological Interpretation". For a summary of Curtin and an account of the discussion immediately preceding the Biblical Commission's deliberations, see Prior, *Historical Critical Method in Catholic Exegesis*, 161-228.

[13] Reference has already been made to Ratzinger's public criticisms of the historical-critical method. On the other side, both Brown, a former Commission member, and Fitzmyer, who participated in producing the *IBC*, were outspoken advocates of the historical-critical method. One gets an idea of the spirit among the historical-critical comrades in arms in Fitzmyer's dedication to Brown of *The Soul of Theology* (1994) which lauds Brown as an "Indefatigable Interpreter of the Sacred Page and Staunch Defender of the Historical-Critical Method of Biblical Interpretation".

[14] Ratzinger had referred to the situation as a "crisis" ("Biblical Interpretation in Crisis" and *Schriftauslegung im Widerstreit*).

sterility in what concerns Christian life and, by its technical complexity, of preventing access to the Bible to all except a small group of specialists (Intro A.f). At various points in the document the Commission criticizes historical-critical exegesis as it has been practiced in the past. In its conclusion, the Biblical Commission echoes the complaints of many when it warns against the tendency to remain at the level of "sources and stratifications of texts" or "to become lost... in the sands of a hypercritical analysis" (Conclusion d,e).

Despite its acknowledgment of these criticisms, there is no doubt that the Biblical Commission wished to assert the necessity of the historical-critical method. The very first sentence of the *IBC* after the Introduction declares, "The historical-critical method is *the* indispensable method for the scientific study of the meaning of ancient texts" (I.A.a, emphasis added). The same paragraph concludes, "[Scripture's] proper understanding not only admits the use of this method but actually requires it". The endorsement of the historical-critical method is one of the most obvious characteristics of the *IBC*, and most reviewers of the document have commented on it. Understood in the context of so much criticism of the historical-critical method, the Commission's strong endorsement is correctly interpreted as a spirited defense[15].

It is worth noting that Pope John Paul II confirms the value of the historical-critical method in his "Address" officially receiving the *IBC*: "The Church of Christ takes the realism of the incarnation seriously, and this is why she attaches great importance to the "Historico-critical" study of the Bible" (Address 7)[16]. Although previous magisterial documents had affirmed the value of critical procedures in the study of Scripture[17], this is the first instance in which a Pope explicitly approved the historical-critical method by name. He adds some important qualifications, similar to those which the Biblical Commission itself proposes:

> Catholic exegesis does not have its own exclusive method of interpretation, but starting with the historico-critical basis *freed from its philosophical*

---

[15] Vanhoye acknowledges that the document intends to defend the historical-critical method, but also, he adds, to defend the method against its own temptations, namely, historicism and getting lost "in the sands of hypercritical analysis" ("Riflessione circa un documento", 12-13, quoting Conclusion e; cf. Vanhoye, "Catholicism and the Bible", 38).

[16] The translator of the Pope's "Address" uses the term "historico-critical" while the translator of the *IBC* uses the expression "historical-critical" to translate the identical French term, "historico-critique".

[17] In the same paragraph Pope John Paul II goes on to cite Leo XIII's support of "artis criticae disciplinam" and Pius XII's endorsement of textual criticism. For a brief summary of other precedents in official church documents see Fitzmyer, "Historical Criticism", 255-257, or for a more detailed study, see Prior, *Historical Critical Method in Catholic Exegesis*, 89-159.

presuppositions or those contrary to the truth of our faith, it makes the most of all the current methods…. (Address 13, emphasis added)[18]

He also adds,

Catholic exegesis *does not focus its attention on only the human aspects* of biblical Revelation, which is sometimes the mistake of the historico-critical method, or on only the divine aspects as fundamentalism would have it…. (Address 14, emphasis added)

It is the opinion of this reviewer that the Biblical Commission's treatment of the historical-critical method provides an important defense against an anti-intellectual fideist approach to Scripture on the one hand (e.g., fundamentalism), and against a non-historical or subjectivist interpretation on the other. The reaffirmation of the importance of the literal sense, and the reaffirmation of the historical-critical method as a rational means of establishing it, are efforts to uphold the objective and historical character of the Christian revelation contained in the Bible. This defense is necessary, since strong trends in contemporary interpretation reject the notion of objective meaning in the biblical text[19] or advocate a notion of biblical meaning divorced either from the interventions of God in history[20] or from the meaning of texts for their original authors and readers[21].

7. A "Properly-Oriented" Historical-Critical Method

At first sight it might appear that the Biblical Commission has given an unqualified endorsement to the historical-critical method as the means suited to ascertaining the literal sense of Scripture. Many reviewers, both sympathetic and critical of the historical-critical method, interpreted the *IBC* this way. However, this study will argue that a more careful reading of the document reveals that the Commission criticizes, and in some important

---

[18] Here a slight difference from the Biblical Commission's document may be noted. The *IBC* excludes the use of the movement with philosophical presuppositions contrary to faith, but states that the historical-critical method "implies of itself no *a priori*" (I.A.4.b). The Pope's wording is more open to the view that the method itself entails problematic presuppositions from which it must be freed.

[19] For example, post-modernism, some reader-response criticism, and some contextual or "ideological" criticism justify reading meanings into the text and resist the authority of a meaning inherent in the text.

[20] Some literary and theological approaches approach the Bible exclusively as "story", as religious fiction, whose truth value is unrelated to the truth or falsity of affirmations of the text about events in space and time.

[21] On the literary side, structuralism and new criticism do not attend to the meaning of texts to their authors and original audiences. Some approaches based on philosophical hermeneutics do likewise.

ways, redefines and re-dimensions the historical-critical method it endorses. In a word, the Biblical Commission had considered and accepted many (though not all) of the criticisms which have been raised against the historical-critical method. Although readers must ultimately decide whether the evidence warrants this conclusion, the comments of two Commission members should be heard in support of this interpretation. Speaking of the *IBC*, Brendan Byrne states,

> The historical-critical method, has indeed, the leading place, but is placed in the context of all the other methods as just another method. This is one of the most significant features of the document: its relativization of the historical-critical method, while insisting upon its necessity and indeed according it a place of privilege[22].

Commission Secretary Vanhoye makes a similar comment: "The document as a whole 'redimensions' the position and function of the historical-critical method, affirming its value, but denying its sufficiency"[23].

It is the Pontifical Biblical Commission's view that not just any use of the historical-critical method will be fruitful for Catholic exegesis. In this regard Fitzmyer speaks of the need for a "properly-oriented" use of the historical-critical method[24]. This study will adopt Fitzmyer's term, "properly-oriented",

---

[22] Byrne, email to author, 8 December 1999.

[23] Vanhoye, "Catholicism and the Bible", 38. Several reasons may explain why many readers failed to see the redimensioning aspect of the document's treatment of the historical-critical method. First, chapter one of the *IBC* which describes and evaluates the various methods and approaches monopolized the attention of many readers on account of its novelty and length (39% of the whole). It gave the impression that the document was mainly about methods, and that among these the historical-critical method had pride of place both by explicit entitlement and by the amount of text devoted to it (more than twice that given to any other method). Second, a consequent neglect of chapter three on the characteristics of Catholic interpretation led some readers to overlook the hermeneutical context in which all the methods may contribute. Third, the *IBC* itself sounds a note of ringing endorsement regarding the method, undoubtedly reflecting the polemical situation which preceded the document ("Too ringing!", said Commission member Byrne when commenting about the effects of the document [conversation with the author, 9 August 1999]). This writer's interpretive interests illuminated the nuances in the Biblical Commission's position: first, the quest for the principles of Catholic interpretation led to recognizing chapter three as the interpretive key to the document; second, his interest in pastoral actualization drew his attention to the ways the Commission seeks to remove the impediments to actualization which have traditionally characterized the use of the historical-critical method.

[24] Fitzmyer criticizes "a kind of halfway use of the method" which has led to skepticism about it: "Some of its practitioners think that their job is finished if they can sort out the sources of a certain text, tell you something about its prehistory, or about its synoptic relation… or something about its form-critical character, without going the further step of accounting adequately for what the text means, what sort of theological or religious meaning is being conveyed or what sense the word of God has in that passage" (Fitzmyer and Stahel,

to refer to the distinctive approach to the historical-critical method endorsed by the Biblical Commission, without claiming to use the term in exactly the sense Fitzmyer intends it[25].

The Biblical Commission's properly-oriented approach to the historical-critical method 1) excludes errors for which the method has been known, 2) defines the object of historical-critical study in a particular manner, and, 3) places the historical-critical method in a hermeneutical context.   Because most of the individual points which constitute these three aspects of the *IBC*'s approach are treated elsewhere in this study, this section will only list and summarize the particular characteristics of a "properly-oriented" historical-critical method.

a)   Excludes Certain Errors

The *IBC* introduces the historical-critical method by recounting its history before going on to describing it "at the present stage of its development" (I.A.3.a). This enables the Biblical Commission to disassociate the use of the method it recommends from problematic tendencies attributable to earlier stages of the historical-critical method's development. Furthermore, the Commission criticizes some tendencies of contemporary practitioners of the historical-critical method. By means of these criticisms, the *IBC* affirms that a sound use of the historical-critical method in Catholic exegesis will avoid the following errors:

1.   Dissecting and dismantling the text in order to identify sources while failing to pay sufficient attention to the final form of the text and its message (I.A.1.b).

2.   Combining the method with presuppositions hostile to or inadequate to Christian faith such as rationalism (IV.A.3.c),

---

"Interview", 10). In *Scripture, the Soul of Theology*, 31, Fitzmyer says that it is "faith presuppositions" which characterize a "properly-oriented" use of the historical-critical method. In his commentary on the *IBC*, Fitzmyer states, "Both faith and the guidance of the community by [the] Holy Spirit enrich the interpretation, and these are part of the presuppositions with which the historical-critical method becomes properly oriented" (*The Biblical Commission's Document*, 69). In an article published just as the Biblical Commission was beginning its work Fitzmyer writes, "by reason of [faith presuppositions] it [the historical-critical method] becomes a *properly-oriented* method of interpretation, for none of the elements of the method is pursued in and for itself. They are used only to achieve the main goal of discerning what the biblical message was that the sacred writer sought to convey..."("Historical Criticism", 255).

[25] What is presented here is more detailed than any description Fitzmyer has given to "properly oriented" historical-critical exegesis. Fitzmyer might wish to define this term differently.

historical positivism (II.A.2.c), historicism (I.A.4.f), atheism (I.D.3.e), and materialism (I.E.1.l).

3. Employing hermeneutical theories that are inadequate for interpreting Scripture by enclosing it within the constraints of a particular philosophy or by emptying it of its objective reality (II.A.2.d)[26].

4. Restricting the search for the meaning of a text to its historical circumstances and failing to attend to subsequent development of meaning (I.A.4.d; II.B.1.e; Conclusion d).

5. Maintaining the view that a text can only have one single meaning (II.B.b-c; II.B.1.d);

6. Paying excessive attention to the form of a text while paying too little attention to its content (I.A.4.e).

7. Basing interpretation on hypothetical historical reconstructions of what the texts were allegedly designed to hide, rather than upon the content of the inspired text (I.E.2.l)[27].

Thus according to the Biblical Commission, a properly-oriented use of the historical-critical method avoids a set of errors which have at times characterized its use.

b) Defines the Object of Study In a Particular Manner

One of the characteristics of the Biblical Commission's approach to the historical-critical method that distinguishes it from the approach of many historical-critical scholars is the way the IBC defines biblical exegesis' object of study. In part this follows from the *IBC* understanding of the literal sense.

1. The text in its final stage, rather than its earlier editions, is the proper object of study, since it is the expression of the word of God

---

[26] The *IBC* cites the example of Bultmann's Heideggerian existentialist hermeneutic and his "excessive demythologization" (II.A.2.d).

[27] This occurs in the discussion of feminist exegesis but it applies to any historical-critical interpretations which employ a similar hermeneutic of suspicion. According to the Biblical Commission, this form of argumentation is weak, since it is *ex silentio*. Also, "this does not correspond at all to the work of exegesis properly so called. It entails rejecting the content of the inspired texts in preference for a hypothetical construction, quite different in nature" (I.E.2.l). Fitzmyer adds, "it cannot be a substitute for the story told in the inspired text of the New Testament itself...[and therefore] can never be taken as a norm of Christian faith and praxis" (*The Biblical Commission's Document*, 100-101).

(I.A.4.f)[28]. For this reason, a synchronic analysis of texts completes the historical-critical method and is an essential element of redaction criticism (I.A.4.f)[29].

2. The literal sense is the meaning that "has been expressed directly by the inspired human authors" (II.B.1.c). This definition avoids explicit reference to the author's intention and confines itself to what is evidenced in the text[30].

3. The literal sense of some texts possesses a *dynamic aspect*; historical-critical exegesis should seek to determine the direction of thought expressed by the text, so as to recognize extensions of its meaning (II.B.1.e)[31].

Therefore a properly-oriented historical-critical method is one which is clear about the nature of its object.

c) Places the Historical-Critical Method in a Hermeneutical Context

Finally, in the *IBC* the Biblical Commission re-dimensions the historical-critical method by placing it in the overall context of Catholic interpretation. Many of the criticisms that have been raised against the historical-critical method can be understood as criticisms of an allegedly neutral practice of the method (in reality, often influenced by hidden philosophical commitments),

---

[28] Many historical-critical scholars would not agree that the final form deserves to be the privileged object of study, preferring the sources as they are able to reconstruct them, e.g., the Yahwist, the prophet Jeremiah, or "Q", over the redactions which comprise the final form of the biblical writings.

[29] Not all practitioners of the historical-critical method concern themselves with a synchronic analysis. Not all regard a synchronic study of the final text as a defining characteristic of redaction criticism; instead, some redaction critics only take an interest in how the final redactor has modified his sources. For instance, Fitzmyer himself, in describing redaction criticism's role in the historical-critical method in 1989, makes no mention of a synchronic study of the final text as an aspect of redaction criticism, although he urges study of the text's final form (see Fitzmyer, "Historical Criticism", 251, 254).

[30] See the discussion on the literal sense and authorial intention beginning p. 165 of this work. This contrasts with a common tendency among some historical-critical exegetes to explain a text's literal meaning as the author's intention, ascertained by a historical construction of circumstances or motives that lie behind the text. Thus, for example, for some interpreters the meaning of pentateuchal texts attributed to "P" lies in the economic and political motives of a particular group.

[31] In the same paragraph the Commission acknowledges that this is not typical of historical-critical exegesis, and that it "has too often tended to limit the meaning of texts by tying it too rigidly to precise historical circumstances" (II.B.1.e).

rather than of a method that consciously begins from a pre-understanding of Christian faith. The Commission describes the presuppositions and the appropriate context for all the methods which Catholic exegesis employs in chapter III, "Characteristics of Catholic Interpretation". The following statement sums up this context and these presuppositions: "What characterizes Catholic exegesis is that it deliberately places itself within the living tradition of the Church, whose first concern is fidelity to the revelation attested by the Bible" (III.b).

This fundamental hermeneutical choice shapes how the historical-critical method functions in Catholic exegesis in a number of important ways.

1. A hermeneutic of faith recognizes that God has spoken and is speaking through the human language of Scripture. The historical-critical method can thus become "an instrument for understanding the central object of all interpretation: the person of Jesus Christ and the saving events accomplished in human history" (II.A.d)[32].

2. The interpretive context of "the living tradition of the Church" establishes the canon of Scripture and the basic doctrinal orientations of the Church Fathers. This provides Catholic historical-critical exegesis with its object of study and the fundamental faith affirmations which orient Catholic exegesis.[33]

3. The biblical tradition of interpretation demonstrates that biblical meaning develops over time as the Scriptures are actualized in new circumstances. The New Testament makes clear that the OT takes on new meaning in the light of the paschal mystery of Christ. These precedents guide interpretation in the Church and exclude an excessively narrow or historicist definition of biblical meaning[34].

4. The recognition that in addition to the literal sense Scripture bears canonical, christological, and ecclesial meanings (III.C.1.c), and that some texts possess spiritual or fuller senses (none of which can be ascertained by the historical-critical method) contradicts the notion that the historical-critical method provides a sufficient means of understanding Scripture[35].

---

[32] See principle #6. In their context in the *IBC* the words in quotation marks refer to what a hermeneutical theory ought to be, in contrast to Bultmann's hermeneutic which failed due to inadequate presuppositions and the misuse of philosophy. But the potential of the historical-critical method as an instrument for grasping revelation is expressed elsewhere in the document (e.g., I.A.3.d, I.A.4.g).

[33] See principles #7 and #10.

[34] See principles #8 and #9.

[35] See principles #13 and #14.

5. The recognition that the texts of Scripture were composed, preserved and are read today for a religious purpose requires that an adequate interpretation explain what they *mean* and not exclusively what they *meant*. In other words, exegesis must explain the contemporary religious meaning of the text, or it has failed to complete its task[36].

6. The fact that historical-critical exegesis takes place in the Church for the nourishment of the people of God means that it is oriented to the *use of the Bible* in the Church (in preaching, teaching, catechetics, liturgy, *lectio divina*, theology and ecumenism)[37].

7. The recognition that exegesis is above all a theological discipline protects against reducing it to a purely historical or literary discipline[38].

8. The fact that Catholic exegesis does not claim any one scientific method as its own (III.a) and that many other methods and approaches may make their contribution denies any claim of sole validity to the historical-critical method (III.D.1.a).

A properly-oriented use of the historical-critical method employs it in the service of Christian faith. The principles of Catholic interpretation implicit in the *IBC* provide a context for the historical-critical method, a context which permits the method to fulfill its noblest task, to help make clear the word of God.

This section has argued that the Biblical Commission has made important strides in responding to criticisms of the historical-critical method and showing how it may be successfully integrated into Catholic exegesis. The

---

[36] In this regard consider these two strong statements of the Biblical Commission: (1) "Exegesis is truly faithful to proper intention [sic] of biblical texts when it goes not only to the heart of their formulation to find the reality of faith there...but also seeks to link this reality to... faith in our present world" (II.A.2.b). (2) "Their [Catholic exegetes']common task is not finished when they have simply determined sources, defined forms or explained literary procedures. They arrive at the true goal of their work only when they have explained the meaning of the biblical text as God's word for today. To this end, they must take into consideration the various hermeneutical perspectives which help toward grasping the contemporary meaning of the biblical message and which make it responsive to the needs of those who read Scripture today" (III.C.1.b). See principles #11, #17 and #18.

[37] See principle #20.

[38] Vanhoye describes this as one of the temptations of the historical-critical method against which the Biblical Commission sought to defend it ("Riflessione circa un documento", 12-13). See principle #6.

remainder of this chapter will explain how two aspects of the Commission's approach to the historical-critical method remain unsatisfactory, namely 1) its treatment of the method's presuppositions, and 2) its neglect of the problem regarding the relationship between faith and history.

8.   The Problem of Presuppositions

The challenge to the historical-critical method which the Biblical Commission could not escape confronting was the public criticism which its President, Cardinal Ratzinger, delivered at the Rockford Conference in New York in 1988. The Cardinal's lecture touched on many issues, but what came through most clearly was a criticism of the presuppositions of historical criticism epitomized in the influential work of Martin Dibelius and Rudolf Bultmann. Underlying the approach of these exegetes, Ratzinger discerned the philosophical influence of Immanuel Kant, characterized by a "restriction to the positive, to the empirical, to the 'exact' science, which by definition excludes the appearance of what is 'wholly other'..."[39]. In the discussion following the Cardinal's presentation and in a published addendum to his own paper at the conference, Raymond Brown disputed the continuing influence of Dibelius and Bultmann, at least on American exegesis, and denied that the historical-critical method is taught in a manner tied to any philosophical system[40]. Brown relegated the problems raised by the Cardinal to the past or to the philosophical commitments of particular practitioners of the historical-critical method. The Commission took Brown's point of view[41], and it seems that Cardinal Ratzinger deferred to the judgment of the Commission members that neither Dibelius nor Bultmann's work determines the historical-critical method as it is practiced today.

---

[39] Ratzinger, "Biblical Interpretation in Crisis", 5. Ratzinger's paper said much more, perhaps too much, to receive an adequate response to all the points he raised. See Prior, *Historical Critical Method in Catholic Exegesis*, 204-208, for an excellent summary. Ratzinger's presentation and the other papers delivered at the same 1988 conference in New York are available in Ratzinger, *Schriftauslegung im Widerstreit*; and Neuhaus, *Biblical Interpretation in Crisis*. Ratzinger's paper is also available in Italian (de la Potterie, "L'esegesi biblica, scienza della fede"). Only the German and Italian versions include the Cardinal's entire written text. See also Wicks, "Biblical Criticism Criticized", for a critical review of the conference and the papers delivered there.

[40] Brown, "Contribution to Ecumenical Church Discussion", 41 and 40-46.

[41] In response to a question about Ratzinger's criticisms and participation in the development of the *IBC*, Vanhoye explained, "We responded to his concerns by indicating that, in its essence, the historical-critical method is not tied to the *a priori* assumptions of Bultmann and Dibelius, and that it is necessary to employ this method in a manner that liberates it from any *a priori* assumption that would be contrary to the faith of the Church" ("Catholicism and the Bible", 35).

The Biblical Commission took quite a firm position both excluding any presupposition that is contrary to Christian faith from Catholic interpretation, and affirming that the historical-critical method

> implies of itself no *a priori*. If its used is accompanied by *a priori* principles [i.e., inconsistent with Christian faith], that is not something pertaining to the method itself, but to certain hermeneutical choices which… can be tendentious (I.A.4.b).

Furthermore, the Biblical Commission suggests that the inclusion of philosophical presuppositions contrary to Christian faith in the method was a problem in the past, but not the present:

> The early confrontation between traditional exegesis and the scientific approach, which initially consciously separated itself from faith and at times even opposed it, was assuredly painful; later however it proved to be salutary: once the method was freed from external prejudices, it led to a more precise understanding of the truth of Sacred Scripture (cf. *Dei Verbum*, 12). (I.A.4.c)

> For a long time now scholars have ceased combining the method with a philosophical system (I.A.4.e).

This section will argue that the Commission's evaluation of the current practice of the historical-critical method is overly positive. Or to put it another way, the report of the demise of the "classic" historical-critical method with its Enlightenment bias against faith has been greatly exaggerated. Consequently the *IBC* fails to adequately address the problem of presuppositions in the historical-critical method as it is widely understood and practiced.

There is considerable evidence of the continued use of the historical-critical method accompanied by presuppositions that are prejudicial to religious faith. The most obvious evidence is the "Third Quest" for the historical Jesus, which, along with some very solid historical research about Jesus, has produced some very tendentious results in the name of the historical-critical method[42]. The research associated with the Jesus Seminar, in particular, has been flawed in this respect. Another indication that the "classic" historical-critical method is alive and well is the issuance of the new *Journal of Higher Criticism*, which boasts that it is carrying out historical

---

[42] See Evans, "Third Quest: A Bibliographical Essay", for a succinct balanced overview of the "Third Quest". See Green, "Quest of the Historical"; Johnson, *The Real Jesus*; Witherington, *The Jesus Quest*, for critical evaluation of the methodologies and biases of the leading works.

criticism in the tradition of F.C. Baur[43]. Further evidence that contemporary biblical scholarship still often employs the historical-critical method in a biased manner appears in a spate of recent publications by respected critically-trained exegetes of various confessions[44].

The most *interesting* indication that the historical-critical method continues to rely on presuppositions problematic for Christian belief occurs in an article by a distinguished Catholic exegete, John J. Collins[45]. Collins' position is intriguing since it is the mirror opposite to that of the Biblical Commission. Instead of arguing that historical criticism, now purified of *a priori* viewpoints incompatible with faith, may be used in Catholic exegesis that begins with a pre-understanding of faith, Collins asserts that the presuppositions of historical criticism and faith assumptions are mutually incompatible, and that exegetes should systematically exclude all propositions based on faith in order to produce a purely critical biblical theology[46]. To ease the "perennial tension between biblical theology and the historical-

---

[43] "The *Journal of Higher Criticism* was initiated in 1994 as a forthright attempt—in a time of scholarly neo-conservatism—to hark back to the bold historical hypotheses and critical interpretations associated with the great names of F.C. Baur and Tübingen" (Journal of Higher Criticism, "Homepage"). The *Journal* is published by the Institute for Higher Criticism at Drew University.

[44] See, for instance, Donfried, "Alien Hermeneutics"; Harrisville, "Critique of Current Biblical Criticism"; Harrisville and Sundberg, *The Bible in Modern Culture*; Harrisville, "The Loss of Biblical Authority"; Johnson, "Crisis in Biblical Scholarship" and "What's Catholic About It?"; Levenson, *The Hebrew Bible, the Old Testament*; and Noble, *The Canonical Approach*, 81-144.

[45] Collins, "Critical Biblical Theology". Collins, author of numerous articles and books on apocalyptic literature and *Daniel* in the Hermeneia series (1994), now teaches at Yale. He is a recent past president of the Catholic Biblical Association of America (1996-1997) and has taught at St. Mary of the Lake Seminary (Mundelein, IL), DePaul University, and Notre Dame, and was a contributor to the *NJBC*. Because of his prominence, Collins' views are significant: it is likely that both his understanding of the historical-critical method and his views about the role of faith in the exegetical enterprise would be shared by many other Catholic exegetes.

[46] Although Collins addresses himself to biblical theology while the Biblical Commission concerns itself with exegesis, the difference is not significant. Exegesis, taken in its narrow sense, is more basic than biblical theology. Thus, if Collins holds that at the higher level of abstraction (i.e., biblical theology) considerations of faith are to be excluded for the sake of a critical biblical theology, *a fortiori* they must be excluded at the more fundamental level of exegesis. Collins' article belongs to an ongoing discussion about the boundaries and methodology of biblical theology which will be touched upon in the discussion of the relationship of exegesis with other theological disciplines (chapter 17). Collins, along with Krister Stendahl and others, holds that biblical theology should be an exclusively descriptive and historical discipline (see Stendahl, "Biblical Theology" and "Method in Biblical Theology").

critical method"[47], Collins urges a more consistent adherence to the latter's principles.

Collins lays out the fundamental principles of historical criticism and their implications for biblical theology as they find expression in the writings of Ernst Troeltsch and Wilhelm Wrede[48]. He summarizes Ernst Troeltsch's "classic formulation" of the principles of historical criticism:

> (1) The principle of criticism or methodological doubt: since any conclusion is subject to revision, historical inquiry can never attain absolute certainty but only relative degrees of probability. (2) The principle of analogy: historical knowledge is possible because all events are similar in principle. We must assume that the laws of nature in biblical times were the same as now. Troeltsch refers to this as "the almighty power of analogy." (3) The principle of correlation: the phenomena of history are inter-related and interdependent and no event can be isolated from the sequence of historical cause and effect. To these [Collins writes] should be added the principle of autonomy, which is indispensable for any critical study. Neither church or state can prescribe for the scholar which conclusions should be reached.[49]

Wrede, applying these principles to biblical theology, objected to the influence "of a faith perspective derived from dogmatic theology. This entailed the profession that the biblical writings were inspired or revealed and should be regarded as normative"[50]. Collins quotes Wrede,

> "For logical thinking there can be no middle position between inspired writings and historical documents." Equally: "It is impossible to continue the dogmatic conception of the canon," since canonical status is not intrinsic to the biblical writings but only represents the judgement of the Church Fathers"[51].

---

[47] Collins, "Critical Biblical Theology", 1.

[48] What is at issue is how the historical-critical method is defined. Collins looks to the principles articulated by two of its modern founders, Troeltsch and Wrede. He then updates some of Wrede's judgments by incorporating corrections brought by philosophical hermeneutics including the awareness that historical criticism is not capable of rendering "objective facts". Although Collins accepts that historical criticism "is a tradition, with its own values and presuppositions, derived in large part from the Enlightenment and western humanism" ("Critical Biblical Theology", 7), he fails to think critically enough about the implications of this fact for biblical theology.

[49] Collins, "Critical Biblical Theology", 2, citing Troeltsch, "Über historische und dogmatische Methode", 729-753. Troeltsch's essay is available in English: see Troeltsch, "Historical and Dogmatic Method".

[50] Collins, "Critical Biblical Theology", 3.

[51] Collins, "Critical Biblical Theology", 3. Collins cites Wrede, "Task and Methods", 69-70.

a)   The Principle of Criticism and the Exclusion of Faith

According to Collins, the fatal flaw of the biblical theology of the first three quarters of the 20th century (he names Eichrodt, G.E. Wright, von Rad and Bultmann) was its "confessional faith, which was understood to require some measure of *a priori* belief and conviction"[52]. Collins rejects a pre-understanding of faith on the basis of its inconsistency with Troeltsch's first principle, the principle of criticism:

> There does, in fact, seem to be an inherent contradiction between theology so conceived and…the principle of criticism, by which any conclusion or conviction must be subject to revision in the light of new evidence. Historical criticism, unlike traditional faith does not provide for certainty but only for relative degrees of probability. Many of the convictions most dearly cherished by biblical theologians were challenged by historical criticism: the historicity of crucial events, the unity of the Old Testament, the uniqueness of Israel…, or the view that the Old Testament is best understood as a process leading to Christ. A biblical theology that takes historical criticism seriously will have to forego any claim of certainty on these matters.[53]

Collins urges the exclusion from biblical theology of "the postulate of divine revelation"[54]. In the conclusion of his article Collins makes his position clear: "Historical criticism, consistently understood, is not compatible with a confessional theology that is committed to specific doctrines on the basis of faith"[55].

The unsuitability for Christian interpretation of the Bible of the principle of criticism applied in this manner is obvious. For example, Catholic exegesis aims at understanding the word of God as it is expressed in the canonical text. Collins' use of Troeltsch's "principle of criticism" is incompatible with that aim, since it refuses to grant any quality to the biblical text that transcends human and cultural factors. Collins, however, insists that Enlightenment

---

[52] Collins, "Critical Biblical Theology", 5.

[53] Collins, "Critical Biblical Theology", 5.

[54] Collins, "Critical Biblical Theology", 9. See also Collins, "Review: 'The Hebrew Bible, The Old Testament…'".

[55] Collins continues, "It is, however, quite compatible with theology, understood as an open-ended and critical inquiry into the meaning and function of God-language" ("Critical Biblical Theology", 14). Collins is aware that most theologies begin with the postulate of revelation (p. 9; see also Collins, "Review: 'The Hebrew Bible, The Old Testament…'") and meet the classic definition of theology, *fides quaerens intellectum*. Essentially Collins proposes a "critical" theology based on reason alone, of which a "critical" biblical theology would form a sub-discipline. In each instance, being "critical" requires the systematic exclusion of assertions grounded on faith.

scholarship is not prejudiced, since the principle of criticism remains open to proofs of the divine dimension of Scripture.   Criticizing Brevard Childs' interpretation in faith, Collins writes,

> Any scholar who wishes to assert any more than what is commonly accepted in the community of scholars must assume the burden of proof or provide appropriate arguments. All shades of theological opinion agree that the Bible belongs to the arena of human experience to some degree. Those who wish to assert with Childs that it transcends human experience need to explain how this is so[56].

But for Christian interpretation which seeks the meaning of the word of God in Sacred Scripture, this is like requiring that before a calculus problem may be solved, Euclid's postulates of geometry must be proven.   There are two problems with such a requirement: First, it requires constantly having to start from the absolute beginning.   Second, and more importantly, postulates are self-evident statements which normally cannot be proven, but if granted, have great explanatory power[57].   What kind of proof can conclusively demonstrate either that Scripture is divinely inspired or that it is not?   Traditional historical criticism as advocated by Collins shows bias in placing the burden of proof on whoever recognizes that Scripture transcends human experience, and exempting from argument whoever does not recognize it.   The "principle of criticism" can indeed be useful to believing exegesis, but only after faith's first principles have been admitted.

Collins advocates an approach to biblical theology that is remote from the principles of interpretation embodied in the *IBC*.   But more to the point, Collins' article illustrates how learned Catholic exegetes might retain quite a different understanding of the presuppositions inherent in the historical-critical method than the *IBC* asserts[58].   Second, Collins' article helps to identify some of the prejudicial presuppositions of the historical-critical method as it is still commonly understood which must be taken into account

---

[56] Collins, "Review: 'The Hebrew Bible, The Old Testament...'", 745.

[57] For readers who do not remember their geometry, Euclid's five postulates, together with five axioms, are the foundation of geometry. Euclid's postulates are: 1) Two points determine one and only one straight line. 2) A straight line extends indefinitely far in either direction. 3) A circle may be drawn with any given center and any given radius. 4) All right angles are equal. 5) Given a line k and a point P not on the line, there exists one and only one line m through P that is parallel to k. From Miller, Heeren and Hornsby, *Mathematical Ideas*, 423.

[58] In fact, although he does not cite Bultmann and Dibelius, Collins' approach embodies the Kantian heritage in exegesis which Ratzinger described as characterized by "a restriction to the positive, to the empirical, to the 'exact' science, which by definition excludes the appearance of what is 'wholly other'..." ("Biblical Interpretation in Crisis", 5).

by interpretation that begins from a pre-understanding of faith. The section that follows will address other problematic presuppositions of the historical-critical method which believing exegetes have recently criticized.

b)   The Principle of Analogy and the Exclusion of Miracles

Various authors have pointed out the problem with Troeltsch's principle of analogy as it has been applied to miracles or to such theologically significant events as the virginal conception or resurrection of Christ[59]. As summarized by Collins (above), the principle of analogy states that "historical knowledge is possible because all events are similar in principle. We must assume that the laws of nature in biblical times were the same as now". Troeltsch explains its application:

> Analogy with what happens before our eyes and what is given within ourselves is the key to criticism.... Agreement with normal, ordinary, repeatedly attested modes of occurrence and conditions as we know them is the mark of probability for the occurrences that the critic can either acknowledge really to have happened or leave on one side.[60]

Since virginal conceptions and resurrections of the dead are not "repeatedly attested modes of occurrence" among us, this grants the historicity of the biblical testimony very little probability. Noble points out the fallacy in this kind of historical reasoning:

> Troeltschian analogy decides by *a priori* decree matters which ought only to be settled by appealing to the relevant historical evidence.... Although Troeltsch proposes analogy as a *methodological* principle, it in fact allows one to draw *substantive historical conclusions*—that Jesus was not born of a virgin, did not raise Lazarus from the dead, and did not return to life himself, etc.—without needing to look at a shred of historical evidence...[61].

---

[59] Abraham, *Divine Revelation and the Limits of Historical Criticism*; Noble, *The Canonical Approach*, 111-116; Pannenberg, "Redemptive Event and History". In a similar vein, Levenson points out that the naturalist *a priori* of historical critics excludes the possibility of foreknowledge, of predictive prophecy, which the Bible attributes to the prophets (Blowers, Levenson and Wilken, "Three Views", 43).

[60] As quoted in Pannenberg, "Redemptive Event and History", 43-44, and cited by Noble, *The Canonical Approach*, 112n.

[61] Noble, *The Canonical Approach*, 113. For a fuller discussion of the principle of analogy and Pannenberg's critique of it, see pp. 111-116. Van A. Harvey advances a more sophisticated principle of historical criticism along the lines of Troeltsch's principle of analogy in Harvey, *The Historian and the Believer*. In *The Canonical Approach*, Noble critiques Harvey's arguments as being question-begging, foundationalist, and atomistic in a discussion informed by the philosophy of science and the history of discovery (116-132). Among other things, Noble argues that the naturalist's claim that the laws of science apply everywhere and

The proper way to make judgments of historicity is to assess the relevant evidence.

Although most historical critical scholars today acknowledge with philosophical hermeneutics that interpretation without pre-understanding cannot exist, and that there are no uninterpreted "facts", the myth persists that the historical-critical method of itself yields results which are objective and neutral[62]. Noble, however, points out that in the case of alleged miraculous occurrences in the Bible, a faith-neutral interpretation is impossible. While a simple description of what the text says may be faith-neutral, as soon as the exegete begins to evaluate the truthfulness or historical significance of what happened, faith neutrality is impossible to him or her. Taking the example of the New Testament accounts of Jesus' resurrection from the dead, Noble argues,

> The impossibility is methodological: An investigation such as this has to make an evaluation of the various claims to have seen Jesus alive, of the various explanations that have been offered for Jesus' tomb being empty, etc.; and this is impossible unless the investigator begins with some prior beliefs that are "strong enough" [in the sense of having a significant degree of substantive content] to interact critically with the pertinent data. Someone with no particular views about whether there is a god, whether nature is lawlike, and whether its laws could be broken would be completely out their depth in such a debate. Far from a neutral investigator being the ideally objective historian, they would be unable even to enter the discussion![63]

According to Noble, an interpreter may be a believing Christian or an atheist (or a Moslem or Hindu), and will conduct the descriptive exegetical task from one or another prior "faith-commitment", but the interpreter's initial stance simply cannot be neutral.

c) Historicism

One of the most consistent criticisms leveled at the historical-critical method today is the charge of historicism[64]. Ricoeur defines historicism as

---

always is as much an "ultimate claim" as the supernaturalist's claim of the possibility of divine intervention.

[62] Fitzmyer frequently speaks of the "neutrality" of the method (e.g., "Historical Criticism", 255, and *Scripture, the Soul of Theology*, 36). However, when he explains himself more fully, it is clear that Fitzmyer recognizes that the historical-critical method has led to different results depending on the presuppositions with which it has been used.

[63] Noble, *The Canonical Approach*, 134.

[64] See the earlier brief discussion of historicism under principle #3, p. 57ff.

"...the epistemological presupposition that the content of literary works and in general of cultural documents receives its intelligibility from its connection to the social conditions of the community that produced it or to which it was destined"[65]. M. Mandelbaum defines historicism as "the belief that an adequate understanding of the nature of anything and an adequate assessment of its value are to be gained by considering it in terms of the place it occupied and the role it played within a process of development"[66]. Perhaps the most important element to note here is the belief in the *adequacy* of historical study for understanding and evaluation of reality. According to Johnson, this leads many scholars to an "epistemological monism" that focuses on history alone[67]. Levenson speaks of the "totalistic" claims of historical criticism[68]. According to these scholars and others, other means of access to truth—such as tradition, religious experience, or literary analysis—are excluded or relativized before the absolute of historical analysis[69].

Various consequences for exegesis follow from a historicist presupposition. A historicist mentality often reduces the interpretation of a text to its *genetic* meaning, i.e., the pre-history of a text, whether in its sources or its *Sitz im Leben*. Or it treats biblical texts as mere *sources* to a historical reality behind the text where meaning is sought, rather than as the bearers of meaning themselves and the proper object of the exegete's reflection. When the meaning of the text itself is considered, historicist exegesis may confine it to the one meaning it had in its moment of origin, without due consideration of the meaning the text bore for the redactors who included it in the biblical

---

[65] Ricoeur, *Interpretation Theory*, 89-90.

[66] From "Historicism" in *Dictionary of Philosophy*, vol. IV, 1967, as quoted in Morgan, "Historicism [*DBI*]", 291.

[67] Johnson, "Crisis in Biblical Scholarship", 20.

[68] Levenson, *The Hebrew Bible, the Old Testament*, 123.

[69] Levenson quotes Leo Strauss on the irony of historicism's blindness to its own limits: "Historicism asserts that all human thoughts or beliefs are historical, and hence deservedly destined to perish; but historicism itself is a human thought; hence historicism can be of only temporary validity, or it cannot be simply true. To assert the historicist thesis means to doubt it and thus to transcend it.... Historicism thrives on the fact that it inconsistently exempts itself from its own verdict about all human thought.... We cannot see the historical character of 'all' thought—that is, of all thought with the exception of the historicist insight and its implications—without transcending history, without grasping something trans-historical" (Strauss, *Natural Right and History*, 25). Levenson comments, "The belief that the real meaning of religious phenomena is available only to the outside observer is a secular analogue to religious revelation. If so, then a system of thought like historicism which 'exempts itself from its own verdict,' is a secular equivalent to fundamentalism. For though it subjects all else to critique, it asserts axiomatically its own inviolability to critique. Demanding to be the norm by means of which truth and error are disclosed, this type of thinking, by definition, can never be in error" (*The Hebrew Bible, the Old Testament*, 116-117).

book, or for the subsequent generations who included the book in the canon of Scripture.   As has been mentioned already, the Biblical Commission acknowledges the historicist tendency of the historical-critical method[70].

d) Other Tendencies and Implications

Levenson has noted other biases of historical-critical study of the Bible which limit its usefulness for communities of faith which seek the Bible's religious meaning. Here is a list of some of them[71]:

1. Exegesis which concentrates on the human dimension of Scripture (which is the only dimension for which historical-criticism is competent), often leads to neglect of the divine dimension, a "desacralization" of biblical studies[72].

2. Historical-critical study casts doubt upon (or denies) the unity of the Bible and of the tradition which accompanies and issues from it[73].

3. Focusing on the human dimension of Scripture results in a "tendency to dissolve text into culture and the Bible into the history that preceded its synthesis"[74]. A specific instance of this problem is the tendency toward an ideological interpretation of Scripture, which sees biblical texts as the legitimization of the economic or political subjugation of one group by another[75].

4. A secular attitude pervades historical-critical exegesis which leads practitioners to suppress their particularist community loyalties and to restrict the questions to be considered in the interests of minimizing religious differences[76].

5. There are intrinsic tensions between historical-critical analysis and the acceptance of a canon of Scripture[77]. First, when historical critical study

---

[70] "Historical-critical exegesis has too often tended to limit the meaning of texts by tying it too rigidly to precise historical circumstances" (II.B.1.e). A little later after speaking of the new light which the paschal mystery sheds on 2 Sam 7:12-13, the Commission contrasts their approach to the historicist interpretation: "Exegetes who have a narrow, 'historicist' idea about the literal sense will judge that here is an example of an interpretation alien to the original. Those who are open to the dynamic aspect of a text will recognize here a profound element of continuity as well as a move to a different level..." (II.B.2.a).

[71] The ideas are Levenson's; the list is the author's.

[72] Blowers, Levenson and Wilken, "Three Views", 42. See also Levenson, *The Hebrew Bible, the Old Testament*, 75.

[73] Blowers, Levenson and Wilken, "Three Views", 43.

[74] Levenson, *The Hebrew Bible, the Old Testament*, 111.

[75] Levenson specifically discusses Coote and Coote, *Power, Politics, and the Making of the Bible*, (*The Hebrew Bible, the Old Testament*,111-114).

[76] Levenson, *The Hebrew Bible, the Old Testament*, 118, 122.

[77] Levenson, *The Hebrew Bible, the Old Testament*, 122-123, 125-126.

exclusively considers the original meaning of the text, it fails to take into account the importance of recontextualization within the canon to biblical meaning. Second, historical-critical analysis views the canon as having no more than an accidental or historico-cultural foundation (i.e., it is what the Church Fathers or rabbis decided). From this perspective canonical meanings do not make sense. But if, as Jews and Christians believe, the canon is the product of divine intention, the new divinely-willed context of canon requires a pan-canonical treatment of themes.

6.   The more the study of the Bible is pursued on "neutral value-free" grounds, the more the value of the enterprise comes into question. The more the canon is treated as merely a historical and cultural product, the less reason there is to study these particular books over other ancient books[78].

e)   A Model, A Tradition

Both Johnson and Levenson maintain that there is more to the historical-critical method than a profane method which can be put to sacred use by means of purifying it of a few tendentious presuppositions[79]. Johnson insists that the historical-critical method is a "model", i.e., "an imaginative construal of the subject being studied, as well as a structured picture of both process and product: a model is a paradigm within which the data pertinent to a discipline makes sense"[80]. In New Testament study, the object being studied is the history of early Christianity including its founder, and the goal is a critical reconstruction of that period. The New Testament writings have value as *sources*, but apart from that are not terribly important. Johnson does not object to the historical model in itself, although he doubts that there is enough evidence available for it to achieve its goal[81]. More to the point, a historical

---

[78] Levenson, *The Hebrew Bible, the Old Testament*, 109-110.

[79] Vignolo wonders whether the document of the Biblical Commission marks the passage from a historicist-positivist to a hermeneutic-theological model, or whether, despite its declared assumption, the *IBC* represents a juxtaposition and faulty harmonization of both. A footnote on this point calls for the recognition of presuppositions not only on the part of interpreters, but also of methods, which bear implicit pre-understandings of the nature of the texts they are examining, the object to research, etc., which influences their results. According to Vignolo, "Whether it intends to or not, every method has its own *a priori*; it presupposes an ontology (if not an ideology!) and a certain idea of the meaning of the text..." ("Questioni di ermeneutica [*Commento*]", 294-295; cf. Marucci, "Presentazione del recente documento", 590-591).

[80] Johnson, *The Real Jesus*, 171-172.

[81] "The writings of the New Testament are too few, too fragmentary, and too lacking in chronological and geographical controls to enable a truly comprehensive reconstruction of Christian origins" (Johnson, *The Real Jesus*, 172).

model is too narrow to fulfill the task of interpretation of the Bible[82]. It might be added that the difficulty of adopting techniques from one "model" for use in another requires an explicit understanding of both models and the roles various elements play in each.

Levenson follows up on Collins' admission that historical criticism is itself a tradition "with its own values and presuppositions, derived in large part from the Enlightenment and western humanism"[83]. If historical criticism itself bears historically-conditioned presuppositions, rather than replacing tradition with pure scientific reason as the Enlightenment claimed to do, should not its presuppositions also be criticized[84]? Should it not abandon its totalistic claims and accept on an equal footing other (religious) traditions whose foundational assumptions are similarly not self-evident or free of cultural particularism[85]? After challenging historical criticism's pretensions, Levenson makes a proposal for its role:

> The tradition of historical criticism should not be abandoned within pluralistic settings, but only reconceived to recognize the challenge of pluralism.... Room must be made for other senses of the text, developed by other traditions, and historical criticism must learn to interact more creatively with those other traditions, neither surrendering to them nor demanding that they surrender to historical criticism.... It will also have to recognize that it corresponds to a *community of interpretation*. It is a very special kind, however, one dependent upon other communities of interpretation for the very object of its inquiry.... Historical critics thus constitute a secondary community; they engage in second-order reflection upon the primary language of the religious communities they study [emphasis original][86].

Whether or not one agrees with Johnson's and Levenson's analyses and proposals, their criticism demonstrates that there is more to the historical-critical method *as it is commonly understood and practiced* than a collection of neutral methods that can simply be incorporated into interpretation of the Bible in the Church. The "properly-oriented" use of the historical-critical

---

[82] Johnson proposes an experience/interpretation model that responds to the texts anthropologically, historically, in their literary complexity and integrity, and religiously (*The Real Jesus*, 173-174).

[83] Collins, "Critical Biblical Theology", 7.

[84] Levenson, *The Hebrew Bible, the Old Testament*, 119-120. Bartholomew provides a very helpful analysis of the tradition of historical criticism and draws out its implications for interpretation in *Reading Ecclesiastes: Old Testament Exegesis and Hermeneutical Theory*, 53-68, 81-97.

[85] Levenson, *The Hebrew Bible, the Old Testament*, 120-122.

[86] Levenson, *The Hebrew Bible, the Old Testament*, 123.

method commended by the Biblical Commission succeeds at articulating a viable alternative.   However, it is doubtful that a "properly-oriented" approach to the historical-critical method can take hold on a wide scale unless its supporters openly acknowledge the defective presuppositions that commonly characterize its use and unless they give due consideration to historical criticism's past and present as a "model" and an interpretive tradition.

9.   More On The Relationship of History to Interpretation in the Church

One of the common criticisms of the historical-critical method has been the way that critical history has served to undermine faith in traditional Christian doctrine and in the trustworthiness of the Bible[87].   Surprisingly, despite the Biblical Commission's awareness of this criticism[88], the *IBC* does not address to this issue. Perhaps the Commission felt that problems of this kind are a holdover from the past and that they will resolve themselves as a more unbiased use of the historical-critical method takes hold. Yet some of the questions have pressing pastoral implications. The *IBC* makes only a few assertions about the relation between history and exegesis[89], and these do not resolve the more vexing questions.

Here are some of the important unresolved questions which, hopefully, a future Biblical Commission document will take up:

1.   How important is the veracity of the history recounted in the Bible? Can most of it (excluding the death and resurrection of Christ) be

---

[87] A common way for the relation of history to biblical interpretation to present itself occurs in debunking exegesis which assumes a form roughly analogous to the antitheses of Matthew 6: "You have heard it said [in your church or synagogue].... But critical study of the Bible demonstrates...." Debunking exegesis of this sort abounds in the Jesus Seminar writings and in introductory courses on Scripture in secular and religious university programs. Johnson and Levenson both describe this as a contemporary phenomenon (Johnson, "What's Catholic About It?", 15; Levenson, "Unexamined Commitments of Criticism", 106-108; Blowers, Levenson and Wilken, "Three Views", 42).

[88] See, for instance, Intro 3: "They [the opponents of the historical-critical method] insist that the result of scientific exegesis is only to provoke perplexity and doubt upon numerous points which hitherto had been accepted without difficulty. They add that it impels some exegetes to adopt positions contrary to the faith of the Church on matters of great importance, such as the virginal conception of Jesus and his miracles, and even his resurrection and divinity".

[89] The Biblical Commission asserts that 1) Scripture bears witness to a historical reality; 2) historical circumstances shaped what was written and must be taken into account to determine a text's meaning (Conclusion c); and 3) not everything written in the past tense is historical (contra fundamentalism, I.F.e) and "a story need not belong to the genre of history but [could] be instead a work of imaginative fiction" (II.B.1.b). See principle #3, "Catholic Exegesis and History".

regarded as fiction without important theological loss? Some say the biblical narrative, accepted on its own terms, is the proper basis for theology, and that questions about historicity are irrelevant[90]. Other scholars would say that the truth value of the Bible depends upon its being reliable in its fundamental historical affirmations (taking into account the difference in modern and ancient historical genres). Yet among those who hold this view, some do not consider historical issues relevant to the exegete's work[91]. Others, both on the theological left and right, are very concerned about historical facticity.

2. How should the historical discipline be defined and what may reasonably be expected from it? Some define it in a way that necessarily excludes supernatural explanations of what it investigates. Thus, Robert Morgan and John Barton claim that it is an axiom of the historical discipline that "acts of God cannot be spoken of, let alone established, by historical research", and that a historical explanation is "a rational,...non-supernatural account"[92]. Still others, like Johnson, argue for a more modest reckoning of history's powers, seeing it as mode of knowing limited by the data available, the capabilities of historians, and its object, namely a "human event in time and space"[93]. Since the resurrection, defined as "the passage of the human Jesus into the power of God" exceeds history's competence, Christ's resurrection is seen as real, but not historical[94]. On the other hand, some authors advocate a historical methodology broad enough to take into account natural and supernatural events[95].

---

[90] Frei, *Eclipse of Biblical Narrative*, rightly or wrongly, is commonly interpreted this way (see Comstock, "Truth or Meaning"; Henry, "Narrative Theology"; Olson, "Back to the Bible (Almost)"). According to Collins, "The significance of the paradigm shift from history to story is that it abandons the last claim of biblical theology to certain knowledge of objective reality" ("Critical Biblical Theology", 11).

[91] Noble says this is Childs' position (*The Canonical Approach*, 84, see 84-94 for an analysis of Childs' decoupling of historical reference and theological value).

[92] Morgan and Barton, *Biblical Interpretation*, 70 and 68, as cited by Noble, *The Canonical Approach*, 110-111.

[93] Johnson, *The Real Jesus*, 136.

[94] Johnson, *The Real Jesus*, 136. See pp. 81-140 for Johnson's views of history and its limits.

[95] Thus Pannenberg, for whom "revelation occurs in the events of history, and must therefore be discovered through historical research" (Noble, *The Canonical Approach*, 111; Pannenberg, "Redemptive Event and History"). Noble evaluates and improves upon Pannenberg's model (108-144).

3. What are the implications of the emerging consensus regarding the inescapably perspectival character of historical knowledge for historical-critical exegesis, "historical Jesus" research and theology[96]?

4. In what biblical or theological specialty should foundational historical questions about Christianity be treated (e.g., the resurrection or the relationship of Jesus of the Gospels to the "historical" Jesus)? Should this be the domain of ordinary exegesis in the Church, or should there be a specialization analogous to fundamental theology to evaluate such issues?

5. How should exegetes respond to supposed findings of critical history which disagree with important biblical history, such as those which deny a historical basis to the biblical accounts of the exodus and conquest of Palestine? What principles should guide their response?

6. What is the historical value of the various historical genres in the Bible? What sort of factual accuracy is appropriate to expect from each?

7. What value should historical re-construction of circumstances behind the text have for interpretation in the Church? For example, Brown and others have proposed elaborate hypotheses about the historical situation that lies behind the Gospel and the Letters of John[97]. How much weight should be given to such hypotheses in determining biblical meaning?

8. In terms of historical method, is it a valid use of sources to detach the accounts of events and sayings from their narrative contexts (in

---

[96] See Green, "Quest of the Historical", for a consideration of this issue in regard to "historical" Jesus research; Green's notes refer to recent publications which reflect on the nature of the historical discipline.

[97] It may be significant that in his final work, *Introduction to the New Testament*, Brown devotes only two pages to his reconstruction of the history of the Johannine community (originally set out in *Community of the Beloved Disciple*), and precedes that summary with the following warning: "One should not confuse such reconstructive research with exegesis, which has to do with what the Gospel meant to convey to its readers. The evangelist tells us his purpose in 20:31, and it was not to recount background.... I shall now present a reconstruction of the community history, warning that while it explains many factors in the Gospel, it remains a hypothesis and 'perhaps' needs to be added to every sentence" (374). In his forward Brown makes clear that he intends to concentrate on the NT, not on "early Christianity", and that he likewise focuses on the extant text of the NT and not its prehistory (viii-ix).

the Gospels or Acts) in order to construct an alternative historical portrait of Jesus or the early Church[98]?

9. How is historical development within the biblical tradition (and then within the tradition of the Church) to be evaluated theologically? When is the earlier tradition more authoritative, when is the later[99]?

10. Reprise

The "Discussion" of principle #15 on "The Use of the Historical-Critical Method" has made several points. First, the Pontifical Biblical Commission, with the support of the Pope, takes a position in the century-long controversy regarding the suitability of the historical-critical method for exegesis in the Catholic Church. The *IBC* endorses the use of the historical-critical method as indispensable to Catholic exegesis.

But at the same time, the Commission presents a unique approach to the historical-critical method which takes into account many of the criticisms which have been voiced over the years. Their document excludes certain problematic tendencies for which the method has been known and defines the object of study in a way that differs from the practice of many exegetes. Finally, the *IBC* re-dimensions the historical-critical method by placing it in the overall context of Catholic interpretation, which has its own principles. Borrowing Fitzmyer's expression, this study has described the Biblical Commission' approach to the historical-critical method as a "properly-oriented" use of the historical-critical method.

Despite the Biblical Commission's achievement in articulating an approach to the historical-critical method that is compatible with Catholic principles of interpretation, this section has identified two weaknesses in the Biblical Commission's treatment of this topic. First, the *IBC* glosses over problematic presuppositions that still often accompany the use of the historical-critical method and that are considered by some scholars to be intrinsic to it. Unfortunately, by failing to distinguish sharply enough

---

[98] Johnson succeeds in raising reasonable questions about this procedure (Johnson, *The Real Jesus*, 92-104, 124-126).

[99] Alternatively, does Christian interpretation in light of the canon have a counterpart to the Eighth Principle of Judaism's "literary simultaneity of Scripture"? See Levenson, "The Eighth Principle of Judaism" and *The Hebrew Bible, the Old Testament*, 62-81. Levenson believes that the application of a diachronic perspective to Scripture seriously undermines the principle that the Bible is a unity (*Hebrew Bible*, 70-71). Can the diachronic principle, linked to the theological notion of progressive revelation, be applied alongside of the principle of the unity of Scripture?

between the approach to the historical-critical method they endorse and other approaches that enjoy wide currency, the Biblical Commission's position has been widely misunderstood as an almost unqualified endorsement of the historical-critical method.

The second weakness of the *IBC*'s treatment of the historical-critical method was its failure to treat a variety of questions regarding the relation of history to the interpretation of the Bible in the Church. Although this is not a new topic and has been treated at various times in the past, it remains one of the most important problems raised by the historical-critical method, and it has practical ramifications for theology, exegesis, and pastoral care.

Notwithstanding these shortcomings, the *IBC*'s affirmation of the historical-critical method—properly understood and placed in the broader context of Catholic exegesis—is an important step forward.

CHAPTER 16

A Plurality of Methods and Approaches

Principle #16

Catholic exegesis is characterized by openness to a plurality of methods and approaches. Although the historical-critical method retains its primacy, literary methods and approaches based on tradition, the social sciences, or particular contemporary contexts can yield important insights into the meaning of the biblical word. However, the value of these insights will correspond to their harmony with the fundamental principles which guide Catholic interpretation[1].

Explanation

1. The "Openness" of Catholic Exegesis

Catholic exegesis is characterized by openness to a plurality of methods and approaches.

Almost everyone, including Pope John Paul II (Address 13), has praised the "openness" of the Commission document, and with good reason. Rather than restrict access to the biblical word of God narrowly to a single methodology, the Commission chose to throw open the doors to as many ways of approaching the Bible as are consistent with the Christian understanding of its nature. This shows respect for diversity in the mentality

---

[1] The *IBC* addresses the plurality of methods that characterize Catholic exegesis above all in chapter I (I.B.-E.), at the beginning of chapter III (III.a-b), and in its Conclusion (c-d).

of persons and groups approaching the Bible, just as other sections of the document indicate respect for the role of every member of the Church in interpretation (III.B.3), or the contribution of diverse cultures (IV.B. "Inculturation", principle #19) and of various interpretive methods throughout history (see III.B.3, "Patristic Interpretation").

The reason Catholic exegesis can be so "open" in its methodology is explained in the opening section of the document's chapter entitled "Characteristics of Catholic Interpretation."

> Catholic exegesis does not claim any particular scientific method as its own... Catholic exegesis freely *makes use* of the scientific methods and approaches which allow a better grasp of the meaning of texts in their linguistic, literary, socio-cultural, religious and historical contexts....

> What characterizes Catholic exegesis is that it deliberately places itself within the living tradition of the Church, whose first concern is fidelity to the revelation attested by the Bible. (III.a,b, emphasis added)

It is not unanimity regarding method that unifies Catholic exegesis, but, rather, a common hermeneutic of faith in the context of Tradition that is the basis of unity[2]. Methods fulfill an instrumental role helping the community of faith hear more clearly the word of God in Sacred Scripture.

A second reason why Catholic exegesis must be open to various approaches is Scripture's own embrace of diversity within its overall unity:

> Within the New Testament, as already within the Old, one can see the juxtaposing of different perspectives that sit sometimes in tension with one another: for example, regarding the status of Jesus (John 8:29; 16:32 and Mark 15:34) or the value of the Mosaic Law (Matt 5:17-19 and Rom 6:14) or the necessity of works for justification (James 2:24 and Rom 3:28; Eph 2:8-9). One of the characteristics of the Bible is precisely the absence of a sense of systematization and the presence, on the contrary, of things held in dynamic tension. The Bible is a repository of many ways of interpreting the same events and reflecting upon the same problems. In itself it urges us to avoid excessive simplification and narrowness of spirit. (III.A.2.g).

The "absence of a sense of systematization" and the presence "of things held in dynamic tension" characterizes not only the Bible, but also Catholic interpretation of it.

2.   Other Methods and Approaches

Although the historical-critical method retains its primacy, literary methods and approaches based on tradition, the social sciences, or particular

---

[2] See principles #6 and #10.

contemporary contexts can yield important insights into the meaning of the biblical word.

As the previous chapter indicated, the Biblical Commission recognizes that the historical-critical method performs a role in understanding the meaning of the biblical word that is indispensable on account of the historical character of Christian revelation. Nevertheless, it is not sufficient:

> No scientific method...is fully adequate to comprehend the biblical texts in all their richness. For all its overall validity, the historical-critical method cannot claim to be totally sufficient in this respect. It [the historical-critical method] necessarily has to lay aside many aspects of the writings which it studies. Other methods and approaches seek to explore dimensions of the text's meaning which the historical-critical method is not able to recognize. (I.B.a)

The reason other methods and approaches are needed is that no one method can do justice to the richness of the Scripture. So long as the meaning of the biblical text in its historical communication is respected, other approaches— especially those commonly called "synchronic"—can add a great deal:

> To function in a way that will be fruitful, synchronic approaches should accept the conclusions of the diachronic [i.e., historical], at least according to their main lines. But granted this principle, the synchronic approaches (the rhetorical, narrative, semiotic and others) are capable...of bringing about a renewal of exegesis and making a very useful contribution. (Conclusion c,d)

The Biblical Commission makes two important distinctions among the various means employed in the interpretation of Scripture. First, they distinguish "methods" from "approaches":

> By an exegetical "method" we understand a group of scientific procedures employed in order to explain texts. We speak of an "approach" when it is a question of an inquiry proceeding from a particular point of view. (Intro B.c note)

"Methods" are distinguished by "scientific procedures" which seek to be as objective as possible, "approaches" by their beginning from a particular interest or perspective. According to Ruppert, "methods" place the interpreter "over" the text to analyze it, while "approaches" enable the interpreter to encounter the text and ask it questions[3]. Both methods and approaches are valid and important[4].

---

[3] Ruppert, "Kommentierende Einführung", 21-22.

[4] See Sevin, "L'approche des textes bibliques", for an illustration of all the methods and approaches the Biblical Commission discusses applied to Luke 7:11-17.

Of all the means of approaching Scripture considered, the Biblical Commission categorizes only the historical-critical method and three kinds of literary analysis as "methods"—rhetorical analysis, narrative analysis, and semiotic analysis[5]. A common advantage of these last three methods over the historical-critical method is that "they pay greater attention to the internal unity of the texts studied" (I.C.a). The *IBC* describes the basis and contribution of each of these literary methods.

Rhetorical analysis is based on the fact that "all biblical texts are in some measure persuasive in character", a fact that was often overlooked in the past (I.B.1.b,i)[6]. Classical and Semitic rhetorical analyses study texts in terms of the traditions of persuasive speaking and writing they reflect, and thus shed light on what the biblical authors meant and what their first readers understood. The New Rhetoric (a form of rhetorical analysis) draws attention to the power of language to persuade and convince and shows that the Bible bears "a function of communication in a particular context", which comes across with a "certain power of argument and rhetorical strategy" (I.B.1.j).

Narrative analysis is appropriate because the Bible often conveys its message through the forms of story and personal testimony (I.B.2.a)[7]. While historical-critical exegesis holds up a "window" into another time and a particular historical situation, narrative analysis shows how the text functions as "mirror", projecting a "narrative world" which influences readers to adopt certain values (I.B.2.f). It is particularly suited to facilitating the transition from the significance of the text in its historical context to its meaning for the reader of today (I.B.2.h).

Finally, *semiotic analysis* bases itself on the theory that "all language is a system of relationships obeying fixed laws"[8]. Semiotics directs greater attention to the fact that "each biblical text is a coherent whole, obedient to a precise linguistic mechanic of operation" (I.B.3.k). When taught in simple terms it can be pastorally useful in helping Christians begin to study the Bible without their first having to become acquainted with its historical background (I.B.3.m).

After distinguishing "methods" from "approaches", the Commission categorizes the various "approaches" to interpreting Scripture under three

---

[5] For more on the *IBC*'s account of literary methods, see Pitta, "Nuovi metodi di analisi letteraria [*Commento*]"; Weber, "Making the Biblical Account Relevant".

[6] For bibliography on rhetorical criticism, see Fitzmyer, *The Biblical Commission's Document*, footnotes on 54-56, 58.

[7] For works of or about narrative analysis, see Fitzmyer, *The Biblical Commission's Document*, 59n.

[8] For works of or about semiotic analysis, see Fitzmyer, *The Biblical Commission's Document*, 64n.

headings, "Approaches Based on Tradition", "Approaches that Use the Human Sciences", and "Contextual Approaches". Again, the Commission points out the potential benefits in each of these approaches.

The approaches based on tradition have an advantage over literary methods and the historical critical method in that they do not consider writings in isolation, but rather take into account the larger tradition to which biblical books belong (I.C.a)[9]. Approaches based on tradition include 1) the canonical approach, 2) the approach through recourse to Jewish traditions of interpretation, and 3) the approach through the history of the influence of the text ("*Wirkungsgeschichte*").

The *canonical approach* begins from an explicit presupposition of faith interpreting each text in light of the Canon of Scriptures as a whole, i.e., "of the Bible received as the norm of faith by a community of believers" (I.C.1.b). It recognizes the special status of the final form of the text and of "the believing community that provides a truly adequate context for interpreting canonical texts" (I.C.1.g). It seeks a theological understanding of the Scripture valid for today (I.C.1.a-b).

The *approach through recourse to Jewish traditions of interpretation* provides historical insight regarding the Septuagint, Judaism of the first century (the cradle of Christianity), and methods of interpretation found both in the Bible and in other ancient Jewish writings. Jewish interpretation also provides important philological and grammatical resources and well as the help of commentators, ancient and modern, in interpreting difficult passages.

The *approach by the history of the influence of the text* *("Wirkungsgeschichte")* is based on the conviction that readers give life to a text when they appropriate it for themselves, and that these interpretations contribute to better understanding the text itself. Those who utilize this approach study the history of the interpretation of a text over time and the role of readers and tradition in relation to it[10], and thus have "a better chance of uncovering all the dimensions of meaning" latent in the text (I.C.3.c-d).

The approaches that use the human sciences (sociology, anthropology, psychology) contribute to interpretation because the word of God took root in human communities and came to us through the psychological dispositions of

---

[9] For more on the *IBC*'s treatment of approaches based on tradition, see Chrostowski, "33 Sympozjum Biblistów Polskich, 1995", 39-54; Mosetto, "Approcci basati sulla tradizione [*Commento*]".

[10] The Commission specifically gives the examples of the interpretation of the Song of Songs in the patristic period, in monastic circles, and in the writings of St. John of the Cross, and of the fruitfulness of the account of the rich young man in Matt 19:16-26 (I.C.3.d).

the biblical writers[11]. The *sociological approach* uncovers data that is useful to historical criticism for understanding the "economic, cultural and religious functioning of the biblical world" (I.D.1.e). It helps explain the relation between biblical texts and the communities that produced them. The *approach through cultural anthropology* seeks to ascertain the cultural characteristics of biblical social contexts, the patterns of daily life, their values, the manner in which social control is exercised, the concepts of family, kinship and other relations, concepts of the sacred and profane, and so on (I.D.2.b). Like sociological criticism, cultural anthropology sheds light on the original situation in which the text arose. These insights can aid in distinguishing the permanent from the contingent elements of the biblical message (I.D.2.c). The *psychological and psychoanalytical approaches* help the texts of the Bible be understood "in terms of experience of life and norms of behavior" (I.D.3.b). They contribute to a deeper understanding of symbol, of religious experience, of cultic rituals and biblical imagery (I.D.3.c-d)[12].

The contextual approaches bring to exegesis points of view that are "responsive to contemporary currents of thought that have not yet been taken sufficiently into consideration" (I.E.a)[13]. The *liberationist approach*, rather than concentrating on what the text said in its original context, reads Scripture from the perspective of the contemporary poor and oppressed, helping them find in the Bible the nourishment that can sustain their hopes and struggles and lead to a Christian praxis of justice and love. The *feminist approach* seeks liberation and equal rights for women, and by the questions it puts to the text, it has elicited new discoveries (I.E.2.a,j). Feminist exegesis has helped bring to light the significance and role of women in the Bible, and has unmasked

---

[11] For more on the *IBC*'s treatment of approaches that use the human sciences, see Chrostowski, "33 Sympozjum Biblistów Polskich, 1995", 55-64; Pesce, "Approcci secondo le scienze umane [*Commento*]".

[12] For brief but helpful bibliographies on these three approaches through the human sciences, see Fitzmyer, *The Biblical Commission's Document*, 84n, 88n, and 89n. Fitzmyer adds a criticism of his own to the *IBC*'s description of the "risks" (I.D.1.f) entailed in the sociological approach to exegesis: "The sociological approach is really more interested in reading between the lines of the biblical text to dig out the positive historical factors that shaped human and community life in biblical times than it is in determining the religious meaning of God's Word itself. In other words, for all the important contribution that the sociological approach has recently made in the study of the Bible, it rarely contributes much to the meaning of the written Word of God itself" (86-87).

[13] For more on the *IBC*'s treatment of contextual approaches, see Chrostowski, "33 Sympozjum Biblistów Polskich, 1995", 65-74 (feminist approach); Fischer, "Frauen und feministische Exegese"; Heidemanns, "Eine 'postkoloniale Kehrtwendung'?"; Segalla, "Scienze umane e interpretazione", 67-92 (feminist approach).

some tendentious interpretations which sought to justify male domination of women (I.E.2.j).

3. Criteria

Amid this diversity it could appear that Catholic exegesis lacks a center of gravity, a particular stance, or point of view of its own from which to evaluate the plethora of methods and approaches. But this is not the case. In each instance the Biblical Commission renders a judgement about the positive features and limitations of each method. In the mind of the Biblical Commission, all these methods and approaches, like the historical-critical method, only bear fruit when used within the overall context of Catholic interpretation, a framework which this study articulates as "principles of Catholic interpretation". The next section will examine the method and criteria employed by the Commission in evaluating the strengths and limitations of these various methods and approaches to interpreting Scripture.

Discussion

4. Discernment of Methods and Approaches

Although the *IBC*'s description and evaluation of various methods and approaches (I.B.-E.) renders a useful service by virtue of its content, it renders an even greater service by the model it provides of discerning methods and approaches. Because methods and approaches for studying Scripture are constantly changing and new methods are constantly being proposed, it is unavoidable that any overview like that of the *IBC* soon becomes dated. For this reason what is most valuable is the model which the *IBC* provides of evaluation from the standpoint of interpretation in the Church.

a) Procedure

The Biblical Commission follows a simple procedure in its consideration of the many methods and approaches: objective description followed by a balanced evaluation according to the fundamental values and principles of Catholic exegesis.

Each method or approach is described without bias in terms that both its proponents and opponents could likely accept. In most cases the description begins by situating each method historically, indicating the problem or insight that led to its development. Then its presuppositions and procedures are described. In each case the Commission distinguishes diverse tendencies within the approach under consideration. Thus, for instance, the *IBC* notes three kinds of rhetorical analysis, the presence in narrative analysis of both

analytic methods and theological reflection, differences between Childs' and
Sanders' versions of the canonical approach, and the existence of three forms
of feminist hermeneutics. The *IBC*'s descriptions of nearly a dozen methods
and approaches are so competently executed, that they elicited little criticism
from the dozens of scholars who reviewed the document.

When the moment arrives for evaluation, the Commission maintains its
fair-mindedness. No approach is granted an unqualified endorsement, since
every method has its limits and no method is deemed sufficient to explain the
richness of the biblical word (I.B.a). On the other hand, no approach is
rejected altogether, and the Biblical Commission has something positive to
say about almost all of the approaches to Scripture it considers[14].

b) Criteria

If one examines the evaluative remarks of the *IBC* regarding the methods
and approaches, one obtains a fairly clear idea of the criteria that guided the
Biblical Commission and that can continue to be useful for evaluating new
methods and approaches that arise. These criteria in large part coincide with
the principles of interpretation which this study proposes. The twenty
principles presented in this study may be summed up by three fundamental
values of interpretation in the Church: *scholarship*, to indicate scientific
reflection on the human dimension of Scripture expressed in principles #2-5
and #15-16; *faith* to refer to the theological principles which specifically treat
Scripture as the word of God in principles #1,6-10 and #12-14; and *pastoral
concern* to reflect the practical orientation of Catholic interpretation to
building up the body of Christ expressed in principles #11, #17-20.

The foundational values of scholarship, Christian faith, and pastoral
concern underlie the Commission's evaluation of all the new methods and
approaches to interpreting Scripture. The following paragraphs illustrate how

---

[14] The Commission's treatment of fundamentalism lacks the equanimity that characterizes
their description of other approaches. One reviewer wrote, "The document displays a measured
and balanced response to other 'methods', including liberation theology and feminism, but
explodes with revulsion toward fundamentalism" (Shea, "Catholic Reaction to
Fundamentalism", 279). Shea has analyzed published Catholic responses to fundamentalism
(including the *IBC*) in *Theological Studies*. He finds many of them, including the *IBC*, to be
marred by defensiveness, superficial knowledge of their subject, derogatory definition,
psychological reductionism, and a lack of interest in dialogue. Some reviews of the *IBC*
vigorously applaud the *IBC*'s treatment of fundamentalism (see p. 61n, for a list of reviews
considering the *IBC*'s treatment of fundamentalism), but these tend to be characterized by the
superficial consideration and lack of interest in serious dialogue with fundamentalism which
Shea describes.

these values (and principles) guide the Biblical Commission's evaluation of the new methods and approaches before them.

Scholarly considerations of a literary nature (principle #4) lead the commission to commend the new methods of literary analysis for their attention to the internal unity of texts (I.B.3.k; I.C.a), while cautioning against merely formal analysis (I.B.1.g; I.B.3.l) or the risk of reading structure into texts (I.B.1.k). Scholarly considerations of a historical nature (principle #3) prompt an appreciation for the background provided through recourse to Jewish traditions of interpretation (I.C.2.b-c), while calling into question some feminist exegesis when it seeks to reconstruct *ex silentio* historical situations the texts themselves (it is supposed) were designed to hide (I.E.l). Scholarly considerations of a hermeneutical nature (principle #5) lead to recognizing the interpretive value of the concerns readers bring to texts, studying the history of a text's effects, and to an openness to contemporary contextual approaches (I.C.3.b-c; I.E.a).

Faith considerations respectful of the "great Tradition" inspire the *caveat* to narrative analysis, not to exclude doctrinal elaboration of the content of biblical narratives, lest it "find itself out of step with the biblical tradition...and also with the tradition of the Church" (principles #8, #10). Faith leads the Commission to welcome the canonical approach's emphasis on the final form of the text (I.C.1.f, principle #1) and its call for interpretation in light of the Canon of Scripture accepted by the Church as the rule of faith (I.C.1.f-g, principle #7). Christian faith leads the Commission to point out that Christian interpretation of the Old Testament distinguishes itself from Jewish canonical interpretation by the decisive significance of Christ's paschal mystery (I.C.1.i, principle #10).

Pastoral concern motivates the Commission to applaud the potential of narrative analysis (I.B.2.h,g) and semiotic analysis (I.B.3.m) to help readers grasp Scripture's significance for their lives today (principles #11, #18). It leads the Commission to caution against traditional interpretations that produce effects contrary to evangelical charity and justice (I.C.3.e; I.E.2.m). Pastoral concern leads to commending liberationist exegesis for practicing "a reading of the Bible which is oriented to the needs of the people" (I.E.1.b,i), and to cautioning against "one-sided" readings or neglect of the "transcendent dimensions of biblical eschatology" (I.E.1.k,m).

It would not be difficult to multiply examples. Everything the Biblical Commission says in evaluation of the new methods and approaches reveals these underlying criteria: scientific rigor in scholarship, fidelity to Christian revelation, a deep pastoral concern, and the principles of Catholic interpretation which we have been considering. This pattern of competent and unbiased description, followed by an evaluation based on fundamental principles, provides a model by which new methods and future developments in old methods should be evaluated[15].

5. The Interrelation of Methods According to Vittorio Fusco

However commendable it may be from a pastoral point of view to welcome many methods and approaches, from a scientific and scholarly perspective, it can be problematic. Vittorio Fusco comments, "This proliferation appears to some as a sign of creativity and richness, but to others...a sign of fragility and superficiality"[16]. Fusco argues that the multiplication of methods and approaches undermines the unity of scientific exegesis and tends toward a subjective pluralism. In the past new methods built on one another like the segments of a cane of bamboo, each attending to discrete moments in the exegetical task. But the methods of the last twenty years have sprung up like branches of a tree, each growing in its own direction as autonomous possibilities. They give the impression that an interpreter may simply choose among them as he or she prefers, much as one chooses among the channels of a television set. Fusco questions why procedures which in history or literature do not constitute discrete methods should be established as separate methods in biblical studies. If the aim of exegesis is to understand texts, and if a given element (whether literary, sociological, or psychological) helps, should it not be taken into consideration in any normal exegesis of the text, rather than be named an alternative method?[17]

The *IBC* does not say much about the interrelation of the various methods it describes and evaluates, nor does it propose an overall hermeneutical model into which they may be integrated. While a subjective pluralism in method would clearly contradict the Biblical Commission's concern for the objective

---

[15] Vignolo suggests that the document would have profited from a comparison of the critical presuppositions that invariably underlie any method. He refers to the way every method predetermines its outcomes by generalizations about what it is studying and pre-understandings of what it considers important or relevant, and excludes other elements from its field of vision. Unless the application of a method takes the method's fundamental presupposition into account, it tends to flatten the text, conforming it to its expectations ("Questioni di ermeneutica [*Commento*]", 295n).

[16] Fusco, "Un secolo di metodo storico", 376. Vittorio Fusco was bishop of Nardo-Gallipoli in Italy and a member of the Pontifical Biblical Commission when he died in July 1999. Fusco completed a doctorate at the Pontifical Biblical Institute in 1971, writing about the parables in Mark, and was for many years a professor of New Testament at the Pontificia Facoltà Teologica dell' Italia Meridionale, Sezione S. Luigi, in Naples.

[17] Fusco, "Un secolo di metodo storico", 375-376. Fusco expresses his debt for the botanical images to Alonso Schökel, "Trends: Plurality of Methods".

content of Scripture (evident in their insistence on the historical-critical method), it seems that the Commission preferred to emphasize the openness of Catholic interpretation, rather than impose any particular unified model. The only comment in the *IBC* regarding the relation of the various methods and approaches to one another appears in its Conclusion. There the Biblical Commission reaffirms the necessity of the historical-critical method on account of the historical character of revelation and states, "To function in a way that will be fruitful, synchronic approaches should accept the conclusions of the diachronic, at least according to their main lines" (Conclusion c).

But this leaves many questions unanswered. Are there also ways in which diachronic analysis should defer to a synchronic analysis of texts? Furthermore, in relation to the historical-critical method, what is the role in exegesis that should be accorded to the approaches based on tradition, to the approaches derived from the "human" sciences, and to the contextual approaches?

a)   Fusco's Proposal for the Unity of Exegesis

Fusco offers a proposal for restoring the unity of exegesis that takes into account the Biblical Commission's priority on history, its appreciation for the synchronic methods, and its respect for tradition[18].   Fusco accepts the multiplication of methods, approaches and "readings" as responses to the real need to overcome the distance between the text and the contemporary reader. Nevertheless, Fusco thinks that sometimes the problem lies not at the level of method but with the spiritual distance of many modern people from the faith expressed in the Scriptures. Furthermore, he does not think that everything calling itself a method deserves to be so categorized[19]. Readings of Scripture which claim to be all-encompassing, such as some Freudian psychoanalytic and materialist readings, are nothing other than alternatives to Christian interpretation of the Scriptures—they are not exegetical methods. Likewise the liberationist and feminist approaches which the Biblical Commission calls "contextual", are not methods in themselves. Instead they embody the questions put to the biblical text by social movements, and, in fact, these approaches rely on the historical-critical method. Finally, some approaches which have long belonged to the historical-critical method should not be erected as distinct methods alongside it. Fusco puts both sociological analysis

---

[18] The next several pages of this study recap the final section of Fusco, "Un secolo di metodo storico", 377-395.

[19] In this discussion Fusco does not follow the *IBC*'s distinction between methods and approaches, or confine himself to the methods and approaches named in the document.

and rhetorical analysis in this category[20]. In the end, Fusco identifies and discusses two kinds of approaches whose relationship to the historical-critical method he thinks deserve further consideration: 1) synchronic analysis, which attempts to examine the text in greater depth in its own right, and 2) the approaches based on tradition[21].

b) Historical Exegesis

In Fusco's opinion, the reconstruction of the unity of exegesis can best be achieved in the context of the historical method, provided that the method is open to incorporating the results of all the disciplines which concern themselves with the meaning of texts. He gives the example of the challenge of structuralism to the historical-critical method which arose in the seventies, and whose insights now seem to have been successfully integrated into historical exegesis[22]. Fusco clarifies in what sense exegesis should and should not be considered "historical". Although it is legitimate for historians to use texts for reconstructing events, in historical *exegesis* the text can never be reduced simply to a "source" for the reconstruction of historical events or of a text's redactional history[23]. Exegesis concerns itself with the meaning of texts; historical exegesis occurs whenever the final text is understood in a historical framework. It is an inescapable fact that a biblical text's language, its categories of thought, and its literary forms belong to a specific epoch and culture. The excessive attention to the prehistory of a text that has sometimes characterized historical exegesis should not be identified with the method itself but with its misuse. Fusco criticizes the Biblical Commission's use of the term "diachronic" in some instances where diachronic analysis seems to

---

[20] In regard to rhetorical criticism, Fusco cites Kennedy, *New Testament Interpretation through Rhetorical Criticism*, 3.

[21] Fusco, "Un secolo di metodo storico", 380-382.

[22] Fusco observes that in fact structuralism has resulted in two different tendencies, both proceeding from the need to escape the exclusive domination of text and to recognize the role of the reader. On the one hand, there is deconstructionist post-structuralism, in which the inexhaustible multiplicity of readings leads to relativism and nihilism. On the other hand, there are the various points of view which recognize a relation between a text's structure and the readers to whom it was originally addressed. But by attending to the reader, structuralism has met with an unexpected result: "By means of the reader reality beyond the text, the much-criticized history, formerly driven from the door, has now re-entered through the window" ("Un secolo di metodo storico", 385-386).

[23] Fusco acknowledges that the reconstruction of a text's redactional history can sometimes aid in determining the text's meaning. He also recognizes that research on the historicity of some decisive events may be important for theology, even though historical reconstruction can never replace the text as a norm of faith ("Un secolo di metodo storico", 387).

be accorded priority, which "contradicts the commonly accepted rule today of the priority of synchronic analysis"[24].

c) Synchronic Methods

Fusco believes synchronic analysis can be integrated into a properly-conceived historical exegesis. Just as the study of the structure of texts remains an irreversible acquisition of historical exegesis from structuralist analysis[25], so also narratology adds necessary insight to the historical understanding of texts. Both the analyses of structures and of narratives require history to be understood. In order to understand the structure of, for instance, the Acts of the Apostles, one needs to consider the structure of other ancient works of similar genre. Similarly, one requires some historical knowledge to penetrate the narrative dynamics of "implicit reader" and "point of view". This holds even for the "deep" structures of narratives which semiotics seek out. If, for example, the reader ignores the historical-political datum of the hostility between the Jews and Samaritans in Luke 10:35-37, he or she will not be able to recognize the opposition between fellow countryman and enemy. Thus, even a semiotic study of the text is impossible to the reader who wants to exclude history[26].

---

[24] Fusco, "Un secolo di metodo storico", 388. In this writer's opinion the problem is that in some instances the *IBC* uses "diachronic" in its fundamental etymological sense (*dia* + *chronos*) to mean "historical", giving the misimpression that the Commission was asserting the priority of studying the redaction history of a text before studying its final form. (See the discussion of the *IBC*'s use of "diachronic" and "synchronic" on p. 221n of this study). When Fusco speaks of the "commonly accepted rule today of the priority of synchronic analysis", he refers to one of the most significant influences of "synchronic" literary analysis on the historical-critical method in the last fifteen years. Ever since the Wellhausen hypothesis and the analogous source criticism of many biblical books, exegetes have tended to, first, analyze a work into its hypothetical sources, and then explain each section of the text in terms of its supposed provenance. However, the lack of hard evidence regarding sources has resulted in the multiplication of theories regarding the origin of texts without a clear basis for judging among them. Moreover, literary analysis has succeeded in demonstrating the unity of many texts by explaining seeming incoherences, repetitions, etc., thus refocusing attention on the meaning of the final literary product and, in many cases, calling into question the results of earlier source criticism. This has led the majority of exegetes to reverse the order of their procedures, first subjecting the final form of the text to synchronic analysis, and then employing "diachronic" means (i.e., source criticism) to explain the tensions and incoherences which remain in the text. For discussion and examples of this development, see Conroy, "Literary Analysis of 1 Kings 1:41-53" and Conroy, "Reflections on the Exegetical Task"; Moberly, *At the Mountain of God*; Noble, "Synchronic and Diachronic Approaches" and *The Canonical Approach*; Alonso Schökel, "Of Models and Methods".

[25] Fusco acknowledges that the desired integration between history and the structuralism of the Greimas school has not occurred ("Un secolo di metodo storico", 390).

[26] Fusco, "Un secolo di metodo storico", 390-391.

d) Approaches Based on Tradition

Fusco considers the relation between historical exegesis and approaches based on tradition[27] to be a complex, yet potentially fruitful, field of inquiry. From its beginnings historical exegesis has defined itself over against traditions which were perceived as an obstacle to attaining the original sense of the text. But today in both philosophical and literary reflection tradition has been re-evaluated and accorded a more positive hermeneutical role. Quite apart from the theological value of tradition (and the Church Fathers) for Christian exegesis, and quite apart from the enlightening historical perspective that readers closer in time to the writing of a text can bring, modern hermeneutics conceives interpretation as a dialogue between reader and text. The reader brings something personal and creative to this dialogue, making it possible for every reading to draw out of the text something that was present in it but not explicitly formulated. For genuine interpretation to occur it is necessary that neither the text nor the reader overpower the other in this dialogue[28].

The implication of this way of thinking is that the meaning of a text cannot be reduced to that which was consciously formulated by the author and perceived by the first recipients of the text. The more a text is read, the more it can reveal its riches[29]. For believers, the study of the tradition of Scripture's interpretation should not be simply the object of a successive or parallel study, since it is indispensable to understand themselves and their history and in this way also brings illumination to the interpretation of the text. As such the study of the history of interpretation should not be an appendix to, but a premise of, Christian exegesis[30].

Nevertheless, Fusco insists that the study of the tradition of interpretation should not be viewed as an alternative to historical exegesis, nor should it lead to a return to pre-critical exegesis. There remains a need to verify traditional interpretations by the text itself. This does not mean simply giving the final word to modern critical means of analysis. Again the problem must be resolved by dialogue, not looking at Augustine, Thomas or Luther in place of the text, but looking at the text and the tradition of interpretation together.

---

[27] Fusco only treats the canonical approach and *Rezeptions- und Wirkungsgeschichte*, not commenting on Jewish traditions of interpretation, which he may regard as useful primarily for their historical value.

[28] Fusco, "Un secolo di metodo storico", 392-393.

[29] Fusco states that this is the case with any human text, but it is even more true in regard to a believer's reading of Scripture. As Gregory the Great noted, *divina eloquia cum legente crescunt* (Fusco, "Un secolo di metodo storico", 393).

[30] Fusco, "Un secolo di metodo storico", 393.

Fusco envisions interpretation as a kind of alternating rhythm between hearing interpretations and hearing the text directly[31].

As to the canon, apart from theological considerations, Fusco sees the canonization of biblical writings as decisive moments in their effective history, their *Wirkungsgeschichte*, which provide a foundation to the view that a text must not be interpreted in isolation from the context of the whole of Scripture. Thus, canonical interpretation has a rational basis independent of theological considerations. But on whatever basis and however strictly a canonical approach is pursued, it does not escape historical exegesis. The linguistic and culture codes of biblical texts that differ from our own must be reconstructed with the help of the familiar historical-philological means. The whole of Scripture cannot be interpreted apart from the smallest units which compose it. Especially between the Old and New Testaments there is a circularity required in understanding one in light of the other. Only a reading which respects history will permit each of the scriptural voices to be heard and their unity to be accurately perceived[32].

In summary, Fusco proposes that the synchronic methods should be integrated into historical exegesis, and that approaches based on tradition (at least the canonical approach and *Wirkungsgeschichte*) have an important place in the overall hermeneutical enterprise. The hermeneutical enterprise cannot limit the meaning of a text to what was formulated consciously by its author and perceived by its first recipients. Rather interpretation requires that the interpreter listen simultaneously to the text (illumined by historical exegesis that employs literary analysis) and to the history of its interpretation.

What can be said of Fusco's proposal to unify exegesis as a broadly-conceived historical method placed within a hermeneutical framework that takes into account the tradition of interpretation? Clearly it is a step forward. Fusco is right in believing that a fruitful methodological pluralism will be found not in the simple affirmation of one method against another, but rather in proposals that seek to integrate the various elements into a comprehensive hermeneutical model[33]. Fusco's insistence on the necessity of history to understand Scripture, no matter what method is being used, echoes the Biblical Commission's. His argument for including synchronic literary analysis and insights from other disciplines within historical exegesis is reasonable.

---

[31] Fusco, "Un secolo di metodo storico", 393-394.
[32] Fusco, "Un secolo di metodo storico", 394-395.
[33] Fusco, "Un secolo di metodo storico", 395-396.

However, the weakness in Fusco's proposal stems from the underdevelopment of its hermeneutic dimensions[34]. First, he does not say enough about the role of the reader and the reader's presuppositions and interests. Although Fusco does not say so himself, it appears that his conception of the hermeneutical enterprise leaves room for contextual approaches since they express the questions and concerns some interpreters bring to the text. Second, it is not obvious that Fusco's hermeneutical framework responds adequately to the need to bring the text and its message into the present. Historical exegesis, even when it incorporates the interpretive tradition, focuses on the past and requires an additional hermeneutical step to actualize the message of the text[35]. Finally, the relation between Fusco's hermeneutic model and *interpretation in the Church*, i.e., exegesis from the perspective of Christian faith, is problematic. On the one hand, Fusco clearly believes faith is an important prerequisite for the exegete[36]. On the other hand, at the points in the discussion when Fusco considers the interpretive role of the Canon, Tradition, and the Fathers— which he recognizes are very important for Christian exegesis—he consistently chooses not to engage the "theological" questions[37]. Fusco appears to regard even the interpretive role of the canon as belonging to a different discipline, namely theology, which must be kept separate to preserve the autonomy of exegesis[38]. However, in light of the discoveries of modern

---

[34] Fusco does not claim to present a comprehensive hermeneutical model. The task he sets for himself is to discuss the relation of synchronic literary methods and approaches based on traditions of interpretation to the historical method. But his judgment that the tradition of interpretation belongs in a hermeneutical dialogue beyond the historical exegesis of a text opens the question about what else belongs at the hermeneutical level. Fusco himself says that the various methods and approaches must be considered in light of an overall hermeneutical plan ("Un secolo di metodo storico", 395-396).

[35] Literary methods, on the other hand, focus on the present meaning of a text, and their potential for actualization has been noted both by their advocates (e.g., see Alonso Schökel, "Of Models and Methods", 12-13) and by the Biblical Commission (particularly, narrative analysis and semiotic analysis [I.B.2.h, I.B.3.m]). Is it possible that a synchronic literary exegetical method that respects and incorporates history would prove even more useful than a historical method which incorporates literary insights?

[36] Fusco insists that it is important that the interpreter of today share the faith in Jesus Christ of those to whom the NT writings were addressed ("Un secolo di metodo storico", 376). Later he says it requires a spiritual person to produce spiritual exegesis, and a person with a theological or pastoral mentality to produce exegesis that is theologically or pastorally sensitive (396-397).

[37] Fusco, "Un secolo di metodo storico", 392, 394-395.

[38] Fusco intentionally excludes theological considerations because he thinks they would stand in tension with the demands of history and require a distinctly theological exegesis, which would result in an inappropriate dichotomy between faith and reason. He says, "The

hermeneutics regarding the role of the interpreter's pre-understanding and in view of the religious aim of Catholic exegesis, a rigid separation between exegesis and theology is no longer desirable or tenable.   Rather, Catholic exegetes need to clarify and acknowledge the theological presuppositions which inform their interpretation.   Despite these lacunae in his hermeneutical vision, Fusco has made a valuable contribution toward the recomposition of exegetical method.

---

challenge is not to create other types of exegesis next to 'scientific' exegesis, separate from it—almost as though reason and faith were mutually exclusive—adding a historical exegesis that would not be theological and some other species of exegesis that would instead be theological without being historical. Rather the challenge is that of exercising exegetical rationality within the horizon of faith" ("Un secolo di metodo storico", 397).

Part VI

INTERPRETATION IN PRACTICE

CHAPTER 17

The Task of the Exegete and the Relationship of Exegesis With Other Theological Disciplines

Principle #17

The task of the Catholic exegete is both a work of scholarship and an ecclesial service (III.C.a). Because sound interpretation requires a lived affinity with what is studied and the light of the Holy Spirit, full participation in the life and faith of the believing community (III.A.3.g) and personal prayer are necessary (Address 9).

The primary task of the exegete is to determine as accurately as possible the meaning of biblical texts in their own proper context, that is, first of all, in their particular literary and historical context and then in the context of the wider canon of Scripture (III.D.4.b).

Catholic exegetes arrive at the true goal of their work only when they have explained the meaning of the biblical text as God's word for today (III.C.1.b). Exegetes should also explain the christological, canonical and ecclesial content of biblical texts (III.C.1.c).

Exegesis is a theological discipline, which exists in a relationship of dialogue with other branches of theology (III.D.a)[1].

---

[1] This principle finds expression primarily in chapter III, "Characteristics of Catholic Interpretation", parts C and D, entitled respectively, "The Task of the Exegete" and "Relationships with Other Theological Disciplines".

Explanation

The sections of the *IBC* devoted to the role of the exegete and the relation of exegesis to other theological disciplines are important for several reasons. First, as was noted earlier, the concluding sentence of the document underscores the centrality of the exegete's task to the *IBC*'s purpose: "The present essay hopes to have made some contribution towards the gaining, on the part of all, of a clearer awareness of the role of the Catholic exegete" (Conclusion f). Furthermore, the sections of the *IBC* devoted to these topics (six pages in length) provide the most complete description of the role of the exegete and its relation to theology of any church document to date[2]. Finally, the Biblical Commission's description of the role of the exegete recapitulates and applies to the work of the exegete most of the themes which this study has identified as principles of interpretation that appear elsewhere in the document.

1. Scholarship And Ecclesial Service

> *According to the Biblical Commission, the task of the exegete is both a work of scholarship and an ecclesial service. (III.C.a)*

As a work of scholarship, exegesis finds expression in research, teaching, and publication. Research necessarily entails specialization, because the fields of knowledge useful for understanding the Bible are vast. It follows that interdisciplinary collaboration is a necessity (III.C.2.a). In their scholarly study of the Bible, Catholic exegetes participate in an enterprise that goes well beyond the bounds of the Church and entails interchange with scholars who are not Catholics (III.C.a). Catholic exegetes teach in the theology faculties of universities, seminaries, and religious houses of study (III.C.3.a) as well as in academic institutions which are not Catholic. The primary medium of dialogue, discussion and cooperation among biblical scholars is publication, whether in books, scholarly journals or the new electronic media (III.C.4.a-b).

Although the ultimate purpose of Catholic exegesis is to deepen Christian faith (Conclusion e)[3], this must in no way lead to lowering the standard of Catholic scholarship or involvement in research. Neither, according to the Biblical Commission,

> should it provide excuse for abuse of methodology out of apologetic concern. Each sector of research (textual criticism, linguistic study, literary

---

[2] For a brief account of the development of the role accorded to exegetes in church documents, particularly the background to *DV* 12, see Lambiasi, "Dimensioni caratteristiche [*Commento*]", 348-351.

[3] See principle #11, "The Aim of Interpretation", especially p.151ff.

analysis, etc.) has its own proper rules, which it ought follow with full autonomy. (Conclusion e)

A properly exercised pre-understanding of faith strives to be as objective as possible, respecting the autonomy of the scientific biblical disciplines, and does not predetermine the results of research.

According to the *IBC*, exegesis is an ecclesial task because "it consists in the study and explanation of Holy Scripture in a way that makes all its riches available to pastors and the faithful" (III.C.a). The Biblical Commission's document situates exegesis at the heart of the Church's life with implications for theology, pastoral practice, liturgy, and ecumenism[4]. It is important that there be a sufficient number of well-prepared Catholics available to do research in the various fields of exegetical study for pastoral reasons, both positive and negative. Negatively,

> a lack in this area exposes the Church to serious harm, for pastors and the faithful then run the risk of being at the mercy of an exegetical scholarship which is alien to the Church and lacks relationship to the life of faith. (III.C.2.b)

Positively, the Second Vatican Council indicated the crucial importance of exegetical research by declaring "that 'the *study* of Sacred Scripture' should be 'as it were the soul of theology'" (*DV* 24 cited in III.C.2.b, *IBC*'s italics).

Exegesis makes the riches of Scripture available to pastors and faithful both through teaching and publications at various levels. Seminary instruction emphasizes the role of Scripture in pastoral ministry, while university programs of biblical studies give more consideration to technical aspects of studying Scripture. Academic teaching of Scripture should avoid being one-sided, by failing to provide either doctrinal and spiritual content or historical-critical grounding:

> Teaching should at one and the same time show forth the historical roots of the biblical writings, the way in which they constitute the personal word of the heavenly Father addressing his children with love (cf. *Dei Verbum*, 21) and their indispensable role in the pastoral ministry (cf. 2 Tim 3:16). (III.C.3.b)

The *IBC* stresses the need for publication by exegetes not only at a scholarly level, but also at a popular level. Those who have "a gift for popularization provide an extremely useful and fruitful work" since there is so great a need to communicate Scripture's message widely and to make it real for the people

---

[4] Vignolo considers one of the signal achievements of the *IBC* to be its defining exegesis as a theological discipline whose aim is the deepening of faith and "whose *Sitz im Leben* is the life of the Church" ("Questioni di ermeneutica [*Commento*]", 294).

of today (III.C.4.c). The goal should be to overcome the distance of time and culture and help the men and women of today appropriate the Bible's true "historical and inspired meaning" (III.C.4.c). The fundamental aim of exegesis remains clear: "In all this variety of tasks, the Catholic exegete has no other purpose than the service of the Word of God" (III.C.4.d).

2. *Personal Prerequisites for Catholic Exegetes*

Because sound interpretation requires a lived affinity with what is studied and the light of the Holy Spirit, full participation in the life and faith of the believing community (III.A.3.g), and personal prayer are necessary (Address 9).

This tenet of principle #17 compresses several lines of thought in the *IBC* and in the Catholic tradition of biblical interpretation. First, contemporary hermeneutics teaches the necessity of "belonging" (*Zugehörigkeit*, II.A.1.c), or a "lived affinity" (III.b), between interpreter and text if any text is really to be understood[5]. Second, because of its divine message of salvation through Jesus Christ, Catholics recognize the interpretation of the Bible as a "unique instance of general hermeneutics" and affirm that "particular presuppositions, such as the faith lived in ecclesial community and the light of the Spirit, control its interpretation" (II.A.2.f). Third, the *IBC* affirms that interpretation of the Bible should be characterized by the same dynamics that characterized its writing:

Faith traditions formed the living context for the literary activity of the authors of Sacred Scripture. Their insertion into this context also involved a sharing in both the liturgical and external life of the communities, in their intellectual world, in their culture and in the ups and downs of their shared history. In like manner, the interpretation of Sacred Scripture requires full participation on the part of exegetes in the life and faith of the believing community of their own time. (III.A.3.g)

Scripture's interpreters should be linked to Scripture by an affinity of faith and by participation in the life and worship of the believing community[6].

The affirmation that "the light of the Spirit" is one of the factors that controls Scripture's interpretation recalls *DV* 12, which states, "holy Scripture must be read and interpreted according to the same Spirit by whom it was written"[7]. Pope John Paul II, links the exegete's need for the Spirit's help to

---

[5] See principle #5, "The Contribution of Philosophical Hermeneutics". See also Vignolo, "Questioni di ermeneutica [*Commento*]", 277.

[6] See principle #6, "A Hermeneutic of Faith", especially p. 97ff. and p. 99ff.

[7] See de la Potterie, "Interpretation in the Spirit (*Dei Verbum* 12c)", especially 223-233, and "Reading Holy Scripture 'in the Spirit'".

personal prayer (Address 9).   According to the Pope, it is important that exegetes help the Christian people perceive the word of God in Scripture, and not only its human dimension.   To do so, they themselves must perceive it, and this is possible only if "intellectual work is sustained by a vigorous spiritual life":

> Indeed, to arrive at a completely valid interpretation of words inspired by the Holy Spirit, one must first be guided by the Holy Spirit and it is necessary to pray for that, to pray much, to ask in prayer for the interior light of the Spirit and docilely accept that light, to ask for the love that alone enables one to understand the language of God, who "is love" (1 Jn 4:8, 16). While engaged in the very work of interpretation, one must remain in the presence of God as much as possible. (Address 9)

3.   The Primary Task

So, granting the scholarly and ecclesial character of the task and the personal requirements of the individuals who fulfill it, what is the job description of the exegete?   The definition of the exegete's "primary task" which forms the next paragraph of this principle is taken verbatim from a section of the *IBC* that contrasts the exegetes' task with that of systematic theologians:

> *The primary task of the exegete is to determine as accurately as possible the meaning of biblical texts in their own proper context, that is, first of all, in their particular literary and historical context and then in the context of the wider canon of Scripture. (III.D.4.b)*

Note that the "proper context" of biblical texts is twofold, which leads to a two-step process of determining the meaning of texts.   First an exegete must determine the meaning of a text in its particular literary and historical setting. This is the literal sense, "that which has been expressed directly by the human authors.... [and which] is intended also by God, as principal author" (II.B.1.c).   Second, an exegete must determine the meaning of a text "in the context of the wider canon of Scripture", i.e., the canonical sense[8].   Both the particular literary-historical and the canonical contexts are the proper context

---

[8] Fitzmyer speaks of the *textual meaning* (the sense of the words and phrases), the *contextual meaning* (the sense in a given paragraph or episode), and the *relational meaning* (the sense in relation to the book or corpus as a whole): "This combination of the textual, contextual, and relational meaning of a passage leads to the discovery of its religious and theological meaning—to its meaning as the Word of God couched in ancient human language" ("Historical Criticism", 254).

of every biblical text, since "each individual book [of the Bible] only becomes biblical in the light of the canon as a whole" (I.C.1.f)[9].

The work of the exegete centers on the biblical text to explain its meaning, while the theologian considers a wider array of sources (the patristic writings, conciliar definitions, other magisterial documents, etc.) in the service of a more comprehensive presentation of Christian faith.

An exegete is responsible to expound "the theological meaning of texts when such a meaning is present", but in contrast to the role of dogmatic theologians the Biblical Commission emphasizes the exegete's "historical and descriptive" role (III.D.4.b). Catholic exegetes must "pay due account to the *historical character* of biblical revelation" in both senses of historical (III.C.1.a, emphasis original). Biblical revelation is historical both because it is historically-conditioned (expressed "in human words bearing the stamp of their time") and because it is "historical revelation", recounting the real intervention of God in time and space (III.C.1.a)[10]. The historical character of biblical revelation is the reason the historical-critical method is necessary, even though other methods also contribute to understanding the text.

4. The Hermeneutical Imperative

Equal to the stress on the historical dimension of the exegete's task is the insistence that "Catholic exegetes must never forget that what they are interpreting is the *Word of God*" (III.C.1.b, emphasis original). Scripture is more than a record of God's actions in the past. According to the Biblical Commission,

> The Church...does not regard the Bible simply as a collection of historical documents dealing with its own origins; it receives the Bible as Word of God, addressed both to itself and to the entire world at the present time. (IV.A.a)

The belief that God is still speaking through the Bible makes the hermeneutical task an essential part of Catholic exegesis. The distance between ancient text and contemporary reader must be overcome. The message of the text must be "detached, to some extent, from its historical conditioning in the past and...transplanted into the historical condition of the present. The exegete performs the groundwork for this operation which the systematic theologian continues..." (III.D.2.c). The Biblical Commission stresses this point in its "Principle Guidelines" for exegetes: "*[Catholic*

---

[9] See principle #8, "Interpretation in Light of the Biblical Tradition, the Unity of Scripture, and the Canon", especially p. 121ff.

[10] See principle #3, "Concerned with History".

exegetes] arrive at the true goal of their work only when they have explained the meaning of the biblical text as God's word for today" (III.C.1.b, emphasis added)[11]. Similarly, the *IBC*'s section on the usefulness of philosophical hermeneutics for exegesis speaks of the "absolute necessity" of incorporating literary and historical criticism in a "broader model of interpretation...in a way that permits a correct actualization of the scriptural message..." (II.A.2.a). The Commission does not explain exactly how this is to be done, only that exegetes must "take into consideration the various hermeneutical perspectives" needed to help people grasp its contemporary meaning (III.C.1.b)[12].

5. *Explanation of the Christological, Canonical And Ecclesial Content*

> *"Exegetes should also explain the christological, canonical and ecclesial content of biblical texts" (III.C.1.c).*

This paragraph of principle #17 is also a direct quotation from the *IBC*'s "Principle Guidelines" for exegetes[13]. It is followed by three or four brief paragraphs which repeat what was said at greater length in the *IBC* sections on "Interpretation in the Biblical Tradition" (III.A) and "Interpretation in the Tradition of the Church" (III.B)[14]. Essentially, the Biblical Commission is saying that the distinctive hermeneutic which has characterized Christian interpretation since the beginning should characterize Catholic exegesis.

Christ is at the center of Christian interpretation of the Old Testament. These books prepared the people of God for his coming and they "display

---

[11] One detects here the echo of a statement by Pope Paul VI: "Interpretation has not fulfilled its task until it has demonstrated how the meaning of Scripture may be referred to the present salvific moment, that is, until it has brought out the application to the present circumstances of the Church and the world. Without taking anything away from the value of philological, archeological and historical interpretation of the text—always necessary—we have to lay emphasis on the continuity between exegesis and preaching" (Paul VI, "Address", as quoted in Hahn, "Prima Scriptura", 94).

[12] See the more extensive discussion on the relation of exegesis to actualization in the next chapter, p. 298ff.

[13] This is a change in wording from the official English translation. The English translation speaks of christological, canonical and ecclesial "meanings". It seems to this writer that "the christological, canonical and ecclesial content" better captures the nuance of the French original ("*la portée christologique, canonique et ecclésiale*").

[14] Lambiasi also sees the *IBC*'s "Principal Guidelines" for exegetes as a recap of III.A-B ("Dimensioni caratteristiche [*Commento*]", 351). It may be useful to refer to the principles which relate to these sections: #9, "Interpretation of the OT in Light of the Paschal Mystery", #8, "Interpretation in Light of the Bible's Interpretation of Itself, the Unity of Scripture, and the Canon" (especially p. 121ff), and #10, "Interpretation in the Light of the Living Tradition of the Church".

their full meaning" in the mystery of Christ (III.C.1.d). There is a mutual illumination between the Old Testament and the New Testament, and the Old Testament has in no way lost its value. What is true of the books of the Old Testament holds for each book of the New Testament: "Although each book…was written with its own particular end in view and has its own specific meaning, it takes on a deeper meaning when it becomes part of the *canon* as a whole" (III.C.1.e, italics original). Catholic exegesis is responsible to explain this deeper christological and canonical meaning.

The "ecclesial significance" of the biblical texts is of a somewhat different order. This refers to a recognition of the relationship that exists between the Bible and the Church, an understanding of Scripture that distinguishes Catholic and Orthodox interpretation from *some* Protestant interpretation. It consists of a keen awareness that Scripture originated in the community life of the people of God and that it is intrinsically linked to a living Tradition which "preceded it… accompanies it and is nourished by it" (III.C.1.f). Furthermore, the Bible continues to be "the privileged means which God uses…to shape the building up and the growth of the Church as the People of God" (III.C.1.f). Vanhoye comments on this last dimension: "The Spirit makes us realize that this biblical text forms part of a continuing dialogue between Christ and His Church…. The text ceases to be an object, but becomes a living mediation that deepens and sheds light on our relationship with God"[15]. The ecclesial dimension of Scripture disposes Catholic exegesis to promote the unity of the Church in ecumenism and the fulfillment of the needs and longings of humanity in the Church's universal mission.

6. A Theological Discipline

Exegesis is a theological discipline, which exists in a relationship of dialogue with other branches of theology. (III.D.a)

Catholic exegesis, which begins with presuppositions based on Christian faith, is a theological discipline satisfying theology's classical definition, "*fides quaerens intellectum*"[16] (III.D.a).

The relation between exegesis and other theological disciplines is reciprocal[17]. On the one hand, Scripture provides the "privileged foundation"

---

[15] Vanhoye, "Catholicism and the Bible", 39.

[16] See the discussion of principle #6, "A Hermeneutic of Faith" (especially p. 97ff.).

[17] Lambiasi offers a brief history of the relation of exegesis to Catholic theology, which he divides into three stages. In the patristic era, there was no distinction between the disciplines; biblical commentaries were at the same time theological works on doctrine and morals. The medieval scholastic era separated Scripture from theology, which it began to treat

of theological studies (III.D.2.a); the *study* of Scripture, *Dei Verbum* affirms, is the "soul of theology" (§24). In other words, theology depends on biblical exegesis for its fundamental data[18]. This crucial theological role of exegesis makes it essential that Catholic exegetes, for their part, "pay particular attention to the religious content of the biblical writings" (III.D.2.a). On the other hand, exegesis receives its fundamental presuppositions from systematic theology, for example, its understanding of biblical inspiration, not to mention of God and of the person of Jesus Christ.

By distinguishing the divine message in Scripture from its historical conditioning, exegetes help systematic theologians avoid the extremes of fundamentalism, which confuses the human and divine elements, and dualism, which completely separates a doctrinal truth from its linguistic expression (III.D.2.b-c). Exegetes serve moral theologians by providing assessments of the great variety of instructions about proper conduct contained in Scripture and by responding to moralists' questions about what Scripture says about various ethical issues (III.D.3.a-c)[19]. Scripture, and, therefore, exegesis, serve theology by mounting challenges to theological systems, drawing attention to aspects of divine revelation and human experience which have been neglected (III.D.4.e). Exegesis, however, must

---

in systematic discussions of various topics, using Scriptural citations as evidence. The third stage was characterized by two opposite tendencies, the birth of criticism infected with a rationalist anti-dogmatic attitude and the manualist theology of the post-Tridentine period, which presented doctrines as theses to be defended by reference first to magisterial documents and secondarily to proof texts from Scripture and the Fathers. Finally, Pius XII's *Divino afflante Spiritu* (1943) began the Catholic appropriation of critical methods, and *Dei Verbum* (1965, especially §24) restored Scripture to its fundamental role in theology.

[18] "Basing his work on the major commentaries (Martini, Semmelroth, Stakemeier, Ratzinger), de la Potterie studies the three images used by the Second Vatican Council to define the relationship between Sacred Scripture and theological studies: foundation, life, and soul" (see Lambiasi, "Dimensioni caratteristiche [*Commento*]", 357-358, citing de la Potterie, "Il Concilio Vaticano II e la Bibbia", 26-31).

[19] Lambiasi offers useful commentary on the *IBC*'s treatment of Scripture and moral theology. He distinguishes Scripture's role in communicating the ultimate foundation of Christian behavior (the revelation of the paschal mystery and the triune God), the deep intentionality of Christian morality (faith working through love and hope), and the fundamental imperatives (the Ten Commandments and the law of love). He offers hermeneutical criteria for discerning the continuing relevance of biblical moral teaching that make it possible to avoid the opposite extremes of fundamentalism and liberalism: the fulfillment in Christ and surpassing of some Old Covenant legal requirements; the historical-conditioning of some instructions; the relation Scripture presents between particular ethical teaching and the center of revelation, the gospel; and the possibility of gaining light on new situations from Scripture on a transcendent rather than categorical level. See Lambiasi, "Dimensioni caratteristiche [*Commento*]", 359-361.

allow itself to be informed by theological research to pose perceptive
questions to Scripture and so discover its richness (III.D.4.f).

Discussion

7.   Elements of Exegetical Procedure

For the Biblical Commission "exegesis" means complete interpretation,
drawing out of a biblical text its meaning as the word of God for Christian
faith. This usage contrasts with the common practice of reserving "exegesis"
to refer to the historical or literary analysis of a text and using terms such as
theology, application, or homilizing to refer to the explanation of a text's
religious meaning. The convention is so well established that contemporary
authors add modifiers to the term "exegesis" or adopt other terms when they
wish to refer to an exegesis that encompasses the theological and
hermeneutical dimensions[20].   But in the document of the Biblical
Commission, interpretation of Scripture in this complete sense is simply
"exegesis". The *IBC* never uses the term "exegesis" to refer to the historical-
literary task and a different term to refer to the explanation of a text's
religious message. Perhaps this usage could be distinguished by referring to it
as "exegesis in the Church" or "Catholic exegesis".

The *IBC* identifies the constitutive elements of exegesis in the Church,
and says some things about how the elements are to be ordered. The elements
of an adequate exegesis of a biblical text, according to the *IBC*, can be
summarized as follows:

A. *Pre-understanding*: Catholic exegesis begins from a pre-understanding
of Christian faith as it deliberately takes its place in the living Tradition of
the Church (III.b).

B. *Determination of the meaning of the text in its particular literary and
historical context* (II.B.1.c, III.D.4.b): This is the element in interpretation

---

[20] Thus Gilbert uses the term "integral exegesis" to indicate exegesis that encompasses the
theological or "pneumatic" principles which *Dei Verbum* 12 views as essential (Gilbert,
"Exegesis, Integral").   Martin speaks of a "total reading" when interpretation goes beyond
"what the text *says*", to "what the text *is talking about*" (Martin, "Literary Theory, Philosophy
of History", 587).   Schneiders uses "integral process of interpretation" to include the
hermeneutical dimension, which seeks "understanding in the fullest sense of the word"
(*Revelatory Text*, 127).   She says, "Integral transformative interpretation is an interaction
between a self-aware reader open to the truth claims of the text and the text in its integrity, that
is, an interaction that adequately takes into account the complex nature and multiple
dimensions of the text and reader. Traditional historical critical exegesis, because it deals with
the text only as a historical document, is necessary but not sufficient for integral interpretation"
(3).

in which the historical-critical method and the synchronic literary approaches make their contribution.

C. *Determination of a text's meaning "in the context of the wider canon of Scripture"* (III.D.4.b).

D. *Explanation of a text's meaning for Christian faith*: This is the element that includes explaining "the theological meaning of texts" (III.D.4.b), "the christological, canonical and ecclesial meanings" (III.C.1.c), and "the meaning of the biblical text as God's word for today" (III.C.1.b).

It is important to note two activities which depend on exegesis, but which do *not* form part of it, namely, pastoral actualization of texts and an overall presentation of the Christian faith. The former is the work of preachers and catechists and the latter the work of theologians, who take into account "much other data which is not biblical—patristic writings, conciliar definitions, other documents of the magisterium, the liturgy"—as well as the situation of contemporary culture (III.D.4.c).

Several observations may be made about the "elements" of exegesis presented above. First, it should be clear that these four elements are not steps to be followed sequentially, since they are different in kind. The pre-understanding of Christian faith (A) functions as a presupposition of the entire process. The explanation of a text's meaning for Christian faith (D) functions as the goal, the result which Catholic exegesis seeks.

Second, there is some order that exists among the elements. It is appropriate to consider the meaning of a text first in its literary and historical context (B), and then in its canonical context (C). Also, *determining* the meaning of a text in both its respective contexts (B and C) necessarily precedes *explaining* it (D).

Third, although the explanation of the text's meaning for Christian faith (D) may occur as the final step in the exegesis of a text, it most naturally occurs as the meaning of a text in its immediate and canonical contexts (B and C) is explained.

Finally, it is worth observing that a considerable share of the exegesis taking place, whether in the classroom or in publications, leaves out one or more of the elements of exegesis which the *IBC* regards as essential. The element least often omitted is a determination of a text's meaning in its literary or historical context. Sometimes the pre-understanding of faith is excluded on principle. The determination of a text's meaning in its canonical context is often regarded as the peculiar interest of the canonical approach. And the explanation of a text's meaning for Christian faith is relegated to the domain of pastors or theologians.

It will not be possible for every exegetical work to give equal attention to the literary, historical and canonical contexts of texts. In order to allow greater depth in exploring one dimension or another, other aspects may need to be neglected, resulting inevitably in an incomplete treatment of a text. Nonetheless, it may be hoped that even when the exegetical task cannot be completed in all its dimensions that effort be made to shed light on "the meaning of the text as God's word, since only thus can exegetes "arrive at the true goal of their work" (III.C.1.b).

8. The Theological Character of Catholic Exegesis

The Biblical Commission's conception of the task of the exegete as a theological discipline may have struck a discordant note for some readers. The fact is, only a minority of Catholic exegetes approach their work in the theological manner outlined in the Biblical Commission's document. In practice, many Catholic exegetes of both Testaments confine their efforts to explaining texts in their historical and literary dimensions, without attempting to explain their theological significance, their meaning in the context of the canon, or the significance of biblical texts for the present[21]. Among Old Testament scholars, few attempt to explain the christological meaning of Old Testament texts in their exegesis, even when that is the primary interpretation the New Testament gives them. Although there are hopeful signs that exegesis is again beginning to attend to the theological dimension[22], one has only to examine most Catholic exegetical journals or recent commentaries by Catholic scholars to recognize the presence of the older tendency.

Many Catholic exegetes indeed view exegesis as an ecclesial service, but distinguish it sharply from theology. Some hold a view like that of J.-M. Sevrin, which sees exegesis as part of theology because its object is Sacred Scripture, but insist that exegesis must scrupulously abstain from faith considerations and analyze biblical texts exactly as it would any other human document[23]. Other exegetes who would not strictly separate faith from exegesis would still confine exegesis' role to "scientific" historical or literary description of a text's or work's meaning, leaving to theology assertions

---

[21] See the discussion of principle #18, "Actualization", for a consideration of the relation between exegesis and actualization, p. 298ff.

[22] For instance, the Sacra Pagina commentary series on the New Testament, edited by Daniel Harrington, takes a more vigorous interest in the theological meaning of texts.

[23] See Sevrin, "L' exégèse critique". See also the discussion of Sevrin's position and Vanhoye's critique under principle #6, "A Hermeneutic of Faith", p. 100ff. David S. Yeago points to the problems this approach has led to regarding the connection between the classical doctrines of the Church and the text of Scripture ("The New Testament and Nicene Dogma").

regarding its religious message or meaning in light of the canon. Some of these exegetes would view the theological character that the *IBC* ascribes to exegesis as belonging more properly to the discipline of biblical theology, with exegesis preserving a more strictly "scientific" or "critical" character[24].

In view of the non-theological approach to exegesis taken by many Catholic and non-Catholic biblical scholars, this would seem to have been a convenient solution. A non-theological exegesis could provide a scientific historico-literary common ground which exegetes of all persuasions could share, while biblical theology could assume responsibility for the theological part—to explain the canonical, christological, ecclesial and present-day significance of Scripture. Vanhoye, however, in response to a question along these lines from the author, makes clear that in the mind of the Commission, the theological dimension of exegesis is non-transferable:

> I do not recall a discussion a propos of biblical theology.... But the Biblical Commission would not agree to say "that the theological character the document ascribes to exegesis should instead define biblical theology". It says clearly that Christian exegesis of texts is a theological discipline, *fides quaerens intellectum*, and not simply a historical-philological discipline[25].

Why does the Biblical Commission take this position? Although the lack of consensus about the nature of biblical theology may have contributed something to rejecting this alternative[26], the Biblical Commission's insistence on the theological character of exegesis has a strong basis grounded in contemporary hermeneutics[27], precedent in the Christian tradition of interpretation (exegesis has always been a theological discipline), and the Church's compelling pastoral interests[28]. In addition, magisterial teaching

---

[24] E.g., Pesce, "Rinnovata difesa dell' esegesi storica": "In my opinion, exegesis is not a theological discipline and biblical theology is not a historical discipline" (35; cf. 41-42). From a somewhat different point of view, Vignolo finds the *IBC*'s description of exegesis to be still too positivist and its description of theology too speculative and systematic ("Questioni di ermeneutica [*Commento*]", 297-298). He also proposes a mediating role for biblical theology.

[25] Vanhoye, fax to author, 31 January 2000.

[26] See Beauchamp, "È possibile una teologia biblica?"; Franco, *La teologia biblica: Natura e prospettive*; Hasel, "Nature of Biblical Theology" and "Recent Models of Biblical Theology". More bibliography on this may be found in Vignolo, "Questioni di ermeneutica [*Commento*]", 297n.

[27] See the discussions of philosophical hermeneutics and a hermeneutic of faith in chapters 5 and 6.

[28] See the discussion of the pastoral purpose of exegesis on p. 151ff. The theological character of exegesis is what makes it deserving of the Church's support. Thus, the *IBC* exhorts bishops and religious superiors to provide people and resources for exegetical study, since "a lack in this area exposes the Church to serious harm, for pastors and the faithful then

regarding the task of the exegete of the last century consistently upholds a theological vision of the exegete's role. It is worth recalling briefly what recent popes and the Second Vatican Council have said about exegesis' theological dimension.

9. Church Teaching and the Theological Dimension of Exegesis

As was mentioned in the discussion of the literal sense (see page 179ff.), Pope Pius XII's 1943 encyclical *Divino afflante Spiritu*, which encouraged Catholic exegetes to make use of all the tools of scientific exegesis, also directed them not to neglect theological interpretation of Scripture:

> With special zeal should they apply themselves, not only to expounding exclusively those matters which belong to the historical, archaeological, philological and other auxiliary sciences—as, to Our regret, is done in certain commentaries—but, having duly referred to these, in so far as they may aid the exegesis, they should set forth in particular the theological doctrine in faith and morals of the individual books or texts so that their exposition may not only aid the professors of theology in their explanations and proofs of the dogmas of faith, but may also be of assistance to priests in their presentation of Christian doctrine to the people, and *in fine* may help all the faithful to lead a life that is holy and worthy of a Christian. (DAS 24, *EB* §551)

Pius XII goes on to say that the exegete should explain the spiritual sense as well as the literal sense, explaining the spiritual sense to be what God ordained in the Old Testament to prefigure the new dispensation of grace (DAS 26, *EB* §552). In seminary instruction "exegetical explanation should aim especially at the theological doctrine" (DAS 54, *EB* §567).

Dei Verbum refers to the work of exegetes primarily in three places, sections 12, 23 and 24. Both sections 23 and 24 occur in a chapter dedicated to "Sacred Scripture in the Life of the Church". Section 23 specifically urges that "exegetes... and *other* students of sacred theology, working diligently together and using appropriate means, should devote their energies...to an exploration and exposition of the divine writings [emphasis added]". The Second Vatican Council has a pastoral goal in view: this work should be done in such a way as to prepare "as many ministers of the divine word as possible...to provide the nourishment of the Scriptures for the People of God". Section 24 focuses on Scripture (along with Sacred Tradition) as the inspired word of God and as the foundation of theology and the nourishment of the ministry of the word. Exegesis is again referred to (though not

---

run the risk of being at the mercy of an exegetical scholarship which is alien to the Church and lacks relationship to the life of faith" (III.C.2.b).

exclusively) in the often quoted statement found in this section that "the *study* of the sacred page is, as it were, the soul of sacred theology [emphasis added]"[29].

The most significant description of the work of the exegete occurs in *Dei Verbum* 12, found in the chapter "The Divine Inspiration and the Interpretation of Sacred Scripture"[30]. Again, the goal of the exegesis's work is theological: "In order to see clearly what God wanted to communicate to us", the exegete (here called "the interpreter" [*interpres*]) must "investigate what meaning the sacred writer really intended and...God wanted to manifest by means of their words". The two paragraphs that follow depict two kinds of analysis which are essential to the exegete's task. The first is historical and literary. In order for the interpreter to understand the intention of the biblical authors, he or she must pay attention to the "literary forms" and the "customary and characteristic styles of perceiving, speaking and narrating which prevailed at the time of the sacred writer". The second kind of analysis necessary may be justly described as "theological":

> But since holy Scripture must be read and interpreted according to the same Spirit by whom it was written, *no less serious attention must be given* to the content and unity of the whole of Scripture, if the meaning of the sacred texts is to be correctly brought to light. The living tradition of the whole Church must be taken into account along with the analogy of faith. (*DV* 12, emphasis added)

The elements that distinguish this second part of the exegete's task include openness to the Holy Spirit, interpretation in light of the entire witness of Scripture, and consideration of Tradition and the "analogy of faith". There is no doubt that the Council intends this second "theological"or "pneumatic" procedure to characterize *exegesis*, since the document changes from speaking of "the interpreter" (*interpres*) used to this point in section 12, and in the sentence immediately following speaks explicitly of "exegetes": "It is the task of exegetes [L. *exegetarum*] to work according to these rules toward a

---

[29] The *IBC* interprets *DV* 24 in this way. After quoting these words, it comments, "the Council has also implicitly reminded Catholic exegetes that their research has an essential relationship to theology, their awareness of which must also be evident" (III.C.2.b). See also Vanhoye, "Esegesi biblica e teologia", 274-275.

[30] The ferment regarding the task of the exegete and methods in exegesis has led many authors to reexamine and comment on *DV* 12. Some of these include Barsotti, "Sacra Scriptura eodem Spiritu" and *La parola e lo spirito*; Bonora, "Vent'anni dopo la costituzione dogmatica *Dei Verbum*"; Curtin, "Historical Criticism and Theological Interpretation" (62-82); de la Potterie, "Interpretation in the Spirit (*Dei Verbum* 12c)" and "Il Concilio Vaticano II e la Bibbia"; Gilbert, "Cinquant' anni"; O'Collins, "'Dei Verbum' and Biblical Scholarship"; and Palma, "La Interpretación de la Escritura en el Espíritu".

better understanding and explanation of the meaning of sacred Scripture, so that through preparatory study the judgment of the Church may mature." This section highlights the role of exegesis in deepening the Church's understanding of Scripture and divine revelation.

Pope Paul VI addressed the Pontifical Biblical Commission in 1974 and identified the exegetical task as presenting the message of salvation:

> Your work is not limited...to explaining old texts, reporting facts in a critical way or going back to the early and original form of a text or sacred page. It is the prime duty of the exegete to present to the people of God the message of salvation, to set forth the meaning of the word of God in itself and in relation to men today...[31].

Pope John Paul II spoke in a similar vein when he addressed the Biblical Commission as it began its work on the *IBC* in 1989: "In the church all methods of exegesis must be, directly or indirectly, at the service of evangelization"[32].

So it is the Church which insists that exegesis maintain its theological character. Exegesis must conduct itself as a theological discipline for the simple reason that the Church founds her doctrine and nourishes the people of God on Scripture, and for this pastoral ministry she relies on the service of exegetes. Any exegesis which aims at less than this fails to fulfill its purpose.

---

[31] Paul VI, "Address to the Biblical Commission".
[32] John Paul II, "Address [1989]".

CHAPTER 18

Actualization

Principle #18

The Church receives the Bible as the word of God addressed both to itself and to the entire world at the present time (IV.a). Actualization is possible because of the richness of meaning contained in the biblical text, and it is necessary, because the Scripture was composed in response to circumstances of the past and in language suited to those circumstances. (IV.A.1.b-c)

Actualization presupposes a correct exegesis of a text, part of which is determining its literal sense (IV.A.2.e). The most reliable and fruitful method of actualizing Scripture is to interpret Scripture by Scripture. The actualization of a biblical text in Christian life proceeds in relation to the mystery of Christ and the Church. (IV.A.2.f)

Actualization involves three steps: 1. to hear the Word from within one's own concrete situation; 2. to identify the aspects of the present situation highlighted or put in question by the biblical text; 3. to draw from the fullness of meaning contained in the biblical text those elements capable of advancing the present situation in a way that is productive and consonant with the saving will of God in Christ[1]. (IV.A.2.g)

---

[1] The primary place the *IBC* treats actualization is in section IV.A, at the beginning of the chapter entitled, "Interpretation of the Bible in the Life of the Church", although the groundwork has been laid in the sections dealing with philosophical hermeneutics (II.A) and re-

Explanation

The section of the *IBC* on actualization is one of the most important and well-received sections of the document[2]. The term, "actualize", comes originally from the French, *actuel*, which means "present" or "contemporary". To actualize Scripture means to bring its meaning into the present. Consequently "actualize", as the *IBC* uses the term, has a different nuance than the word "actualize" usually bears in English usage[3]. It is the first time that this term has been employed in an official church document on Scripture.

Although the word "actualization" entered common currency recently (at least in English), the practice of actualization is very old and deeply rooted in the biblical tradition and in the tradition of the Church. The Biblical Commission explains,

> Already within the Bible itself…one can point to instances of actualization: very early texts have been re-read in the light of new circumstances and applied to the contemporary situation of the People of God. (IV.A.a)

In other words, what is elsewhere referred to in the document as re-readings, *relecture*—a constant feature of biblical interpretation—is nothing other than actualization[4]. Far from being a modern idea or even a misuse of an ancient text, actualization, seeking to understand Scripture's meaning for the present, has always characterized the reading and interpretation of believers. Besides its presence in the Bible itself, the Jewish tradition actualized Scripture in its Targums and Midrashim, while the Fathers of the Church had their own techniques for actualizing biblical texts (IV.A.2.b-c).

---

readings in the biblical and ecclesial tradition (III.A-B). Although this principle will cover most of the same material found in IV.A, it will be structured somewhat differently.

[2] Some of the articles which responded favorably to the *IBC*'s attention to actualization include Hebblethwaite, "The Bible in the Church"; Heidemanns, "Eine 'postkoloniale Kehrtwendung'?"; McNamara, "Inspiration and Interpretation of Scripture"; Murphy, "Reflections on 'Actualization'"; Senior, "Church and the Word"; and Williamson, "Actualization: A New Emphasis".

[3] In English "actualize" usually means to "realize", or, to "make real", as in, "their hopes for their son's future were actualized when he finally graduated from medical school". The matter is complicated by the fact that the French term *can* bear the primary meaning of the English term, and vice versa. In general, French usage emphasizes the aspect of time, while English usage emphasizes realization as contrasted with potentiality. When applied to Scripture, the possibility of misunderstanding is compounded by the fact that it is possible to speak of actualizing Scripture in both senses. For example, St. Paul actualized the story of the wilderness journey for the Corinthian community (1 Cor 10); St. Francis actualized the Sermon on the Mount in his life of poverty, humility and penitence. The former is what the Biblical Commission refers to by "actualization".

[4] See the substantial treatment of this theme in the *IBC*, "Re-readings (*relectures*)" (III.A.1).

Another way of saying it is that actualization is what the Church does with Scripture. Raymond Brown points out that the primary interest of the Church has always been not in what Scripture meant, but in what it means[5] (though, of course, what the text means in the present bears an important relation to what it meant originally). It is no accident that the explanation of "actualization" stands at the head of the *IBC*'s chapter on "Interpretation of the Bible in the Life of the Church": the use of the Scripture in liturgy, in *lectio divina*, and in the pastoral ministry—preaching, catechesis, and the biblical apostolate—all entail actualization, the discovery of the meaning of the ancient biblical text for the present.

One may understand the actualization of Scripture either in a broad sense, as the present meaning of biblical text (its religious meaning for Christian faith today), or more narrowly, as a particular application of a text to a contemporary question or circumstance. The *IBC* seems to use the term in both senses, leading to some confusion about what the document was asking of exegetes. Vanhoye clarified the matter by ascribing to preachers and catechists the task of applying the text to contemporary circumstances, and to exegetes, the task of explaining the text's religious meaning:

> The task of scientific exegesis itself is not to actualize the text, but to prepare for actualization. Actualization is a pastoral task. But scientific exegesis must keep in view the ultimate goal of actualization in order to be faithful to the orientation implicit in the written word of God.... If an exegete does his work well, he prepares the way for actualizing the text, because he brings to light the true meaning of the text, yielding a more profound and complete understanding of the word of God, communicated centuries ago, but always capable of inspiring and shaping the lives of men and women[6].

1. Possibility and Necessity

The Church receives the Bible as the word of God addressed both to itself and to the entire world at the present time (IV.a). Actualization is possible because of the richness of meaning contained in the biblical text, and it is necessary, because the Scripture was composed in response to circumstances of the past and in language suited to those circumstances. (IV.A.1.b-c)

---

[5] "The church is primarily concerned with what Scripture means to its people; it is not immediately concerned with what Scripture meant to those who wrote it or first heard it—the literal sense" (Brown and Schneiders, "Hermeneutics [*NJBC*]", 1163, §83).

[6] Vanhoye, "Catholicism and the Bible", 36-37. Vanhoye's clarification corrects a misunderstanding of this point by the author of this study in Williamson, "Actualization: A New Emphasis".

The foundation of the Church's past and present practice of actualization is theological, based on the conviction that Scripture does not merely record the history of God's dealing with his people. Christians believe both that what God has revealed in Scripture is perpetually meaningful and relevant and that God continues to speak to his people through Scripture. The Biblical Commission speaks of the "richness" of meaning in the biblical text, a term that Ricoeur has used to refer to the symbolic character of biblical language "which gives rise to thought ('donne à penser')", pointing to a transcendent reality and awakening human longings (II.A.1.d). Although the way that Scripture reveals its meaning for the present is unique on account of its divine inspiration, parallels exist in the way any great literary work can shed light on the circumstances of readers in a different era. Readers in a later age, such as the present one, bring new questions and concerns to the text. When they do so the Bible sheds light on contemporary issues—such as forms of ministry, the God's attitude toward the poor, or the situation of women—and on values of which the modern world is more conscious—such as human rights, protecting life, ecology or world peace (IV.A.2.h).

It is *necessary* to actualize Scripture because the word of God as we find it in the Bible stands at a certain distance from us in its language, its cultural context, and in the circumstances which it addresses. Because God has not given the historical conditioning of Scripture an absolute value (III.D.2.c), its message must be taken out of the historical conditioning of the past and applied to contemporary circumstances in a language suited to the present (IV.A.1.b-c)[7]. Translations of Scripture are instances of actualization, as are homilies which attempt to apply the text to particular contemporary circumstances.

Although the practice of re-reading the inspired text in the light of present circumstances is as old as Scripture itself, the concept of actualization has emerged only recently. Previous generations of Jews and Christians actualized Scripture reflexively without being conscious of the distance between the biblical text and their own time and cultural circumstances. But the historical consciousness of modern times and the historical critical study of the Bible brought into focus the distance of the biblical text from the present. This development provoked dissatisfaction among believers who were primarily interested in knowing the meaning of the text for Christian life, rather than what it meant at the moment of its composition.

---

[7] "This does not mean, however, that God has given the historical conditioning of the message a value which is absolute. It is open both to interpretation and to being brought up to date—which means being detached, to some extent, from its historical conditioning in the past and being transplanted into the historical conditioning of the present" (III.D.2.c).

Dissatisfaction with a purely historical approach stimulated the discovery of new methods and approaches and provoked hermeneutical reflection. The result has been a recognition that to understand the meaning of the Bible for the present requires a hermeneutical step which entails its own presuppositions and procedures, i.e., actualization.

2. Controls

Obviously actualization poses the risk of arbitary interpretation. This is not a risk of little consequence, since the authority of Scripture for Christians is so extraordinary. The *IBC* addresses this authority and this danger in paragraph IV.A.1.f: "The text of the Bible has authority over the Christian Church at all times...". This applies even to the Magisterium, which the Commission recalls "is not above the Word of God, but serves it, teaching only what has been handed on..." (IV.A.1.f, quoting *Dei Verbum* 10). Therefore, actualization must not mean "manipulation of the biblical text", or "projecting novel opinions or ideologies upon the biblical writings, but of sincerely seeking to discover what the text has to say at the present time" (IV.A.2.f). The *IBC* warns against "tendentious interpretations" which use biblical texts to justify predetermined positions, rather than approaching Scripture in genuine docility, and it cites the example of the sects and of Jehovah's Witnesses in particular (IV.A.3.b).

There need to be controls if Scripture's message is truly to be understood, rather than individuals reading into Scripture meanings that are quite extraneous to it[8]. The Biblical Commission points to three such controls: a) correct exegesis, b) interpretation of Scripture by Scripture, and c) actualization's intrinsic link to the mystery of Christ and the Church.

a) Correct Exegesis

Actualization presupposes a correct exegesis of a text, part of which is the determining of its literal sense. (IV.A.2.e)

This tenet of principle #18 is again a direct quotation from the *IBC*. Exegesis, the explanation of a text's meaning must precede the application of a text to any particular situation or question. This stands to reason and indicates the importance of the exegete's work for the life of the Church. Exegesis begins with determining the literal sense of a text, "that which has

---

[8] This study restructures into two sections entitled "Controls" and "Procedures" the material on actualization that the *IBC* presents somewhat awkwardly under the headings "Methods" and "Limits". The hope is that this presentation expresses the intent of the document more clearly.

been expressed directly by the inspired authors" (II.B.1.c). Discovering the meaning of the word of God for the present begins with understanding what God inspired the human writer to say. This is accomplished by analyzing the text in its literary and historical context. Nevertheless, the Biblical Commission describes determining the literal sense as only "part" of the task of exegesis. As we saw in principle #17 on the task of the exegete, exegesis also considers the meaning of the text in the light of the canon and gives consideration to christological and other theological meanings which may be present.

But the Biblical Commission follows their statement about the priority of a correct exegesis with an important addition:

> Persons engaged in the work of actualization who do not themselves have training in exegetical procedures should have recourse to good introductions to Scripture; this will ensure that their interpretation proceeds in the right direction. (IV.A.2.e)

The addition is important for two reasons. First, it make plain that many people beside exegetes have responsibility to actualize Scripture. In fact this point echoes the Biblical Commission's first sentence of the chapter on "Interpretation in the Life of the Church": "Exegetes may have a distinctive role in the interpretation of the Bible but they do not exercise a monopoly" (IV.a). Every pastoral worker, and indeed, every Christian in his or her personal reading of Scripture is called upon to discover Scripture's meaning for the present. The second reason this is important is that even for non-professionals, correct exegesis is important. Pastors and lay people are not dispensed from serious study and reflection about what the text actually means. The good news is that "by recourse to good introductions to Scripture", Christians who are not exegetes can ensure that their actualization "proceeds in the right direction" (IV.A.2.e).

b) Interpreting Scripture by Scripture

The most reliable and fruitful method of actualizing Scripture is to interpret Scripture by Scripture. (IV.A.2.f)

The second "control" on actualization offered by the Biblical Commission is the use of Scripture to interpret Scripture. This reflects an ancient principle of both the rabbis and the Fathers of the Church. Augustine says that obscure passages are to be explained by those which are more clear. Aquinas says that what is genuinely contained in the spiritual senses of Scripture is elsewhere directly stated as the literal sense. The Reformers, Luther and Calvin, emphasized this method as a means of coming to grips with the message of Scripture[9]. Consulting other Scriptural texts helps to balance interpretations, since different parts of Scripture balance one another. This step tends toward a canonical interpretation of Scripture. According to the *IBC*, contemporary readers stand on the firmest ground when their actualizations follow re-readings found in Scripture (IV.A.2.e). Thus, when Christians compare the manna of Exodus 16 to the gift of the eucharist (John 6), they stand in continuity with a line of actualization found in the Bible itself.

c)   Relation to the Mystery of Christ and the Church

> *Actualization of biblical text in Christian life occurs "in relation to the mystery of Christ and the Church". (IV.A.2.f)*

The third means of controlling actualization which the Biblical Commission recommends is the relation of all actualization of Scripture to Christ and the Church[10]. This is a less obvious kind of control, but is perhaps the most important. At the simplest level, this means actualizing Old Testament texts in light of the fullness of revelation in Jesus Christ. The example the Commission gives is the inappropriateness of relying exclusively on Old Testament models from Exodus or 1-2 Maccabees for Christians struggling for liberation. Through the fullness of revelation in Jesus, the Bible witnesses to a liberation that goes beyond political liberation, and Christian actualization must not stop short of this fullness.

Actualization "in relation to the mystery of Christ and the Church" also means interpreting and applying the Bible for today in "explicit continuity with the communities which gave rise to Scripture and which preserved and handed it on" (IV.A.1.e), i.e., in harmony with tradition[11]. Maintaining a strong link between contemporary application and the tradition of interpretation both protects actualization from erroneous interpretations, and also "ensures the transmission of the original dynamism", i.e., it helps Christians today to proceed in harmony with the Spirit's activity in previous generations (IV.A.1.e). Actualizing Scripture "in explicit continuity with the communities which gave rise to Scripture" and "within the stream of the

---

[9] Murphy, however, overstates the matter when he says, "This statement is surprising since it seems to adopt quite clearly the Reformation principle of *Scriptura sua interpres*: Scripture is its own interpreter" ("Reflections on 'Actualization'", 80).

[10] The Biblical Commission only applies this criterion to the matters treated in the first paragraph of this section. In an effort to present more systematically the "controls" on actualization found in the *IBC*, this author take "the relation to the mystery of Christ and the Church" as a wider criterion.

[11] See chapter 10, "Interpretation in Light of the Living Tradition of the Church".

living Tradition" also entails responsiveness to "the guidance of the Church's Magisterium" so that "false paths [may] be avoided" (IV.A.3.e).

Actualization "in relation to the mystery of Christ" also requires that biblical interpretation be fully in harmony with the content of the gospel expressed in Scripture (IV.A.2.f)[12]. It is on this basis that the Biblical Commission explicitly rules out actualization "grounded in *theoretical principles* which are at variance with the fundamental orientations of the Biblical text" such as rationalism or atheistic materialism (IV.A.3.c, emphasis original). The Commission similarly rejects every attempt at actualization "contrary to *evangelical justice and charity*" such as "the use of the Bible to justify racial segregation, anti-Semitism or sexism whether on the part of men or of women" (IV.A.3.d, emphasis original).

Finally, although the Biblical Commission does not mention it explicitly in this section, actualization in relation to the mystery of Christ means interpreting and applying Scripture under the guidance of the Holy Spirit. Actualization is not merely an intellectual procedure of finding analogies between a biblical text and present circumstances. It is a matter of discerning what the Lord himself wishes to say in the present through a text written long ago. Fruitful actualization requires spiritual discernment, the ability to recognize the voice of the Spirit in reading the sacred text. In this light, reception by a community of Christians alive in the Holy Spirit would suggest a particular actualization of Scripture is authentic.

3. Procedure

The Biblical Commission chose not to be too specific regarding procedures for actualization—the possibilities are too abundant and diverse to prescribe any particular approach[13]. Instead they point out various characteristics of sound actualization, most of which were treated in the preceding section on "Controls". They also allude to the diverse ways that actualization has been carried out in the past by Jewish interpreters in the Targums and Midrashim and by the Church Fathers, all employing interpretive procedures suited to their times. Contemporary actualization

---

[12] The *IBC* does not explicitly discuss the role of the "analogy of faith" which *DV* 12 presents as one of the principal "rules" of interpretation. Nevertheless, one may find the idea implicit in this broader formulation of actualization "in relation to the mystery of Christ and of the Church".

[13] In recent years a number of exegetes have offered suggestions on how to actualize Scripture. See, for example, Betori, *Come leggere un testo biblico*; Burkhard, "The Use of Scripture in Theology and Preaching"; Dreyfus, "L'actualisation à l'intérieur de la Bible"; Manns, "Lire les Écritures en Église"; Morfino, *Leggere la Bibbia con la vita*; Rasco, "La 'Parola vivente' (Eb 4,12)"; Seibold, "Palabra de Dios y Pueblo de Dios".

should bear in mind "both changes in ways of thinking and the progress made in interpretive method" (IV.A.2.d). In other words, actualization today will have a different character, suited to the mentality of modern people[14].

Nevertheless, contemporary hermeneutics helps to recognize the underlying dynamic of applying Scripture in any age. The following paragraph from principle #18 (which quotes the *IBC* directly) indicates the fundamental procedure of actualization:

> *Actualization involves three steps: 1. to hear the Word from within one's own concrete situation; 2. to identify the aspects of the present situation highlighted or put in question by the biblical text; 3. to draw from the fullness of meaning contained in the biblical text those elements capable of advancing the present situation in a way that is productive and consonant with the saving will of God in Christ. (IV.A.2.g)*

4. Illustration of Actualization

In the fall of 1998 this writer had the opportunity to teach principles of Catholic biblical interpretation to 50 students from various disciplines at the University of Vilnius under the auspices of the Center for Religious Studies. When it came time to illustrate the principle of actualization, the author applied the biblical account of Israel's experience in the wilderness after liberation from Egypt to the religious and social situation in post-Soviet Lithuania. (For actualizating the wilderness experience there is plenty of scriptural warrant—both the re-readings found in Deut 6 and St. Paul's comparison of the wilderness journey to the life of the Christian community in 1 Cor 10:1-22.) After God's wonderful and surprising deliverance of Israel from slavery in Egypt, Israel needed to learn God's ways and undergo transformation (Ex 19:6, Lev 20:26) to be fit for life in the promised land. So God led them to an encounter with himself at Sinai, gave them the law, and

---

[14] Fitzmyer interprets the *IBC* section entitled "Methods" as enumerating "four ways...in which actualization...can be carried out": the use of Jewish exegetical techniques, patristic typology and allegory, interpretation of Scripture by Scripture, and philosophical hermeneutics (*The Biblical Commission's Document*, 173-175). However, it seems unlikely that the Commission wished to present rabbinic or patristic models as available methods. Rather than an enumeration of the "various methods" referred to in the topic sentence, it seems more coherent to divide the section in three parts: 1) an illustration of the variety of possible methods by reference to rabbinic and patristic precedents; 2) advice about actualization (pay attention to the contemporary ways of thinking and methods, begin with the literal sense, seek correlation in Scripture); 3) an analytic view of what actualization entails, drawn from philosophical hermeneutics. For yet another reading of the structure of the "Methods" section, see Làconi, "Nella vita della chiesa [*Commento*]", 365-366, who, as this study does, views the references to Jewish and patristic methods at the beginning of the section to be illustrative precedents.

tested and purified them in the wilderness (Deut 8:2,16). Similarly, Lithuanians experienced a remarkable deliverance from Soviet occupation. Since that time many had come to a personal experience of God and a renewal in the life of their Church, imperfect and incomplete as it might be. Yet just as in Israel's case, the end of political oppression for Lithuania did not immediately lead to ease and prosperity for the Church or nation. Instead, tremendous social, economic, political and spiritual challenges remain. These include both vestiges of the past (the carryover of negative features of Soviet culture) and new temptations to idolatry (in the form of Western consumerism). Like Israel of old, Lithuania faces the temptation to return to the security of its past servitude (Ex 16:3). The Lord is inviting Lithuanians, as he once invited Israel in the wilderness, to trust and obey him with undivided hearts as he trains them as a father disciplines his son (Deut 8:5). If they are faithful to the Lord in the face of these trials and temptations, God will prosper them, their Church and their nation.

Discussion

5. Actualization and Exegesis

Although the Biblical Commission affirms that actualization must begin from a valid exegesis of the text, important questions remain about the relation of actualization to exegesis. Is there an intrinsic relation between exegesis and actualization, or are they two separate operations? Should all exegesis issue in actualization? What does the *IBC* mean when it says, "[Exegetes] arrive at the true goal of their work only when they have explained the meaning of the biblical text as God's word for today" (III.C.1.b)?

Ugo Vanni takes up some of these questions in "Exegesis and Actualization in the Light of *Dei Verbum*"[15], published in a volume devoted to assessing the significance of the Second Vatican Council twenty-five years later[16]. This book appeared in Italian in 1987, in time to be read by Commission members and to influence their work. Vanni's chapter offers suggestive insights on the relation of exegesis to actualization that go beyond, but are compatible with, what the *IBC* states.

---

[15] Vanni, "Exegesis and Actualization". Vanni also evaluates the relative merits of the historical-critical method and structuralist exegesis in relation to what *Dei Verbum* says about exegesis and actualization. However, this study will confine the account of Vanni's article to its most essential elements.

[16] Latourelle, *Vatican II, Assessment and Perspectives*.

Vanni defines actualization as "all those ways in which the written word of God is made meaningful and effective in the present, with particular reference to the liturgical experience" (344-5). He notes that *Dei Verbum* marked a significant turning of the Church toward actualization, indicated by many efforts to appropriate the meaning of the biblical word for the present. However, he notes among those interested in actualization at the time of his writing a surprising lack of reference to exegesis or to the relation between the two proposed by *Dei Verbum*. On the contrary, since the Council, some authors, such as F. Refoulé and F. Dreyfus, had written about a "chasm" and an "abyss" which they perceived existing between actualization and scientific exegesis[17]. Vanni examines *Dei Verbum* in search of insights there that may illumine the problem.

Vanni begins by analyzing the description of the task of the exegete found in *Dei Verbum* 12. He finds two dimensions of exegesis expounded there, the "historical-literary" dimension, and what he calls the "pneumatic" dimension[18]. The former consists of attention to the literary forms and contemporary styles of communicating by which the biblical authors expressed their meaning. The latter consists of an attention to the Holy Spirit who inspired the biblical authors, through reflecting on the text in light of the content of Scripture as a whole, the living Tradition, and the analogy of faith. Both "historical-literary" and "pneumatic" dimensions are strictly necessary: "If either of these elements were ignored, we would have a reductive exegesis, which would lose its wholeness and specificity, and would therefore be inadequate and hence unscientific"[19].

Although actualization is not explicitly referred to in *Dei Verbum* 12, according to Vanni, it is the primary theme of chapter VI, entitled "Sacred Scripture in the Life of the Church". The chapter begins by affirming that the Church draws its life equally from the Eucharist and the word of God, the liturgy being the privileged place for this life-giving encounter. In the preceding chapters of *Dei Verbum* Scripture is described as a communication from God to the human race, but the verbs are almost always in the past tense. This communication is understood historically, as what God has revealed in the past. But chapter VI speaks of the continuing communication between God and human beings, and here the document uses present tense verbs:

---

[17] See Refoulé, "L'exégèse en question"; Dreyfus, "Exégèse en Sorbonne" or an Italian translation in Refoulé and Dreyfus, *Quale esegesi oggi?*

[18] See also the discussion of *Dei Verbum* in the section on the task of the exegete, p. 286ff.

[19] Vanni, "Exegesis and Actualization", 349.

> Inspired by God and committed once and for all to writing, [the Scriptures]
> *impart* the word of God Himself without change, and *make* the voice of the
> Holy Spirit resound in the words of the prophets and apostles.... For in the
> sacred books, the Father who is in heaven *meets* his children with great love
> and *speaks* with them.... (*DV* 21, emphasis added)

So even though the term "actualization" is not used, the concept is very much
present. When *Dei Verbum* discusses the transition from writings of the past
to the present it speaks of the work of exegetes and "ministers of the divine
word":

> Catholic exegetes then and other students of sacred theology, working
> diligently together and using appropriate means, should devote their
> energies...to an exploration and exposition of the divine writings. This
> should be done *in such a way* that as many ministers of the divine word as
> possible will be able effectively to provide the nourishment of the
> Scriptures for the People of God, thereby enlightening minds, strengthening
> their wills, and setting men's hearts on fire with the love of God. (*DV* 23,
> emphasis added)

Commenting on this text, Vanni explains that the roles of exegetes and
ministers of the word are distinguished, from one another, but serve the
common purpose of providing "nourishment...for the People of God":

> Exegesis must retain its own character and perform its task with the tools
> proper to it (*aptis subsidiis...investigent*). However, both the research and
> the explanation (*ita investigent et proponant*) entailed in the task of exegesis
> must be carried out in such a way as to enable (*ut possint*) the immediate
> servants to carry out their task in an adequate manner. Any exegesis that
> did not have such an application in view would not be accepted as such by
> the Constitution[20].

Actualization depends on exegesis, and exegesis is oriented to actualization.
Subsequent paragraphs of *Dei Verbum* emphasize the necessity that Scripture
study animate all theology and pastoral work. Theology must be rooted in
"the study of the sacred page" (§ 24) and priests, deacons and catechists (all
who are ministers of the word) must "hold fast to Scripture through diligent
sacred reading and careful study" (§ 25).

Vanni draws several conclusions about the "indissoluble" relationship
between exegesis and actualization[21]. Exegesis and actualization must retain

---

[20] Vanni, "Exegesis and Actualization", 351.

[21] Vanni, "Exegesis and Actualization", 352. Vanni's *L'Apocalisse: ermeneutica, esegesi,
teologia*, published the same year as his essay about exegesis and actualization, illustrates
Vanni's approach to interpretation. The first part of the work is devoted to method and
includes the following explanation of the respective roles of exegesis and actualization:

their distinctive characteristics. Exegesis must maintain both its historical-literary dimension and its pneumatic dimension. Without the former it would lose its objectivity, and without the latter it would lose its capacity for actualization. Actualization, even though it needs exegesis, has its own inner dynamism in the life of the Christian people: "There is a life that is lived, guided, and organized by the Spirit, and that absorbs into itself the content proposed by exegesis"[22]. If the life of the individual Christian or Christian community is chronically weak and debilitated, not even the best exegesis can be actualized and assimilated. The element that *unites* exegesis and actualization in the Christian community is the life of the Holy Spirit which inspires them both. The continuity between exegesis and actualization means that actualization does not call for some filtered type of content—it takes the real results of exegesis, the understanding of what Scripture really says, and makes that the basis of life. Finally, there is a reciprocal movement by which actualization may shed light on exegesis itself. The dynamic is already present in the pneumatic dimension of exegesis which receives light from the living Tradition and the analogy of faith.

Vanni concludes by commenting on the current state of exegesis and by making an intriguing suggestion. He notes a tendency toward actualization which is superficial and not linked to study and exegesis: "People want to listen to the word directly and hear its immediate sound, without what they see as the screen constituted by exegesis.... [But] an impoverished reading of the Bible inevitably leads to a partial actualization". Vanni also notes the partiality and inadequacy of some scientific exegesis which fails to make itself complete through the "pneumatic dimension". Vanni's intriguing suggestion is that just as exegesis provides a verification for any actualization of Scripture, so also might actualization provide a means of verifying authentic exegesis:

> If a given exegetical proposition were seen to be completely irrelevant for the life of the Church, because of its heterogeneity or its lack of openness to actualization, it would therefore be suspected of being inadequate or partial. And if a formulation of exegetical content were seen to be capable of setting authentic actualization in motion, this would constitute positive confirmation, and be a certain proof of its scientific correctness.

"Exegesis, that is, the exposition of a biblical text, is an exposition carried out for the sake of life. At this point hermeneutics enters in, which makes possible the passage from the abstract level of a message, of a content, to the level of a living assimilation. That which the text says it says, concretely to life. When one reaches life, one has carried out the *hermeneutical actualization* of a text" (p. 19).

[22] Vanni, "Exegesis and Actualization", 353.

In summary, those whose primary responsibility is actualization must seek out sound exegesis to provide the basis of their actualization. Correspondingly, those whose primary responsibility is exegesis must not forget the goal of their work and the measure of their success, namely to serve those who make the word of God meaningful and effective in the present[23].

---

[23] Recently more exegetes are seeking to actualize texts. Some examples include Buzzetti, "L'attualizzazione di una parabola"; Cuvillier, "Evangile et traditions chez Paul"; Dillmann, "Die Bedeutung der semantischen Analyse"; Fleckenstein, *Ordnet euch einander unter in der Furcht Christi*; Gourgues, "Le père prodigue (*Lc 15*,11-32)", *Jean, de l'exégèse à la prédication, vols. 1 and 2*, and *Luc, de l'exégèse à la prédication*; Gradara, *Luca: il Vangelo degli ultimi*; and Landier, Pécriaux and Pizivin, *Voici l'homme*.

CHAPTER 19

Inculturation

Principle #19

The foundation of inculturation is the Christian conviction that the word of God transcends the cultures in which it has found expression. The word of God can and must be communicated in such a way as to reach all human beings in their own cultural contexts. (IV.B.b)

The first stage of inculturation consists in translating Scripture into another language (IV.B.c). Then comes interpretation, which sets the biblical message in more explicit relationship with the ways of feeling, thinking, living and self-expression proper to the local culture. Finally, one passes to other stages of inculturation, leading to the formation of a local Christian culture, encompassing all aspects of life. (IV.B.e)

The relation between the word of God and the human cultures it encounters is one of mutual enrichment. The treasures contained in diverse cultures allow the Word of God to produce new fruits, while the light of the word of God allows helpful and harmful elements in cultures to be discerned[1]. (IV.B.f)

---

[1] All the elements of this principle of interpretation may be found in section IV.B, "Inculturation".

Explanation

Just as actualization makes Scripture fruitful for people living in various periods in time, so inculturation makes Scripture fruitful for the peoples living in different places. The concept of "inculturation" as it is used in the *IBC* includes the interpretation of Scripture, but goes beyond it in two respects. First, inculturation is concerned not only with Scripture but with the Christian message itself in its entirety. This is why the Biblical Commission uses the term "the Word of God" in its discussion of inculturation rather than "Scripture" or "biblical texts" as it usually does in the rest of the document. Second, inculturation refers not only to an *interpretation* of the Christian message in a particular cultural setting, it refers to the successful *embodiment* of that message in the life of a people. Nevertheless, inculturation belongs in a discussion of interpretation of the Bible in the Church since the interpretation of Scripture plays a central role in inculturation.

1. Foundation

> *The foundation of inculturation is the Christian conviction that the word of God transcends the cultures in which it has found expression. The word of God can and must be communicated in such a way as to reach all human beings in their own cultural contexts. (IV.B.b)*

Just as actualization is founded on the Christian conviction that through the Bible God addresses human beings at all times, so inculturation is grounded on the conviction that the revelation contained in Scripture transcends particular cultures. This is a biblical perspective beginning in Genesis, which shows God as the creator of the entire human race, giving human beings dominion over all the earth (1:27-28) and promising that all the nations of the world will be blessed through Abraham and his offspring (12:3; 18:18). The New Testament confirms the universal orientation of the Bible in its insistence that the gospel be preached to all nations (Mt 28:18-20; Rom 4:16-17; Eph 3:6).

Inculturation had already begun in Judaism with the translation of the Hebrew Scriptures into Greek and Aramaic. Jewish scholars such as Philo took the process still further, interpreting Israel's Scriptures in ways accessible to Platonic and Stoic philosophy. The New Testament, written in Greek rather than in Aramaic, is "characterized in its entirety by a dynamic of inculturation...in its transposition of the Palestinian message of Jesus into Judeo-Hellenistic culture" (IV.B.d)[2].

---

[2] The inculturation present in the NT itself has drawn the attention of many scholars in recent years. See, for instance, Bossuyt and Radermakers, "Rencontre de l'incroyant et

Other developments in the early Church laid the basis for inculturation. The outpouring of the Spirit at Pentecost and the "devout Jews from every nation under heaven" who heard the apostles speaking "in [their] own languages" symbolized the direction of the future (Acts 2:5,11). The decision early on to not require Gentile Christians to keep the entire Mosaic law marked a decisive step in this direction, reducing the Mosaic regulation to the legal code of a particular people (III.A.2.e). The entire mission to the Gentiles depicted in the Acts of the Apostles, the commission to be Jesus' witnesses "in Jerusalem... and to the ends of the earth" (1:8) the re-formulation of the gospel in terms accessible to the pagan world (14:8-18; 17:16-33), and the gospel's itinerary from Jerusalem to Rome (1-28), implied inculturation. The gospel was not to be limited to a particular place or to a particular ethnic group. Rather the word of God must be announced to all nations in terms adapted to their understanding, without compromising its essential content.

2. Stages

> The first stage of inculturation consists in translating Scripture into another language (IV.B.c). Then comes interpretation, which sets the biblical message in more explicit relationship with the ways of feeling, thinking, living and self-expression proper to the local culture. Finally, one passes to other stages of inculturation, leading to the formation of a local Christian culture, encompassing all aspects of life. (IV.B.e)

A successful inculturation of Scripture and its message begins with translation. Translation means more than simply substituting words in one language for words in another. The ways in which the Bible's meaning is expressed may need to be changed in order for the message to be intelligible in a different cultural setting[3]: "concepts are not identical and symbols have a different meaning, for they come up against other traditions of thought and ways of life" (IV.B.c). L. Luzbetak illustrates this in *The Church and Cultures*:

> The beautiful expression 'Lamb of God' in reference to Christ leaves the Melanesian cold and unmoved, for sheep are not sacrificial animals in the

---

inculturation"; Cova, "La parola alle genti"; Czajkowski, "Die Inkulturation des Evangeliums"; Manicardi, "Bibbia e inculturazione"; Pastore, *La inculturación del evangelio*; and Söding, "Eucharistie und Mysterien".

[3] For recent discussions dealing with cultural issues in translation, see Combrink, "Receiving Matthew in Africa"; Dhavamony, "The Lord's Prayer in Sanskrit"; Gispert-Sauch, "St. John's Nectar in Indian Flavour"; and Ponchaud, "L'Évangile en khmer".

native life-way; in fact, the ancestors would be terribly disappointed if such an inferior animal were offered to them[4].

Inculturation is a topic particularly relevant to Christian missions[5], but its three essential stages can be illustrated from the history of Christianity's development from a Palestinian Jewish sect to the dominant religion of the late Roman Empire[6]. The inculturation of the gospel in the Roman Empire began with its translation from the Aramaic language of Palestine into the koine Greek of New Testament, the *lingua franca* of the day. The second stage of inculturation, the interpretation of the Christian message in relation to the thought forms of the surrounding culture, took place over several centuries, beginning with the interpretation of the gospel for Gentiles by Paul, a diaspora Jew and Roman citizen familiar with both Jewish tradition and Hellenistic culture. It continued in the Apologists such as Justin Martyr, who held that "everything good in paganism belonged equally to Christians, because all truth accords with the Word in some way.... In Christ Christians possess the truth of all philosophy in an eminent form, for philosophy is never anything other than sharing in the Logos"[7]. Clement of Alexandria, Origen and many of the Fathers continued the process of interpreting Christianity and Scripture so as to make it intelligible to the Greco-Roman culture of their day, while great Councils gave expression to the New Testament testimony about Jesus' human and divine natures in terms derived from Greek philosophy. Gradually, and especially after the conversion of Constantine, the Christian message produced a Christian culture extending to all aspects of life—forms of prayer, work, social life, customs, legislation, art, philosophical and theological reflection (IV.B.e). In doing so it incorporated elements of Greco-Roman culture—for example, Stoic concepts of virtue and vice, iconic art forms, and philosophical terminology—which it enriched with new meaning.

Four observations about the process of inculturation may be noted. First, it is not an extrinsic imposition of Christian standards on an alien culture. Transformation of culture works from the inside out, beginning with the translation, interpretation and appropriation of Scripture and its essential message. The goal is an inner transformation of culture rather than merely

---

[4] Luzbetak, *The Church and Cultures*, 246.

[5] This may be deduced in that the *IBC*'s only three references to Vatican II's *Ad Gentes* appear in the discussion of inculturation.

[6] This classical instance of inculturation has drawn the attention of numerous authors. See, for instance, Kretschmar, "Early Church and Hellenistic Culture"; Neuner, "Die Hellenisierung des Christentums als Modell"; and Prinzivalli, "Incontro e scontro fra 'classico' e 'cristiano'".

[7] Pelland, "Apologists", 42.

external conformity. Second, while it begins with missionaries who do their best to understand the culture they are evangelizing, inculturation achieves its goal only when people of the cultural group themselves succeed in expressing Scripture's message in terms of their culture. The Biblical Commission comments,

> Missionaries, in fact, cannot help [but] bring the Word of God in the form in which it has been inculturated in their own country of origin. New local churches have to make every effort to convert this foreign form of biblical inculturation into another form more closely corresponding to the culture of their own land. (IV.B.g)

Third, the outcome of successful inculturation of the Christian message is a culture of a distinct and recognizable character which the Biblical Commission refers to as "local Christian culture" (IV.B.e). The presence of the modifier "local" recognizes the reality of different Christian cultures in different places. Finally, inculturation of the Bible is relevant not only to missionary situations but everywhere the Church already exists, since cultures continue to evolve. The immense challenge for the Church today is to inculturate the message of Scripture in modern (and post-modern) technological, secular and religiously-diverse cultures[8].

3. Mutual Enrichment and Discernment

> *The relation between the word of God and the human cultures it encounters is one of mutual enrichment. The treasures contained in diverse cultures allow the Word of God to produce new fruits, while the light of the word of God allows helpful and harmful elements in cultures to be discerned* [9]. *(IV.B.f)*

The *IBC* employs the biblical metaphor of a seed to describe the dynamic activity of the word of God in human cultures:

> The Word of God is, in effect, a seed, which extracts from the earth in which it is planted the elements which are useful for its growth and

---

[8] Examples of inculturation efforts in particular cultures include Combrink, "Reception of Matthew in Africa"; Ezeogu, "Bible and Culture in African Christianity"; Hilary, *Acts 15: An Inspiration for the Igbo Church Today*; Osei-Bonsu, "Biblically/theologically-based Inculturation". Reflections on method in inculturation include Cothenet, "Discernement prophétique"; Theobald, "Paulus und das Problem der Inkulturation"; Tiessen, "Hermeneutic for Discerning Universal Moral Absolutes"; Trimaille, "Exégèse et inculturation"; Ukpong, "Rereading the Bible with African Eyes" and "Parable of the Shrewd Manager (Luke 16:1-13): Essay in Inculturation". Attempts to apply inculturation principles to feminist concerns include Berger, "A Female Christ Child", and Bilezikian, "Hierarchist and Egalitarian Inculturations".

[9] The ideas of this paragraph of principle #19 found in paragraphs IV.B.e-g of the *IBC* come from Vatican II's *Ad Gentes* 22.

fruitfulness (*Ad Gentes* 22).... The treasures contained in diverse cultures allow the Word of God to produce new fruits… (IV.B.e-f).

Implicit in this metaphor is a positive appraisal of the potential of the soil in which the seed of the word is planted. The *IBC* speaks of the "treasures contained in diverse cultures" and "riches God, in his generosity, has bestowed on the nations" (IV.B.e). Not only can there be found the particular genius or talent of various nations which can be brought to the service of the gospel, but "every authentic culture is…in its own way the bearer of universal values established by God" (IV.B.a). The presence of these universal values in various cultures is the reality which Justin Martyr called (using a different metaphor) "seeds of the Word" sown in the earth.

Nevertheless, some elements in cultures are not compatible with the gospel and the inculturation of Scripture means rejecting these harmful elements: "The light of the Word allows for a certain selectivity with respect to what cultures have to offer" (IV.B.f). Thus Scripture exercises a certain critical function in relation to cultures as well as a transforming function[10]. The Biblical Commission names two "false solutions" to be avoided in inculturation of Scripture's message: on the one hand, a *"superficial 'adaption'"*, which fails to enter deeply into the life of the people; on the other, *"syncretistic confusion"*, which fails to discern adequately what in a given culture is incompatible with the word of God (IV.B.f, emphasis added)[11]. Besides recourse to "the light of the Word", how are these dangers to be avoided? Rather than propose a method to safeguard inculturation from error, the Biblical Commission identifies a subjective prerequisite in the one who inculturates the message of Scripture, namely, "total fidelity to the person of Christ, to the dynamic of his paschal mystery and to his love for the Church" (IV.B.f).

---

[10] Klauck accurately describes the background of this discussion to be the dialectic between the inculturation of the gospel and the evangelization of culture ("Das neue Dokument: Darstellung und Würdigung", 86).

[11] The *IBC* makes reference here to *Ad Gentes* 22, which expresses the same point in a slightly different manner: "As a result [of fresh theological investigation of each socio-cultural area in the light of Scripture, the Fathers and Magisterium], avenues will be opened for a more profound adaption in the whole area of Christian life. Thanks to such a procedure, every appearance of *syncretism* and of *false particularism* can be excluded, and Christian life can be accommodated to the genius and the dispositions of each culture [emphasis added]".

Discussion

4. A New Focus of Attention

The presence of a section on inculturation in a Biblical Commission document on interpretation reflects a new awareness of the relation between culture and the Gospel. Translators of the Bible and missionaries have always found it necessary to decide about how the word of God should be expressed and embodied in diverse cultures. Sometimes those judgments were made on the basis of an inadequate understanding or respect for other cultures, and criticisms of some missionary approaches have heightened the Church's sensitivity to cultural issues. In addition, modern means of communication that reveal the diversity of cultures have raised cultural awareness. Finally, profound social and religious changes in the last century have aroused interest in the reciprocal influence of culture and religion.

Beginning with the Second Vatican Council the magisterium of the Church has given this theme considerable attention, an attention which has continued in synod documents and in the teaching of Popes Paul VI and John Paul II[12]. In 1979 the Pontifical Biblical Commission studied the theme of inculturation of faith in the light of Scripture, and the International Theological Commission (ITC) addressed this subject in its 1984 document on ecclesiology and in its 1988 document entitled, *Faith and Inculturation* (*FI*)[13]. The procedure of looking to the Bible to shed light on inculturation appears not only in the documents of the Biblical Commission, but in *Gaudium et Spes*, the ITC's *Faith and Inculturation* and other magisterial documents as well.

Christianity's approach to inculturation distinguishes it from the other great monotheistic religions, Judaism and Islam. Insofar as Judaism receives converts, it seeks to gather them into the people of Israel and to introduce them to the customs, laws and cultic language of a particular nation. Islam, like Christianity, announces its message to people in every nation, but, unlike Christianity, it seeks to spread the particular customs and language of the

---

[12] Among the documents of Vatican II, the concern for the relation of the Gospel to culture is evident in *Gaudium et Spes*, *Ad Gentes*, and *Nostra Aetate*. The synods' and popes' preoccupation with this topic appears in *Evangelii Nuntiandi* (especially §18-20), *Catechesi Tradendae* (e.g., § 53), the Report of the Extraordinary Synod for the 20th Anniversary of the Closing of the Second Vatican Council, and Pope John Paul II's encyclical *Apostoli Slavorum*.

[13] See Pontificia Commissione Biblica, *Fede e cultura alla luce della Bibbia*, International Theological Commission, "Select Themes of Ecclesiology" (278-284), and International Theological Commission, "Faith and Inculturation".

middle-Eastern culture in which it originated. Only Christianity seeks to preserve the cultures it encounters while transforming them from within.

Christian inculturation has its own logic which the International Theological Commission's *Faith and Inculturation* spells out[14]. Culture is the natural outworking of human nature, created in God's image, as human persons joined in community seek to better themselves. Its domain is broad, entailing knowledge, arts, work, customs and institutions. Cultures reflect humanity's search for God, even though cultures also manifest humanity's pride and selfishness. According to the International Theological Commission,

> A single principle explains the totality of relations between faith and culture: Grace respects nature, healing in it the wounds of sin, comforting and elevating it.... The process of inculturation may be defined as the church's efforts to make the message of Christ penetrate a given sociocultural milieu, calling on the latter to grow according to all its particular values, as long as these are compatible with the Gospel. (*FI* I, 10-11)

Inculturation is manifest in the history of salvation. Although God chose Israel for a special role in his plan of salvation, from the beginning God's plan embraced all of creation. Jesus lived the life of Israel, observing its customs and laws and taking part in its spiritual tradition. Yet he did not hesitate to challenge and correct ideas which history, religious tradition, and culture taught about God and his ways. Ultimately,

> The death and resurrection of Jesus, on account of which the Spirit was poured out into our hearts, have shown the shortcomings of completely human wisdoms and moralities and even of the law (nonetheless given by God to Moses), all of which were institutions capable of giving knowledge of the good, but not the force to accomplish it.... (II, 11)

Jesus Christ transcends every particular culture, including that of Israel, which experienced God's particular grace in its history and prepared the way for his coming.

Nevertheless, because the Son of God became incarnate and lived in a particular time, place, and culture, Christ is present to culture and cultures:

> "By his incarnation the Son of God has united himself in some fashion with every man".... The transcendence of Christ does not therefore isolate him above the human family but renders him present beyond all restriction. (*FI* II, 18 quoting *GS* 22)

---

[14] The following paragraphs rely on this document; citations in parentheses refer to section and paragraph numbers. The text is available in English in *Origins*, vol. 18, 800-807.

The Word assumed human nature and raised it to a divine dignity.

In the body of Christ the many different human cultures are complementary, insofar as they are renewed by grace and faith. According to the Theological Commission, "They permit us to see the multiform richness of which the teachings and energies of the same Gospel are capable..." (*FI* II, 21). The Church recognizes "resources of truth and love", *semina Verbi*, which God has placed in human cultures (*FI* II, 22—without denying that cultures often also reflect human rejection of God's truth and love). At Pentecost a new humanity of many cultures came into being, a new "race" which enjoys a divine unity, a *koinonia* in the Spirit. In this context, "the Holy Spirit does not establish a superculture, but is the personal and vital principle which will vivify the new community" in its members (II, 24).

Principle #19 drawn from the *IBC*'s brief treatment of inculturation remains an important general principle.   Nevertheless, it must be supplemented in order to decide the hard questions about the Gospel and culture which arise. Whether Bible translations for Melanesians should refer to Jesus as something other than the "Lamb of God", given the problems of this symbolism for that culture[15], requires careful consideration. A decision must be made when peoples should be instructed in the meaning of first-century Jewish culture of the New Testament, and when other symbols or concepts should be substituted. Perhaps initial evangelization and subsequent catechesis call for different strategies. Similar challenges arise when religious practices must be evaluated in a culture undergoing evangelization. What constitutes syncretism, or, at the opposite extreme, merely superficial adaption of the Christian message within a culture? Cultural patterns of the New Testament require discernment as well. Which early Church practices regarding sexual ethics, family relations, and structures in the Church should be viewed as particular to a culture and which as intrinsic to the Gospel or to God's design for human life?   How should the universal elements be expressed and embodied in contemporary Western culture? The principle of inculturation found in the *IBC*, while important, is only a beginning. Additional principles are needed to tackle the difficult questions which inculturation poses.

---

[15] See above, p. 306.

CHAPTER 20

The Use of the Bible in the Church

Principle #20

Interpretation occurs in all the ways in which the Church uses the Bible—in the liturgy, lectio divina, *pastoral ministry and ecumenism.*

In principle, the liturgy brings about the most perfect actualization of the biblical texts since it is Christ himself who "speaks when Sacred Scripture is read in the church" (SC 7). The liturgy gives a privileged place to the Gospels, and the cycle of Sunday readings, which associate an Old Testament text with a Gospel reading, often suggests a typological interpretation. (IV.C.1.b-c)

Lectio divina *is a reading of Scripture as the word of God, which leads, with the help of the Holy Spirit, to meditation, prayer and contemplation. (IV.C.2.a)*

Pastoral ministry makes use of the Bible in catechesis, preaching, and the biblical apostolate (IV.C.3.a). Scripture provides the first source, foundation and norm of catechetical teaching and preaching, where it is explained in the light of Tradition (IV.C.3.b). The role of the homily is to actualize the word of God (IV.C.1.d).

In ecumenism, the same methods and analogous hermeneutical points of view permit exegesis to unite Christians by means of the Bible, the common basis of the rule of faith. (IV.C.4.c,e)[1]

Explanation

In a time like the present in which many motives for the study of Scripture have been proposed, whether theological, literary, psychological, or political, it is worth remembering that the Christian approach to the Bible is characterized by an intense interest in the *use* of Scripture in the life of the Church. The classic text on the inspiration of Scripture, 2 Tim 3:16-17, in fact devotes more attention to the usefulness of the biblical word than to its inspiration: "All scripture is inspired by God and is *useful* for teaching, for reproof, for correction, and for training in righteousness, so that everyone who belongs to God may be proficient, equipped for every good work [emphasis added]".

Thus, it is not surprising that in its final chapter dedicated to "The Interpretation of the Bible in the Life of the Church" the *IBC* takes up the concrete forms that interpretation assumes in the Church's use of the Bible. The Biblical Commission introduces its theme by saying that although exegetes "have a distinctive role in the interpretation of the Bible... they do not exercise a monopoly" (IV.A.a)[2]. Furthermore, interpretation in the context of the Church's life "has aspects which go beyond the academic analysis of texts" (IV.a). After laying out the principles of actualization (IV.A) and inculturation (IV.B), the document treats the primary *uses* of the Bible (IV.C), beginning with the interior sources of the Church's life in the liturgy and *lectio divina* and working outwards to pastoral ministry and ecumenism. The explanation of this principle will not comment on everything that the *IBC* says about these topics, but will concentrate on how the Church's use of the Bible manifests principles of interpretation.

1. Liturgy

According to the *IBC*, Scripture and liturgy belong together for several reasons. First, reading Scripture has been central to the liturgical worship of the Church since her beginning, as it had been a vital element of synagogue worship. Second, the liturgy is still the primary place where most Catholic

---

[1] All the elements of this principle of interpretation may be found in section IV.C, "Use of the Bible". Some additional material on preaching appears in III.B.3.

[2] Rather, all the members of the Church have a role in interpreting Scripture (see principle #7).

Christians encounter Scripture. Third, "the liturgy of the word is a crucial element in the celebration of each of the sacraments of the Church" (IV.C.1.f). Fourth, the liturgy (especially the Liturgy of the Hours) uses biblical language, symbolism and the psalms in the service of Christian prayer. Fitzmyer adds an additional reason for the mutual belonging of Scripture and liturgy, i.e., the fact that many biblical texts originated in a liturgical context[3].

The Christian liturgy's use of Scripture manifests principles of interpretation which are summarized in the following paragraph of principle #20[4]:

> In principle, the liturgy brings about the most perfect actualization of the biblical texts since it is Christ himself who "speaks when Sacred Scripture is read in the church" (SC 7). The liturgy gives a privileged place to the Gospels and the cycle of Sunday readings, which associate an Old Testament text with a Gospel reading, often suggests a typological interpretation. (IV.C.1.b-c)

The *IBC* declares that "the sacramental liturgy, the high point of which is the Eucharistic celebration, brings about the most perfect actualization of the biblical texts" (IV.C.1.b). As we have seen, to actualize Scripture means to bring its meaning into the present. However, here actualization refers to more than a mere re-reading of the text in a new situation. Instead this re-reading of Scripture occurs in the context of a *divine encounter*. Christian faith understands liturgical worship as a meeting with God the Father, through Jesus Christ, in the Holy Spirit. According to *Sacrosanctam Concilium* §7, Christ is present in the Eucharistic celebration in the person of the sacramental minister, in the Eucharistic elements, and in the worshipping community (Mt 18:20), and "it is he himself who speaks when Sacred Scripture is read in Church.... Written text thus becomes living word" (IV.C.1.b). Perhaps, rather than the Church's "re-reading", one should speak of Jesus' re-addressing the words of Scripture to his disciples in their particular circumstances by his Spirit. After the readings, the homily, an integral part of the liturgy, continues the movement of actualization by

---

[3] Fitzmyer, *The Biblical Commission's Document*, 179. He names as examples the psalter, Jonah 2:3-10, Luke 1:46-55, 1:68-79, Phil 2:6-11, Eph 1:3-10, Rev 5:9-10, 11:16-18. Fitzmyer also points out the influence of the salvation-history emphasis of Luke-Acts on the liturgical calendar.

[4] For recent reflection on Scripture and liturgy, including responses to what the *IBC* says on this topic, see Beuken, Freyne and Weiler, *Bible and its Readers*; Bradshaw, "Use of the Bible in Liturgy"; Höslinger, "Vom Gebrauch der Bibel in der Liturgie"; Jensen, "Prediction-Fulfillment in Bible and Liturgy" and "Old Testament in the New Testament"; Langsfield, "The Worship of God and Teaching"; Stevenson, "A Liturgist's Response".

applying the proclaimed word explicitly to the needs of the congregation (IV.C.1.d).

Besides actualizing scripture in a unique way, liturgical biblical interpretation is christological interpretation. The *IBC* explains that the triple cycle of Sunday readings centers around the Gospels "in such a way as to shed light on the mystery of Christ as principle of our salvation" (IV.C.1.c)[5]. Often the choice of Old Testament texts that correspond to the Gospel of the day calls for interpretation "moving in the direction of typology", even though this is not the only way of interpreting the text (IV.C.1.c)[6]. The Biblical Commission categorizes typology as an aspect of the spiritual sense of Scripture (see II.B.2.i) and defines the spiritual sense as "the meaning expressed by the biblical texts when read, under the influence of the Holy Spirit, in the context of the paschal mystery of Christ and of the new life which flows from it" (II.B.2.i). Typology is sometimes lumped with allegorical interpretation as pre-critical eisegesis, belonging to the hermeneutic tools of another age and the *IBC* expresses reserve about the suitability of ancient allegorical methods for modern people (II.B.2.i, III.B.2.i,k). In this light the Commission's acceptance of "scriptural interpretation moving in the direction of typology" is significant (IV.C.1.c). Typology and allegory differ from one another. When typology bases itself on the way in which the New Testament describes an Old Testament reality, "one can speak of a meaning that is truly scriptural" (II.B.2.i).

The Christian liturgy's "interest" in its interpretation of Scripture is clearly religious, and might be said to have three specific aims: (1) to explain the mystery of salvation in Jesus Christ; (2) to actualize Scripture by considering its meaning for today in the context of a divine encounter; and (3) to provide language for prayer, praise and worship.

2. *Lectio Divina*

In *lectio divina*, the spiritual reading of Scripture, the religious interest of interpretation is the same as it is in the liturgy but with greater emphasis on the last two aspects, actualization and prayer[7]. The following paragraph of

---

[5] *DV* §18 speaks of the pre-eminence of the Gospels because they are the principal witness to the life and teaching of Jesus.

[6] Jensen makes the point that, strictly speaking, the liturgy's association of OT texts and gospel texts often reflects *thematic* rather than typological linkage (Jensen, "Beyond the Literal Sense", 56-57). For more on typology in this work, see "Typology", p. 194ff.

[7] In recent years *lectio divina* has been experiencing a renaissance. Recent writings on this topic include Chrostowski, "34 Sympozjum Biblistów Polskich, 1996", 51-55; Gargano, *Iniziazione alla 'Lectio divina'*; Hall, *Too Deep For Words*; Martini, "Teaching the Scriptures

principle #20 presents the wording of the *IBC*'s definition of *lectio divina* virtually verbatim:

> Lectio divina *is an individual or communal reading of Scripture as the word of God, which leads, at the prompting of the Holy Spirit, to meditation, prayer and contemplation. (IV.C.2.a)*

Let us examine each of its elements. First, *lectio divina* may be either done individually or in a group. The document briefly traces the history of regular or daily reading of Scripture in the Church by groups (first attested by Origen in the third century) and by individuals (especially in monasticism). It recalls that *Dei Verbum* §25 prescribes "assiduous" reading and study of Scripture for clergy and urges frequent spiritual reading of Scripture for the laity. The Biblical Commission's document emphasizes *how* one reads Scripture in the course of *lectio divina*. The text is to be "received as the Word of God" (IV.C.2.a), in other words, with a pre-understanding of Christian faith and with a readiness to hear what God is saying at the present time. The person or group engaging in *lectio divina* expects the Holy Spirit to be present and active in the reading, and this spiritual reading "leads, at the prompting of the Spirit, to meditation, prayer and contemplation" (IV.C.2.a)[8]. Here the Biblical Commission gives expression to the traditional teaching about the spiritual reading of Scripture which distinguishes three elements which follow the reading (*lectio*): *meditatio*, *oratio*, and *contemplatio*. The Biblical Commission's mention of the "prompting of the Spirit" underscores that this is not merely a mechanical procedure.

3. *Pastoral Ministry*

Besides the use of Scripture in the liturgy and *lectio divina*, which nourish the Church's prayer, Scripture nourishes the people of God through its use in pastoral ministry. Following Acts 6:4, *Dei Verbum* §24 refers to pastoral ministry as "the ministry of the word". The *IBC* offers quite a bit of advice about how Scripture is to be interpreted in the context of pastoral ministry. Its most important elements are summarized in the following paragraph of principle #20:

> *Pastoral ministry makes use of the Bible in catechesis, preaching, and the biblical apostolate (IV.C.3.a).* Scripture provides the first source, foundation and norm of catechetical teaching and preaching, where it is

---

to a Diocese"; Russell, "Paul Ricoeur on *Lectio Divina*"; Salvail, *At the Crossroads of Scripture*; Teani, "Tornare alla Bibbia".

[8] This corresponds well to Schneiders' recognition of Scripture as "the revelatory text", the privileged place of encounter with God. The weakness of Schneiders' approach is its reluctance to affirm much regarding Scripture's determinate revealed content. See note, p. 34.

explained in the light of Tradition (IV.C.3.b). The role of the homily is to
actualize the word of God (IV.C.1.d).

a) Catechesis

The most striking characteristic of the Biblical Commission's teaching about catechesis is how authoritative and substantial a role Scripture assumes[9]:

> The explanation of the Word of God in catechesis (*Sacros. Conc.*, 35; *Gen.*
> *Catech. Direct.*, 1971,16) has Sacred Scripture as first source. Explained in
> the context of the Tradition, Scripture provides the starting point,
> foundation and norm of catechetical teaching. One of the goals of catechesis
> should be to initiate a person in correct understanding and fruitful reading
> of the Bible. This will bring about the discovery of the divine truth it
> contains and evoke as generous a response as is possible to the message
> God addresses through his word to the whole human race. (IV.C.3.b)

Here Scripture is described as fulfilling both a *normative* and a *material* role. Because Scripture is the "first source" and "starting point", Scripture provides the norm for catechesis not merely by functioning as an extrinsic standard against which catechetical teaching may be measured. Rather catechesis occurs through the communication of the content of Scripture[10]. For this reason, the *IBC* says that teaching people to read Scripture fruitfully must be a goal of catechesis.

The Biblical Commission addresses both the method and the content of Scripture's use in catechesis[11]. As regards *method*, catechesis should begin

---

[9] Although "catechesis" is the topic under consideration, the intent is to express the relation between Scripture and the ministry of the word in general, including preaching. This is indicated in the following section beginning with IV.C.3.g, where the *IBC* explicitly states, "analogous remarks apply to the ministry of *preaching* [emphasis added]". Also the church documents cited by the Commission here, *SC* §35 and *Gen Catech. Direct.*, 1971, §16 (see also §14), both treat the relation of Scripture to ministry of the word more generally.

[10] Làconi, commenting both on the *IBC* and on the Italian episcopal conference's pastoral commentary (especially Conferenza Episcopale Italiana, *Nota Pastorale*), summarizes the point this way: "The Bible, therefore, is not merely a resource of catechesis, or even a privileged resource from which to draw content or themes. It is 'the book' of Christian catechesis in its basic presentation" (Làconi, "Nella vita della chiesa [*Commento*]", 374-375). Recognizing both the considerable progress that has been achieved and the fact that the goal has not yet been attained, Làconi offers various suggestions, including a closer collaboration between exegetes and catechists, and the development of "an exegesis that flows into catechesis" (citing Seghedoni, "Accostarsi alla Bibbia").

[11] For some recent reflections on Scripture and catechesis, see Hahn, "Prima Scriptura"; Langsfield, "The Worship of God and Teaching"; Ralph, "The Bible and the Adult Roman

with "the historical context of divine revelation so as to present persons and events of the Old and New Testaments in the light of God's overall plan" (IV.C.3.c). In other words, catechesis conveys an overview of God's action in time to fulfill his purposes through various individuals and circumstances. But it is not enough to merely give a chronological presentation of the persons and events in the Bible. Catechesis must "move from biblical text to its salvific meaning for the present time" (IVC3.d) by commenting on Scripture. For this purpose it may avail itself of whatever hermeneutical procedures will serve best. In the words of the Biblical Commission, "the presentation of the Gospels should be done in such a way as to elicit an encounter with Christ..." (IV.C.3.f). The aim of commenting on texts is to communicate Scripture's religious message which should lead to experiential knowledge of God and awareness of Scripture's meaning for the present. Likewise, the words of the prophets and of the New Testament writers should be presented as a message "addressed to Christians now" (IV.C.3.f).

As regards the *content* of catechesis, some portions of Scripture will be more useful than others. Undoubtedly confirmed by recent insights into the evocative power of narrative, the Biblical Commission urges the use of *stories* both from the Old and New Testaments. The Decalogue should be taught, as should some "prophetic oracles, the wisdom teaching, and the great discourses in the Gospels, such as the Sermon on the Mount" (IV.C.3.e).

Finally, what the Biblical Commission says about Scripture providing the "starting point, foundation and norm of catechetical teaching" is qualified by the phrase "explained in the context of the Tradition" (IV.C.3.b). In an earlier section the *IBC* indicates that what distinguishes Catholic exegesis "is that it deliberately places itself within the living tradition of the Church" (III.b), and Tradition supplies one of Catholic interpretation's fundamental principles[12]. Here the sense is stronger still. Not only does the catechist begin with a pre-understanding formed by Catholic belief, but he or she *explains* the Scripture in the context of Catholic Tradition. The difference has to do with the pastoral character of catechesis in contrast to the scholarly character of exegesis. The research of the Catholic exegete might lead him or her to criticize church traditions or even authoritative doctrinal definitions which fall short of fully conveying the message of the inspired Scriptures. But the cathechist (and preacher) leans more heavily on Tradition to shape his or her

Catholic"; Seghedoni, "Accostarsi alla Bibbia"; Terra, *A interpretação da Bíblia na Igreja*; and Weber, "Making the Biblical Account Relevant".

[12] "What characterizes Catholic exegesis is that it deliberately places itself within the living tradition of the Church..." (III.b). See principles #6 and #10, on a hermeneutic of faith and on interpretation in light of Tradition, respectively.

interpretation. Concretely, the "context of tradition" might mean making use of church teaching (e.g., the *Catechism of the Catholic Church)*, the Fathers of the Church, or writings by or about the saints to shed light on a text. According to the *IBC*, Tradition functions both negatively and positively in actualizing Scripture: "On the one hand, it provides protection against deviant interpretations; on the other hand, it ensures the transmission of the original dynamism" (IV.A.1.e).

b) The Homily

The Biblical Commission's comments on preaching concern the homily at eucharistic celebrations[13]. Therefore, most of what the Biblical Commission has said about the interpretation of the Bible in the liturgy applies to the homily. Furthermore, the Biblical Commission states that what was said about catechesis applies in an analogous way to preaching (IV.C.3.g). From this we may conclude that Scripture provides the content and norm of preaching. In addition, preachers should explain the salvific meaning of the events recounted including the christological significance of the Old Testament. Like catechists, preachers are to explain Scripture in the light of Tradition.

The *IBC* treats preaching both in its discussion of the roles of priests and deacons in interpretation (III.B.3) and in its discussion of Pastoral Ministry (IV.C.3.g-k). According to the Biblical Commission, several traits characterize the interpretation of the Bible in liturgical preaching. The first is *actualization*: "Gifted with a particular charism for the interpretation of scripture", priests and deacons "apply the eternal truth of the Gospel to the concrete circumstances of daily life" (III.B.3.c). They "draw from the ancient texts spiritual sustenance adapted to the present needs of the Christian community" (IV.C.3.g). On the one hand, the emphasis in actualization is the active role of the ministers of the word to *apply* the text to the situations of their congregations. On the other hand, preachers help their congregations to encounter God in Scripture:

> Their principal task... [is] not simply to impart instruction, but also to assist the faithful to understand and discern what the Word of God is saying to them in their hearts when they hear and reflect upon the Scriptures. Thus

---

[13] Recent discussions of the passage from text to preaching include Bailey, *Hermeneutics for Preaching*; Burkhard, "The Use of Scripture in Theology and Preaching"; Goldingay, "Preaching on the Stories" and *Models for Interpretation*; Gormley, "Opening the Mystery of Christ"; Langsfield, "The Worship of God and Teaching"; Parmisano, "Preaching and Contemporary Exegesis".

the *local church* ...becomes a community which knows that it is addressed by God.... (III.B.3.d, emphasis original)

Second, *faithfulness to the text* characterizes good liturgical preaching. The homilist needs to invest adequate time in preparation so as to avoid the communication of what are merely his own ideas, whether moralizing or discussing contemporary issues without "shed[ding] upon them the light of God's Word" (IV.C.3.i). Third, *coherence with the biblical message as a whole* is important to the homily. Specifically,

Preachers should certainly avoid insisting in a one-sided way on the obligations incumbent upon believers. The biblical message must preserve its principal characteristic of being the good news of salvation freely offered by God. (IV.C.3.j)

The Biblical Commission adds further pastoral advice. Because the eucharistic celebration does not permit a detailed examination of texts, the homilist should focus his remarks on the main point of the texts and "that which is most enlightening for faith and most stimulating for the progress of the Christian life" (IV.C.3.i). Priests and deacons should make sure the people understand the unity of Word and Sacrament in the ministry of the Church (III.B.3.c). Thus, pastoral considerations shape homiletic biblical interpretation.

c) The Biblical Apostolate

The biblical apostolate works to draw attention to the Bible as the word of God and source of life[14]. It achieves its goals by translating the Bible into many languages, distributing it as widely as possible, and establishing groups, conferences and a myriad of activities that lead people to a deeper knowledge of Scripture. The Biblical Commission applauds this promotion of the Bible in the life of the Church.

The *IBC* calls particular attention to church associations and movements which emphasize reading Scripture "within the perspective of faith and Christian action"[15]. Obviously, "the perspective of faith and Christian action" is an appropriate and excellent point of view from which to read and interpret

---

[14] Some recent publications illustrative of the biblical apostolate include Hinnebusch, "Bible in the Charismatic Movement"; Martin, "Bible in the Retreat Movement"; Milligan, "The Bible as Formative"; Murray, "The Biblical Apostolate"; Swetnam, "German Catholics and the Bible", "Zimbabwean Catholics and the Bible"; and "The Word of God and Pastoral Theology".

[15] Besides the reference to "basic Christian communities" which follows this quote, the Biblical Commission does not point to any specific church associations and movements, probably because this practice is so widespread.

Scripture, since the Christian Scriptures were written and preserved by communities with similar aims. The document makes particular mention of "basic Christians communities [which] focus their gatherings upon the Bible and set themselves a threefold objective: to know the Bible, to create community and to serve the people" (IV.C.3.m). Again, these goals provide a valid approach to interpretation closely related to Scripture's overall message.

In the context of discussing the interpretation of the Bible in "basic Christian communities", the Commission makes two comments that reflect its fundamental principles. First, it observes that at this popular level "exegetes can render useful assistance in avoiding actualizations of the biblical message that are not well grounded in the text" (IV.C.3.m). Genuine actualization of Scripture does not consist in discussing the Bible and using it as a springboard to make whatever comments seem relevant. Actualization must penetrate and apply the real meaning of the text to the circumstances and questions of contemporary life. In their popular writing and teaching exegetes can provide necessary background to resolve difficulties and explain texts to help ordinary readers grasp Scripture's authentic meaning and actualize it correctly.

The second comment, however, illustrates the Biblical Commission's conviction that interpreting the Bible is not an activity reserved for elites in the Church:

> But there is reason to rejoice in seeing the Bible in the hands of people of lowly condition and of the poor; they can bring to its interpretation and to its actualization a light more penetrating, from the spiritual and existential point of view, than that which comes from a learning that relies upon its own resources alone (cf. Matt 11:25). (IV.C.3.m)[16]

The biblical reference is to Jesus' praising the Father for hiding the truths of the Kingdom from the wise and learned and revealing them to "infants". Despite their own considerable learning the members of the Biblical Commission assert that the keys to understanding the Bible "from the spiritual and existential point of view" are humble dependence on God and the enlightening grace of the Spirit.

4. Ecumenism

Since its beginning the ecumenical movement has been a profoundly scriptural movement. Texts such as John 17 (especially vv.11, 20-23) have aroused deep longing among Christians for the unity for which John's Gospel tells us Jesus prayed. After citing a number of New Testament texts on the

---

[16] See also principles #6, "A Hermeneutic of Faith" and #7, "The Community of Faith Interprets Scripture".

ideal of Christian unity, the Biblical Commission says that "Scripture provides its theological foundation (Eph 4:4-6; Gal 3:27-28), the first apostolic community its concrete, living model (Acts 2:44; 4:32)" (IV.C.4.a). In addition, the *IBC* points out that "most of the issues which ecumenical dialogue has to confront are related in some way to the interpretation of biblical texts" (IV.C.4.b)[17].

What is the connection between ecumenism and Catholic principles of interpretation? The final paragraph of principle #20 summarizes the Commission's position:

> In ecumenism, the same methods and analogous hermeneutical points of view permit exegesis to unite Christians by means of the Bible, the common basis of the rule of faith. (IV.C.4.c,e)

Because all Christians acknowledge Scripture as normative for Christian doctrine (albeit in different ways), it provides an important common ground for dialogue. But the Biblical Commission's point is that alongside the common regard for Scripture, contemporary exegesis' common methods and analogous hermeneutical perspectives contribute to Christian unity. In the face of criticism by theologians and others, the methods of contemporary exegesis are validated by the contribution they have made to the Church's ecumenical quest[18]:

> Through the adoption of the same methods and analogous hermeneutical points of view, exegetes of various Christian confessions have arrived at a remarkable level of agreement in the interpretation of Scripture, as is shown by the text and notes of a number of ecumenical translations of the Bible, as well as other publications. (IV.C.3.c)

Besides ecumenical translations of the Bible[19], one can cite the remarkable consensus that prevails regarding the text of the Bible (evident in the ability of

---

[17] Recent discussion of the Bible in ecumenism includes Chrostowski, "34 Sympozjum Biblistów Polskich, 1996", 91-107; Meeking and Stott, *Evangelical-Roman Catholic Dialogue*; Muddiman, "Light on Biblical Authority"; Reumann, "After Historical Criticism, What?"; Reumann and Fitzmyer, "Scripture as Norm for our Common Faith"; and Wainwright, "Towards an Ecumenical Hermeneutic".

[18] This is an argument which has been advanced by Brown and Fitzmyer in defense of the historical-critical method. See Brown, "Contribution to Ecumenical Church Discussion"; Fitzmyer, *Scripture, the Soul of Theology* and "Historical Criticism".

[19] For example, *The Oxford Annotated Bible with the Apocrypha: Revised Standard Version*, ed. H.G. May and B.M. Metzger (New York: Oxford University, 1965); *Traduction oecuménique de la Bible*, ed. J.Potin (Paris: Cerf/Les Bergers et les Mages, 1975; repr.1985); *Die Bibel: Einheitsübersetzung der Heiligen Schrift, Altes und Neues Testament*, ed. O. Knoch et al. (Stuttgart: Katholisches Bibelanstalt/Deutsche Bibelstiftung, 1979-1980); and *La Bibbia*

the United Bible Society to publish a text of the Greek New Testament that enjoys general acceptance) and a growing convergence on some theological issues.

What are these "same methods" and "analogous hermeneutical points of view"? Above all the common use of the historical critical method has enabled Christians of various persuasions to overcome historical differences about biblical interpretation leading to convergence in doctrine. The recent "Joint Declaration on the Doctrine of Justification", which representatives of the Catholic Church and the Lutheran World Federation signed in Augsburg on 31 October 1999, offers an excellent example. The accord followed several years of dialogue between exegetes and theologians from both sides. *Justification by Faith*, the book which publishes the results of the United States Lutheran-Roman Catholic dialogue affirms that "in recent decades *developments in the study of Scripture* have brought Catholics and Lutherans to a fuller agreement about the meaning of many passages controverted at least since the sixteenth century [emphasis added]"[20].

Although the Biblical Commission does not explain what it means by "analogous hermeneutical views" which have contributed to ecumenical agreement in interpretation, three possibilities suggest themselves. First, Christians of different confessions share a pre-understanding of faith by receiving Scripture as inspired by God and authoritative; these perspectives are "analogous" rather than identical since the specific interpretive traditions of Christian churches differ. Second, exegetes of various churches have incorporated insights from philosophical hermeneutics (especially the writings of Gadamer and Ricoeur) regarding the relationship between Scripture and tradition. While Catholics regard Tradition as authoritative in biblical interpretation, Protestants increasingly acknowledge the important function of tradition. Finally, just as a common use of the historical-critical method has served as an ecumenical bridge between Catholics and Protestants, a common regard for the role of Tradition and the Fathers of the Church in biblical interpretation provides a basis for Catholic-Orthodox rapprochement.

---

concordata: Tradotta dai testi originali, con introduzione e note, ed. S. Cipriani et al. (Milan: Mondadori, 1968).

[20] Anderson, Murphy and Burgess, *Justification by Faith*, 58. See also Reumann, *"Righteousness" in the New Testament*, which contains responses by Fitzmyer and J.D. Quinn.

Discussion

5. Different Procedures for Different Purposes

Some readers of the *IBC* may have been surprised by the inclusiveness of the interpretive procedures endorsed by the Biblical Commission in the document's final chapter, "The Interpretation of the Bible in the Life of the Church". After having described scientific historical and literary methods and subtle insights from philosophical hermeneutics and after having re-asserted the priority of the historical-critical method, the Biblical Commission might seem to have reverted in its final chapter to an unscientific approach to Scripture. That chapter calls for actualization and inculturation—which could seem to imperil the original historical meaning of the text. It says that the poor and "people of lowly condition" can bring to Scripture's interpretation "a light more penetrating" that many learned people bring. It says that catechists and preachers should explain Scripture in light of Tradition and confirms a place for typology in the liturgical homily. Finally, it refers to the activity of the Spirit and the experience of communication with God in the liturgy, *lectio divina*, catechesis and preaching. How can this apparent oscillation between "scientific" and "religious" interpretive procedures be justified?

The answer is simple. Different tasks call for different tools. Different purposes require different procedures. When the task is ascertaining as closely as possible what the biblical author meant for the sake of translation or theological precision, critical tools will be primary. But when the purpose is more directly pastoral—nourishing the people of God with the word of God—interpretive procedures that actualize the message of the text, that highlight its salvific meaning, that relate it to Tradition, and that cooperate with the dynamic of divine communication and human response will be primary.

The common element which the Biblical Commission urges for pastoral as well as for scholarly purposes is faithfulness to the text itself and its message. It is this concern for the primacy and authority of the text itself that makes the role of exegetes essential for the interpretation of Scripture in the Church. This holds true both for scientific exegetical and theological work which is the particular responsibility of exegetes, and for pastoral work for which exegetes prepare and assist ministers of the word by their teaching, publications and other resources.

The members of the Biblical Commission give good example to their fellow exegetes by recognizing the legitimacy of procedures suited to pastoral interpretation and giving practical advice about the use of Scripture in catechesis and preaching. In the past some biblical scholars have cast aspersions on the interpretation that takes place in pastoral settings because it does not employ the procedures or make the distinctions that belong to their own scholarly labors. In other instances Scripture professors who recognize the legitimacy of pastoral actualization teach exclusively scientific exegesis to their students, often seminarians, deacon candidates, or lay people being trained for the ministry of the word. They erroneously assume ,that the pastoral and theological implications are obvious, or inappropriate to the classroom, or that their students will learn them elsewhere, perhaps in homiletics, catechetics or ministry courses.   The unintended result is a complete disconnect in the mind of many ministers of the word between the scientific explanation of texts they heard in Scripture courses and the pastoral task of interpreting and applying Scripture they are called to fulfill. Perhaps this is why the Biblical Commission defines the task of exegetes to include explaining "the meaning of the biblical text as God's word for today" and "the christological, canonical, and ecclesial meanings" of Scripture (III.C.1.b-c). These meanings not only convey the Church's understanding of Scripture: they also illustrate procedures for interpreting the Bible suited to the use of the Bible in the Church.

CONCLUSION

This conclusion will assess what the Pontifical Biblical Commission has accomplished in *The Interpretation of the Bible in the Church*, will consider some areas that need more attention, and will reflect on the challenge that confronts Catholic biblical interpretation at the beginning of a new millennium.

A. The Achievement of *The Interpretation of the Bible in the Church*

The Biblical Commission's document on interpretation in the Church has made a significant contribution to Church literature on the interpretation of Scripture at an important moment in the history of Catholic exegesis. While not claiming to be exhaustive, the next section sums up the Commission's achievement under seven headings.

1. Clarifying the Distinctive Traits of Catholic Interpretation

In their 1993 document the Biblical Commission has provided a more complete statement than any previous Church document of how Catholics interpret Scripture.

Analyzing the *IBC* and formulating the principles of biblical interpretation expressed within it has brought the characteristics of Catholic exegesis into clearer relief. On the one hand, these principles make it possible to identify the elements that Catholic exegesis holds in common with non-Catholic academic study of the Bible. Catholic interpretation recognizes the human, historical and literary character of the Bible, and the consequent necessity of investigating biblical texts with every scientific means available (principles #2, #3, #4, #15). It also recognizes that new light can be shed on ancient texts by viewing them in the light of the questions of contemporary readers, and that the richness of the biblical text requires a plurality of methods and approaches to explain it (principles #5, #16).

On the other hand, the principles found in the *IBC* which are discussed in part III of this study distinguish Catholic interpretation in varying ways from secular, Protestant and Jewish interpretation. Catholic exegesis approaches Scripture with a conscious pre-understanding of Christian faith (principle #6). It considers the Church as a whole to be the truly adequate interpreter of Sacred Scripture with each member of the Church sharing in this task according to his or her role in the body of Christ (principle #7). Catholic exegesis interprets Scripture in continuity with the pattern of interpretation found within it, recognizing Scripture's essential unity (without denying its diversity), and interpreting individual texts in the light of the entire canon (principle #8). In harmony with the New Testament writings, Catholics regard the Old Testament writings as inspired Scripture and interpret them in light of the death and resurrection of Jesus, while continuing to appreciate the meaning the texts conveyed at earlier stages of the history of salvation (principle #9). Catholic exegesis deliberately places itself within the stream of the living Tradition of the Church, accepting the canon of Scripture, remaining faithful to the revelation attested to by Scripture and to the basic orientations the Church Fathers gave to the doctrinal tradition of the Church (principles #6, #10). Finally, the primary aim of Catholic interpretation is not academic but religious and pastoral: to nourish and build up the body of Christ with the word of God (principle #11).

Furthermore, the principles found in the *IBC* regarding the senses of Scripture and regarding the practice of interpretation in the Church also distinguish characteristics of Catholic interpretation from secular academic interpretation. Academic interpretation which is based on reason alone is not able to recognize the literal sense as inspired and "intended by God, as principal author" (II.B.1.c). Nor can secular academic interpretation perceive the spiritual sense—the meaning Scripture takes on in light of the paschal mystery—or the fuller sense—a deeper meaning of the text intended by God that goes beyond the intention of the human author (principles #13 and #14). Similarly, while secular interpretation recognizes the legitimacy of actualizing an ancient text, it cannot recognize in that re-reading, as Catholic exegesis does, the continuing activity of the same Spirit who inspired the writing of Sacred Scripture (principles #18, #19, #20).

2. *Confirming But Redimensioning the Historical-Critical Method*

In the wake of a century of controversy, the Pontifical Biblical Commission, with the agreement of Pope John Paul II, has given the historical-critical method the strongest endorsement it has ever received in an official church document. This reaffirmation of the historical-critical method is a legitimate defense to maintain the historical and objective character of the Christian revelation contained in the Bible. Nevertheless, the *IBC* takes a carefully nuanced approach to the historical-critical method, defining it in a particular manner, excluding certain common errors, and placing the method in a broader hermeneutical context. The Biblical Commission has taken into account many valid criticisms that have been raised and has redimensioned the role of the historical-critical method by recognizing the limits of historical criticism and by welcoming the contribution of other methods and approaches.

However, the *IBC*'s treatment of the historical-critical method is not an unqualified success. At points the intensity of the document's rhetoric in defense of the method obscures the nuances of the Biblical Commission's position. In addition, this study has proposed two criticisms. First, by asserting that the method "implies of itself no *a priori*" (I.A.4.b) the *IBC* fails to consider serious questions that have been raised about the presuppositions and biases intrinsic to the method itself. Second, the *IBC* neglects important issues raised by the historical-critical method regarding the relation of history and believing exegesis.

3. Incorporating Philosophical Hermeneutics

The Interpretation of the Bible in the Church is the first official church document on Scripture that takes into account the insights of the last century in philosophical hermeneutics. The contribution of this field turns out to be important, providing as it does an antidote to some of the excesses of historical criticism and a philosophical basis for approaching Sacred Scripture in the light of faith. Contributions of philosophical hermeneutics to Catholic interpretation include recognizing the role of pre-understanding and the importance of an affinity between interpreter and text, criticizing historicism and historical positivism, appreciating that the meaning of a text may develop, and bridging the gap between the past and present.

4. Opening to New Methods and Approaches

Another achievement of the *IBC* is its successful incorporation of a wide variety of methods and approaches for interpreting Scripture in the Church. No previous church document has been as explicit and detailed about scholarly methods of interpretation. The document manifests a remarkable openness regarding methods and approaches that can contribute to understanding the Bible. However, this openness is not uncritical; instead, it is guided by Catholic exegesis' "fidelity to the revelation attested by the

Bible" (III.b) and by the values of scholarship, faith, and pastoral concern embodied in its principles.

5. Rehabilitating the Senses of Scripture

In its quest to incorporate the insights of modern critical methods during the last half-century, Catholic exegesis has focused its attention on the literal sense and paid little attention to the spiritual sense despite its important role in the tradition of Christian interpretation. It is significant, therefore, that the Biblical Commission has chosen to offer a definition of the spiritual sense and to endorse an understanding of the fuller sense. The Biblical Commission makes a point of distinguishing these valid senses of Scripture from arbitrary eisegesis or from the allegorical extremes that sometimes characterized interpretation by the Fathers and by others during the Middle Ages. Although the *IBC* section treating the senses is very brief and needs further clarification and elaboration, it moves the discussion forward and re-opens the way for Catholics to profit from these ways of interpreting Scripture that have proved fruitful in the past.

6. Emphasizing the Meaning for Today

While historical-critical study concerns itself with what the text *meant* to its author and original readers, the Church's interest in Scripture centers on what the text *means* today as a living word for Christian faith. Although the meaning of Scripture for today is essentially related to what the text meant in its historical setting, interpretation in the Church must always make the hermeneutical transition from the original to the present meaning. This is because the Church "receives the Bible as the Word of God, addressed both to itself and to the entire world at the present time" (IV.a). In light of this conviction, interpretation in the Church stresses both the theological meaning of Scripture and pastoral actualization. The contemporary meaning of Scripture is one of the major themes of the *IBC*, and this re-orientating message for exegesis stands as one of the defining characteristics of the document.

7. Recognizing the Value of Non-Specialist Interpretation

Exegesis has been accused of making the interpretation of Scripture so technical that it has become the exclusive reserve of a small number of specialists. One of the achievements of the document of the Biblical Commission has been to affirm the value of Scriptural interpretation by pastors and lay people who lack professional training. The Commission has accomplished this without detracting from the importance of interpretation that proceeds from a sound exegesis of the text or of the distinctive role of exegetes.

B. An Agenda for Further Discussion

Despite the significant contributions of the *IBC*, several areas would benefit from further discussion by Catholic scholars and perhaps by the Biblical Commission. On the basis of this study this writer would like to propose four issues for future discussion regarding the interpretation of the Bible in the Church.

8. To Clarify the Implications of the Dual Nature of Scripture

More reflection on the nature of Scripture and its implications for interpretation is needed. First, an adequate hermeneutic should begin with consideration of the object to be interpreted. This was always the traditional approach to explaining Scripture's interpretation. The importance of this step is especially true in the case of Scripture since the distinguishing characteristics of Catholic biblical interpretation depend so heavily on Scripture's divine inspiration and its relation to revelation. Second, the analogy of Scripture to the Incarnate Word, i.e., the way in which Scripture is both human and divine, is susceptible to widely different interpretations, so greater clarity is needed. Clarifying the implications of the nature of Scripture for its interpretation is an interdisciplinary task that will require the cooperation of systematic theologians, exegetes, and philosophers. Finally, the hermeneutical implications of the fact that God is the author of Scripture require more explicit consideration. How is the message of the divine author related to that of the various human authors, and how may it be distinguished?

9. To Clarify the Nature of Biblical Theology in the Church

In its deliberations about exegesis and interpretation in the Church, the Biblical Commission did not take up the question of biblical theology. Nevertheless, the principles of interpretation contained in the *IBC* illuminate a possible path for biblical theology as a discipline of interpretation in the Church. It is no secret that biblical theology has been foundering because of a lack of clarity about its foundational principles. A biblical theology conducted according to the principles of interpretation implicit in the *IBC* would begin with an explicit pre-understanding of faith. It would not confine itself exclusively to historical description of what biblical writings *meant*, but, as a normative theological discipline, biblical theology would address itself to what Scripture *means* for Christian life today. Other principles, especially those touching exegesis and Christian faith (part III), would provide a basis for development.

Such a biblical theology would differ from exegesis because its field of vision would be broader. Rather than focusing primarily on individual pericopes or biblical books, it might study the themes and issues that unite sections of the canon or the Bible as a whole. At the same time it would explore tensions and differences of outlook where they occur, since these also enrich the Church's understanding of the word of God. While exegesis confines itself to the biblical text itself (III.D.4.b), biblical theology could give greater scope to the tradition of interpretation, drawing from the rich biblical theologies found in the liturgy, the Fathers of the Church, medieval commentators, the Reformers, and modern authors. Because of its wider scope, such a biblical theology would have a great deal to contribute to systematic theology as well as to preaching and catechesis.

These are simply ideas springing from the principles of interpretation found in the *IBC*. It would be helpful if the Biblical Commission itself would consider the field of biblical theology in the Church and define a role for it in relation to exegesis and systematic theology.

10. To Clarify Various Questions Regarding History and Faith

One of the most consistent criticisms of the historical-critical method has been that it has undermined confidence in the historical reliability of the Bible. In the 1990's historical questions about the gospels came to new prominence as a result of the "Third Quest" for the historical Jesus. The *IBC* does not address this problem which has dominated discussion of the Bible in the media in the 1990's. In addition, other questions about the relation of the Bible and biblical interpretation to history have been raised in this study[1], which have implications for the relation of Christian faith to history. In the opinion of this writer, these questions and others like them could provide a useful topic for future study by the Pontifical Biblical Commission.

11. To Consider the Relation of Catholic Exegesis to the Secular Academy

The *IBC* devotes its entire attention to the interpretation of the Bible inside the bounds of Church. This study has referred to this interpretation as "Catholic exegesis" since it is within the Church's life that Catholic exegesis acquires its definitive character. However, much of the exegesis carried out by Catholics takes place in non-Catholic settings. Furthermore, even when the setting is Catholic—as in Catholic universities, seminaries or scholarly

---

[1] See p. 248ff.

journals—often the terms of discourse are determined more by the discussion in the secular academy than in the Church. This fact presents a problem since so much of what defines Catholic exegesis follows from its presupposition of faith, while the secular academy begins from entirely different presuppositions that often exclude and sometimes oppose the interests of faith.

The principles by which believing scholars do exegesis within the secular or inter-confessional academy must be taken up. Essentially the options reduce to two. Either believing exegetes, whether Jewish or Christian, must leave their fundamental presuppositions at the door and attempt to discuss the Bible apart from their beliefs and motives, or the academy must acknowledge that there is no such thing as presuppositionless interpretation and require that scholars disclose their presuppositions and interests along with the results of their research. Although the first of these approaches has dominated until now, this writer is convinced that only the second approach in the long run can preserve both scholarly and religious integrity[2]. In order to succeed, however, exegetes of all persuasions need to consider how to conduct a discussion among scholars whose fundamental paradigms differ[3].

C. The Challenge Ahead

This study has examined the explicit and implicit principles of interpretation expressed the Pontifical Biblical Commission's document, *The Interpretation of the Bible in the Church*. This concluding section briefly discusses some of the challenges to be encountered if these principles are to be realized in the Church's life.

---

[2] Some of the exegetes who think along these lines and offer useful suggestions include Levenson, *The Hebrew Bible, the Old Testament*, 106-126; Noble, *The Canonical Approach*, 130-132, 350-353; Vanhoye, "Catholicism and the Bible", 36-38; Watson, *Text, Church and World* and "Bible, Theology and the University". Noble draws promising insights from Thomas Kuhn's discussion of ways of handling competing paradigms in the natural sciences in *Structure of Scientific Revolutions*.

[3] Dividing the field between believing and non-believing exegetes does not do justice to the diversity of fundamental commitments and interests which inform biblical exegesis. Radical feminist, Marxist, and deconstructionist interpreters have joined an already diverse exegetical community of Catholics, liberal and conservative Protestants, Jews, atheists, and agnostics. This diversity of presuppositions in the exegetical community has led to greater recognition that the differing commitments and interests interpreters bring to the biblical text must be accepted and taken into account.

12. To Reflect on the Principles of Catholic Interpretation

Sandra Schneiders has observed that contemporary exegesis knows *how* to do what it does, but often does not know *what* it is doing[4]. Discussion of biblical interpretation commonly centers on methods, rather than on fundamental principles. The need for thoughtful reflection about the aims, presuppositions, and procedures of Scriptural interpretation extends not only to exegetes, but to everyone who reads Scripture—theologians, clergy, catechists, and lay people. Whether they realize it or not, all interpreters of Scripture are guided by principles of interpretation. It is a great advantage to be aware of what those principles are and to consciously reflect upon them. It is useful for all who are engaged in interpreting the Bible to ask themselves questions such as these: What is the aim of this interpretation? What presuppositions are appropriate? In light of the text under consideration, what methods will be most useful?

This study has sought to stimulate discussion of Catholic interpretation's essential principles. Readers must judge for themselves whether what is presented here accurately represents the principles explicit or implicit in the *IBC*. Furthermore, they must consider what additional principles apply to specific interpretive tasks, such as preaching, catechesis, and theological reflection, since exegesis itself is the primary concern of the *IBC* and of this study. Insofar as these principles are faithful to the Biblical Commission's document, and if they are put to work, the principles proposed here can help exegetes, preachers, catechists, and lay readers evaluate interpretations and resources on the Bible, and in some cases, supply what is lacking. Finally, the discussion and use of explicit principles of Catholic interpretation can lead to the development of more adequate principles and to interpretation that achieves its purpose of faithfully explaining the meaning of the word of God.

13. To Be (Or Not To Be) a Theological Discipline

If taken seriously, the Biblical Commission's document challenges Catholic exegetes, biblical associations, journals and theology faculties to a choice regarding the practice of exegesis: Will exegesis function as a theological discipline, or will it not? The position of the Biblical Commission is unambiguous on this point: "Catholic exegesis should... maintain its identity as a theological discipline, the principal aim of which is the deepening of faith" (Conclusion, e). Because the Bible consists of writings composed by human beings, exegesis must make use of history, literary analysis and other scientific disciplines, respecting the autonomy of their

---

[4] See note on p. 85 and accompanying text.

procedures and not distorting their results for apologetic reasons[5]. However, because Scripture communicates the word of God, exegesis must employ theological principles such as those articulated in parts III and IV of this study. Since the "study of sacred letter is the soul of theology", exegesis must be capable of theological assertion, rather than exclusively historical or literary assertion. The adequate pre-understanding for reading the Christian Scriptures is a hermeneutic of faith, one that recognizes Scripture as the word of God and that "deliberately places itself within the living tradition of the Church, whose first concern is fidelity to the revelation attested by the Bible" (III.b). In fact, "An authentic interpretation of Scripture...involves in the first place a welcoming of the meaning that is given in the events and, in a supreme way, in the person of Jesus Christ" (II.A.2.d). The view that regards exegesis as a theological discipline is both traditional (it was held by Origen and Jerome and the rest of the Fathers, Thomas Aquinas and medieval tradition, as well as the Reformers) and modern, in that the Second Vatican Council and Popes Pius XII, Paul VI and John Paul II have insisted upon it.

However, there exists in the exegetical community a profound wariness about the intimate relationship between theology and exegesis, the former considered to be biased and dogmatic and the latter regarded as scientific. This wariness reflects a lingering reaction to an excessive dominance by dogmatic theology and church authority in the past. This reaction and the Church's new openness to scientific methods since Vatican II has led to a tendency for exegesis to pitch its tent in the realm of positivistic science, and to refrain from discussing Scripture's theological implications or its religious message for Christian faith. This has influenced seminary and university courses on Scripture which often confine themselves to historical or literary analysis. Not a few exegetes make their lack of "theological bias" a point of principle. A prominent Old Testament scholar at a Catholic university in the United States told this writer, "The first day of class I inform my students that I'm a priest and a Franciscan, but that from that point on, they can expect me to approach the biblical texts exactly as I would any other ancient document".

A wall of separation between exegesis and theology can be found among older Catholic scholars who are personally devout, but who were taught to practice their discipline in an "objective" manner, uncontaminated by considerations of its relation to Christian life. A younger generation of scholars has reacted against the aridity of this approach, seeking Scripture's

---

[5] "This does not mean a lesser involvement in scholarly research of the most rigorous kind, nor should it provide excuse for abuse of methodology out of apologetic concern. Each sector of research (textual criticism, linguistic study, literary analysis, etc.) has its own proper rules, which it ought follow with full autonomy" (Conclusion, e).

existential relevance. This has led both to a renewed interest in the Christian tradition and to the adoption of philosophical or ideological hermeneutic models which are less compatible with Scripture's message. Most Catholic exegetes today have not been trained in a theological approach to their craft[6]. Most have never engaged in scholarly reflection about how exegesis should prepare for actualization. Most Catholic exegetes were never taught how to interpret Old Testament texts in the light of the death and resurrection of Jesus while doing justice to their pre-paschal canonical meaning (I.C.1.i), nor how to relate contemporary exegetical insight to the Catholic tradition of interpretation. In order to implement the understanding of exegesis as a theological discipline which the Biblical Commission urges, there needs to be a change in the academic formation of Catholic exegetes[7].

The difficulty of Catholic exegesis acquiring a theological outlook should not be underestimated. In the opinion of this writer, it will not occur on account of the *IBC* or magisterial instruction pointing in the same direction. Rather, the outcome will be determined by the choices of the individual exegetes and institutions which comprise Catholic exegesis as a whole. Insofar as Catholic exegetes continue in the direction of practicing exegesis primarily as a literary or historical discipline, the Church will need to find ways to train "ministers of the divine word" (*DV* 23) in another way—perhaps by developing a Catholic biblical theology distinct from exegesis as Pesce and others prefer[8]. On the other hand, insofar as Catholic exegetes remember their theological vocation to explain the word of God, the scientific advances of the last half-century will produce a rich harvest for theology, preaching and the life of the Church. For the Church's good, the only approach which must be excluded is the present false one in which exegesis is a theological discipline in theory, but predominantly a historical-literary discipline in practice.

---

[6] This is to be distinguished from not having been trained in theology. In the past most Catholic biblical scholars received a substantial theological formation at Catholic institutions, although exegesis' relation to faith and theology remained problematic. In recent years, however, many Catholic scholars receive their Scriptural training in secular institutions, and theological training is widely considered irrelevant.

[7] Commission Secretary Vanhoye acknowledges this implication ("Catholicism and the Bible", 37).

[8] But even in that case, in the opinion of this writer, Catholic exegesis beginning from a conscious pre-understanding of faith will re-emerge, since Catholic biblical theology cannot advance without scientific exegesis proceeding from faith at its base.

14. To Make Scripture the Spiritual Nourishment of the People of God

The Church has made great strides forward since the Second Vatican Council regarding the place of the Bible in the life of the Church. Nevertheless, the hope "for a new surge of spiritual vitality from intensified veneration of God's word" expressed in *Dei Verbum* 26 remains only partially fulfilled and must be ardently pursued. The Biblical Commission's document, and the principles which this study derives from it, help illumine the road ahead.

The *IBC* and its explicit and implicit principles provide a vision, above all, for the renewal of exegesis and the role of the exegete (Conclusion f). Scholarship which devotes itself only to the human dimension of the biblical texts cannot fulfill the Church's need to have Scripture as a wellspring of its life. Above all, Catholic seminaries, universities, and centers of religious formation require academic teaching of the Bible that explains the word of God without ignoring the fact that the divine word comes to us in human language. Those who have responsibility for Catholic educational institutions should hire those who teach Scripture in such a way as to make clear its religious message.

Probably it is pastors and catechists who love Scripture and interpret it soundly who will make the greatest single contribution to "a new surge of spiritual vitality from intensified veneration of God's word". Familiarity with the *IBC* and these principles, especially those pertaining to the practice of interpretation in the Church, can strengthen them in making Scripture the first source, foundation and norm of preaching and catechesis. Their work of pastoral actualization and inculturation will be decisive for the Church's future in the new millennium.

Finally, by an attentive listening to Scripture in the liturgy and in *lectio divina* and by a readiness to believe and obey the word of God, every member of the Church can hasten that new springtime of Christianity which Pope John Paul II has predicted will unfold in the third millennium "if Christians are docile to the action of the Holy Spirit"[9].

It is this writer's fervent hope that the principles of Catholic interpretation and their explanation and discussion proposed in this study may contribute toward that bright future for the Church of Jesus Christ. In the words of the Biblical Commission,

> The aim is that the Word of God may become more and more the spiritual nourishment of the members of the People of God, the source for them of a

---

[9] John Paul II, *Tertio Millennio Adveniente*, §18.

life of faith, of hope and of love—and indeed a light for all humanity (cf. *Dei Verbum*, 21). (Intro B.b)

APPENDIX

Catholic Principles for Interpreting Scripture in the Document of the Pontifical Biblical Commission, *The Interpretation of the Bible in the Church* (1993)

I. The Foundational Principle

1. The Word of God in Human Language.

Sacred Scripture is the word of God expressed in human language (I.A.a). The thought and the words belong at one and the same time both to God and to human beings in such a way that the whole Bible comes at once from God and from the inspired human authors (III.D.2.c).

It is the canonical text in its final stage which is the expression of the word of God. (I.A.4.f)

Because it is the word of God, Scripture fulfills a foundational, sustaining, and critical role for the Church, for theology, for preaching and for catechesis. Scripture is a source of the life of faith, hope and love of the People of God and a light for all humanity (Intro B.b).

II. "In Human Language": Catholic Exegesis and Human Knowledge

2. Catholic Exegesis and Science

Biblical texts are the work of human authors who employed their own capacities for expression and the means which their age and social context put at their disposal. Consequently, Catholic exegesis freely makes use of scientific methods and approaches which allow a better grasp of the meaning of texts in their literary, socio-cultural, religious and historical contexts. (III.a)

Catholic exegesis should be carried out in a manner which is as critical and objective as possible.

Catholic exegesis actively contributes to the development of new methods and to the progress of research (III.a). In this enterprise Catholic scholars collaborate with scholars who are not Catholic (III.C.a).

3. Catholic Exegesis and History

Catholic exegesis is concerned with history because of the historical character of biblical revelation. Although the Bible is not a history book in the modern sense and although it includes literary genres that are poetic, symbolic and imaginative, Scripture bears witness to a historical reality, i.e., the saving actions of God in the past which have implications for the present.

Interpretation of a biblical text must be consistent with the meaning expressed by the human authors. (II.B.1.g)

Historical study places biblical texts in their ancient contexts, helping to clarify the meaning of the biblical authors' message for their original readers and for us.

Although Catholic exegesis employs a historical method it is not historicist or positivist, confining its view of truth to what can be demonstrated by supposedly objective historical analysis.

4. The Use of Philological and Literary Analysis

Because Scripture is the word of God that has been expressed in writing, philological and literary analysis are necessary in order to understand all the means biblical authors employed to communicate their message.

Philological and literary analysis contributes to determining authentic readings, understanding vocabulary and syntax, distinguishing textual units, identifying genres, analyzing sources, and recognizing internal coherence in texts (I.A.3.c). Often they make clear what the human author intended to communicate.

Literary analysis underscores the importance of reading the Bible synchronically (I.A.3.c; Conclusion c-d), of reading texts in their literary contexts, and of recognizing plurality of meaning in written texts (II.B.d).

5. The Contribution of Philosophical Hermeneutics

Because interpreting the Bible entails an act of human understanding like the act of understanding any other ancient writing, it is fitting that philosophical hermeneutics inform Catholic interpretation.

It is not possible to understand any written text without "pre-understanding," i.e., presuppositions which guide comprehension (II.A.1.a). The act of understanding involves a dialectic between the pre-understanding of the interpreter and the perspective of the text (II.A.1.c). Nevertheless, this pre-understanding must be open to correction in its dialogue with the reality of the text (II.A.1.a).

Since interpretation of the Bible involves the subjectivity of the interpreter, understanding is only possible if there is a fundamental affinity between the interpreter and his object. (II.A.2.c)

Some hermeneutical theories are inadequate due to presuppositions which are incompatible with the message of the Bible. (II.A.2.d)

Philosophical hermeneutics corrects some tendencies of historical-criticism, showing the inadequacy of historical positivism (II.B.2.c), the role of the reader in interpretation, possibilities of meaning beyond of a text's historical setting, and the openness of texts to a plurality of meaning (II.B.c; Conclusion d).

Because in the Bible Christians seek the meaning of ancient writings for the present, literary and historical criticism must be incorporated in a model of interpretation which overcomes the distance in time between the origin of the text and our contemporary age (II.A.2.a). Both the Bible itself and the history of its interpretation demonstrate a pattern of re-reading texts in the light of new circumstances (II.A.2.b).

III. "The Word of God": Catholic Exegesis and Christian Faith

6. A Hermeneutic of Faith

Biblical knowledge cannot stop short at an understanding of words, concepts and events. It must seek to arrive at the reality of which the language speaks, a transcendent reality, communication with God. (II.A.1.d)

Reason alone is not able to fully comprehend the events and the message recounted in the Bible. In order to truly understand the Bible one must welcome the meaning given in the events, above all, in the person of Jesus Christ (II.A.2.d). Because the Bible is the word of God, it must be approached in the light of faith in order to be properly understood. Therefore, exegesis is a theological discipline.

The light of the Holy Spirit is needed to interpret Scripture correctly. As someone grows in the life of the Spirit, his or her capacity to understand the realities of which the Bible speaks also grows. (II.A.2.f)

7. The Role of the Community of Faith

The believing community, the People of God, provides the truly adequate context for interpreting Scripture (I.C.1.g). Scripture took shape within the traditions of faith of Israel and the early Church, and contributed in turn to the development of their traditions (III.A.3.f).

The Scriptures belong to the entire Church (III.B.3.i) and all of the members of the Church have a role in the interpretation of Scripture (III.B.3.b). People of lowly status, according to Scripture itself, are privileged hearers of the word of God (III.B.3.f).

Various special roles in interpretation belong to clergy, catechists, exegetes and others (III.B.3.i). Church authority is responsible to see that interpretation remains faithful to the Gospel and the Great Tradition, and the Magisterium exercises a role of final authority if occasion requires it (I.C.1.g).

8. Interpretation in Light of the Biblical Tradition, the Unity of Scripture, and the Canon

Catholic exegesis seeks to interpret the Sacred Scripture in continuity with the dynamic pattern of interpretation found within the Bible itself. In the Bible later writings often depend on earlier texts when their authors re-read what had been written before in light of new questions and circumstances (III.A.1.a). Catholic exegesis seeks both to be faithful to the understanding of faith expressed in the Bible and to maintain dialogue with the generation of today (III.A.3.h).

Catholic exegesis recognizes the essential unity of Scripture, which encompasses differing perspectives (III.A.2.g), yet presents an array of witnesses to one great Tradition (I.C.a, III.A.a).

Catholic exegesis interprets individual texts in the light of the whole canon of Scripture. (I.C.b; III.D.4.b)

9. Interpretation of the Old Testament in Light of the Paschal Mystery

The Church regards the Old Testament as inspired Scripture, faithfully conveying God's revelation (III.A.2.a; III.B.1.b).

The New Testament interprets the Old Testament in the light of the paschal mystery (I.C.1.i). Jesus' life, death and resurrection fulfill the Old Testament Scriptures (III.A.2.a). Jesus' own interpretation of the Old Testament and that of the Apostles expressed in the New Testament under the inspiration of the Spirit are authoritative, even if some of the interpretive procedures employed by New Testament authors reflect the ways of thinking of a particular time period (III.A.2.f).

Christians do not limit the meaning of the Old Testament to the ways in which it prepares for the coming of Christ. Rather the Church esteems the canonical interpretation of the Old Testament before the Christian Passover as a stage in the history of salvation (I.C.1.i). Christians continue to draw sustenance from the inspired message of the Old Testament (III.A.2.e).

10. Interpretation in Light of the Living Tradition of the Church

Catholic exegesis deliberately places itself within the stream of the living Tradition of the Church (III.b) and seeks to be faithful to the revelation handed on by the great Tradition, of which the Bible is itself a witness (Conclusion e).

Within this living Tradition, the Fathers of the Church have a foundational place, having drawn from the whole of Scripture the basic orientations which shaped the doctrinal tradition of the Church, and having provided a rich theological teaching for the instruction and spiritual sustenance of the faithful (III.B.2.b). However, Catholic exegesis is not bound by the Fathers' exegetical methods (II.B.2.h; III.B.2.k).

11. The Aim of Interpretation: To Explain Scripture's Religious Message

The primary aim of Catholic exegesis is to explain the religious message of the Bible, i.e., its meaning as the word which God continues to address to the Church and to the entire world (IV.a, III.C.1.b). The ultimate purpose of Catholic exegesis is to nourish and build up the body of Christ with the word of God.

IV. The Meaning of Inspired Scripture

12. The Literal Sense

The literal sense of Scripture is that which has been expressed directly by the inspired human authors. Since it is the fruit of inspiration, this sense is also intended by God, as principal author. One arrives at this sense by means of a careful analysis of the text, within its literary and historical context (II.B.1.c).

The literal meanings of many texts possess a dynamic aspect that enables them to be re-read later in new circumstances (II.B.1.e).

13. The Spiritual Sense, Typology

The spiritual sense of Sacred Scripture is the meaning expressed by the biblical texts when read under the influence of the Holy Spirit in the context of the paschal mystery and of the new life which flows from it. (II.B.2.b)

The spiritual sense is always founded on the literal sense. A relationship of continuity and conformity between the literal and the spiritual sense is necessary in order for the literal sense of an Old Testament text to be fulfilled at a higher level in the New. (II.B.2.e)

Typology is an aspect of the spiritual sense. (II.B.2.i)

14. The Fuller Sense

The fuller sense (*sensus plenior*) is a deeper meaning of the text, intended by God but not clearly expressed by the human author (II.B.3.a). It has its foundation in the fact that the Holy Spirit, principal author of the Bible, can guide human authors in the choice of expressions in such a way that the latter will express a truth, the fullest depths of which the authors do not perceive (II.B.3.c).

The existence of a fuller sense to a biblical text can be recognized when one studies the text in the light of other biblical texts or authoritative doctrinal traditions which utilize it. (II.B.3.a)

V. "In Human Language": Methods and Approaches

15. The Use of the Historical-Critical Method

The historical-critical method is the indispensable tool of scientific exegesis to ascertain the literal sense in a diachronic manner. (I.A.4.g, I.A.a)

In order to complete this task, it must include a synchronic study of the final form of the text, which is the expression of the word of God. (I.A.4.f)

The historical-critical method can and must be used without philosophical presuppositions contrary to Christian faith. (I.A.4.b-c)

Despite its importance, the historical-critical method cannot be granted a monopoly, and exegetes must be conscious of its limits. Exegetes must recognize the dynamic aspect of meaning and the possibility that meaning can continue to develop (Conclusion d).

16. A Plurality of Methods and Approaches

Catholic exegesis is characterized by openness to a plurality of methods and approaches. Although the historical-critical method retains its primacy, literary methods and approaches based on tradition, the social sciences, or particular contemporary contexts can yield important insights into the meaning of the biblical word. However, the value of these insights will correspond to their harmony with the fundamental principles which guide Catholic interpretation.

VI. Interpretation in Practice

17. The Task of the Exegete and the Relationship of Exegesis with Other Theological Disciplines

The task of the Catholic exegete is both a work of scholarship and an ecclesial service (III.C.a). Because sound interpretation requires a lived affinity with what is studied and the light of the Holy Spirit, full participation in the life and faith of the believing community (III.A.3.g) and personal prayer are necessary (Address 9).

The primary task of the exegete is to determine as accurately as possible the meaning of biblical texts in their own proper context, that is, first of all, in their particular literary and historical context and then in the context of the wider canon of Scripture (III.D.4.b).

Catholic exegetes arrive at the true goal of their work only when they have explained the meaning of the biblical text as God's word for today (III.C.1.b). Exegetes should also explain the christological, canonical and ecclesial content of biblical texts (III.C.1.c).

Exegesis is a theological discipline, which exists in a relationship of dialogue with other branches of theology (III.D.a).

18. Actualization

The Church receives the Bible as the word of God addressed both to itself and to the entire world at the present time (IV.a). Actualization is possible because of the richness of meaning contained in the biblical text, and it is necessary, because the Scripture was composed in response to circumstances of the past and in language suited to those circumstances. (IV.A.1.b-c)

Actualization presupposes a correct exegesis of a text, part of which is determining its literal sense (IV.A.2.e). The most reliable and fruitful method of actualizing Scripture is to interpret Scripture by Scripture. The actualization of a biblical text in Christian life proceeds in relation to the mystery of Christ and the Church. (IV.A.2.f)

Actualization involves three steps: 1. to hear the Word from within one's own concrete situation; 2. to identify the aspects of the present situation highlighted or put in question by the biblical text; 3. to draw from the fullness of meaning contained in the biblical text those elements capable of advancing the present situation in a way that is productive and consonant with the saving will of God in Christ. (IV.A.2.g)

19. Inculturation

The foundation of inculturation is the Christian conviction that the word of God transcends the cultures in which it has found expression. The word of God can and must be communicated in such a way as to reach all human beings in their own cultural contexts. (IV.B.b)

The first stage of inculturation consists in translating Scripture into another language (IV.B.c).   Then comes interpretation, which sets the biblical message in more explicit relationship with the ways of feeling, thinking, living and self-expression proper to the local culture.   Finally, one passes to other stages of inculturation, leading to the formation of a local Christian culture, encompassing all aspects of life. (IV.B.e)

The relation between the word of God and the human cultures it encounters is one of mutual enrichment.   The treasures contained in diverse cultures allow the Word of God to produce new fruits, while the light of the word of God allows helpful and harmful elements in cultures to be discerned. (IV.B.f)

20. The Use of the Bible in the Church

Interpretation occurs in all the ways in which the Church uses the Bible—in the liturgy, *lectio divina*, pastoral ministry and ecumenism.

In principle, the liturgy brings about the most perfect actualization of the biblical texts since it is Christ himself who "speaks when Sacred Scripture is read in the church" (SC 7).   The liturgy gives a privileged place to the Gospels, and the cycle of Sunday readings, which associate an Old Testament text with a Gospel reading, often suggests a typological interpretation. (IV.C.1.b-c)

Lectio divina is a reading of Scripture as the word of God, which leads, with the help of the Holy Spirit, to meditation, prayer and contemplation. (IV.C.2.a)

Pastoral ministry makes use of the Bible in catechesis, preaching, and the biblical apostolate (IV.C.3.a). Scripture provides the first source, foundation and norm of catechetical teaching and preaching, where it is explained in the light of Tradition (IV.C.3.b). The role of the homily is to actualize the word of God (IV.C.1.d).

In ecumenism, the same methods and analogous hermeneutical points of view permit exegesis to unite Christians by means of the Bible, the common basis of the rule of faith. (IV.C.4.c,e)

BIBLIOGRAPHY[*]

Abbott, Walter M., ed. *The Documents of Vatican II*. New York: America, 1966.

Abraham, William J. *Divine Revelation and the Limits of Historical Criticism*. Oxford: Oxford University Press, 1982.

Adam, A.K.M. *What Is Postmodern Biblical Criticism?* Guides to Biblical Scholarship. Minneapolis: Fortress, 1995.

Alonso Schökel, L. *Commentarios a la constitución "Dei Verbum"*. Madrid: Biblioteca de autores cristianos, 1969.

____. "Considerazioni sulla *Dei Verbum* a trenta anni dal concilio". *Firmana [Fermo]* 11 (1995), 11-27.

____. "Of Models and Methods". *Vetus Testamentum Supplements* 36 (1985), 3-13.

____. "Trends: Plurality of Methods, Priority of Issues". *Vetus Testamentum Supplements* 40 (1988), 285-292.

Alter, Robert. *The Art of Biblical Narrative*. New York: Basic Books, 1981.

____. *The Art of Biblical Poetry*. New York: Basic Books, 1985.

Anderson, H.G., T.A. Murphy, and J.A. Burgess, eds. *Justification by Faith*, Lutherans and Catholics in Dialogue 7. Minneapolis, MN: Augsburg, 1985.

Angelini, Giuseppe, ed. *La Rivelazione Attestata: La Bibbia fra Testo e Teologia*. Milan: Glossa, 1998.*

Aquinas, Thomas. *Summa Theologica*. Translated by Thomas Gilby. Vol. 1. 60 vols. New York: McGraw-Hill, 1964.

---

[*] This bibliography includes two kinds of entries. First, it includes all works cited in this study. Second, it includes entries for published editions of the Biblical Commission's document as well as reviews, books and articles which discuss *The Interpretation of the Bible in the Church*. Entries of the second kind are indicated by an asterisk.

Arens, E. "Los evangelios y el magisterio". *Paginas* 21, no. 141 (1996), 97-110.*

____. "Roma y la interpretación de la Biblia". *Paginas* 128 (1994), 64-77.*

Asurmendi, J. "Cien años de exégesis católica". *Salmanticensis* 41, no. 1 (1994), 67-82.*

Ayres, Lewis, and Stephen E. Fowl. "(Mis)Reading the Face of God: *The Interpretation of the Bible in the Church*". *Theological Studies* 60 (1999), 513-528. *

Bailey, R., ed. *Hermeneutics for Preaching: Approaches to Contemporary Interpretations*. Nashville, TN: Broadman, 1992.

Balás, David L., and D. Jeffrey Bingham. "Patristic Exegesis of the Books of the Bible". In *IBCom*, 64-115, 1998.

Barr, James. "Jowett and the 'Original Meaning' of Scripture". *Religious Studies* 18 (1982), 433-437.

____. "Jowett and the Reading of the Bible 'Like Any Other Book'". *HBT* 4 (1985), 1-44.

____. "The Literal, the Allegorical, and Modern Biblical Scholarship". *Journal for the Study of the Old Testament* 44 (1989), 3-17.

Barsotti, Divo. *La parola e lo spirito: Sagi sull' esegesi spirituale*. Milan, 1971.

____. "Sacra Scriptura eodem Spiritu quo scripta est etiam legenda et interpretanda (*Dei Verbum* 12)". In *Costituzione conciliare Dei verbum (Atti della XX Settimana Biblica)*, 301-320. Brescia, 1970.

Bartholomew, Craig G. *Reading Ecclesiastes: Old Testament Exegesis and Hermeneutical Theory*. Vol. 139. Analecta Biblica. Rome: Pontificio Istituto Biblico, 1998.

Beauchamp, Paul. "È possibile una teologia biblica?". In *La Rivelazione Attestata: La Bibbia fra Testo e Teologia*, ed. Giuseppe Angelini, 319-332. Milano: Edizioni Glossa, 1998.

Beentjes, P. "Pauselijke Bijbelcommissie Doet van zich Spreken". *Collationes* 24, no. 4 (1994), 401-409.*

Begley, J. "Modern Theories of Interpretation". *Australian Catholic Record* 73, no. 1 (1996), 81-91.*

Bergant, D. "Fundamentalism and the Biblical Commission". *Chicago Studies* 34, no. 3 (1995), 95. *

Berger, T. "A Female Christ Child in the Manger and a Woman on the Cross, Or: The Historicity of the Jesus Event and the Inculturation of the Gospel". *Feminist Theology* 11 (1996), 32-45.

Betori, G. "Modelli interpretativi e pluralità di metodi in esegesi". *Biblica* 63 (1982), 305-328.

____. ed. *Come leggere un testo biblico*. Vol. 11, Bibbia e Catechesi. Bologna: Dehoniane, 1987.

Bertuletti, Angelo. "Esegesi biblica e teologia sistematica". In *La Rivelazione Attestata: La Bibbia fra Testo e Teologia*, ed. Giuseppe Angelini, 133-157. Milano: Glossa, 1998.*

Beuken, Wim, Seán Freyne, and Anton Weiler. *The Bible and its Readers*. Concilium, 1991/1. London: SCM, 1991.

Bilezikian, G. "Hierarchist and Egalitarian Inculturations". *Journal of the Evangelical Theological Society* 30, no. 4 (1987), 421-426.

Blondel, Maurice. "Histoire et dogme: Les lacunes philosophiques de l'exégèse moderne". *La Quinzaine* 56 (1904), 145-167; 349-373; 433-458.

Blowers, Paul, Jon D. Levenson, and R.L. Wilken. "Interpreting the Bible: Three Views". *First Things* 45 (August/September 1994), 40-46. *

Bonora, A. "Vent'anni dopo la costituzione dogmatica *Dei Verbum*: il metodo esegetico (critica e teologia)". *Teologia* 10, no. 4 (1985), 287-306.

Bonsor, Jack A. *Athens and Jerusalem: The Role of Philosophy in Theology*. New York: Paulist, 1993.

Borg, M.J. "A Temperate Case for a Non-Eschatological Jesus". *Forum* 2 (1986), 81-102.

Bossuyt, P., and J. Radermakers. "Rencontre de l'incroyant et inculturation: Paul à Athènes (*Ac 17*, 16-34)". *Nouvelle Revue Théologique* 117, no. 1 (1995), 19-43.

Braaten, C.E. and R.W. Jenson, ed. *Reclaiming the Bible for the Church*. Grand Rapids: Eerdmans, 1995.

Bradshaw, Paul. "The Use of the Bible in Liturgy: Some Historical Perspectives". *Studia Liturgica* 22 (1992), 35-52.

Brown, Raymond E. *The Community of the Beloved Disciple*. Mahwah, NJ: Paulist, 1979.

____. "The Contribution of Historical Biblical Criticism to Ecumenical Church Discussion". In *Biblical Interpretation in Crisis: The Ratzinger Conference on Bible and Church*, ed. Richard John Neuhaus, 24-49. Grand Rapids: Eerdmans and the Rockford Institute Center on Religion and Society, 1989.

____. *The Critical Meaning of the Bible*. New York: Paulist, 1981.

____. "Hermeneutics". In *The Jerome Biblical Commentary*. Englewood Cliffs, NJ: Prentice Hall, 1968.

____. *An Introduction to New Testament Christology*. New York: Paulist, 1994.

____. *An Introduction to the New Testament*. Anchor Bible Reference Library, ed. David Noel Freedman. New York: Doubleday, 1997.

____. *The Sensus Plenior of Sacred Scripture*. Baltimore: St. Mary's University, 1955.

____. *The Virginal Conception and the Bodily Resurrection of Jesus*. New York: Paulist, 1973.

Brown, Raymond E., and Thomas Aquinas Collins. "Church Pronouncements". In *NJBC*, 1166-1174, 1990.

Brown, Raymond E., and Sandra Marie Schneiders. "Hermeneutics". In *NJBC*, 1146-1165, 1990.

Brown, Raymond E., Joseph A. Fitzmyer, and Roland E. Murphy, eds. *The Jerome Biblical Commentary*. Englewood Cliffs, NJ: Prentice Hall, 1968.

Brown, Raymond E., et al. *Mary in the New Testament*. New York: Paulist, 1978.

Brown, Raymond E., Joseph A. Fitzmyer, and Roland E. Murphy, eds. *The New Jerome Biblical Commentary*. Englewood Cliffs, NJ: Prentice Hall, 1990.

Bultmann, Rudolf. *Jesus and the Word*. New York: Scribner's & Sons, 1958.

____. "New Testament and Mythology". In *Kerygma and Myth: A Theological Debate*, ed. Hans Werner Bartsch. London: SPCK, 1962, 1964.

____. *Theology of the New Testament*. 2 vols. London: SCM, 1952, 1955.

Burkhard, John J. "The Use of Scripture in Theology and Preaching: Experience, Interpretation and Ecclesial Identity". *New Theological Review* 8 (January 1995), 30-44. *

Buzzetti, C. "Per l'attualizzazione di una parabola: la guida di due applicazioni precedenti". *Rivista Biblica* 40, no. 2 (1992), 193-212.

Byrne, Brendan. Email to Peter Williamson, 8 December 1999.

____. "A New Vatican Document on the Bible". *Australian Catholic Record* 71, no. March (1994), 325-329.*

Caballero Cuesta, J.M. *Hermenéutica y Biblia*. Estella [Navarra]: Verbo Divino, 1994.*

Campbell, Antony F., and James W. Flanagan. "1-2 Samuel". In *NJBC*, 145-159, 1990.

Campbell, Antony F., and Mark O'Brien. "1-2 Samuel". In *IBCom*, 572-607, 1998.

Carroll, Robert P. "Cracks in the Soul of Theology". In *The Interpretation of the Bible in the Church*, ed. J.L. Holden, 142-155. London: SCM, 1995.*

Carson, D.A. "The Tabula Rasa Fallacy". *Modern Reformation*, July/August 1999, 29-32, 43.

Chadwick, Henry. "Augustine". In *DBI*, 65-69, 1990.

Childs, Brevard S. "Critical Reflections on James Barr's Understanding of the Literal and the Allegorical". *Journal for the Study of the Old Testament* 46 (1990), 3-9.

____. "Interpretation in Faith". *Interpretation* 18 (1964), 432-449.

____. *Old Testament Theology in a Canonical Context*. London: SCM, 1985.

____. "The *Sensus Literalis* of Scripture: An Ancient and Modern Problem". In *Beiträge zur Alttestamentlichen Theologie*, ed. H. Donner and et al., 80-93. Göttingen: Vandenhoeck & Ruprecht, 1977.

____. "Toward Recovering Theological Exegesis". *Pro Ecclesia* 6, no. 1 (1997), 16-26.

Chrostowski, W., et al. "Dokument Papieskiej Komisji Biblijnej 'Interpretacja Biblii w Kosciele': 33 Sympozjum Biblistów Polskich, Szczecin, 14-15.IX.1995". *Collectanea Theologica* 66, no. 1 (1995), 5-101.*

Chrostowski, W., et al. "Dokument Papieskiej Komisji Biblijnej 'Interpretacja Biblii w Kosciele': 34 Sympozjum Biblistów Polskich, Radom, 11-13 IX 1996". *Collectanea Theologica* 67, no. 1 (1997), 5-115.*

Cipriani, S. "L'interpretazione della Bibbia nella chiesa". *Asprenas [Naples]* 42, no. 1 (1995), 5-20.*

Collins, John J. "Is a Critical Biblical Theology Possible?" In *The Hebrew Bible and Its Interpreters*, ed. William Henry Propp, Baruch Halpern and David Noel Freedman, 225. Winona Lake, IN: Eisenbrauns, 1990.

____. "Review: The Hebrew Bible, The Old Testament and Historical Criticism: Jews and Christians in Biblical Studies". *Christian Century*, 28 July 1993, 743-745.

Collins, Raymond F. "Hearing the Word: Methods of Biblical Interpretation". *Living Light* 31, no. 1 (1994), 3-9.*

____. "Inspiration". In *NJBC*, 1023-1033, 1990.

Combrink, H.J.B. "The Reception of Matthew in Africa". *Scriptura* 58 (1996), 285-303.

____. "Translating or Transforming - Receiving Matthew in Africa". *Scriptura* 58 (1996), 273-284.

Commission Biblique Pontificale. *Bible et Christologie*. Paris: Cerf, 1984.

____. "L'interprétation de la Bible dans l'Église". *Biblica* 74, no. 4 (1993), 451-528.*

____. *L'interprétation de la Bible dans l'Église. Allocution de Sa Sainteté le pape Jean-Paul II et document de la Commission Biblique Pontificale.* Paris: Cerf, 1994.*

____. *Unité et diversité dans l'Eglise: Texte officiel de la Commission Biblique Pontificale et travaux personnels des Membres.* Città del Vaticano: Libreria Editrice Vaticana, 1989.

Comstock, G.L. "Truth or Meaning: Ricoeur versus Frei on Biblical Narrative". *HervTeolStud* 45, no. 4 (1989), 741-766.

Conferenza Episcopale Italiana. *Nota pastorale: La Bibbia nella vita della Chiesa*. Bibbia: Proposte e metodi. Torino: Elle Di Ci, 1996.*

Congregation for the Doctrine of the Faith. *Instruction on the Ecclesial Vocation of the Theologian*. Rome, 1990.

Conroy, Charles. "A Literary Analysis of 1 Kings 1:41-53". *Vetus Testamentum Supplements* 36 (1985), 54-66.

____. "Reflections on the Exegetical Task: Apropos of Recent Studies on 2 Kings 22-23". In *Pentateuchal and Deuteronomistic Studies*, 255-268. Louvain: Leuven University Press, 1990.

____. "Reflections on the Present State of Old Testament Studies". *Gregorianum* 73, no. 4 (1992), 597-609.

Coote, Robert B., and Mary P. Coote. *Power, Politics, and the Making of the Bible*. Philadelphia: Fortress, 1990.

Coppens, Joseph. "Le problème d'un sens biblique plénier". In *Problèmes et méthode d'exégèse théologique*, ed. L. Cerfaux, J. Coppens and J.Gribomont, 11-19. Louvain: Desclée de Brouwer, 1950.

Costacurta, Bruna. "Esegesi e lettura credente della scrittura". *Gregorianum* 73, no. 4 (1992), 739-745.

Cothenet, E. "Commission Biblique Pontificale: L'interprétation de la Bible dans l'Église". *Esprit & Vie* 104, no. 8 (1994), 1121-1126.*

____. "Discernement prophétique dans le Nouveau Testament". *Spiritus* 33, no. 128 (1992), 362-371.

Cova, G.D. "La parola alle genti: Comunità credente e culture tra Antico e Nuovo Testamento". *SacDoc* 41, no. 3-4 (1996), 21-33.

Culler, J. *Structuralist Poetics*. Ithaca: Cornell University, 1975.

Curtin, Terence R. "Historical Criticism and the Theological Interpretation of Scripture". Dissertation, Pontificia Universitas Gregoriana, 1987.

Cuvillier, E. "Evangile et traditions chez Paul: Lecture de Romains 6,1-14". *Hokhma* 45 (1990), 3-16.

Czajkowski, M. "Die Inkulturation des Evangeliums Jesu im Neuen Testament und heute". *Collectanea Theologica* 58, no. special issue (1988), 29-38.

D'Ambrosio, Marcellino. "Henri de Lubac and the Critique of Scientific Exegesis". *IntCathRev/Communio* 19, no. 3 (1992), 365-388.

Davies, Philip R. *Scribes and Schools: The Canonization of the Hebrew Scriptures*. Louisville: Westminster John Knox, 1998.

____. *Whose Bible Is It Anyway?* Vol. 204. Journal For The Study Of The Old Testament Supplement. Sheffield: Sheffield Academic Press, 1995.

de la Potterie, Ignace. "Il Concilio Vaticano II e la Bibbia". In *L'esegesi cristiana oggi*, ed. Ignace de la Potterie. Casale Monferrato: Edizioni Piemme, 1991.

____. "Interpretation of Holy Scripture in the Spirit in Which It Was Written (*Dei Verbum* 12c)". In *Vatican II, Assessment and Perspectives: Twenty-five Years After*, ed. René Latourelle, vol. 1, 220-266. New York: Paulist, 1988.

____. "L'Istituto Biblico negli ottant'anni della sua storia". *Civiltà Cattolica* 140, no. 3344 (1989), 166-172.

____. "L'esegesi biblica, scienza della fede". In *L'esegesi cristiana oggi*, ed. Ignace de la Potterie, 127-165. Casale Monferrato: Edizioni Piemme, 1991.

____. "Reading Holy Scripture 'in the Spirit': Is the Patristic Way of Reading the Bible Still Possible Today?" *International Catholic Review/Communio* 13, no. 4 (1986), 308-325.

____. "The Spiritual Sense of Scripture". *Communio* 23 (1996), 738-756.

____. "Storia e mistero". *30 Giorni*, no. 1 (1998), 76-77.

____. *Storia e mistero: Esegesi cristiana e teologica giovannea*. Roma: Trenta Giorni Società Cooperativa, 1997.

de Lubac, Henri. *Medieval Exegesis: The Four Senses of Scripture (Ressourcement)*. Translated by Mark Sebanc. Grand Rapids: Eerdmans, 1998.

____. *The Sources of Revelation*. Translated by Luke O'Neill. New York: Herder and Herder, 1968.

Dhavamony, M. "The Lord's Prayer in the Sanskrit Bible". *Gregorianum* 68, no. 3-4 (1987), 639-670.

Dillmann, R. "Die Bedeutung der semantischen Analyse für die Textpragmatik". *Biblische Notizen* 79 (1995), 5-9.

Dirscherl, E. "Pluralität ja - Fundamentalismus nein! Vom Umgang mit der Bibel in 'postmodernen' Zeiten". *Bibel und Liturgie* 70, no. 3 (1997), 208-212.*

Dohmen, Christoph. "Die gespaltene Seele der Theologie. Zum Verhältnis von Altem und Neuem Testament". *Bibel und Liturgie* 68, no. 3-4 (1995), 154-162.*

____. "Was Gott sagen wollte...Der *sensus plenior* im Dokument der Päpstlichen Bibelkommission". *Bibel und Liturgie* 69, no. 4 (1996), 251-254.*

Donahue, John R. "The Literary Turn and New Testament Theology: Detour or New Direction?" *Journal of Religion* 76, no. 2 (1996), 250-275.

Donfried, Karl P. "Alien Hermeneutics and the Misappropriation of Scripture". In *Reclaiming the Bible for the Church*, ed. C.E. Braaten and R.W. Jenson, 19-45. Grand Rapids: Eerdmans, 1995.

Doré, J. "L'interprétation de la Bible dans l'Eglise". *Études* 382, no. 2 (1995), 227-232.*

____. "Méthodes exégétiques et enseignement de l'exégèse: Sur l'Instruction de la Commission biblique pontificale, L'interpretation de la Bible dans l'Église". *Revue de l'Institut Catholique de Paris* 52 (1994), 33-40.*

Dreyfus, F. "Exégèse en Sorbonne, exégèse en Église". *Revue Biblique* 82 (1975), 321-359.

____. "L'actualisation à l'intérieur de la Bible". *Revue Biblique* 83 (1976), 161-202.

____. "L'actualisation de l'Ecriture: I. Du texte à la vie". *Revue Biblique* 86 (1979), 5-58.

____. "L'actualisation de l'Ecriture: II. L'action de l'Esprit". *Revue Biblique* 86 (1979), 161-193.

____. "L'actualisation de l'Ecriture: III. La place de la Tradition". *Revue Biblique* 86 (1979), 321-384.

Dulles, Avery. "The Interpretation of the Bible in the Church: A Theological Appraisal". In *Kirche sein: Nachkonziliare Theologie im Dienst der Kirchenreform*, 29-37. Freiburg: Herder, 1994.*

Dumais, Marcel. "Sens de l'Écriture: Réexamen à la lumière de l'herméneutique philosophique et des approches littéraires récentes". *New Testament Studies* 45 (1999), 310-331.*

Edwards, M. *Towards a Christian Poetics*. London: Macmillan, 1984.

Ellis, E. Earle. "Interpretation of the Bible Within the Bible Itself". In *IBCom*, 53-63, 1998.

Evans, Craig A. "The Third Quest of the Historical Jesus: A Bibliographical Essay". *Christian Scholar's Review* 28, no. 4 (1999), 532-543.

Ezeogu, E.M. "Bible and Culture in African Christianity". *International Review of Mission* 87, no. 344 (1998), 25-38.

Fabris, Rinaldo. "Lettura fondamentalista". In *Commento*, ed. Giuseppe Ghiberti and Francesco Mosetto, 243-260, 1998.*

Fernández, Andrea. "Hermeneutica". In *Institutiones Biblicae*. Rome: Pontifical Biblical Institute, 1927.

Filippi, Alfio, and Erminio Lora, eds. *Enchiridion Biblicum*. Bologna: Dehoniane Bologna, 1993.*

Fischer, G. "Kann aus Rom etwas Gutes kommen?" *Bibel und Liturgie* 69, no. 3 (1996), 171-173.*

Fischer, I. "Frauen und feministische Exegese im Dokument der Päpstlichen Bibel-kommission 'Die Interpretation der Bibel in der Kirche'". *Bibel und Liturgie* 70, no. 1 (1997), 53-56.*

Fitzmyer, Joseph A. *The Biblical Commission's Document "The Interpretation of the Bible in the Church": Text and Commentary.* Vol. 18. Subsidia Biblica, ed. James Swetnam. Rome: Pontifical Biblical Institute, 1995.*

____. *A Christological Catechism: New Testament Answers.* New York: Paulist, 1991.

____. "Historical Criticism: Its Role in Biblical Interpretation and Church Life". *Theological Studies* 50 (1989), 244-259.

____. "The Interpretation of the Bible in the Church Today". *Irish Theological Quarterly* 62 (1996-1997), 84-100.*

____. "Problems of the Literal and Spiritual Senses of Scripture". *Louvain Studies* 20, no. 2-3 (1995), 134-146.*

____. *Scripture and Christology: A Statement of the Biblical Commission with a Commentary.* New York: Paulist, 1986.

____. *Scripture, the Soul of Theology.* New York: Paulist, 1994.*

____. "The Senses of Scripture Today". *Irish Theological Quarterly* 62 (1996-1997), 101-116.*

Fitzmyer, Joseph A., and Thomas J. Stahel. "Scripture, the Soul of Theology: An Interview with Joseph A. Fitzmyer, SJ". *America* 172, no. 16 (1995), 8-12.*

Fleckenstein, K.-H. *Ordnet euch einander unter in der Furcht Christi: Die Eheperikope in Eph 5,21-33.* Vol. 73. Forschung zur Bibel. Würzburg: Echter, 1994.

Focant, C. "L'interprétation de la Bible dans l'Église". *Revue théologique de Louvain* 25 (1994), 348-354.*

Forestell, J.T. "The Church and the Bible: *The Interpretation of the Bible in the Church". Canadian Catholic Review [Saskatoon]* 13, no. 7 (1995), 11-21.*

Fowl, Stephen E. *Engaging Scripture: A Model for Theological Inquiry.* Cambridge, MA: Blackwells, 1998.

Franco, E., ed. *La teologia biblica: Natura e prospettive.* Rome: Ave, 1989.

Frei, Hans. *The Eclipse of Biblical Narrative*. New Haven: Yale University Press, 1974.

Froehlich, Karlfried. *Biblical Interpretation in the Early Church*. Sources of Early Christian Thought, ed. William G. Rusch. Philadelphia: Fortress, 1984.

Frye, Northrop. *The Great Code: The Bible and Literature*. New York: Harcourt Brace Jovanovich, 1982.

Fuchs, O. "Päpstliche Bibelkommission versöhnt zwischen Freiheit und Verbindlich-keit". *Bibel und Liturgie* 71, no. 1 (1998), 55-60.*

Fusco, Vittorio. "Un secolo di metodo storico nell' esegesi cattolica". *Studia Patavina* 41, no. 2 (1994), 37-94.*

Gadamer, Hans-Georg. *Philosophical Hermeneutics*. Berkeley, CA: University of California Press, 1976.

____. *Truth and Method*. Translated by Joel Weinsheimer and Donald G. Marshall. 2nd revised ed. New York: Crossroad, 1989.

Gargano, I. *Iniziazione alla 'Lectio divina': Indicazioni metodologiche con l'esemplificazione di alcuni brani presi dal Vangelo secondo Matteo*. Conversazioni bibliche. Bologna: Dehoniane, 1992.

Gelin, A. "La question des 'relectures' à l'intérieur d'une tradition vivante". *Sacra Pagina I (BEThhL XII) Gembloux* (1958), 303-315.

Ghiberti, Giuseppe. "Il metodo storico-critico". In *Commento*, ed. Giuseppe Ghiberti and Francesco Mosetto, 105-146, 1998.*

Ghiberti, Giuseppe, and Francesco Mosetto, eds. *L'interpretazione della Bibbia nella Chiesa: Commento*. Torino: Elle Di Ci, 1998.*

Gilbert, Maurice. "Cinquant' anni di magistero romano sull' ermeneutica biblica". In *Chiesa e Sacra Scrittura: Un secolo di magistero ecclesiastico e studi biblici*, vol. 17, 11-33. Rome: Pontifical Biblical Institute, 1994.

____. "Exegesis, Integral". In *Dictionary of Fundamental Theology*, ed. René Latourelle and Rino Fisichella, 291-298. New York: Crossroad, 1995.

____. "New Horizons and Present Needs". In *Vatican II, Assessment and Perspectives: Twenty-five Years After*, ed. René Latourelle, vol. 1, 321-343. New York: Paulist, 1988.

Gillman, John. "Faith and Science Together: The Work of the Pontifical Biblical Commission". *Living Light* 31, no. 1 (1994), 10-15.*

Girard, R. "Is There Anti-Semitism in the Gospels?" *BibInt* 1, no. 3 (1993), 339-352.

Gispert-Sauch, G. "St. John's Nectar in Indian Flavour". *Vidyajyoti* 51, no. 9 (1987), 421-424.

Goldingay, J. *Models for Interpretation*. Grand Rapids: Eerdmans, 1995.

____. "Preaching on the Stories in Scripture". *Anvil* 7, no. 2 (1990), 105-114.

Gormley, Joan. "Opening the Mystery of Christ in the Scriptures". In *The Church and the Universal Catechism: Proceedings from the Fifteenth Convention of the Fellowship of Catholic Scholars*, ed. Anthony J. Mastroeni, 55-68. Steubenville, OH: Franciscan University, 1992.

Gourgues, M. *Jean, de l'exégèse à la prédication: Vol. 1, Carême et Pâques, Année A*. Vol. 97. Lire la Bible. Paris: Cerf, 1993.

____. "Le père prodigue (*Lc 15*,11-32): De l'exégèse à l'actualisation". *Nouvelle Revue Théologique* 114, no. 1 (1992), 3-20.

____. *Luc, de l'exégèse à la prédication: Carême et Pâques, Année C*. Vol. 103. Lire la Bible. Montréal: Fides, 1994.

Gradara, R. *Luca: il Vangelo degli ultimi*. Bologna: Dehoniane, 1991.

Graffy, A. "How Should I Interpret the Bible". *Priests & People* 9, no. 6 (1995), 234-237.*

Grant, Robert, and David Tracy. *A Short History of the Interpretation of the Bible*. 2nd ed. Philadelphia: Fortress, 1984.

Grech, Prosper. "L'ermeneutica biblica nel XX secolo". *Studia Patavina* 41, no. 2 (1994), 399-411.*

____. *Ermeneutica e teologia biblica*. Rome, 1986.

____. "Hermeneutics". In *DFT*, ed. René Latourelle and Rino Fisichella, 416-425, 1994.

Green, Joel B. "In Quest of the Historical: Jesus, the Gospels, and Historicisms Old and New". *Christian Scholar's Review* 28, no. 4 (1999), 544-560.

Gross, W. "Rom gegen den Fundamentalismus". *Theologische Quartalschrift* 174 (1994), 232-234.*

Haag, H. "Bilanz eines Jahrhunderts: Ein Lehrschreiben der Päpstlichen Bibel-kommission". *Orientierung* 58, no. 11 (1994), 129-132.*

Hahn, Scott. "Prima Scriptura: Magisterial Perspectives on the Primacy of Scripture for Catholic Theology and Catechetics". In *The Church and the*

Universal Catechism: Fifteenth Convention of the Fellowship of Catholic Scholars, ed. Anthony J. Mastroeni, 69-79. Steubenville, OH: Franciscan University, 1992.

Hall, Thelma. *Too Deep For Words: Rediscovering Lectio Divina*. New York: Paulist, 1988.

Harrisville, Roy A. "A Critique of Current Biblical Criticism". *WordWorld* 15, no. 2 (1995), 206-213.

____. "The Loss of Biblical Authority and Its Recovery". In *Reclaiming the Bible for the Church*, ed. C.E. Braaten and R.W. Jenson, 47-61. Grand Rapids: Eerdmans, 1995.

Harrisville, Roy A., and W. Sundberg. *The Bible in Modern Culture: Theology and Historical-Critical Method from Spinoza to Käsemann.* Grand Rapids: Eerdmans, 1995.

Harvey, Van A. *The Historian and the Believer: The Morality of Historical Knowledge and Christian Belief.* New York: Macmillan, 1966.

Hasel, G.F. "The Nature of Biblical Theology". *Andrews University Seminary Studies* 32 (1994), 203-215.

____. "Recent Models of Biblical Theology: Three Major Perspectives". *Andrews University Seminary Studies* 33 (1995), 55-75.

Hasitschka, M. "Wörtlicher und geistlicher Sinn der Schrift". *Bibel und Liturgie* 70, no. 2 (1997), 152-155.*

Hayes, John H., and Carl R. Holladay. *Biblical Exegesis: A Beginner's Handbook*. Revised ed. Atlanta: John Knox, 1987.

Hebblethwaite, Peter. "The Bible in the Church". *The Tablet*, 2 April 1994, 444-445.*

Heidemanns, K. "Eine 'postkoloniale Kehrtwendung'? Anmerkungen zum Dokument der Päpstlichen Bibelkommission aus missionswissenschaftlicher Sicht". *Bibel und Liturgie* 70, no. 1 (1997), 57-61.*

Henry, Carl F. "Narrative Theology: An Evangelical Appraisal". *TrinJourn* 8, no. 1 (1987), 3-19.

Hilary, M. *Inculturation Theology of the Jerusalem Council in Acts 15: An Inspiration for the Igbo Church Today*. Vol. 50. European University Studies, Series 23: Theology. Frankfurt: Lang, 1995.

Hinnebusch, Paul. "The Bible in the Charismatic Movement". In *IBCom*, 156-159, 1998.

Hirsch, E.D., Jr. *The Aims of Interpretation*. Chicago: University of Chicago Press, 1976.

____. "Meaning and Significance Reinterpreted". *Critical Inquiry* 11 (1984), 202-224.

____. "Transhistorical Intentions and the Persistence of Allegory". *New Literary History* 25 (1994), 549-567.

____. *Validity in Interpretation*. New Haven: Yale University Press, 1967.

Holman, Jan. "A Dutch Catholic Perspective". In *The Interpretation of the Bible in the Church*, ed. J.L. Holden, 129-134. London: SCM, 1995.*

Höslinger, N.W. "Vom Gebrauch der Bibel in der Liturgie: Impulse im Dokument 'Die Interpretation der Bibel in der Kirche' (1993)". *Bibel und Liturgie* 68, no. 3-4 (1995), 216-220.*

Houlden, J.L. "An Anglican Reaction". In *The Interpretation of the Bible in the Church*, ed. J.L. Holden, 107-111. London: SCM, 1995.*

____., ed. *The Interpretation of the Bible in the Church*. London: SCM, 1995.*

International Theological Commission. "Faith and Inculturation". *Origins*, 4 May 1989, 800-807.

____. "Select Themes of Ecclesiology on the Occasion of the Eighth Anniversary of the Closing of the Second Vatican Council". In *International Theological Commission: Texts and Documents 1969-1985*, ed. Michael Sharkey, 267-304. San Francisco: Ignatius, 1989.

Jeanrond, Werner G. "After Hermeneutics: The Relationship Between Theology and Biblical Studies". In *The Open Text*, ed. Francis Watson, 95-101. London: SCM, 1993.

____. *Text and Interpretation as Categories of Theological Thinking*. New York: Crossroad, 1988.

Jensen, Joseph. "Beyond the Literal Sense: The Interpretation of Scripture in the *Catechism of the Catholic Church*". *Living Light [Washington, DC]* 29, no. 4 (1993), 50-60.

____. "The Old Testament in the New Testament and in the Liturgy". *TBT* 28, no. 207-212 (1990), .

____. "Prediction-Fulfillment in Bible and Liturgy". *Catholic Biblical Quarterly* 50 (1988), 646-662.

John Paul II. "Address". *L'Osservatore Romano*, 17 April 1989.

____. *Fides et Ratio*. Rome: L'Osservatore Romano, 14 October 1998.

____. *Tertio Millennio Adveniente*. Vatican City: Libreria Editrice Vaticana, 1994.

Johnson, Luke Timothy. "The Crisis in Biblical Scholarship". *Commonweal* 120, no. 21 (1993), 18-21.

____. *The Real Jesus: The Misguided Quest for the Historical Jesus and the Truth of the Traditional Gospels*. New York: HarperCollins, 1995.

____. "So What's Catholic About It? The State of Catholic Biblical Scholarship". *Commonweal*, 16 January 1998, 12-16.

____. "Who Is Jesus? The Academy vs. the Gospels". *Commonweal* 122, no. 22 (1995), 12-14.

Journal of Higher Criticism. "Homepage". 1999. Accessed Web site. Available from www.depts.drew.edu/jhc/.

Kennedy, G.A. *New Testament Interpretation through Rhetorical Criticism*. Chapel Hill: University of North Carolina, 1984.

Kertelge, K. "Die Interpretation der Bibel in der Kirche. Zum gleichnamigen Document der Päpstlichen Bibelkommission vom 23. April 1993". *Trierer Theologische Zeitschrift* 104, no. 1 (1995), 1-11.*

Klauck, Hans-Josef. "Das neue Dokument der Päpstlichen Bibelkommission: Darstellung und Würdigung". *Biblische Zeitschrift* 39, no. 1 (1995), 1-27.*

____. "Der Katechismus der Katholischen Kirche: Rückfragen aus exegetischer Sicht". In *Ein Katechismus für die Welt. Informationen und Anfragen*, ed. E. Schulz, vol. 150, 71-82. Düsseldorf, 1994.*

____. "Das neue Dokument der Päpstlichen Bibelkommission: Darstellung und Würdigung". In *Die Interpretation der Bibel in der Kirche: das Dokument der Päpstlichen Bibelkommission vom 23.4.1993 mit einer kommentierenden Einführing von Lothar Ruppert und einer Würdigung durch Hans-Josef Klauck*, vol. 161, 62-90. Stuttgart: Verlag Katholisches Bibelwerk, 1995.*

Kogler, F. "Das Verhältnis von AT – NT in jüngeren römischen Dokumenten: Novum Testamentum in Vetere latet, et in Novo Vetus patet". *ProtokolleBibel* 5, no. 2 (1996), 109-143.*

Kremer, J. "Die Interpretation der Bibel in der Kirche. Marginalien Zum neusten Dokument der Päpstlichen Bibelkommission". *Stimmen der Zeit* 212, no. 3 (1994), 151-166.*

Kretschmar, G. "The Early Church and Hellenistic Culture". *International Review of Mission* 84, no. 332-333 (1995), 33-46.

Kristeva, Julia. *Semiotikè: Recherches pour une sémanalyse.* Paris: Seuil, 1969.

Kuhn, Thomas S. *The Structure of Scientific Revolutions.* 2nd ed. Chicago: Chicago University, 1970.

Làconi, Mauro. "Interpretazione della Bibbia nella vita della chiesa". In *Commento*, ed. Giuseppe Ghiberti and Francesco Mosetto, 364-380, 1998.*

Lambiasi, Francesco. "Dimensioni caratteristiche dell' interpretazione cattolica". In *Commento*, ed. Giuseppe Ghiberti and Francesco Mosetto, 299-363, 1998.*

Landier, J., F. Pécriaux, and D. Pizivin. *Voici l'homme: Pour accompagner une lecture de l'Évangile de Jean, chapitres 13 à 21.* Paris: Éditions Ouvrières, 1990.

Lang, B. *Die Bibel neu entdecken. Drewermann als Leser der Bib.* Munich: Kösel, 1995.*

Langsfield, Paul J. "The Worship of God and Teaching of His Word". A paper delivered at the Fifteenth Convention of the Fellowship of Catholic Scholars, Pittsburgh, PA, 1992.

Larraín, E. Pérez-Cotapos. "El valor hermenéutico de la eclesialidad para la interpretación de la Sagrada Escritura". *Teología y Vida (Santiago)* 36, no. 3 (1996), 169-185.*

Lategan, Bernard C. "Hermeneutics". In *ABD*, vol. 3, 149-154, 1992.

Latourelle, René. "Positivism, Historical". In *DFT*, 785-788, 1995.

____. ed. *Vatican II, Assessment and Perspectives: Twenty-five Years After.* New York: Paulist, 1988.

Lentricchia, F. *After the New Criticism.* London: Methuen, 1980.

Leo XIII. *Vigilantiae*, 30 October 1902.

Levenson, Jon D. "The Bible: Unexamined Commitments of Criticism". *First Things* 30 (1993), 24-33.

____. "The Eighth Principle of Judaism and the Literary Simultaneity of Scripture". *Journal of Religion* 68, no. 2 (1988), .

____. *The Hebrew Bible, the Old Testament, and Historical Criticism: Jewish and Christians in Biblical Studies*. Louisville, KY: Westminster/John Knox Press, 1993.

Levoratti, Armando J. "How to Interpret the Bible". In *IBCom*, 9-38, 1998.*

L'Hour, Jean. "Pour une lecture 'catholique' de la Bible". *Biblical Interpretation* 5, no. 2 (1997), 113-132.*

Lindbeck, George. "Scripture, Consensus and Community". In *Biblical Interpretation in Crisis: The Ratzinger Conference on Bible and Church*, ed. Richard John Neuhaus, 74-101. Grand Rapids: Eerdmans and the Rockford Institute Center on Religion and Society, 1989.

Longman, Tremper, III. *Literary Approaches to Biblical Interpretation*. Grand Rapids: Zondervan, 1987.

Loza Vera, J. "La interpretación de la Biblia en la Iglesia". *AnáMnesis [Xochimilco, Mexico]* 4, no. 2 (1994), 77-117.*

Luzbetak, Louis J. *The Church and Cultures*. 2nd, reprint ed. William Carey Library Series on Applied Cultural Anthropology. Pasadena, CA: William Carey Library, 1977.

Mack, Burton L. *A Myth of Innocence: Mark and Christian Origins*. Minneapolis: Fortress, 1988.

Manicardi, E. "Bibbia e inculturazione della fede". *SacDoc* 41, no. 3-4 (1996), 227-236.

Manns, F. "Lire les Écritures en Église". *RevSciRel* 69, no. 4 (1995), 436-452.

Marböck, J. "Ermutigung aus Rom". *Theologisch-Praktische Quartalschrift* 142, no. 4 (1994), 378-382.*

Marchadour, A. "Recontre entre psychanalyse et Bible". *Chronique* 4 (1997), 25-36.*

Marshall, I.H. "Review: 'The Interpretation of the Bible in the Church'". *Scottish Bulletin of Evangelical Theology* 13, no. 1 (1995), 72-75.*

Marthaler, Bernard L. "Interpreting the Scriptures". *Living Light* 31, no. 1? (1994), 1-2.*

Martin, Francis. "The Bible in the Retreat Movement". In *IBCom*, 160-161, 1998.

____. "Literary Theory, Philosophy of History and Exegesis". *Thomist* 52, no. 4 (1988), 575-604.

Martini, Carlo Maria. *La Parola di Dio alle origini della Chiesa*. Rome, 1980.

____. "Teaching the Scriptures to a Diocese". *Priests and People* 6, no. 6 (1992), 225-229.

Martins, J. Saraiva. "La sacra scrittura nella formazione teologica a trent'anni dalla 'Dei Verbum'". *Alpha Omega* 1, no. 1 (1998), 63-74.*

Marucci, C. "L'interpretazione della Bibbia nella Chiesa: Presentazione del recente documento dalla Pontifica Commissione Biblica". *Rassegna di Teologia* 35, no. 5 (1994), 587-594.*

McEvenue, Sean E. *Interpretation and Bible: Essays on Truth in Literature.* Collegeville, MN: Liturgical, 1994.

McEvenue, Sean E., and Ben F. Meyer. *Lonergan's Hermeneutics: Its Development and Application.* Washington DC: Catholic University of America, 1989.

McGrath, A.E. "Luther". In *DBI*, 414-416, 1990.

McNamara, M. "Inspiration and Interpretation of Scripture: Some Centennial Reflections". *Scripture in Church* 25 (1995), 107-119.*

McNeil, Brian. "*Sensus Plenior*". In *DBI*, 621-622, 1990.

Meeking, Basil, and John Stott. *The Evangelical-Roman Catholic Dialogue on Mission.* Exeter: Paternoster, 1986.

Mejía, Jorge. "Antisemitism in the Bible and After". In *IBCom*, 307-308, 1998.

Metzger, Bruce M. *Textual Commentary on the Greek New Testament.* 2nd ed. Stuttgart: Deutsche Bibelgesellschaft, 1994.

Meyer, Ben F. *Reality and Illusion in New Testament Scholarship: A Primer in Critical Realist Hermeneutics.* Collegeville, MN: Liturgical, 1994.

Miller, Charles D., Vern E. Heeren, and E. John Hornsby, Jr. *Mathematical Ideas.* New York: HarperCollins, 1990.

Milligan, M. "The Bible as Formative in a Basic Christian Community in Brazil". *Studies in Formative Spirituality* 13, no. 2 (1992), 145-149.

Moberly, R.W.L. *At the Mountain of God: Story and Theology in Exodus 32-34.* Vol. 22. JSOTS. Sheffield: Journal for the Study of the Old Testament, 1983.

Montague, George T. *Understanding the Bible: A Basic Introduction to Biblical Interpretation.* New York: Paulist, 1997.*

Morfino, M.M. *Leggere la Bibbia con la vita. La lettura esistenziale della Parola: un aspetto comune all'ermeneutica rabbinica e patristica.* Magnano: Qiqajon, 1990.

Morgan, Robert, and John Barton. *Biblical Interpretation.* The Oxford Bible Series. Oxford: Oxford University Press, 1988.

Morgan, Robert T. "Historicism". In *A Dictionary of Biblical Interpretation*, ed. R.J. Coggins and J.L. Houlden, 290-291. London: SCM, 1990.

Mosetto, Francesco. "Approcci basati sulla tradizione". In *Commento*, ed. Giuseppe Ghiberti and Francesco Mosetto, 162-194, 1998.*

Motyer, S. "Is John's Gospel Anti-Semitic?" *Themelios* 23, no. 2 (1998), 1-4.

Muddiman, John. "Light on Biblical Authority: Anglican-Roman Catholic Dialogue". In *The Interpretation of the Bible in the Church*, ed. J.L. Holden, 135-141. London: SCM, 1995.*

Muilenburg, J. "Form Criticism and Beyond". *Journal of Biblical Literature* 88 (1969), 1-18.

Muñoz León, Domingo. "La relación entre Antiguo y Nuevo Testamento en el documento de la Pontificia Comisión Bíblica (1993)". *Miscelánea Comillas* 52, no. 101 (1994), 249-74.*

____. "Los sentidos de la Escritura. Perspectivas del Documento de la Pontificia Comisión Bíblica (1993) sobre "La Interpretación de la Biblia en la Iglesia". *Script Theol* 27, no. 1 (1995), 99-122.*

Murphy, Roland E. "The Paschal Mystery: The Primary Hermeneutical Principal?" *Theological Studies* 60 (2000), 139-146.*

____. "Reflections on 'Actualization' of the Bible". *Biblical Theology Bulletin* 26, no. 2 (1996), 79-81.*

____. "The Testament(s): Continuities and Discontinuities". *Biblical Theology Bulletin* 29, no. 3 (1999), 112-117.*

____. "What Is Catholic About Catholic Biblical Scholarship?—Revisited". *Biblical Theology Bulletin* 28, no. 3 (1998), 112-119.*

Murray, D. "The Biblical Apostolate in Today's World". *DocLife* 41, no. 10 (1991), 507-516.

Neuhaus, Richard John, ed. *Biblical Interpretation in Crisis: The Ratzinger Conference on Bible and Church*, Encounter Series. Grand Rapids: Eerdmans and the Rockford Institute Center on Religion and Society, 1989.

Neuner, J., and J. Dupuis, eds. *The Christian Faith in the Doctrinal Documents of the Catholic Church*. New York: Alba, 1996.

Neuner, P. "Die Hellenisierung des Christentums als Modell von Inkulturation". *Stimmen der Zeit* 213, no. 6 (1995), 363-376.

Noble, Paul R. *The Canonical Approach: A Critical Reconstruction of the Hermeneutics of Brevard S. Childs*. Vol. 16. Biblical Interpretation Series. Leiden: E.J. Brill, 1995.

____. "The *Sensus Literalis*: Jowett, Childs, and Barr". *Journal of Theological Studies* 44, no. 1 (1993), 1-23.

____. "Synchronic and Diachronic Approaches to Biblical Interpretation". *LitTheol* 7, no. 2 (1993), 130-148.

O'Collins, Gerald. "'Dei Verbum' and Biblical Scholarship". *Scripture Bulletin* 21, no. 2 (1991), 2-7.

O'Collins, Gerald, and Edward G. Farrugia. *A Concise Dictionary of Theology*. New York: Paulist, 1991.

Olson, R.E. "Back to the Bible (Almost)". *Christianity Today* 40, no. 6 (1996), 31-34.

Orecchia, Carlo. "Univocità e polisemia del testo biblico nella storia dell'interpretazione". In *La Rivelazione Attestata: La Bibbia fra Testo e Teologia*, ed. Giuseppe Angelini, 99-132. Milano: Glossa, 1998.*

Osei-Bonsu, J. "Biblically/theologically-based Inculturation". *African Ecclesiastical Review* 32, no. 6 (1990), 346-358.

Palma, M.A. Molina. "La Interpretación de la Escritura en el Espíritu: Estudio historico y teologico de un principio hermenéutico de la Constitución 'Dei Verbum' 12". Dissertation, Pontifical Biblical Institute, 1985.

Palmer, Richard E. *Hermeneutics: Interpretation Theory in Schleiermacher, Dilthey, Heidegger, and Gadamer*. Evanston: Northwestern University Press, 1969.

Pannenberg, Wolfhart. "Redemptive Event and History". In *Basic Questions in Theology*, 15-80. London: SCM, 1970.

Parmisano, S. "Preaching and Contemporary Exegesis". *Homiletic & Pastoral Review* 89, no. 3 (1988), 21-25.

Pastore, C., ed. *La inculturación del evangelio*. Caracas: Iter, 1988.

Paul VI. "Address of His Holiness, 25 September". *L'Osservatore Romano*, 8 October 1970.

___. "Address to the Pontifical Biblical Commission". *L'Osservatore Romano*, 18 April 1974.

___. Motu proprio, *Sedula cura*, 27 June 1971.

Pelland, Gilles. "Apologists". In *DFT*, 41-44, 1995.

Pesce, Mauro. "Approcci secondo le scienze umane". In *Commento*, ed. Giuseppe Ghiberti and Francesco Mosetto, 195-221, 1998.*

___. "Rinnovata difesa dell' esegesi storica ed esigenze di un'interpretazione teologica". In *Scienze umane e interpretazione della Bibbia*, ed. G. Segalla and I. De Sandre, vol. 43, 25-42, 1996.*

Pilch, J.J. "Psychological and Psychoanalytical Approaches to Interpreting the Bible in Social-Scientific Context". *Biblical Theology Bulletin* 27, no. 3 (1997), 112-116.*

Pitta, Antonio. "Nuovi metodi di analisi letteraria". In *Commento*, ed. Giuseppe Ghiberti and Francesco Mosetto, 145-161, 1998.*

Pius X. *Praestantia Scripturae Sacrae*, 18 November 1907.

Ponchaud, F. "L'Évangile en khmer: Inculturation et traduction". *Études* 380, no. 2 (1994), 229-234.

Pontifical Biblical Commission. *The Interpretation of the Bible in the Church*. Boston: St. Paul Books & Media, 1993.*

___. "The Interpretation of the Bible in the Church". *Origins* 23, no. 29 (1994), 497-524.*

___. *The Interpretation of the Bible in the Church: Address of His Holiness Pope John Paul II and Document of the Pontifical Biblical Commission*. Rome: Libreria Editrice Vaticana, 1993.*

Pontificia Commissione Biblica. *Fede e cultura alla luce della Bibbia: Atti della Sessione Plenaria 1979 della Pontificia Commissione Biblica*. Torino: Leumann, 1981.

Pottmeyer, Hermann J. "Tradition". In *DFT*, 1119-1126, 1995.

Powell, Mark Allan. *Fortress Introduction to the Gospels*. Minneapolis: Fortress, 1998.

Prinzivalli, E. "Incontro e scontro fra 'classico' e 'cristiano' nei primi tre secoli: aspetti e problemi". *Salesianum* 56, no. 3 (1994), 543-556.

Prior, Joseph G. *The Historical Critical Method In Catholic Exegesis*. Vol. 50. Tesi Gregoriana, Serie Teologia. Rome: Gregorian University, 1999.*

Propp, V. *Morphology of the Folktale*. Translated by L.A. Wagner. 2nd ed. Austin: University of Texas Press, 1968.

Ralph, M.N. "The Bible and the Adult Roman Catholic: A Missing Piece in Adult Parish Catechesis". *Living Light* 30, no. 2 (1993), 43-50.

Ramm, Bernard. *Protestant Biblical Interpretation*. Boston: W.A. Wilde, 1956.

Rasco, E. "La 'Parola vivente' (Eb 4,12): dallo studio alla vita. La mediazione ermeneutica". *Gregorianum* 73, no. 4 (1992), 689-695.

Ratzinger, Joseph. "Biblical Interpretation in Crisis: On the Question of the Foundations and Approaches of Exegesis Today". In *Biblical Interpretation in Crisis: The Ratzinger Conference on Bible and Church*, ed. R. J. Neuhaus, 1-23. Grand Rapids: Eerdmans and the Rockford Institute Center on Religion and Society, 1989.

____. "Dogmatische Konstitution über die göttliche Offenbarung: Einleitung". In *Lexicon für Theologie und Kirche: Das zweite Vatikanische Konzil*, 498-503. Freiburg, 1967.

____. "Modernità atea religiosità post-moderna". *Il Regno-Attualità* 1994, no. 4 (1994), 65-70.*

____. ed. *Schriftauslegung im Widerstreit*. Vol. 117, Quaestiones Disputatae. Freiburg: Herder, 1989.

Raurell, F. "El método histórico-crítico frente a las lecturas fundamentalistas e integristas de la Biblia". *Laurentianum* 35, no. 2-3 (1994), 273-318.*

Refoulé, F. "L'exégèse en question". *Le Supplément* 111 (1974), 391-423.

Refoulé, F., and F. Dreyfus. *Quale esegesi oggi nella Chiesa?* Vol. 38-41. Sussidi Biblici. Reggio Emilia: San Lorenzo, 1992.

Reumann, J. "After Historical Criticism, What?   Trends in Biblical Interpretation and Ecumenical, Interfaith Dialogues". *Journal of Ecumenical Studies* 29, no. 1 (1992), 55-86.

____. *"Righteousness" in the New Testament: "Justification" in the United States Lutheran-Roman Catholic Dialogue*. Philadelphia: Fortress, 1982.

Reumann, J., and James A. Fitzmyer. "Scripture as Norm for our Common Faith". *Journal of Ecumenical Studies* 30, no. 1 (1993), 81-107.

Ricoeur, Paul. *The Conflict of Interpretations: Essays in Hermeneutics*. Evanston, IL: Northwestern University, 1974.

____. *Essays on Biblical Interpretation*. Philadelphia: Fortress, 1980.

____. *Interpretation Theory: Discourse and the Surplus of Meaning*. Fort Worth, TX: Texas Christian University Press, 1976.

Rogerson, John W., and Werner G. Jeanrond. "Interpretation, History of". In *ABD*, vol. 3, 424-443, 1992.

Rome and the Study of Scripture. 7th ed. St. Meinrad, IN: Grail, 1962.

Ruppert, Lothar. "Kommentierende Einführung in das Dokument". In *Die Interpretation der Bibel in der Kirche: das Dokument der Päpstlichen Bibelkommission vom 23.4.1993 mit einer kommentierenden Einführung von Lothar Ruppert und einer Würdigung durch Hans-Josef Klauck*, vol. 161, 9-61. Stuttgart: Verlag Katholisches Bibelwerk, 1995.*

____. "Neue Impulse aus Rom für die Bibelauslegung — Zum neuesten Dokument der Päpstlichen Bibelkommission". *Bibel und Kirche* 49, no. 4 (1994), 202-213.*

Russell, K.C. "Paul Ricoeur on *Lectio Divina*". *Église et Théologie* 26, no. 3 (1995), 331-344.

Ryken, L. *How to Read the Bible as Literature*. Grand Rapids: Zondervan, 1984.

Salvail, Ghislaine. *At the Crossroads of Scripture: An Introduction to Lectio Divina*. Boston: Pauline Books & Media, 1996.

Schanks, Hershel. "The Catholic Church & Bible Interpretation". *Bible Review* 10, no. 4 (1994), 32-35.*

Schneiders, Sandra Marie. "Church and Biblical Scholarship in Dialogue". *Theology Today* 42 (1985), 353-358.

____. *The Revelatory Text: Interpreting the New Testament as Sacred Scripture*. 2nd ed. Collegeville, MN: Liturgical Press, 1999.

____. "Scripture as the Word of God". *Princeton Seminary Bulletin* 14, no. 1 (1993), 18-35.

Scholtissek, Klaus. "Relecture – zu einem neu entdeckten Programmwort der Schriftauslegung (mit Blick auf das Johannesevangelium)". *Bibel und Liturgie* 70, no. 4 (1997), 309-315.*

Schweitzer, Albert. *The Quest of the Historical Jesus: A Critical Study of Its Progress from Reimarus to Wrede*. London: Black, 1910.

Schwöbel, C. "Calvin". In *DBI*, 98-101, 1990.

Scullion, J.P. "Experience Encounters the Sacred Text: The Interpretation of the Bible in the Church". *NewTheology Review* 8, no. 1 (1995), 18-29.*

Seckler, Max. "Theology and Science". In *Dictionary of Fundamental Theology*, ed. René Latourelle and Rino Fisichella, 1069-1075. New York: Crossroad, 1994.

Segalla, Giuseppe. "Introduzione: Cento anni di studi biblici (1893-1993)". *Studia Patavina* 41, no. 2 (1994), 3-10.

____. "Storia del documento". *Studia Patavina* 43 (1996), 19-23.*

Segalla, Giuseppe, et al. "Cento anni di studi biblici (1893-1993)". *Studia Patavina* 41, no. 2 (1994), 3-152.*

Segalla, Giuseppe, et al. "Scienze umane e interpretazione della Bibbia". *Studia Patavina* 43 (1996), 15-105.*

Seghedoni, I. "Accostarsi alla Bibbia". In *La Bibbia*, 3209-3210. Casale Monferrato: Piemme, 1995.

Seibold, J.R. "Palabra de Dios y Pueblo de Dios: La actualización de la Sagrada Escritura en la Evangelización de América Latina". *Stromata* 46, no. 1-2 (1990), 3-63.

Senior, Donald. "The Church and the Word of God". *Origins* , no. 3 (1996), 577-583.*

Sequeri, PierAngelo. "La struttura testimoniale delle scritture sacre: teologia del testo". In *La Rivelazione Attestata: La Bibbia fra Testo e Teologia*, ed. Giuseppe Angelini, 3-28. Milano: Glossa, 1998.*

Sevin, M. "L'approche des textes bibliques". *LumVit* 50, no. 3 (1995), 253-260.*

Sevrin, J.-M. "L' exégèse critique comme discipline théologique". *Revue théologique de Louvain* 21 (1990), 146-162.

Shea, W.M. "Catholic Reaction to Fundamentalism". *Theological Studies* 57, no. 2 (1996), 264-285.*

Simian-Yofre, Horacio. "Esegesi, Fede e Teologia". In *Metodologia dell' Antico Testamento*, ed. Horacio Simian-Yofre, 9-21. Bologna: Dehoniane, 1995.

____. "Old and New Testament: Participation and Analogy". In *Vatican II, Assessment and Perspectives: Twenty-five Years After*, ed. René Latourelle, vol. 1, 267-298. New York: Paulist, 1988.

Simonetti, M. *Biblical Interpretation in the Early Church: An Historical Introduction to Patristic Exegesis.* Translated by J. A. Hughes. Edinburgh: T.&T. Clark, 1994.

Smalley, Beryl. *The Study of the Bible in the Middle Ages.* 3rd ed. Oxford: Blackwell, 1983.

Söding, T. "Eucharistie und Mysterien: Urchristliche Herrenmahlstheologie und antike Mysterienreligiosität im Spiegel von 1Kor 10". *Bibel und Kirche* 45, no. 3 (1990), 140-145.

Stendahl, Krister. "Biblical Theology, Contemporary". In *The Interpreter's Dictionary of the Bible*, vol. 1, 418-432. New York: Abingdon, 1962.

____. "Method in the Study of Biblical Theology". In *The Bible in Modern Scholarship*, ed. J.P. Hyatt, 196-209. London: Carey Kingsgate, 1966.

Stevenson, Kenneth. "A Liturgist's Response". In *The Interpretation of the Bible in the Church*, ed. J.L. Holden, 156-163. London: SCM, 1995.*

Stowasser, M. "'...damit das Urteil der Kirche reife': Von 'Providentissimus Deus' zur 'Interpretation der Bibel in der Kirche'". *Theologische Quartalschrift* 175, no. 3 (1995), 202-214.*

Strauss, Leo. *Natural Right and History.* Chicago: University of Chicago, 1950.

Stuart, D. "Exegesis". In *ABD*, vol. 2, 682-688, 1992.

Studer, Basil. "Neuerscheinungen zur Exegese der Kirchenväter". *Theologische Revue* 93, no. 2 (1997), 91-94.

____. "Die patristische Exegese, eine Aktualisierung der Heiligen Schrift (Zur hermeneutischen Problematik der frühchristlichen Bibelauslegung)". *Revue des Études Augustiniennes* 42, no. 1 (1996), 71-95.*

Stylianopoulos, Theodore G. *The New Testament: An Orthodox Perspective.* Vol. 1. Scripture, Tradition, Hermeneutics. Brookline, MA: Holy Cross Orthodox Press, 1997.

Swetnam, James. "German Catholics and the Bible". *Bible Today* 25, no. 5 (1987), 315-318.

____. "The Word of God and Pastoral Theology in the Contemporary Church". In *Vatican II, Assessment and Perspectives: Twenty-five Years After*, ed. René Latourelle, vol. 1. New York: Paulist, 1988.

____. "Zimbabwean Catholics and the Bible". *Bible Today* 26, no. 3 (1988), 168-172.

Tábet, Miguel Ángel. "L'interpretazione della Bibbia nella Chiesa', un documento della PCB". *Annales Theologici* 8, no. 1 (1994), 23-68.*

____. "Il senso litterale e il senso spirituale della Sacra Scrittura: un tentativo di chiarimento terminologico e concettuale". *Annales Theologici* 9 (1995), 3-54.*

Tafferner, A. "Was trauen wir der Bibel in der Seelsorge zu?" *Bibel und Liturgie* 69, no. 4 (1996), 255-257.*

Teani, M. "Tornare alla Bibbia". *Civiltà Cattolica* 147, no. 3504 (1996), 562-573.

Terra, J.E.M., ed., ed. *A interpretação da Bíblia na Igreja*. Vol. 18, Revista de Cultura Bíblica. São Paulo: Edições Loyola, 1994.*

Theobald, M. "'Allen bin ich alles geworden . . .' (1 Kor 9, 22b): Paulus und das Problem der Inkulturation des Glaubens". *Theologische Quartalschrift* 176, no. 1 (1996), 1-6.

Thiselton, Anthony C. *New Horizons in Hermeneutics: The Theory and Practice of Transforming Biblical Reading*. London: HarperCollins, 1992.

____. *The Two Horizons*. Grand Rapids: Eerdmans, 1980.

Tiessen, T. "Toward a Hermeneutic for Discerning Universal Moral Absolutes". *Journal of the Evangelical Theological Society* 36, no. 2 (1993), 189-207.

Trimaille, M. "Exégèse et inculturation". *Revue de. l'Institut Catholique de Paris* 52 (1994), 21-26.

Troeltsch, Ernst. "Historical and Dogmatic Method in Theology". In *Religion in History*, 11-32. Edinburgh: T & T Clark, 1991.

____. "Über historische und dogmatische Methode in der Theologie". In *Gesammelte Schriften*. Tübingen: J.C.B. Mohr, 1913.

Ukpong, J.S. "The Parable of the Shrewd Manager (Luke 16:1-13): An Essay in Inculturation Biblical Hermeneutic". *Semeia* 73 (1996), 189-210.

____. "Rereading the Bible with African Eyes: Inculturation and Hermeneutics". *JournTheolSAfric* 91 (1995), 3-14.

Utzschneider, H. "Exegese als ökumenische Chance. Überlegungen eines lutherischen Alttestamentlers zum Dokument der Päpstlichen Bibelkommission". *Bibel und Liturgie* 71, no. 1 (1998), 61-65.*

Vanhoozer, Kevin J. "'But That's Your Interpretation': Realism, Reading and Reformation". *Modern Reformation* 8, no. 4 (1999), 21, 24-28, 43.

____. *Is There a Meaning in this Text? The Bible, the Reader, and the Morality of Literary Knowledge*. Grand Rapids: Zondervan, 1998.

____. "Language, Literature, Hermeneutics, and Biblical Theology: What's Theological about a Theological Dictionary?" In *New International Dictionary of Old Testament Theology and Exegesis*, ed. Willem A. VanGemeren, vol. 1. Grand Rapids, MI: Zondervan, 1997.

Vanhoye, Albert. "Catholicism and the Bible". *First Things* 74 (June/July 1997), 35-40.*

____. Conversation with Peter Williamson on the Senses of Scripture and Other Topics, 22 February 1999.

____. "Dopo la *Divino afflante Spiritu*: Progressi e problemi dell'esegesi cattolica". In *Chiesa e Sacra Scrittura: Un secolo di magistero ecclesiastico e studi biblici*, 35-52. Rome: Pontifical Biblical Institute, 1994.

____. "Esegesi biblica e teologia: la questione dei metodi". *Seminarium* 43, no. 2 (1991), 267-278.

____. Fax response to questions from Peter Williamson, 31 January 2000.

____. "L'interpretazione della Bibbia nella Chiesa: Riflessione circa un documento della Commissione Biblica". *Civiltà Cattolica* 145, no. #3457 (1994), 3-15.*

____. "Passé et présent de la Commission Biblique". *Gregorianum* 74 (1993), 261-275.*

Vanni, Ugo. *L'Apocalisse: ermeneutica, esegesi, teologia*. Vol. 17. Supplementi alla Rivista Biblica. Bologna: Edizioni Dehoniane Bologna, 1988.

____. "Exegesis and Actualization in the Light of *Dei Verbum*". In *Vatican II, Assessment and Perspectives: Twenty-five Years After*, ed. René Latourelle, vol. 1, 344-363. New York: Paulist, 1988.

Vesco, Jean-Luc. "Présentation". In *L'interprétation de la Bible dans l'Église*, ed. Commission Biblique Pontificale, i-xxiii. Paris: Cerf, 1994.*

Vignolo, Roberto. "Metodi, ermeneutica, statuto del testo biblico: Riflessione a partire da 'L'interpretazione della Bibbia nella Chiesa' (1993)". In *La Rivelazione Attestata: La Bibbia fra Testo e Teologia*, ed. Giuseppe Angelini, 29-97. Milano: Glossa, 1998.*

____. "Questioni di ermeneutica". In *Commento*, ed. Giuseppe Ghiberti and Francesco Mosetto, 261-298, 1998.*

Wainwright, G. "Towards an Ecumenical Hermeneutic: How Can All Christians Read the Scriptures Together?" *Gregorianum* 76, no. 4 (1995), 639-662.

Warzecha, J., and et al. "Sympozjum bibijne—4.04.1995 r. Zagajenie". *Studia Theologica Varsaviensia* 33, no. 2 (1995), 137-188.*

Watson, Francis. "Bible, Theology and the University". *Journal for the Study of the Old Testament* 71 (1996), 3-16.

____. *Text, Church and World: Biblical Interpretation in Theological Perspective*. Grand Rapids: Eerdmans, 1994.

Weber, Kathleen. "Making the Biblical Account Relevant: A Narrative Analysis". *Living Light* 31, no. 1 (1994), 16-19.*

Wicks, Jared. "Biblical Criticism Criticized". *Gregorianum* 72 (January 1991), 119-128.

____. *Introduction to Theological Method*. Casale Monferrato: Piemme, 1994.

____. "Rule of Faith". In *DFT*, 959-961, 1994.

Williamson, Peter S. "Actualization: A New Emphasis in Catholic Scripture Study". *America* 172, no. 18 (1995), 17-19.*

Wimsatt, W.M., and M.C. Beardsley. "The Intentional Fallacy". In *On Literary Intention*, ed. Newton-De Molina, 1-13. Edinburgh: Edinburgh University Press, 1976.

Witherington, Ben, III. *The Jesus Quest: The Third Search for the Jew of Nazareth*. 2nd ed. Downers Grove, IL: Intervarsity, 1997.

Witherup, R.D. "Is There a Catholic Approach to the Bible?" *Priest* 51, no. 2 (1995), 29-35.*

____. "A New *Magna Carta* for Catholic Biblical Studies?" *Bible Today* 32, no. 6 (1994), 336-341.*

Wolterstorff, Nicholas. *Divine Discourse: Philosophical Reflections on the Claim that God Speaks*. Cambridge: Cambridge University, 1995.

____. "The Promise of Speech Act Theory for Biblical Interpretation". A paper delivered at the Open Book and Scholarship Conference, Redeemer University College, Ancaster Ontario, August 16-19 2000.

Wrede, Wilhelm. "The Task and Methods of New Testament Theology". In *The Nature of New Testament Theology*, ed. R. Morgan, 68-116. London: SCM, 1973.

Yeago, David S. "The New Testament and Nicene Dogma: A Contribution to the Recovery of Theological Exegesis". *Pro Ecclesia* 3 (1994), 152-164.

Zenger, Erich. *Der Erste Testament: Die jüdische Bibel und wir Christen*. Düsseldorf, 1991.

____. "Weisse Flecken im neuen Dokument der Bibelkommission". *Bibel und Liturgie* 69, no. 3 (1996), 173-176.*

INDEX

Readers are encouraged to also consult the detailed table of contents, since the structure of chapter topics and subheadings found there is not repeated in the index.

GLOSSARY*

actualization: The reading of a text for its meaning in the present. Actualization may refer to the pastoral application of a text to a specific situation or community, or it may refer more generally to the meaning of a text for Christian faith. Sometimes "actualization" refers to the re-reading of texts in the past, e.g., by later biblical writers or Church Fathers, in order to discover Scripture's meaning for their day.

allegorical interpretation: Interpretation in which persons, objects and actions depicted in a text are taken as representing other things not present in the text. The Fathers of the Church were fond of employing allegorical interpretation of the Old Testament to show how the entire Jewish Scriptures pointed to Christ, to explain texts that might otherwise seem scandalous (e.g., questionable actions of Old Testament heroes), and to give a pastoral application to texts that might otherwise seem obsolete. The terms "allegory" or "allegorical interpretation" have also been used more broadly to refer to interpretation of the Old Testament in the light of Jesus Christ.

analogy of faith: The inner unity of the truths of faith with one another and with Christian revelation as a whole (see *CCC* § 114). *Dei Verbum* 12 presents the analogy of faith as a criterion for authentic interpretation of Scripture.

approach: A way of studying Scripture which proceeds "from a particular point of view" (Intro B.e, footnote). The Biblical Commission distinguishes approaches from methods (see below) and identifies various approaches: those based on tradition (e.g., the canonical approach,

---

* This glossary provides a brief guide for students and non-specialists to the meaning of terms as they are used in the present study and in *The Interpretation of the Bible in the Church*. A deeper understanding may be obtained by consulting the index entries of terms which also appear there. Readers should be aware that some of these terms are used in different senses by other authors.

Wirkungsgeschichte), those that rely on the human sciences (e.g., sociological, psychological and psychoanalytical approaches), and contextual approaches (liberationist and feminist approaches).

authorial intention: What the human author of a biblical text wanted to communicate when he wrote.

biblical theology: Theology which draws its content and, usually, its categories from Scripture.   In contrast, systematic theology draws from sources besides the Bible—such as patristic writings, magisterial documents, the liturgy, philosophy, and the social and cultural situation of the modern world—and aims to present a holistic contemporary understanding of Christian faith.   Biblical theology differs from exegesis in that it concerns itself with the entire Bible or at least larger portions of the biblical literature rather than confining itself to particular texts or books.   Authors disagree about the aim and nature of biblical theology. Some believe it should provide only historical description while others believe it should function as a normative theological discipline.

biblical tradition of interpretation: The pattern and content of interpretation found within the Bible when earlier texts are interpreted by later texts in the light of new questions and circumstances.   This includes the New Testament's reading the Old Testament in the light of the death and resurrection of Jesus.

canon: The list of books that comprise the Christian Scriptures accepted by the Church as a norm of faith.

canonical approach: Interpretation which seeks to understand biblical texts in light of the whole canon of Scripture (see I.C.1.b).   The *IBC* describes two versions of the canonical approach.   Brevard S. Childs' approach focuses on the final canonical form of the text (whether book or collection); that of James A. Sanders (called *"canonical criticism"*) focuses on the "canonical process" by which the Scriptures take shape as a normative authority for the believing community.

canonical sense: The meaning of a text when read in the light of its *canonical context*, i.e., the context of the whole Bible.   "Although each book of the Bible was written with its own particular end in view and has its own specific meaning, it takes on a deeper meaning when it becomes part of the *canon* as a whole" (I.C.1.e).

Catholic exegesis: Exegesis that accords with Catholic principles of interpretation.

christological analogy: A comparison of the human and divine aspects of Sacred Scripture to the two natures of Christ manifest in the incarnation.

christological sense: The meaning of Old Testament texts in light of the "mystery of Christ" (Eph 3:4), especially the paschal mystery. While in many places the New Testament reveals the authentic christological sense of the Old Testament, patristic and medieval Christian exegesis has been criticized for sometimes overemphasizing *christological interpretation* to the detriment of other dimensions of the Old Testament's meaning.

critical: When used to modify "methods", "research" or similar terms, "*critical*" means "scientific" or "scholarly" and implies the use of analytical procedures aimed at objectivity and precision. Although in its quest for objectivity some "critical" biblical scholarship has at times systematically excluded religious faith, philosophical hermeneutics has recognized "the impossibility of interpreting a text without starting from a pre-understanding of one type or another" (III.b). Catholic critical exegesis begins with a pre-understanding of Christian faith.

deconstruction: A skeptical school of philosophy and literary analysis which began to influence biblical interpretation in the late 20th century. Deconstruction denies that words refer to extra-textual realities, and instead regards words as signs which endlessly signify other signs and never come to rest in any determinate meaning. Advocates of deconstruction take interest in the endless play of meaning that results from indeterminate signs interpreted in light of the uniquely personal context which every reader brings to the text.

diachronic study: The historical study of a text's meaning. The term "diachronic" is derived from the Greek words *dia + chronos*, which literally mean "through time". Often, though not always, diachronic study of a text refers to the attempt to identify sources that lie behind the final form of the text.

dynamic aspect of meaning: The capacity of the literal sense of some texts to be re-read in new circumstances; the direction of thought or trajectory opened up by such texts. The *IBC* offers the example of the royal psalms: "In speaking of the king, the psalmist evokes at one and the same time both the institution as it actually was and an idealized vision of kingship as God intended it to be" (II.B.1.e).

ecclesial significance: The meaning of Scripture in light of the special relationship that exists between the Bible and the Church. To grasp the ecclesial meaning of Scripture is to understand that Scripture originated in the community life of the people of God, that it is intrinsically linked to the living Tradition of that people, and that Scripture remains "the privileged means which God uses yet again in our own day to shape the building up and the growth of the Church" (III.C.1.f).

exegesis: The explanation of the meaning of a text. Although the *IBC* often uses this term interchangeably with "interpretation", "exegesis" usually connotes the scientific or scholarly study of Scripture. For the Biblical Commission exegesis does not end with historical or literary analysis but includes an explanation of the text's religious message. The term "exegesis" also refers to the discipline which studies the meaning of Scripture.

final form: The last stage of the text of the Bible which has been officially accepted as canonical by the Church in contrast to earlier versions of biblical writings which are known or thought to have existed. Catholic exegesis concerns itself with the final form of the biblical text which it recognizes as divinely inspired Scripture.

fuller sense (*sensus plenior*): "A deeper meaning of the text, intended by God but not clearly expressed by the human author" (II.B.3.a). This deeper meaning emerges through divine interventions which reveal the meaning of earlier texts or through the reading of texts in the context of the canon of Scripture (see II.B.3.c).

hermeneutic of faith: The interpretation of Scripture beginning from a presupposition of Christian faith. A hermeneutic of faith may be contrasted to a interpretive stance that approaches Scripture no differently than it would approach any other ancient text.

hermeneutic: Interpretation proceeding from particular presuppositions or a particular hermeneutical theory: e.g., a feminist hermeneutic, a hermeneutic of faith, a rationalist hermeneutic, etc.

hermeneutics: The science of interpretation. "Hermeneutics" may also denote the process of interpretation through which the distance is bridged between an ancient author's original communicative action and the meaning of a text for readers today.

historical criticism: (1) The application of the historical-critical method (see below) to ancient documents. (2) An evaluation of the historicity or historical significance of reported events.

historical positivism: The belief that "objective" historical study (i.e., not "biased" by religious faith) can obtain scientifically-precise historical information about events recounted in the Bible by the use of "objective" methods and sources, and that only such historical information is worthy of credence.

historical-critical method: A general term to describe the set of methods and analytical procedures scholars use to interpret ancient documents including the Bible. The method is historical in that it "seeks to shed light upon the historical processes which gave rise to biblical texts" (I.A.2.b). It is critical because "it operates with the help of scientific criteria that seek to be as objective as possible" (I.A.2.c). In describing the historical-critical method at its current stage of development, the *IBC* lists the following steps: textual criticism, linguistic and semantic analysis, literary criticism, genre criticism, tradition criticism, redaction criticism, and historical criticism.

historicism: A belief in the adequacy of historical study for understanding and evaluating literary works in general and Scripture in particular. Historicist biblical interpretation locates and confines the meaning of a text within the historical circumstances of its origin.

historicity: The historical actuality or facticity of reported events, i.e., whether or not a particular event actually occurred. "Historicity" can also refer to the location in history of authors and readers and the consequent uniqueness and limitation of their respective points of view.

incarnation analogy: See "christological analogy".

inculturation: The expression of the Christian message in a manner and in terms that are consonant with the mentality of a particular culture.

inerrancy: The doctrine that Scripture does not err because it is divinely inspired. While the fundamentalist understanding of biblical inerrancy encompasses scientific and historical matters, the Catholic doctrine, expressed in *Dei Verbum* 11, is more circumscribed: "Therefore, since everything asserted by the inspired authors or sacred writers must be held to be asserted by the Holy Spirit, it follows that the books of Scripture must be acknowledged as teaching firmly, faithfully and without error that truth which God wanted put into the sacred writings for the sake of our salvation".

interpretation: An understanding or explanation of the meaning of something.   The *IBC*, referring to biblical interpretation, often uses "interpretation" interchangeably with "exegesis".

intertextuality: A relationship between texts, whether of allusion, explicit citation, re-reading, or shared literary conventions.

*lectio divina***:** Literally, "divine reading", a traditional term for the spiritual reading of Scripture.   This kind of reading of Scripture is to be accompanied by *meditatio* ("meditation"), *oratio* ("prayer"), and *contemplatio* ("contemplation").

liberationist approach: Interpretation beginning from the viewpoint of liberation theology.   Liberationist interpretation maintains that exegesis cannot be neutral but must take sides on behalf of the poor; it seeks an actualization of Scripture that can be the basis of "authentic Christian praxis, leading to the transformation of society through works of justice and love" (I.E.1.c).

literal sense: The meaning of Scripture "which has been expressed directly by the inspired human authors" (II.B.1.c).

literary analysis: The scholarly study of literary works and of how texts function, i.e., how they communicate a message, tell a story, persuade, etc. Generally, literary analysis of Scripture concerns itself with the final form of the text, rather than its pre-canonical stages. The *IBC* briefly discusses three methods of literary analysis: rhetorical analysis, narrative analysis, and semiotic analysis.

literary criticism: In biblical studies, either (1) source criticism or (2) literary analysis. In older usage, literary criticism referred to the search for sources such as the Yahwist, Elohist, or Q. More recently "literary criticism" refers to the application to the Bible of methods developed in the study of literature.

method (exegetical): "A group of scientific procedures employed in order to explain texts" (see Intro B.e, footnote).   The Biblical Commission distinguishes "methods" from "approaches" (see above) and recognizes the following as methods: the historical-critical method, rhetorical analysis, narrative analysis, and semiotic analysis.

narrative analysis: A method of interpreting biblical narratives with the help of literary theory. Narrative analysis, also called "narrative criticism", attends to literary features such as plot, characterization, point of view in narration, etc., and considers how a text tells a story and involves the reader in its "narrative world".

patristic exegesis: The biblical interpretation of the Fathers of the Church.

philology: The study of words, morphology, and syntax and how they convey meaning in texts (referred to as "linguistic study" in the *IBC*). In this study "philological and literary analysis" refers to the totality of literary disciplines employed in the interpretation of texts. "Historical philology" is the study of the evolution of words and their meanings through time.

philosophical hermeneutics: Scholarly reflection on human communication and interpretation which addresses topics such as signs and what they refer to, semantics, epistemology, metaphysics, and the quest for truth in human existence.

pre-understanding (*precomprehension*): The presuppositions which an interpreter brings to a text. Without some prior understanding of the words, concepts, and realities to which a text refers, understanding is impossible.

principles of Catholic interpretation: The presuppositions and procedures appropriate to interpreting Scripture in the context of the Catholic Church.

redaction criticism: The critical study of the editing process through which a biblical text attained its final form ("*Redaktionsgeschichte*"). According to the *IBC*, redaction criticism culminates in a synchronic analysis of the final form of the text (I.A.3.c).

referentiality: The reference of a text to a reality that is outside it. Some theories of interpretation such as structuralism or deconstruction are unconcerned about or deny the referentiality of texts to historical reality beyond themselves.

relectures: See "re-readings".

religious message: The meaning of Scripture as the word of God, as divine communication and revelation, for Christian faith; the religious meaning of Scripture.

re-readings (*relectures*): The interpretation of earlier biblical writings by later ones through allusion, citation, commentary or the re-telling of stories, usually for the sake of actualizing the message of earlier texts.

Re-readings, arising from new circumstances or new questions, "develop new aspects of meaning" (III.A.1.a).

rhetorical analysis: A group of exegetical methods which study how texts employ literary devices (and other means) to persuade their readers.

scientific exegesis: Critical or scholarly biblical interpretation, i.e., exegesis which employs critical methods.

semiotic analysis: A method of literary analysis which studies how signs convey meaning in texts through the observance of linguistic rules and conventions. Semiotic analysis attends exclusively to the text under consideration without considering "external" data such as the author, audience or historical circumstances.

sensus plenior: See "fuller sense".

source criticism: The detection and study of the written and oral sources which preceded the final form of a text. Thus, scholarship that proposes hypotheses regarding earlier versions than the canonical texts, for instance, of the Pentateuch or Synoptic Gospels, engages in source criticism.

speech-act theory: A theory of communication that studies what the speaker or writer is *doing* (e.g., warning, asserting, promising, informing, etc.) when he or she says something. Proponents of speech-act theory believe that it overcomes problems inherent both in semiotic interpretation and in interpretation grounded in authorial intention.

spiritual sense: "The meaning expressed by the biblical texts when read under the influence of the Holy Spirit in the context of the paschal mystery and of the new life which flows from it" (II.B.2.b). The spiritual sense of Old Testament texts often means their christological sense. This term is used variously by different authors.

structuralism: A school of literary criticism which employs insights into the sign nature of language and the rules or "grammar" which govern literary works (especially narratives) to interpret the final form of a text. Structuralists locate the meaning of a work in the narrative conventions employed by its author in the text.

subjective interpretation: Interpretation stemming from personal inspiration, imagination, speculation, or bias rather than finding its basis in the text itself.

synchronic study: (1) The study of a text in its final form. (2) The study of a text without regard for historical considerations. The term "synchronic" is derived from the Greek words *syn + chronos* which mean "with time", "without regard to historical considerations", or "simultaneous". The new literary methods generally emphasize synchronic study of the text.

textual criticism: The examination of various ancient manuscripts or translations of a biblical text to determine as accurately as possible its original wording.

textual meaning: The meaning of the words of the text itself (independent of consideration for the author's intention).

Tradition: The living presence of the word of God in the life of the Church through time. As the communication of divine revelation, Tradition must be distinguished from various theological, disciplinary, liturgical or devotional *traditions* that have arisen that seek to give expression to it. Tradition entails both the *content* of divine revelation and the *process* of its communication in the Church. The *content* of Tradition is everything Christ revealed to the Apostles and what the Holy Spirit enabled them to understand later. The *process* of handing on Tradition's content occurs in the life of the Church by the activity of her members as the Church "in her teaching, life and worship, perpetuates and hands on to all generations all that she herself is, all that she believes" (*DV* 8). The Church's understanding of divine revelation develops and deepens under the guidance of the Spirit with the passing of time.

typical sense (typological sense): The deeper meaning of the persons, places and events in the Bible (types) when they are seen to have foreshadowed subsequent persons, places, and events (anti-types) in God's work of salvation. The *IBC* views the typical sense as an instance of the spiritual sense. (See "typological interpretation".)

typological interpretation: Interpretation which recognizes the typical sense (see above). The New Testament provides many examples of typological interpretation of Old Testament realities which foreshadow Christ or the realities of the New Covenant. These include Adam as a figure of Christ (Rom 5:14; 1 Cor 15:45-49) and the flood and crossing of the Red Sea as types of baptism (1 Pet 3:20-21; 1 Cor 10:1). "Typological" can also be used more generally to mean "figurative".

Wirkungsgeschichte: An approach to biblical interpretation which studies how a text has been appropriated by individuals or communities through history in order to better understand the meaning latent in the text. The *IBC* proposes the history of the interpretation of the Songs of Songs by patristic, monastic and mystical writers as an example of how *Wirkungsgeschichte*—literally, "history of the effect"—sheds light on a text's meaning.

STAMPA: Febbraio 2008

presso la tipografia
"Giovanni Olivieri" di E. Montefoschi
ROMA • info@tipografiaolivieri.it